Mr. Echard

The Roman History

Vol. III

Mr. Echard

The Roman History
Vol. III

ISBN/EAN: 9783337122966

Printed in Europe, USA, Canada, Australia, Japan

Cover: Foto ©ninafisch / pixelio.de

More available books at **www.hansebooks.com**

THE ROMAN HISTORY,

From the Removal of the

Imperial Seat

BY

Constantine the Great,

To the Total Failure of

The Western Empire

IN

AUGUSTULUS.

Containing the Space of 146 *Years.*

VOL. III.

Being a Continuation of Mr. *ECHARD's* History; with his Recommendatory PREFACE.

LONDON,
Printed for *Jacob Tonson,* within *Grays-Inn* Gate, next *Grays-Inn* Lane, 1704.

Mr. ECHARD's
PREFACE.

Aving resolv'd not to concern my self further in the *Roman History*, I am desir'd to write a Line or two in Relation to this *Third Volume,* which is written by One whose Person is unknown to me. I dare not presume to set up for a Judge in Matters of this Nature; but, according to my Opinion, I believe it to be a very well digested, useful and entertaining History; especially to all such as have thought fit to read over the two first Volumes upon this Subject. The Author's Method seems to be clear and natural, his Transitions neat and illustrating, and his Reflections and Observations judicious and instructive; particularly in Page 170, 171, and the Conclusion.

Mr. Echard's Preface.

His Stile, in the main, I take to be Grave, Manly, and proper for the Greatness of the Subject; in which there is Perspicuity without Meanness, Strength without Stiffness, and Politeness without Affectation. This is what it appears to me, after a careful Perusal of this Work: But, as I wanted Opportunity of examining it with the Ancient and Original Authors, from whence it was taken; so all that I can say as to that Matter is, That I have no Reason to think it unfaithful or defective: And I am glad to find my own Design so well incourag'd, and so advantagiously pursu'd.

Louth in Lincolnshire,
Novemb. 6. 1703.

Lau. Echard.

THE

The Author's
PREFACE.

THE *great Succeſs the two Firſt Volumes of the* Roman *Hiſtory met with in the World, tho' it was no more than what was due to the Author's Merit, was however an undeniable Inſtance of its extraordinary Uſefulneſs and Entertainment. As the Subject was great and peculiar, ſo was it written with a Genius equal to it; and the ſeveral Excellencies of thoſe ancient Authors that have been made uſe of in the framing this Hiſtory ſeem blended together, and dreſs it out in all the Beauties of Antiquity. Theſe obvious Conſiderations made me think, that at leaſt the vulgar Readers might probably*

The Author's Preface.

bably *defire* to know what was the **End** of that State, which had been fo extraordinary in its Beginning; and to leave it with the Second Volume look'd, in my Opinion, like a Ceremony too much in practice amongft fome Men, who ftick faft to their Friends in their Profperity, but drop 'em with the firft Opportunity, when once Fortune has forfaken 'em. The Roman Greatnefs appear'd too Majeftick, even in its Ruins, not to require our Attention; for Great Men, as whilft living they are gaz'd upon with Admiration, fo when dead are they ufually attended with a folemn Reverence to their Graves: But another more prevailing Motive made me wifh a Continuation of this Hiftory. The Enemies of Chriftianity have imputed the Downfal of the Roman Empire to the Principles of our Religion, as if it choak'd in its Profeffors the Courage, Vigour and Generofity of their Fore-fathers, and taught 'em to be fluggifh, unactive, and

no

The Author's Preface.

no otherwise than passively Valiant; that it was inconsistent with that Greatness of Mind, which so eminently distinguish'd the ancient Romans *from the rest of their Co-temporaries, and introduc'd a Poorness of Spirit, that made 'em careless and insensible of their ancient Glory.*

This was not only glanc'd at by the Heathen Writers of those Times, but is too frequently insisted upon in common Discourse by some Men of this Age, who think themselves wiser than the rest of Mankind, and assume a Privilege of condemning the Sense of all those whose Reason won't suffer 'em to concur with them in their airy Fancies, and ill-grounded Imaginations. The Reader, upon a Perusal of the following Sheets, will find the Fallacy of those Insinuations, and that the Downfal of the Roman *Empire was owing to other Causes than what have been suggested by these Men;*

The Author's Preface.

Men; and that both Principles and Practices, very opposite to those enjoin'd by the Gospel, occasion'd its Ruin.

As soon as I understood that he, who was best able, intended to concern himself no farther in it, I was persuaded to undertake this Third Volume; but by that time I had diligently consulted the Original Authors, from whom I was to be supply'd, and had recourse to those Modern Writers, upon whose Assistance I in a great measure depended, I quickly found how much Difficulty there was in the Attempt. However, the Encouragement I receiv'd from some who had the Perusal of the First Part of it, and who were Men of too much Learning and Judgment to be deceiv'd themselves, and of too much Integrity to deceive me, made me proceed with great Chearfulness; nor, 'till the Publick Censure of the World has condemn'd me, will I repent of my Undertaking.

The Author's Preface.

I have throughout this Third Volume aim'd at so much Sincerity, the very Life of History, that I may presume to tell the English *Reader he must not think himself conversing with a Modern Writer in the following Sheets, but with* Ammianus Marcellinus *himself, with* Zosimus, Aurelius Victor, Eutropius, Cassiodorus, *and the rest; the substance of whose Histories, as far as they related to my present Design, I endeavour'd faithfully to recite, divested of that Partiality, which, upon an unbias'd Enquiry, appear'd too notorious in some of the best among 'em, and are a manifest Instance to us of Human Frailty. Nor must I omit the great Helps I receiv'd from Monsieur* Le Seur, *and Doctor* Howell, *who at least directed me in my Enquiries, and often help'd me out in my Method and Observations.*

As

The Author's Preface.

As I am ready to confess my self far from being perfect in my Performance, so, by way of Excuse, may I be allow'd to reply, that neither are these my Guides infallible; they are most of 'em distinguish'd by some peculiar Failings, which I have endeavour'd to avoid, because I knew I was to be answerable for Faults enow of my own. I have interserted so much of the Church Affairs, as I thought would appear to be of a piece with the Body of the History. If the Reader finds my time not ill spent, my Design is answer'd, nor will I be concern'd at the Opinion of some Men, with whom Learning is of so small a value, that a bare Pretention to, or Acquaintance with it, is an unanswerable Objection with them, as if that Man was unfit to thrive in the World, who entertain'd Thoughts that soar'd above the Dregs of it.

The Author's Preface.

I hope the Errors of the Press will appear to be very few; the most material are these that follow, which the Reader is desir'd to correct with his Pen before he proceeds.

ERRATA.

PAGE 14. line 10. for *Daughter* read *Sister*, p. 18. l. 20. f. *guilty of* r. *punishable with*, p. 27. l. 4. f. *but* r. *for*, l. 13. f. *led* r. *offer'd*, p. 38. l. 16. f. *eminent* r. *imminent*, p. 41. l. 1. dele *to*, p. 56. l. 4. r. *Besançon*, p. 93. l. 25. after *King* r. *of*, p. 101. l. 28. f. *and* r. *his Father*.

A TABLE OF THE EMPERORS.

Uguſtulus and *Zeno*, } 53d Emp. pag. 375.

Anthemius and *Leo*, } 52d Emp. p. 359, to 366.

Arcadius and *Honorius*, } 48th Emp. p. 232, to 312.

Avitus and *Martian*, } 51ſt Emp. p. 353, and 354.

Conſtantine the Great, 41ſt Emp. p. 1, to 6.

Conſtantine II. *Conſtantius, Conſtans,* } 42d Emp. p. 8, to 65.

Glycerius and *Leo*, } 52d Emp. p. 369.

Gratian, 46th Emp. p. 185, to 199.

Jovian, 44th Emp. p. 90, to 99.

Julian,

A Table of the Emperors.

Julian, 43d Emp. p. 66, to 87.
Leo, 52d Emp. p. 355, to 370.
Majorianus and *Leo*, } 52d Emp. p. 355, to 357.
Martian, 51st Emp. p. 337, to 355.
Maximus and *Martian*, } 51st Emp. p. 349, to 351.
Nepos and *Zeno*, } 53d Emp. p. 371, to 375.
Severus and *Leo*, } 52d Emp. p. 357.
Theodosius the Great, 47th Em. p. 190, to 231.
Theodosius II. 49th Emp. p. 263, to 336.
Valentinian I. and *Valens*, } 45th Emp. p. 102, to 182.
Valentinian II. and *Gratian*, } 46th Emp. p. 163, to 221.
Valentinian III. 50th Emp. p. 315, to 348.
Zeno, 53d Emp. p. 372, ad finem.

CONTENTS.

VOL. III.

CHAP. I.

FROM the Removal of the Imperial Seat by Constantine the Great, to the Admission of the Goths into Thrace; containing about 45 Years.   Page 1

CHAP. II.

From the Admission of the Goths into Thrace, to the Death of Theodosius the Great; containing about the Space of 19 Years.
    Page 170

CHAP. III.

From the Death of Theodosius the Great, 'till the Taking of Rome the First Time by

The Contents.

by the Goths; *containing the Space of almost* 16 *Years.* Page 232

CHAP. IV.

From the Taking of Rome *by the* Goths, *to the Total Failure of the Western Empire in* Augustulus; *containing the Space of* 66 *Years.* Page 296

THE
Roman History.

VOL. III.

From the Removal of the Imperial Seat by Constantine *the Great, to the total Failure of the* Western *Empire in* Augustulus.

Containing the Space of about 146 *Years.*

CHAP. I.

From the Removal of the Imperial Seat by Constantine *the Great, to the Admission of the* Goths *into* Thrace.

Containing about 45 *Years.*

I. HOW prevalent soever the Reasons that induced *Constantine* to settle the Imperial Seat at *Byzantium* appear'd then to him, Experience has since shown they were weak and impolitick; for undoubtedly by that the *Roman* Great-

A.D. 330.

ness

ness received a fatal Stroke: And the Reader will find, in the Prosecution of this History, which we intend, God willing, to continue down to the total Failure of the *Western* Empire in *Augustulus*, that it never after appeared in its natural Vigour; but, like Flowers transplanted into a Foreign Clime, languish'd by degrees, and shrunk at length into nothing.

However, as he design'd to fix his own Court there for the future, so he desired it might be honour'd with the ordinary Residence of the succeeding Emperors; for which purpose he omitted no Cost or Labour, that might render it either beautiful or convenient, and by that Means invite 'em thither. He divided it into fourteen Regions, built a Capitol, made a *Circus Maximus*, an Amphitheatre, several *Forums*, *Porticus*'s, and other publick Works; which, together with the many Churches built upon a Religious Account, added much to the Lustre of the City. The Magnificence of which when he found it answerable to the Greatness of his Design, in a very solemn Dedication he consecrated it *To the God of the Martyrs*; encourag'd the Inhabitants by many Acts of Grace, secur'd them by many wholesome Laws, and Royal Immunities; for finding himself for two or three Years past disengag'd from War, he had more leisure to pursue his other Designs; but the Year following he was drawn by the *Sarmatians* into their Quarrel with the *Goths*, who finding *Constantine* had evacuated all the Garrisons along the *Danube*, made new Irruptions into *Mœsia* and *Thrace*, where they committed unheard of Cruelties, and ravaged the Country; but the Emperor, by his Son *Constantine*, obtain'd a memorable Victory over 'em, and finish'd the War with that Success, that near 100000 of the Enemy were destroy'd by Hunger and Cold, besides those that fell

A.D. 332.

by

by the Sword; upon which they were conftrain'd to sue for Peace, and deliver up Hoftages to the Emperor, among whom was their King's Son.

The *Sarmatæ* thus deliver'd from the Inroads of the *Goths*, were, two Years after, more cruelly opprefs'd by their own Slaves, whom in their Extremities they had been forc'd to arm againft their Enemies, and who by that means grown fenfible of their Strength, threw off the Yoke, and turn'd their Arms againft their Mafters, for whofe Defence they had been entrufted in their Hands; and herein they fucceeded fo well, that they forc'd 'em, to the number of 300000 of both Sexes, all Ages and Conditions, to fly for Refuge to the Emperor; by whom they were difpos'd in feveral Parts of *Thrace*, *Scythia*, *Macedonia*, and *Italy*, but fuch among 'em as were fit for Service, he incorporated in his Legions. This Example being follow'd by feveral of the fucceeding Emperors, prov'd very pernicious to the Empire; for thefe Barbarians growing too ftrong for the natural Inhabitants, among whom they were fettled, by degrees difpoffefs'd their Landlords, and became Mafters of the Country. This Year *Syria* and *Cilicia* were grievoufly afflicted with a Peftilence and Famine, which fwept off an infinite number of People, as likewife a great many were deftroy'd by an Earthquake in *Cyprus*.

A. D. 333.

And as thefe Parts of the Body Politick labour'd under thofe civil Calamities, fo was the Church no lefs afflicted with inteftine Diftractions; for about this time we find *Athanafius*, Bifhop of *Alexandria*, cruelly perfecuted by the prevailing *Arrians*, and formally condemn'd in the Council of *Tyre*, for feveral pretended Crimes objected againft him: From whence we may learn, how fatal the Profperity the Church then enjoy'd prov'd to her, how it open'd the Gates of the Sanctuary it felf to Corruption, and infatuated so many of her Teachers with Envy, Malice, and Ambition.

These things happen'd in the thirtieth Year of this Emperor's Reign, at which time *Calocerus*, a Man of great Authority in the Island of *Cyprus*, procur'd himself to be declared Emperor: But *Dalmatius* being sent with an Army against him, defeated him, and took him Prisoner; and having settled all things in that Island, he carry'd him to *Tarsus* in *Cilicia*, where he was burnt alive.

For this Service he was created *Cæsar*, together with *Constans* the Emperor's third Son, in the same Year, being the thirtieth of *Constantine*'s Reign, which he celebrated at *Constantinople* with great Magnificence: And the Year following *Constantius* his second was married to *Eusebia* a Lady of an illustrious Birth, and extraordinary Knowledge for one of her Sex. The Nuptials were solemnized with all imaginable Splendor, the Men and Women feasted apart, and the Emperor, in honour thereof, bestowed Gifts upon all Nations and Cities. These Feastings were prolonged by the Arrival of some Embassadors from the *East-Indies*, who brought him Presents of great Value, but greater Rarity; not only precious Stones, but several Animals unknown before to the Western parts of the World; intimating, as my Author has it, that his Empire extended to the utmost Bounds of the Ocean, and that as *Britain*, the Limits of the West, submitted to him at his first Promotion, so now at last the *Indians* in the East acknowledged his Sovereign Authority.

A. D. 336.

Having receiv'd this Homage from the *Indian* Embassadors, he divided the Government of the Empire in this manner; *Constantine* the Eldest commanded in *Gaul*, and some Western Provinces; *Constantius* govern'd *Africk* and *Illyricum*; and *Constans* rul'd in *Italy*. *Dalmatius* was sent to defend those
Parts

Parts that border'd upon the *Goths*; and *Annibalianus* had the Charge of *Cappadocia*, and *Armenia* the lefs. This Divifion was not made by *Conftantine*, as if he intended by that to diveft himfelf of his Sovereignty, but for the better Government of the Empire, and Education of his Sons, tho' it feem'd indeed an Ominous Introduction to that Partition, which was made in little more than a Year after. He was now near Sixty Years of Age, and yet was fo healthy and vigorous as to endure Exercife, Riding and Travel; of fo perfect an Underftanding as to be able ftill to Compofe Prayers and Orations, and affift with much Dexterity at the framing his Laws both Civil and Military.

Not long before his Death he made a Funeral Oration, in which he difcours'd much of the Immortality of the Soul, and the Rewards and Punifhments of another Life; by thefe, and fuch like Methods, preparing for himfelf an eafie Difmiffion out of this; 'till his Meditations were interrupted by the Difturbance the *Perfians* made in the Eaft, of which, as foon as he receiv'd an Account, he rais'd a powerful Army, intending, as he faid, to make this his laft Victory; but the Enemy being advertis'd of his fudden Expedition, and fearing to be engag'd in a War with him, difpatch'd away their Embaffadors, who upon an humble Defire of his Friendfhip, and a Promife to make good whatever Satiffaction fhou'd be requir'd, obtain'd a Peace. After this, finding himfelf feavourifh and diftemper'd, he made ufe of the warm Baths of the City, but receiving no Benefit from thence, he remov'd for change of Air to *Helenopolis* (a City built by him in Memory of his Mother) and from thence to *Nicomedia*; in the Suburbs of which Place, call'd *Achyrona*, he was Baptiz'd, declaring he defign'd to have receiv'd that Seal of his Salvation in the Wa-

A. D. 337.

ters of *Jordan*, but God in his infinite Wisdom had otherwise dispos'd of him. Then having partaken of the Holy Eucharist, he departed this Life on the two and twentieth Day of *May*, in the 62d Year of his Age, and 32d of his Reign (tho' the punctual time as to both is not fully agreed upon) the first Year of the 279th *Olympiad*, the 1090th Year of *Rome*, *An. Dom.* 337. *Fab. Tatianus* and *Felicianus* being Consuls, and about seven Years after the Removal of the Imperial Seat to *Constantinople*. Thus dy'd *Constantine* the Great, to the unexpressible Grief of the whole Empire, especially of the Church, which he had freed from Tyranny, and a most horrible Persecution. The Character of this Emperor is variously describ'd according to the various Passions and Affections of those Authors who have writ concerning him; the Heathen Writers wounding his Memory with all the Virulence imaginable, and the Christians beautifying it with accumulated Honours and Encomiums; however they all agree in this, that he was a Prince of innumerable Excellencies both of Body and Mind, ambitious of Military Glory, fortunate in War, but not more Fortunate than Industrious; a great Promoter of Learning, and of himself much addicted to Read, Write, and Meditate; if he was sometimes over credulous, as in the Case of his Wife *Fausta*, and the *Eusebiens*, by whose artificial Insinuations he was induced to Discountenance St. *Athanasius*, and the Orthodox Christians, it proceeded more from the Easiness than Malignity of his Nature, and was a Fault in others rather than in himself. His improvident Removal to *Constantinople*, and fatal Division of the Empire at his Death, are indeed Errors too apparent to be vindicated: But then his Zeal for the Gospel, and the Protection he gave it throughout his Dominions, made

Constantine dies.

His Character.

Chap. I. XLI. Constantine *the Great*.

made his Subjects and Posterity a Compensation more than equivalent, by opening to 'em the Gates of everlasting Life, and giving 'em a Title to a better Kingdom, of an Eternal Duration.

The Soldiers so soon as they heard of the Emperor's Death tore their Cloaths, fell prostrate on the Ground, knock'd their Heads against the Walls, and gave other Publick Testimonies of their Sorrow, as were agreeable to so general a Calamity; whilst their Officers in mournful and passionate Expressions call'd him their *Preserver, Deliverer and common Parent;* and the Townsmen joining with the rest in the Solemnity of Woe, ran like Mad-men about the Streets, or sate at home bewailing their Loss, dejected and oppress'd with Sorrow. When Grief wou'd give 'em leave, the Soldiers took up the Body, and, covering it with Purple, carry'd it in a solemn manner to *Constantinople*, where it was exposed in the Palace, with Lights burning round it, and Attendants watching it. Here Court was kept as if he had been still living; the great Officers that were wont to adore or salute, doing their Duty to him now as formerly; the Senate and all the Magistrates paid him the same Respect, and the Citizens were not wanting to testifie their deep Sense of his Loss, who had been so Noble a Founder and Benefactor to their City. Nor did Old *Rome* forget to sympathize with the New; for as soon as they heard of his Death all their Shops and Publick Baths were shut up, their Sports and Recreations which were us'd in times of Prosperity were intermitted. So publick was the loss of one Prince, who in his Life had been so general a Blessing.

II. *Constantius* (while his Brethren were absent) arrived at *Nicomedia* soon after his Father's Decease, and his first Act of Authority was his

his putting to Death his Uncle *Constantius Dalmatius,* and his Sons *Constantius Cæsar,* and *Anaballianus:* Tho' some think he no more than barely permitted, rather than order'd these Executions; yet they who plead by way of Excuse his Father's Command in his last Will, because they attempted to poison him, as some have improbably reported, and the Danger of Competition (for three Brothers were thought sufficient for the Government of the Empire) leave no room to doubt of the large share he had in 'em. However it were, this Act no way deterr'd the Soldiers from declaring him and his Brethren *Augusti,* or Emperors, which they did on the Fifth of the *Ides* of *September;* and sometime after the Division of the Empire was confirm'd between 'em at *Sirmium* in *Pannonia.* In which Division, *Gaul, Spain, Britain,* and part of *Africa Proconsularis* fell to *Constantine* the eldest; to *Constans* the youngest, *Italy,* with the rest of *Africk, Illyricum, Macedonia* and *Greece,* and those Parts that border'd upon the *Euxine* Sea; and to *Constantius, Mœsia, Thrace,* with *Constantinople, Asia, Egypt,* and the Eastern Empire, as far as from *Illyricum* to *Nisibis.* This Partition, tho' founded upon their Father's Testament, was not made without some Heat and Dissatisfaction, which, tho' compos'd for some time by *Constantius,* proved in the end fatal to the eldest, who thinking his Share too little for an elder Brother, demanded of *Constans* no less than the rest of *Africk,* and all *Italy;* and to make good his Claim Invaded his Brother's Territories with a powerful Army, and was Slain near *Aquileia,* in the third Year of his Reign.

A. D. 338.
In the mean time *Constantius* removed into *Syria* against *Sapor* King of *Persia;* who presuming upon *Constantine*'s Death, and the mean Opinion he had of his Children, had ravaged *Mesopotamia,* and was
sate

sate down before *Nisibis*, which *Constantius* was resolved to relieve, but the Work was done to his Hands before his Arrival; for *Sapor* despairing of Success had rais'd the Seige, and was retiring back. This was attributed to the Sanctity of *James* the Bishop, during whose Life and Residence there all his Designs against that City were ineffectual.

After this *Constantius*, that he might have leisure to attend other Affairs, incited the *Arabians* to Invade King *Sapor*, and divert him elsewhere; whilst he intent upon such Regulations in that Country as he found necessary, issued out several Edicts to that purpose, by one especially inhibiting all Incestuous Marriages, under no less a Penalty than that of Death. Here we shall leave him 'till the Affairs in *Italy* call upon him to revenge the Murder of his Brother *Constans*, who was now become sole Emperor of the West by the Death of *Constantine*, and in the Year 341. gain'd a Battel against the *Franks* in *Gaul*, and the Year following overthrew and quieted them; from thence he came over into *Britain* to punish the *Scots* and *Picts*, who had started out into Rebellion. The Particulars of this Expedition, which were recorded in the former part of *Ammianus Marcellinus* his History, are with that Peice lost to Posterity. After this he return'd into *Gaul*, and having obtain'd to himself a quiet Possession of his Brother's Provinces he grew remiss, and through his Intemperance contracted an ill Habit of Health, which render'd him very unfit for Business, and regardless of the State; nor did he take care to supply it with honest and able Ministers, but preferr'd those to the most profitable Employments, who were able to lay down the most Mony for 'em, and who for that reason oppress'd the People by an irregular Administration; the Odium of which, as it is customary in such Cases,

A. D. 341.
Constans his Wars in Gaul.

flew

A. D. 349.

Magnentius Rebels.

flew back upon himself. This, together with his Inactivity, which had render'd him disagreeable to the Army, and the Absence of *Constantius*, who was employ'd in the *Persian* War, encourag'd *Magnentius*, who had the Command of two Legions, to set up for himself, in which he was assisted by *Marcellinus* Præfect of the Treasury. *Marcellinus* in Honour of his Son's Birth-day had invited *Magnentius*, and several among the chief of the Army, to a Supper; and about Midnight, whilst they were in the height of their Jollity, *Magnentius* upon a pretence of some necessary Occasion withdrew, but a short time after return'd in the Imperial Robes attended by a Guard. Those of the Company who were privy to the Design immediately saluted him with the Title of Emperor, and the rest who at first look'd on it as no other than a Play or a Jest, (and as such it's probable, had the Plot miscarry'd, they intended it should pass) surpriz'd with the thing, at last follow'd their Example. Several of the chief Citizens of *Autun*, where this Scene was acted, were then in Company, who concurring with the rest induced the Inhabitants to salute and own him as *Augustus*; by which means he seized on the Palace, and distributed Mony among the Multitude, they who continued Loyal to their Prince being too weak to oppose him. Having proceeded thus far, he sent *Gaiso*, a Principal Commander in the Army, with a Party of Men to dispatch *Constans*; who being advised of what had pass'd, threw off the Imperial Robe, thinking to make his Escape, but was Murder'd by *Gaiso* himself in a Place call'd *Helena*, a little Village at the Foot of the *Pyrenees*. Thus fell *Constans* in the Tenth Year after the Death of *Constantine* his Brother, in the Consulship of *Sergius* and *Nigrinianus*, *An. Dom.* 350. His violent End may seem a just return of Providence upon

Procured Constans to be Murder'd.

A. D. 350.

Chap. I. XLII. Conſtantius.

upon him for the Murder of his Brother, and his loofe intemperate Life. At his firſt entrance upon the Government his Adminiſtration was both juſt and vigorous; and it may be ſaid of him throughout his whole Reign, that all the Provinces under his Juriſdiction enjoy'd a continued Serenity; for he kept the Neighbouring Nations in Peace about him, which was attributed rather to his Art in procuring of Hoſtages, than the Terror of his Arms: But his Tyrannical Deportment after his Brother's Death, his Licentious Life, and the little Care he had to ſee the Diſcipline of the Army ſtrictly obſerv'd, encourag'd *Magnentius* to riſe up againſt him, and Crown his Rebellion with his Death. But the People quickly found themſelves the Loſers in this unhappy Change, for *Magnentius* was of a cruel barbarous Nature, and being elevated with his Succeſs cauſed all the Magiſtrates in the Country, whom he had ſent for in *Conſtans* his Name, before his Death was known, to be Murder'd upon the Road; nor could he reſtrain his Hands from the Blood of ſome of thoſe who were Conſpirators with him. Notwithſtanding all theſe his Cruelties, and tho' he had declar'd his two Brothers, *Decentius* and *Deſiderius*, *Cæſars*, and at the ſame time diſpatch'd 'em to make ſure of *Gaul* and *Spain*, yet was his Sovereignty frail and precarious; for no ſooner had *Nepotianus*, the Nephew of *Conſtantine* the Great, heard of the Death of *Conſtans*, but he went with a Company of Gladiators, and ſeveral others of broken and deſperate Fortunes, who had eſpouſed his Cauſe, to ſeize on *Rome*, which ſome of *Magnentius* his Party had ſecured before, wherefore he ſate down before the City and Beſieg'd it; but engaging with *Marcellinus*, whom *Magnentius* had ſent with an Army againſt him, he was defeated, and loſt his Head, after he had pleas'd himſelf with the

A. D. 350.

Magnentius his Cruelty.

Nepotianus ſets up for himſelf.

Nepotianus defeated and ſlain.

the Title of Emperor Twenty seven Days. But Heaven, which thought fit to punish *Magnentius* for his perfidious Ingratitude to his Master, rais'd him up another Competitor in the Person of *Veteranio*, General of the Foot in *Pannonia*. He fearing least *Magnentius*, who was now become Master of *Italy*, shou'd break into *Pannonia*, and possess himself of that Country too, assumed the Imperial Robe, and was saluted Emperor by the Legions under his Command, by whose assistance he secured that Province, and fix'd his Head Quarters at *Mursa*, a Town belonging to it. Some say he advertis'd *Constantius* of his Proceedings, promising to assist him against *Magnentius*, which will not seem improbable if we consider the kind Usage he afterwards met with from that Emperor, who receiv'd the News of his Brother's Death, and *Magnentius* his Usurpation, with a Resentment that became him, and was fully resolv'd to chastise the Treason; but was at present deeply engag'd in the *Persian* War. For *Sapor* taking an Advantage from the Disturbances in the West, had miserably ravaged *Mesopotamia*, and was sate down before *Nisibis*; and finding the Besieged resolute to defend it, he drew the River off from the Town, thinking by that means they wou'd be constrain'd to surrender; which when he found ineffectual, for the Defendants digg'd very deep Wells, and had Fountains within sufficient to supply that want, he turn'd the River against the Town, and made a Breach in the Wall, which however was by an extraordinary Industry repair'd; despairing therefore of Success, and hearing the *Massagets* were making Inroads into his own Country, he return'd home after he had lost a considerable part of his Army.

Whereupon *Constantius* removed the following Year into *Pannonia*, and in his way from *Constantinople* was

was met by Messengers from *Magnentius* with Offers of Accommodation. 'Tis said that whilst *Constantius* was deliberating on the Answer he should return, his Father appeared to him in a Dream the Night following, holding *Constans* in his Hand, bidding him revenge the Death of a Prince descended from so many Emperors, upon a Tyrant and Murderer, and therein vindicate the Imperial Throne from so foul an Abuse: Whereupon committing the Messengers to Custody, he went with all Expedition to *Sardica,* a Town in *Dacia*. *Veteranio* surprized at his Diligence, and having before entertain'd an Inclination for his Service, went out to meet the Emperor, and receive him at his Approach; who glad of the Advantage, and pleased that he should not have two Enemies to deal with at once, embraced him, called him Father, carried him with him to *Sirmium,* set him at his Table, and consulted with him how to prosecute the War.

But some time after, when both ascended the Tribunal to harangue the Army, and *Constantius* from the Dignity of his Birth had the Precedency of Speech given him; he reminded the Soldiers, in a very eloquent Address, how much they were obliged to his Father, whose Liberality had been so extraordinary towards them, and before whom they had taken so many Oaths of Duty and Allegiance to his Sons: That therefore they were bound to revenge upon *Magnentius* his Brother's violent Death, and vindicate the Off-spring of their Patron and Benefactor from Treason and Assassination. Upon this the Soldiers, sensibly touch'd by so pathetical a Representation, disdaining an Usurper should sit on the Throne of *Constantine* the Great, pull'd *Veteranio* down from the Tribunal, and deprived him of the Imperial Robes, who thereupon threw himself at *Constantius* his Feet, and obtain'd an easie Pardon

Veteranio deposed by the Soldiers.

from

from the Emperor; who in Compassion to his extream Age, allow'd him a Revenue suitable to his Quality, confining him to *Prusias*, a City in *Bithynia*, where he spent the Residue of his Days without ever intermeddling in the Affairs of the Empire. After this *Constantius*, finding the Administration of Power and Authority in Countries at so great a distance a Burden too unequal for one Man, and despairing now of any Male Issue, married *Gallus*, his Uncle *Constantius*'s Son, to his own Daughter *Constantina*, and conferr'd on him the Title of *Cæsar*; who in his Absence was to have an Eye upon the *Persians*, and take care of the Eastern Provinces, whilst he was intent upon the Usurpation of *Magnentius*, and settling the Affairs of the Empire in the West. But *Magnentius* apprehensive of the Emperor's Intentions, chose rather to meet him abroad, than expect him in those he called his own Dominions, and thereupon advanc'd with his Army to *Noricum*, and thence into *Pannonia*, where he took *Sciscia* by Assault, and laid it even with the Ground. After this he wasted the Country lying upon the *Save*, and sate down before *Sirmium*, but being repuls'd from thence by the couragious Defence of the Inhabitants, he removed, and laid close Seige to *Mursa*, which *Constantius* was resolved to relieve; of whose Approach when *Magnentius* was advised, he disposed an Ambuscade of 4000 *Gauls* in a Wood adjoining, with Orders to fall upon the Enemy's Rear when they found both Armies engaged: Of this the besieged found means to acquaint the Emperor, who thereupon sent away two Tribunes with a strong Detachment to stop up all the Avenues to the Place, by which means the whole Party was cut off.

Magnentius seeing his Stratagems ineffectual, gave *Constantius* Battel in the Plains of *Mursa*; and both Armies

Gallus created Cæsar.

A. D. 352.

XLII. Constantius.

Armies fought with that Resolution, that the Emperor, tho' he gained an absolute and entire Victory, was deeply concern'd to see how much the Strength of the Empire was thereby impaired and broken. *Magnentius* is said to have lost 30000 Men in this Fight, but for himself, when he found his Men begin to give Ground, and fearful of falling into the Emperor's Hands, he turn'd his Horse loose, adorn'd as it was with the Imperial Ornaments, that the Enemy might imagine the Rider was slain, and fled with a few of his Party into *Italy*, there to recruit his broken Troops, and try the Fortune of another Battel. *Constantius*, as soon as it was Day (for the Battel continued all Night, with such Animosity did they engage) beheld from an adjoining Eminence the Plain cover'd with dead Bodies, and the River it self, that ran by, choak'd up with them; at which melancholy Sight he cou'd not refrain from Tears, exclaiming against *Magnentius*, who had been deaf to all his Messages of Peace, tho' he had made him an Offer of *Gaul* upon condition he would disarm: He order'd all that were slain to be buried without distinction, and such as were wounded to be attended with Care; after which he retir'd to *Sirmium*, where he resided the rest of this Year, and the greatest part of the next, ordering in the mean time some of his Troops to pursue *Magnentius*, who was retiring in the best Order he cou'd to *Pavia*, where he defeated *Constantius* his Commanders, and removed from thence with an intent of getting into *Rome*, but at his Approach he found the Gates shut against him; upon this he passed over into *Gaul*, and by the Assistance of his two Brothers he rais'd a very considerable Army in these Provinces, which he knew were firm to his Service, and so he was enabled once more to try his Fortune with the Emperor; who hoping by his Presence to redeem the

Magnentius over-thrown.

Flies into Italy.

From thence into Gaul.

A. D. 353.

Losses

Losses he had sustain'd by his Generals, after having published an Act of Oblivion, whereby he granted free Pardon to all such as wou'd return to their Duty, excepting those who were guilty of the many Murders committed during the Rebellion, and another touching the Auxiliary and Provincial Troops, *The Empe-* went in person into *Gaul*, resolving vigorously to *ror mar-* carry on the War against *Magnentius*; who made so *ches a-* resolute an Opposition, that several Encounters hap-*gainst him.* pened between 'em with various Success. At length *Magnentius* being defeated near *Lyons* retreated into the Mountains, where after he had endeavour'd in a set Speech to encourage his Men, whose Spirits began to sink under their ill Fortune, they answer'd the Conclusion of it, as the Custom was, by an Acclamation; but through an unlucky Mistake, instead of *Magnentius Augustus,* saluted him by the name of *Constantius Augustus*. This unlook'd for Omen so exceedingly disheartned him, that he immediately dispatch'd a Person of Senatorian Rank, and after him some Bishops to treat of a Peace with the Emperor, who wou'd not so much as admit 'em to his Presence, thereby teaching *Magnentius* what he was to expect from him; who perceiving there was no room left for Pardon, recruited his Army in the best manner he could, and sent a Villain to murder *Gallus* at *Antioch,* hoping the Emperor would be thereby obliged to go himself in Person against the King of *Persia,* and withdraw his Army from him. But the Person he employ'd unadvisedly discover'd the Secret of his Commission before he could put it in execution, and was thereupon executed as a Traitor. Some time after this happen'd another Engagement, near a Place call'd at this time *Montluel,* in *Magnenti-* which *Magnentius* was entirely routed, and with *us again* much Hazard made his Escape into *Lyons*. Where *defeated.* when he observ'd that the chief of his Followers, despairing

spairing now of any further Success, resolv'd to make their Peace with the Emperor, by throwing him up into his Hands, and for that purpose watch'd the House wherein he was lodg'd; he sent for those Friends and Relations that were near, whom in the Extravagance of Despair he slew with his own Hands, wounded mortally, as he thought, his Brother *Desiderius*, and at last dispatch'd himself, to prevent falling alive into *Constantius* his Power, and to avoid a lingring Death; after he had reign'd three Years and an half. This was the deserv'd End of a Tyrant and Usurper; the first Rebel that brought a Scandal upon Christianity, (of which he made an outward Profession) by the Murder of his lawful Soveraign. He was a Man of a prodigious Stature, and most outragious Morals; for he made both Law and Religion subservient to his Ambition, and in the Pursuit of his aspiring Designs, trampled under foot all the Obligations of Nature and Humanity. His Brother *Decentius* heard of his Death, whilst he was preparing to relieve him; and judging it impossible to obtain his Pardon from the Emperor, hang'd himself on the 18th of *August*, at *Senonæ* in *Gaul*: Tho' *Desiderius* was no sooner cured of his Wounds, but upon a submissive Application he met with an easie Pardon from *Constantius*; who notwithstanding punish'd, with great Severity, the Chief of those who had join'd with *Magnentius* against him. Thus the *Roman* Empire, which *Constantine* the Great had divided among his three Sons, became united in the Person of *Constantius*, the second, in the 17th Year of his Reign, and the 353d after the Birth of our Saviour; he himself being in his sixth, and *Gallus* in his second Consulate.

Kills himself.

III. At *Arles* the Emperor celebrated the *Circensian* Games, upon the account of this important Victory; the News of which, when it was brought to

Rome, was receiv'd with great Demonstrations of Joy and Satisfaction by the Senate and People; *Cerealis*, Præfect of the City, erecting a Statue to *Constantius*, with an Inscription declaring him the Restorer of the City and the Empire, and the Abolisher of the late most pestilent Tyranny; whilst the Emperor in the mean time was busie at *Lyons*, in settling the Peace of those Parts, and restoring them to their former Obedience. He first publish'd a general Pardon, and Act of Oblivion, to all who were not guilty of any Capital Crimes, such as Murder and the like; and then made void all the publick Acts of the Usurper, in several of which he had grievously oppress'd those, who during his Usurpation had stood firm to their Faith and Integrity. And to prevent such Robberies as wou'd otherwise ensue upon disbanding the Army, he by an Edict commanded all those who were to be dismiss'd, to apply themselves either to Tillage, or Merchandize; declaring such as disobey'd guilty of Death.

The rest of this Year, and the former Part of that which followed, he continued either at *Lyons* or *Arles*;

A. D. 354.

but towards the Spring he removed to *Valentia*, where he waited for the Provisions of his Army to be sent thither out of *Aquitain*, and prepared for an Expedition against *Gundomadus* and *Vadomarius*, two Brothers, and Kings of the *Germans*; who by their frequent Incursions wasted the Borders of *Gaul*, and the adjoining Provinces. Here he first received the unwelcome News of *Gallus Cæsar*'s ex-

The extravagant Behaviour of Gallus.

travagant Deportment in the East, who behav'd himself more like a Tyrant and Madman, than a Prince fit to govern the Provinces committed to his Care. His unexpected Advancement, and some slight Advantages obtain'd over the *Jews* and *Persians* at his Entrance upon the Government, had instill'd into him so much Pride and Arrogance, that he broke

out

Chap. I. XLII. Conſtantius.

out into all the Acts of Violence imaginable; which wou'd have ended in the Deſtruction of him that rais'd him, had his Power been equal to his Ambition. And leſt at any time his Paſſions ſhould grow cool, they were kept in a continual Flame by the reſtleſs and turbulent Spirit of his Wife, that *Mega-* *and Con-* *ra* of her Sex, whoſe Thirſt after Blood was as great *ſtantina.* as that of her Husband. Some were murder'd upon bare Suſpicion, others depriv'd of their Eſtates, and turn'd out a begging, without the Appearance of any Accuſer, or ſo much as a Slave, to put the leaſt colour of Juſtice upon their Proceedings. Mens Lives were bought and ſold, without any other Conſideration, than the Pleaſure or Advantage of thoſe who drove the Bargain. Thus *Clematius*, a Nobleman of *Alexandria*, was murder'd by the Procurement of his Wife's Mother. She burning in Luſt towards him, and not able to obtain her unnatural Deſires, turn'd her Love into Hatred, and reſolv'd to ruin what ſhe cou'd not enjoy. To which Purpoſe ſhe apply'd her ſelf to *Conſtantina*, and preſenting her with a Bracelet of great Value, obtain'd a Warrant to *Honoratus*, *Comes* of the Eaſt, to put him to Death, which was executed accordingly.

These Proceedings made *Gallus* his Government inſupportable, and occaſion'd a World of Miſchiefs; which however *Thalaſſius*, the *Præfectus Prætorio*, *Thalaſſius* might in ſome meaſure have prevented, had he gone *his impru-* prudently to work about it; but being himſelf of an *dent Beha-* haughty, arrogant Temper, he oppos'd him with too *viour.* much Heat and Licence, ſending the Emperor Information of all his Actions, not privately, but in publick, and with a Deſign *Gallus* ſhould know he had done it; which, inſtead of reclaiming him, made him act with more Fury and Deſperation. Thus were the Eaſtern Provinces oppreſs'd by their own Prince at home, and at the ſame time inſulted by their Enemies abroad. For the *Isauri*, a People accustomed to a ravenous pilfering Life, made frequent Inroads into the Neighbouring Parts, where they committed all manner of Violence, to revenge, as they pretended, an injurious Affront offer'd their Nation at *Iconium*, a Town in *Pisidia*, where some of their Country-men were expos'd to Wild Beasts upon the Theatre, contrary to the Precepts of Christianity, and the Custom of Christians. After they had rifled all the Merchants Ships they could find riding on the Coast, and from thence proceeded into the Inland Countries, stealing or killing whatever came in their way; they sate down before *Seleucia*, and laid close Siege to it. Of this frequent Complaints being made to *Gallus*, he sent *Nebridius* to relieve the Place, who hasten'd with what Forces he cou'd draw together to raise the Siege; of whose Approach, when the Rovers were advertis'd, they sav'd him the Labour, for they retir'd into the Neighbouring Mountains with Precipitation, and disperss'd themselves.

Nor had the King of *Persia* any better Success at this time in his Attempts upon the Empire; he had order'd *Nohodares* his General to fall upon *Mesopotamia*, who found the Coasts too well secur'd by strong Forts and Garrisons to attempt any thing upon them, and therefore directed his whole Design against *Batne*, a Town famous for a Mart held there every Year about the beginning of *September*, whither the choicest *Indian* Commodities were at that time Imported from other Parts for Sale; this Town he hop'd to surprize by means of a Wilderness that stood near it, but his Intentions were discover'd, and he forc'd to retreat with Loss and Disgrace. The *Saracens* in the mean time were more successful in their Irruptions, roving up and down, and destroying all they met; and then on a sudden

sudden retiring without giving the Enemy time to think upon a Recovery, or Revenge.

During these Transactions *Gallus* so far proceeded in his Outrages at *Antioch*, that he grew a Burden and Plague to all good Men, exercising his Cruelties upon all alike, without regard to Quality, Sex or Age. He had Murder'd the Principal among the Senators, had not *Honoratus*, *Comes* of the East, oppos'd it with an inflexible Resolution; and he was so highly delighted with the bloody Shows, which he exhibited daily upon the Theatre, that he had no regard to the Publick Edicts of the Empire, by which they were expresly forbidden. Of all these his Outrages *Constantius* was inform'd by *Thalassius* and others, and therefore resolv'd to deprive him of his Dignity, but endeavour'd first by fair Means and sober Remonstrances to recal him to his Duty, and commanded *Domitian* the Præfect, upon his Arrival in *Syria*, to try by all gentle Applications to reclaim him. But he, instead of following the Emperor's Instructions, behav'd himself with too much Arrogance and Indiscretion, and provok'd *Cæsar* to that degree, who did not usually meet with such rough Usage, that he procur'd him and *Montius* the Quæstor in a cruel manner to be Murder'd, as he did likewise *Epigonius*, *Eusebius*, *Apollinaris* the Father, and the Son, and several others.

Thus groan'd the Eastern Provinces under the Tyrannical Government of *Gallus*, of which tho' *Constantius* was but too sensible, he was not yet at leisure to repress him; for whilst he resided at *Valentia*, the better to prosecute his *German* Expedition, his Army which lay then at *Cabillon*, was ready to Mutiny for want of Provision, which had like to have prov'd fatal to *Ruffinus*, *Præfectus Prætorio* of these Parts; for he being Uncle to *Gallus* by the Mother's

The Army like to Mutiny in the West for want of Provisions.

Mother's side, was for his sake grown obnoxious to the Soldiers before, and was now requir'd to give them an Account how their Necessaries came to be detain'd so long from them; and if the forwardest among them, and those who were capable of doing the most Mischief, had not been appeas'd by some Presents of Gold sent for that purpose to *Cabillon*, by those who were chiefly concern'd, the Severity of their Inquisition had undoubtedly extended to his Life; but their Fierceness and Animosity being by this means quieted, and Provisions arriving in abundance not long after, the Præfect sav'd his Life, and the Army was in a readiness to march. They met with a vigorous Résistance at *Rauracum*, on the Bank of the *Rhine*, where when the Emperor had order'd a Bridge to be laid over, the Enemy from the other side ply'd the Workmen so warmly with their Darts and Arrows, that it was impossible for them to appear upon the Water; this reduc'd the Emperor to great Straits, for he knew not what Course to take, 'till one unexpectedly offer'd himself for a Guide, and undertook, for a good Reward, to conduct 'em over at a Place where it was fordable, which, in the Obscurity of the Night, he had certainly effected, had not the Design been discover'd by some of their own Country-men, who had Principal Posts of Command in the Army. Notwithstanding which, the *Germans* sometime after, doubtful of the Success of their Arms, if they persisted to the extremity, sent several among the Chief of their Nobility to sue for Pardon and a Peace; to which the Emperor, by the Advice of his Council, and Approbation of his Army readily consented, and so was now at leisure to consult what effectual Methods were to be taken to suppress and ruin his Cousin: The better to accomplish which he writ several obliging Letters to *Constantina*,

Chap. I. XLII. Conftantius.

ftantina, expreffing a mighty Defire to fee her, and invited her by all the tender Infinuations imaginable to come to Court, thinking that the readieft way to draw *Gallus* thither after her. She was too fenfible of what fhe had done not to apprehend the worft from the Emperor; however fhe hop'd by her artful Infinuations, and the Privilege of a Sifter to difarm his Rage, and without any farther Deliberation fet out to attend him, but was overtaken by a Feavour, which put an end to her Journey, and her Life at *Cæni Galliciani* in *Bithynia*. This threw *Gallus* into a great Perplexity, for he had now loft his only Advocate with the Emperor, whom he had too much provok'd, and who he knew was too inclinable to deftroy his Kindred, to liften to any Plea he could make, and was ready to lay hold on any Opportunity to deftroy him. So that had he met with any Encouragement, or cou'd have trufted thofe about him, who now began to defert him in diftruft of his inconftant Temper, and apprehenfion of *Conftantius* his Power, he had certainly affumed the Title of Emperor; but growing every Day more perplex'd in Mind, and being by feveral repeated Meffages importun'd from the Emperor to come with all fpeed into his Prefence, but above all perfuaded to it by *Scudilo* the Tribune, a crafty infinuating Man, who gave him all imaginable Affurances on the Emperor's part; he left *Antioch*, and fet out for *Conftantinople*, where like a Man in the midft of Security he exhibited Publick Shows to the People, and through his confident Behaviour made *Conftantius* more follicitous to provide for his Deftruction; he therefore remov'd all the Garrifons out of the Towns through which he was to pafs, left his Defperation might make him work any thing upon the Soldiers, and kept fuch a ftrict Watch upon him, that when he arriv'd at *Adriano-ple,*

Conftantius *refolves to get rid of* Gallus.

Conftantina *dies.*

ple, and the *Thebean* Legions Quarter'd in those Parts offer'd him their utmost Assistance, the Messengers were so narrowly observ'd, that they could by no means gain an Opportunity of speaking with him.

Here he receiv'd fresh Letters requiring him to hasten away, and ten publick Carriages were provided for the Conveniency of his Equipage, but all the Officers of his Court were left behind, except some few that attended in his Chamber, and waited on him at his Table. In this melancholy Condition he was hurry'd away to *Petow*, or *Petovio* in *Noricum*, cursing his own Easiness that had thus betray'd him into the Hands of his Enemies, and stung with Remorse for his many Murders and causeless Cruelties; in this Agony of his Conscience, that he might no longer doubt of the Designs laid against him, *Barbatio* and *Apodemius* appear'd attended by a Company of Soldiers, whom *Gallus* knew the Emperor had oblig'd so well that they wou'd decline executing nothing he should Command; and *Barbatio* the next Day enter'd his Chamber before it was hardly Light, depriv'd him of the Imperial Robe, and cloath'd him in a common Habit, assuring him in the mean time by repeated Oaths, that nothing worse than what he had already seen and felt was intended by the Emperor against him; but ordering him to rise with all speed he immediately clapp'd him into a close Litter, and convey'd him to a place near *Pola* in *Istria*, whither *Constantius* had sent Commissioners to examine him about those he had put to Death at *Antioch*. He with Looks full of Fear and Confusion endeavour'd the best he cou'd to clear himself, alledging that what had been done proceeded chiefly from the Instigation of his Wife *Constantina*. *Constantius* grew the more enraged at this Answer, which reflected

in

Chap. I. XLII. Conftantius.

in fo high a meafure upon his Sifter, and confequently upon himfelf; for which reafon, placing his whole Security in the Deftruction of *Gallus,* he refolv'd to put an end to his own Fears, and the other's Life together, and accordingly fign'd the Orders for his Death, which was executed upon him as if he had been a common Thief. Thus fell *Gallus Cæfar* in the 29th Year of his Age, and the beginning of the Fourth after his Promotion; he was the Son of *Conftantius,* Brother to *Conftantine* the Great, and of *Galla,* Sifter of *Rufinus* and *Cerealis*; his Death was chiefly owing to his own Tyrannical Deportment, but in a great meafure to the Procurement of *Eufebius* the Eunuch his bitter Enemy, and to *Scudilo* and *Barbatio,* who accufed him of more Crimes than he really was guilty of, for which Villany they met with a juft Reward, as we fhall fee hereafter. He was a comely well-proportion'd Man, of yellow Hair, and a thin Beard, but fo deprav'd in his Morals, that *Ammianus* will have him as much beneath his Brother *Julian* in every thing that was Good and Virtuous, as *Domitian* came fhort of *Titus.* *Gallus* was kill'd in the 1106th Year of the City, the 354th from our Saviour's Nativity, the fecond of the 283d *Olympiad, Conftantius* the feventh, and *Gallus Cæfar* the third time Confuls.

Gallus put to Death.

IV. The Emperor lay at *Milan* when he receiv'd the News of *Cæfar*'s Death, and what with the late Treafons of *Magnentius,* and *Gallus* his infolent Behaviour, he was grown fo jealous and diftruftful, that his Ears were open to all the Accufations, by which his Eunuchs and other infinuating Courtiers procur'd the Ruin of many brave Men. He had by his Severity, and the Death of feveral Perfons, render'd his Victory, obtain'd over *Magnentius,* lefs acceptable to the People, who found

Conftantius grows Jealous and Cruel.

found the Act of Indemnity of no Advantage to whomsoever the Emperor had the least reason to mistrust. Some upon little more than the bare Shaddow of Guilt were first fetter'd like Wild Beasts, and then were put to Death, depriv'd of their Estates, or banish'd, and that without the appearance of any Accuser against them. These Proceedings cast a great Blot upon the Reign of *Constantius*, especially in the Opinion of our Writers; for the Effects of his Jealousie extended as far as this I-

Paul, a Spanish Notary, sent into Britain.

sland, whither one *Paul*, a Notary, born in *Spain*, was sent to reduce such of the Army as had revolted to *Magnentius*. They that were guilty purchas'd their Safety with their Mony, by which way of Traffick, having once tasted the Sweetness

His Behaviour there.

of Riches, like a ravenous Wolf, he ran Headlong into all Villainous Practices, making the most innocent guilty, if they had but Estates, in which he intended to have a share. One *Martin* was at this time Vicar of these Provinces, who being much offended at *Paul's* Oppressions, endeavour'd at first by his Intercessions to stop the Career of his Villany, but finding that ineffectual, he was then forc'd more openly to oppose him; and the Contest grew so high between them, that he resolv'd at length to quit this Place, rather than be a Witness of the daily Outrages that were committed. *Paul* foreseeing this would put an end to his Trade, resolv'd to put him down among those that were to be accused, and us'd all his Interest at Court, that he might be sent for with the rest; of which when *Martin* was inform'd he attempted to kill the Villain, but failing therein he turn'd his Sword against himself, and by that means eased *Paul* of his Apprehensions; who pursu'd his Purpose, and carry'd his Prisoners up in Chains to Court, where some suffer'd a long uncomfortable Imprisonment, others were

Chap. I. XLII. Conſtantius.

were put to Torture; ſome were proſcrib'd and baniſh'd, and others put to Death. This was the uſe the Emperor made of his Succeſs againſt *Magnentius*, but after he found himſelf got rid of *Gallus* he grew exceedingly elevated, and gave himſelf up to the Hyperbolical Encomiums of his Ambitious Flatterers, by whom he was ſo far poiſon'd as to arrogate to himſelf the Title of *Lord of the whole World*; yet whilſt he aſpir'd to tranſcend the Dignity of the greateſt, he outwardly pretended to equal the Morality of the very beſt of Princes. But ſtill his Ears continu'd ſo open to whatever Accuſations were led to him, that Multitudes of People were brought out of the Eaſt in Chains to *Aquileia*, where one *Arbora* and *Euſebius* ſate upon 'em as Judges, and without making any Diſtinction between the Guilty and Innocent paſs'd Judgment equally upon all, ſentencing ſome to the Rack, and after that to Baniſhment; others to Servile Offices in the Army, and the reſt to Death it ſelf; for 'tis obſervable throughout this Emperor's Reign, that few or none eſcaped Condemnation in one of theſe kinds upon the ſmalleſt Preſumption of their Guilt. Theſe venerable Judges having diſpatch'd the Buſineſs for which they were ſent, return'd back in Triumph to *Conſtantius*, who whilſt he was employ'd in making Laws at *Milan*, relating to the Corporations and ſeveral Officers of State, and in too ſtrict an Inquiſition after Offenders, receiv'd Advice that the *Lentienſes*, a People dwelling upon the Borders of *Germany*, made frequent Incurſions into the *Roman* Territories, upon which War was declar'd againſt them. The Emperor ſet out in Perſon againſt them, and having march'd his Army into *Rhætia*, he there call'd a Council of War, wherein it was reſolv'd that *Arbetio*, Maſter of the Horſe, ſhould be ſent before

Conſtantius his Vanity.

with

with a select Body, and fall upon 'em on a sudden near the Lake of *Constance*. *Arbetio* follow'd his Orders, but the Enemy being inform'd of his coming, set upon him at so great an Advantage, that his Men were routed, and by the Favour of the Night most of 'em escap'd back to the Camp. The *Germans* were so elevated with this Success, that they renew'd their Excursions, and before it was Light sallied out almost as far as the *Roman* Camp; but were so warmly receiv'd, first by the *Scutarii* provok'd by their Insolence, and by degrees by the rest of the Army, that the greatest part of them were destroy'd, the rest flying as fast as they could from the Pursuers, leaving the Fields cover'd with the Slain. After the Emperor had obtain'd this signal Victory he return'd in Triumph to *Milan*, and there took up his Winter-Quarters.

There he had not long staid before his groundless Jealousies expos'd him to new Troubles, which were like to have ended in his Ruin. *Sylvanus* at that time commanded in *Gaul*, whither he was sent by the Procurement and Authority of *Arbetio*, who was Consul this Year together with *Lollianus*. *Sylvanus* ow'd this Advancement to the jealous Artifices of Rival Courtiers, who are apt to send those who are able to dispute their Master's Favour with them, far from his Presence upon some dangerous Employment. *Gaul* had of late been very much distress'd by the Inroads of the Barbarous Nations their Neighbours, who laid all waste before them with Fire and Sword. *Arbetio* thought this the most convenient Expedition to remove *Sylvanus*, if not out of the World, at least out of the Emperor's Sight, who as yet highly esteem'd him for his Merit. He was a brave experienc'd Commander, and proceeded with that Conduct against the Enemy, that by his Means *Gaul* was deliver'd from their Incursions. In

A. D. 355.

the

Chap. I.   XLII. Constantius.

the mean time *Dynamius*, a chief Commander in the Army, forged a Letter, directed from *Sylvanus* to his Friends at Court, exhorting them to assist him in his Design, which was no less than the Usurpation of the Empire. This Letter was produced, and *Dynamius* appointed to enquire into the Matter; who immediately apprehended all those named in the Paper who were near at hand, and sent to secure the rest, who were abroad in the several Colonies. The Matter made so great a Noise, and was of such high Consequence, that *Sylvanus* could not but know the dangerous Condition of his Affairs: And tho' upon a stricter Enquiry *Florentius*, great Master of the Houshold, discover'd the whole Intrigue, yet *Sylvanus*, who was well acquainted with the Emperor's credulous Temper, and knew how industrious *Arbetio* was to destroy him, concluded he should be condemn'd absent and unheard, and therefore at first resolv'd to throw himself into the Arms of the Barbarians; but being dissuaded from that by his Friends, he at length assumed the Imperial Habit; encourag'd to it by his Principal Officers, and forc'd upon it for his own Preservation. The News of this Usurpation was brought to the Emperor at *Milan*, who in great Astonishment summon'd his Council in the Dead of Night, to consult with them what was to be done upon so great an Emergency. Every one testified his sense of the Danger, in the Distractions of his Countenance; they found it easier to raise a Storm than to lay it; nor knew they whom they could chuse, able to oppose the Torrent they saw rolling down upon 'em. At length they pitch'd upon *Ursicinus*, an old Soldier, perfectly acquainted in Military Affairs, having serv'd under and with *Constantine* the Great in all his Wars. He had of late been in Disgrace, but was now sent for, and receiv'd with all the Honour

Sylvanus sets up for Emperor.

Against whom, Ursicinus is sent.

they

they thought due to a Deliverer. In employing him the Courtiers proposed to themselves a double Advantage; for if he miscarry'd in the Attempt, then should they be rid of one, from whose Anger they apprehended a Revenge some time or other, for the Injuries he had receiv'd; but if he prevail'd upon *Sylvanus*, then they should be deliver'd from the Danger which at present hung over their Heads.

It was resolv'd in Council, that *Constantius*, as if he knew nothing of *Sylvanus* his assuming the Imperial Title, should send him a Letter by *Ursicinus*, enjoining him to accept of him for his Successor, and return, and enjoy those Places he held before at Court. Hereupon *Ursicinus* received his Dispatches, and taking with him ten Assistants, among whom was *Ammianus Marcellinus* the Historian, he made all the Haste he could, the better to conceal his Expedition from *Sylvanus*; but notwithstanding all his Diligence, the News of it was got before him to *Cologn*, where at his Arrival he found a great Body of Forces drawn together in defence of *Sylvanus*. Upon this *Ursicinus* took other Measures, and endeavour'd to master his Designs by an outward show of Submission and Obedience. This procur'd him a kind Reception from *Sylvanus*, who admitted him to kiss the Purple, as the Custom was of saluting Emperors, and freely open'd all his Thoughts to him, consulting with him what was to be done for their mutual Security; and complaining with great Indignation, how vile, unworthy Persons were preferr'd to the Consulate, from which they had been hitherto most unjustly excluded, and treated with all Inhumanity, the one being stained with false Accusations of Treason, and the other hurried out of the East, and expos'd to the subtle Practices of his Enemies. This Security in *Sylvanus* was of great
Ad-

Advantage to *Ursicinus*, and his Associates; for by degrees they wrought so effectually with some of the Guards, that early one Morning they set upon those who had the Charge of the Palace, and having kill'd 'em, dragg'd *Sylvanus* out of a Chappel, whither he had fled, and cut him in pieces. Thus fell a brave deserving Captain, whom the crafty Malice of his Enemies, join'd with the Emperor's Credulity, had forc'd in his own Defence to usurp the Imperial Title: For tho' there was scarce a Man in the Empire deserv'd more of *Constantius* than himself, both for his Father's Services and his own, yet he knew all would be too little to oppose the natural Jealousie and Credulity of that Prince. *Ammianus* reports, that before he was slain in *Gaul*, the People at *Rome* cry'd out in the *Circus Maximus*, without any known Motive, or certain Grounds, that *Sylvanus* was overthrown.

<small>Sylvanus *murder'd.*</small>

V. *Constantius* express'd an extraordinary Joy at this happy Deliverance, but made a very ill use of it; for he grew more insolent and proud from his Security, and like *Domitian*, who quarrell'd with all that were better than himself; instead of rewarding *Ursicinus* for his extraordinary Service, he call'd him to a strict Account for some Mony which he falsly pretended he had intercepted in *Gaul*; and proceeded with such Rage against *Sylvanus* his Friends, that tho' *Proculus*, a lean infirm Man, endured the Rack with a wonderful Constancy, without accusing or mentioning the Name of any one Person whatsoever, affirming on the contrary, that what *Sylvanus* did was purely out of Necessity, not Ambition; instancing, that when he paid the Army, five Days before he assum'd the Imperial Title, he then us'd the Name and Authority of *Constantius*, exhorting them all to be constant in their Loyalty to him; which he wou'd not have done, had he design'd to set up for himself,

but

but have perverted the Treasure to his own Advantage: And tho' many more were ready to attest this as real matter of Fact, yet was *Proculus* and several others condemn'd and executed.

These his cruel Proceedings against his own Subjects at home, were in some measure reveng'd upon him by his Enemies abroad; for the Barbarous Nations, in Contempt of the Peace lately sign'd, broke in upon *Gaul*, and laid all waste before 'em. This exceedingly perplex'd the Emperor, who continued still at *Milan*, and was at that time unwilling to stir out of *Italy* himself, and therefore he was of Necessity to repress the Barbarians by some other Hand. Upon this he thought of promoting *Julian*, the Brother of *Gallus*, to the Dignity of *Cæsar*, tho' he was therein oppos'd by his Sycophants that were about him; who, when he protested that he was unable to sustain the great Burden of the Empire alone, affirm'd nothing was so difficult but must of necessity give way to his extraordinary Courage and Conduct: And had certainly diverted him from his Design, had not the Empress interposed; who, whether averse to long and dangerous Expeditions, or observing new Troubles arising in *Pannonia*, and that the King of *Persia* was preparing to make good his Claim upon *Armenia* and *Mesopotamia*, concluded it impossible for the Emperor to oppose so many Enemies at once, prevail'd with *Constantius* to pursue his Intentions.

Julian had been lately sent for out of *Achaia*, and had hitherto devoted himself wholly to Study. But now the Emperor, having called the Army together at *Milan*, mounted a Tribunal made for that purpose more conspicuous than ordinary, and placed *Julian* on his Right Hand; then he address'd himself to the Soldiers, told 'em under what Necessities the Empire lay at present, and how much he stood in need of an Assistant; that therefore he

was

was inclinable, with their Approbation, to dignifie his Coufin *Julian* with the Title and Authority of *Cæfar*, who was a young Man of approved Modefty and extraordinary great Hopes. As he was proceeding the Army interrupted him, telling him it was the Will of God, and it fhou'd be fo: Upon which *Julian* was clothed in the Purple Robe, and declared *Cæfar*. Then the Emperor, with a grave and fettled Countenance, faluted him with the Title of *Moft Loving Brother*; telling him, it added much to his Glory, that he could thus confer a Dignity, in a manner Hereditary, to fo near and dear a Relation; that he look'd on him now as his Affociate in the Empire, bound to fhare with him the Cares and Labours that attended it; that he committed *Gaul* to his Protection, and placed him at the Head of a ftout couragious Army; that being a valiant Man himfelf, he made no doubt but he wou'd appear fuch upon Occafion at the Head of his Troops, and animate his Soldiers by his own Courage, and be a Witnefs of theirs; that he might promife himfelf from him all the Love and Affiftance he cou'd expect; concluding, that he made no doubt but by God's Affiftance they fhould govern the *Roman* World with equal Piety, Prudence, and Moderation. Thus *Julian* was created *Cæfar* at *Milan*, on the fixth of *November*, in the Confulfhip of *Arbetio* and *Lollianus*.

Julian created Cæsar

In a few Days after *Julian* was marry'd to *Helena*, the Emperor's Sifter; and having prepared all things requifite for his Journey, he fet out for *Gaul* with a fmall Train on the firft of *November*, the Emperor himfelf attending him part of his way. At *Taurinum* (or *Trent*) he was firft inform'd of the Ruin of *Cologne*, a famous City in the fecond *Germany*, which the Barbarians had taken and levell'd with the Ground. This feem'd an ill Omen to his

And marry'd to Helena, the Emperor's Sifter.

first Undertaking, and made him say, That all the Advantage he was like to receive from his Promotion, was to perish with more Vexation, and to make a greater Noise at his Fall. At *Vienna* he was receiv'd with the general Applause of the People, who welcom'd him with all Expressions of Joy, and embrac'd him as their Deliverer. And when a blind old Woman, who ask'd what Prince was then making his Entrance, was answer'd it was *Julian*, she reply'd, Then this is he that is to restore the Temples of the Gods. Here he enter'd into his first Consulate, the Emperor, now eight times Consul, being his Partner: And before the Winter was well advanc'd he receiv'd Intelligence that *Augustodunum* (now *Autun*) a large City of great Antiquity, was besieg'd by the Barbarians, which he prepared with all speed to relieve; but upon his Approach he found the Enemy had rais'd the Siege, and were retired: Whom with the light part of his Army he pursu'd with such Diligence, that he overtook 'em near *Tricassin*, in Higher *Dauphine*, where they engag'd him in great Multitudes, and some of 'em he took, more he kill'd, and the rest he put to Flight, After this Action he remov'd to *Rheims*, where the main Body of his Army waited in a readiness for him under the Command of *Marcellus* and *Ursicinus*. From hence, after he had held a Council of War, he march'd against the Enemy; who taking the Advantage of a dark wet Night, and their Ignorance of the Way, fell upon his Rear, and had cut off two of his Legions, had not the rest of the Army, alarm'd by the sudden Noise, turn'd back to their Rescue. This made him more cautious in his Marches, and attempt some of the Cities upon the Borders, where when he had master'd 'em he might lye securely, and make Excursions from thence at his pleasure. In order to which he advanc'd towards *Brotomagum*,

A.D. 356.
His Exploits in Gaul.

or

Chap. I. XLII. Constantius.

or *Worms*, which after a succesful Fight against the *Germans*, who endeavour'd to hinder his Designs, he took, as he did several others that proved of great Service to him in the Course of the War. From *Worms* he removed to *Cologne*, which he caus'd to be re-built; and stay'd here long enough to conclude a Peace with the Kings of the *Franks*, who grew weary of the War, and deliver'd him up one of their strong Towns. After this he went to *Triers*, and from thence to *Senonæ*, where he took up his Winter Quarters. Whilst he lay here, the Enemy, who being inform'd that a considerable Part of the Army were absent, or dispers'd through the Country for convenience of their Quarters, came on a suddain and laid Siege to the Town. He with his Officers kept watch Day and Night upon the Walls, and tho' his Numbers were too weak to make a Sally, he defended the Place so long 'till the Enemy despairing to take the Town rais'd the Siege, and drew off. All this while *Marcellus* lay near at hand, and yet he never stir'd to relieve *Cæsar*, or preserve the Place, which he ought to have done tho' *Julian* had not been in it. For this Omission the Emperor, as soon as he was inform'd of it, turn'd him out of his Commission, and confin'd him to his House. This Proceeding made *Marcellus* imagin himself highly injured by *Cæsar*, on whom he was resolv'd to be reveng'd, by instilling into the Emperor's Ears such things as might raise his Jealousie, and end in *Julian*'s Ruin. *Julian* knowing well the Malice of the one, and the supine Credulity of the other, sent *Eutherius* to answer such things as should be objected against him; which he did so effectually, that *Marcellus* his Accusation fell to the Ground. Thus ended the War this Year in *Gaul*, doubtful in the Beginning, but in the Conclusion prosperous.

He is besieg'd in Senonæ.

And raises the Siege.

Being accused by Marcellus he clears himself.

D 2 The

A.D. 357.

The Year following, being the 21st of *Constantius* his Reign, he and *Julian* continued Consuls, the Emperor residing still at *Milan*; where he publish'd an Edict, restraining the Arbitrary Proceedings of the Provincial Officers in the Imposition and Levying of Taxes; allowing those called extraordinary never to be imposed but by the *Præfectus Prætorio* himself, and that only when there was an absolute unavoidable Necessity for it, enjoining him to acquaint the Emperor that he had imposed such a Tax; that what was done might be confirm'd by the Imperial Authority, or receive such Alterations as were judged convenient, before it was collected.

Constantius takes a Progress to Rome.

VI. After this the Emperor finding he had little to do resolv'd to visit *Rome*, where the Senate and all the People came forth to meet him, and so great was the Confluence, that he thought the whole World was there assembled together. He made his Entry in a Golden Chariot, which was adorn'd with such a multitude of sparkling Gems, that it rivall'd the Lustre of the Sun. The Dragons embroider'd upon Purple wanton'd in the Air about him, curling their Heads from the Ends of their Staves that glister'd with Pearl and precious Stones, and when they waved to and fro in the Winds, they seem'd alive by their Hissings, and Tortuosity of their Tails. When he came to the *Rostra* he was amazed at the sight of the *Forum*, that Demonstration of the ancient Power of the Inhabitants, and spake to the Nobility in the Senate House, and made a Speech to the People from the Tribunal. He was wonderfully delighted with the Place, but what he most admired was the Temple of *Jupiter Tarpeius*, the publick Baths, the Amphitheatre, the *Pantheon*, *Pompey*'s Theatre, and other magnificent Ornaments of this *Eternal City*, as *Ammianus* calls it, and as it is stil'd

by

Chap. I.   XLII. Conſtantius.

by the Emperors in moſt of their Edicts: In a Word, he was ſo amaz'd with what he beheld, that he complain'd of Fame, which either through Weakneſs or Malice had given a lame imperfect Account of what related to *Rome*, tho' in other Matters ſhe conſtantly exceeds the Truth; and deſiring to add ſomething of his own to the Ornaments of the City, he intended to erect an *Obelisk* in the *Circus Maximus*, which was done accordingly towards the latter end of the Year.

The Empreſs *Euſebia* had in this Progreſs to *Rome* brought under a ſhow of Friendſhip *Helena Julian*'s Wife along with her; and as ſhe had formerly brib'd the Midwife to deſtroy a Boy, of which ſhe was juſt deliver'd in *Gaul*, by cutting off too much of the Navel String, ſo now ſhe practis'd with ſo much skill upon her, that ſhe prevail'd with her to take ſomething which made her Miſcarry; for being Barren her ſelf ſhe could not endure ſhe ſhould be a Mother; and ſo careful were they, ſaith the Hiſtorian, to deprive that Valiant Man of Iſſue, who notwithſtanding the many Inconveniences he labour'd under in *Gaul*, had in many reſpects been very ſucceſsful againſt the Enemy. *Barbatio*, General of the Foot, was ſent out of *Italy* with a Supply of 25000 Men, and *Julian* had drawn out his Troops Garriſon'd about *Senonæ* in Order to join him, or fall in ſeparate Bodies upon the Enemy, and try if it were poſſible to reſtrain 'em with doubled Forces, and confine 'em within their Bounds, for they had now paſs'd the *Rhine*, and were advancing up into the Country. *Julian*'s Deſign was to encloſe 'em, if he could, between his own Army and that commanded by *Barbatio*, in which he ſucceeded according to his Deſire; for the *Germans*, notwithſtanding this additional Strength, paſſing between the two Camps, in their roving

Julian's *farther Progreſs in* Gaul.

man-

manner proceeded as far as *Lyons*, with an Intent to surprize it; but they were so warmly receiv'd by the Inhabitants, that judging it impossible to take the City they wasted the Country round about, and were returning with a great Booty; when *Julian*, who had notice of what was done, detach'd three strong Parties of Horse to three several places, by which he concluded the Barbarians must return, who accordingly were all cut off, except such as escap'd where *Barbatio*'s Post was assign'd him; for *Barbatio*, as well in this as every thing else, labour'd all he could to oppose and ruin *Cæsar*, and 'tis thought the Instructions he receiv'd from the Emperor were to that purpose, who was said to have sent *Julian* not so much to relieve the Province of *Gaul*, as to expose him to such eminent Danger, under which he must of necessity miscarry; so that when he demanded seven Boats of *Barbatio* to make Bridges over into some Islands upon the *Rhine*, where several of the Barbarians had secured themselves, he having notice of his Design burnt them all, as he did such Corn as had been of course provided, which came his way; for having taken half to himself he constantly burnt the rest; and after he had receiv'd a notable Defeat from the Enemy near *Basle*, who took the greatest part of his Baggage, and pursu'd him as far as the *Rauraci*, he as if the Summer's Expedition was over, sent his Men into Winter Quarters, and return'd to Court, where he persuaded the Emperor that his Army had been Victorious, and did all the ill Offices he could to *Cæsar*; who notwithstanding pursu'd his Designs with Vigour, and having coasted along the *Rhine* came to the *Three Tabernæ*, now *Zaberne*, a Fort lately Demolish'd by the Enemy, which he thought fit to rebuild the better to curb 'em, and hinder their Irruptions into *Gaul*. This Work he finish'd

sooner

sooner than was expected, and stor'd it with Provisions for a whole Year, which he got with much difficulty out of the Enemy's Country. But whilst he was busily employ'd in this Work, the Barbarians animated with their Success, and concluding that *Cæsar* himself was run away through Fear, assembled in great Numbers together, under the Conduct of six Kings, and encamp'd near *Strasbourgh*. Tho' at length they found that *Julian* was still in the Country, yet being inform'd by a Deserter that he had not above 13000 Men with him, they had the Arrogance to send in a menacing, imperious manner, and command him instantly to quit the Country he had Invaded, which was purchas'd by the Valour and Conduct of their Fore-fathers, otherwise that they would denounce open War against him. *Julian* not mov'd with the Message, but laughing at the Insolence of the Barbarians, detain'd the Messengers 'till he had compleated the Work, and then march'd directly against 'em; when he had first by a set Speech encourag'd his Men, who were of their own Inclinations forward enough, and demanded with one Voice to be led on against the Enemy, who inform'd of their Approach, stood in a readiness to receive them. The *Romans*, during the whole Course of this War, had never been so hardly put to it as now; for besides that the Enemy were more than double their Number, they were headed by *Chnodomarius* and *Serapio*, the most Valiant of their Kings, assisted by five others, and ten more of the Royal Families, together with a great number of the Nobility.

The Right Wing of the *Roman* Army consisted of their Cavalry, which the Enemy oppos'd with the choice of their Horse, lining their Ranks up and down with some Foot, who creeping and insinuating themselves here and there, as occasion requir'd, *His Victory over the Barbarians at Argentoratum.*

quir'd, ſtabb'd their Horſes, and put 'em at firſt into a great Confuſion, and at laſt to an abſolute Flight; nor could all the Rhetorick *Julian* was Maſter of perſuade 'em, for a long time, to Rally and Charge a ſecond time upon the Enemy, who were by this time fallen with great Violence upon the Foot, and had cut themſelves a Paſſage through the Legions, 'till they had pierc'ed up as far as the Body of thoſe call'd *Primani*, who being the choiceſt of the *Roman* Infantry took Advantage of their Raſhneſs, and put 'em to a diſorderly and bloody Flight. Many of 'em unable to flie faſt enough for the Heaps of the dead Bodies that choak'd up the Way, ventur'd to take the *Rhine*, wherein moſt of 'em were drown'd, kill'd or taken. Among the reſt *Chnodomarius* endeavouring to paſs the Water was purſu'd and forc'd to yield; they that took him brought him to *Cæſar*, of whom he begg'd Pardon with great Submiſſion, which being granted him, he was ſent to *Rome*, where he dy'd ſome time after of a Lethargy. Of the Enemy ſix thouſand dy'd upon the Place, beſides vaſt numbers of thoſe that periſh'd in the River. The *Romans* loſt no more than 243 Men. After this ſo unexpected a Victory the Army ſaluted *Julian* by the Title of *Auguſtus*; but he abſolutely refus'd it, and reprov'd the Soldiers for it, telling 'em 'twas an Honour belonging to none of Right but *Conſtantius*, who upon the News of his Succeſs attributed this, as he did all the reſt, to his own Fortunate Conduct, as if he had been Fighting himſelf at the Head of his Armies.

Julian, after the Battel, ſent away his Priſoners and all his Booty to *Metz*, whilſt he himſelf advanc'd to *Mayence*, where he built a Bridge over the River, and fell upon the *Germans* in their own Country, which he laid Waſte by way of Retaliation,

tion, and began to repair a Fort to which the Emperor *Trajan* had formerly given his own Name. With this the Barbarians were so exceedingly discourag'd, that they sent and su'd for a Peace, which could not be obtain'd upon any Terms, but a Truce was granted them for ten Months, which they oblig'd themselves inviolably to maintain, and in which time *Julian* concluded the Fortifications he had begun would be finish'd; returning from thence in order to put his Men into Winter Quarters, he was forc'd to chastise some *Franks*, who presuming upon his Absence in *Germany*, had to the number of 600 rifled all the Country about *Rheims*, and hearing of his Return seiz'd on two Forts which had been dismantl'd, and therein fortify'd themselves in the best manner they could. One of these Castles standing upon the *Meuse*, *Julian* besieg'd, and tho' they defended themselves with great Obstinacy for 50 Days together in the midst of Winter, yet he press'd 'em so hard that they were forc'd to surrender, and were all sent away to the Emperor; after which he dispers'd his Men into Winter Quarters, and went himself to *Paris*, where he consulted how to improve the small time of the Truce to the Ease and Refreshment of the exhausted Provinces.

VII. The Year following the *Quadi* under the Command of *Vitrodorus*, and the *Sarmatæ* led by *Zizais* their King, broke with great Violence into *Pannonia*, upon which the Emperor early in the Spring set forward from *Sirmium* with a very good Army; and tho' the *Danube* was at that time swoln very much by reason of a sudden Thaw, he made a Bridge of Boats and pass'd the River. This unexpected Diligence in the Emperor very much perplex'd the Barbarians, who were in no manner prepared to receive him, so that they who were best able

A. D. 358.
The Quadi Invade the Empire.

able to defend their Country, instead of resisting the Enemy, shifted for themselves, and left their Friends and Relations expos'd to the Fury of the *Roman* Soldiers, by which means all that part of *Sarmatia* which lay nearest to *Pannonia Secunda* was entirely ruin'd. This at length provok'd the Inhabitants so far, that being assisted by their Friends the *Quadi*, they try'd their Fortune in several Rencounters, but were as often defeated. This made 'em so desirous of Peace, that they were content to deliver up themselves, their Wives, Children, and Territories into the Emperor's Hands to purchase it, which however they obtain'd upon cheaper Terms, being only oblig'd to restore the Prisoners they had taken, and for the future submit to his Commands.

but are suppress't by Constantius.

This Act of Clemency towards *Zizais* and his Associates had such Operation upon their Neighbours, that those of the *Quadi* who inhabited beyond the Mountains, and the *Sarmatæ* next adjoining to them, in a just Sense of the many Outrages they had committed, came in the greatest Humility to sue for a Pardon and Peace, which they obtain'd upon giving up their Hostages chosen by Lot out of the Sons of the Nobility, and with them such Prisoners as they had taken. There yet remain'd the *Sarmatæ Limigantes*, those who being Slaves had dispossess'd their Masters, as we observ'd before, who had committed such Outragious Villanies as call'd aloud for Punishment; however the Emperor intended to deal more gently with them than they deserv'd, and only to remove 'em farther off, that they might not be tempted by Opportunity so often to infest the Empire. Upon appearance of the *Roman* Army they pretended an extraordinary Fear, as if they expected nothing but Destruction: They begg'd Pardon, and promis'd an yearly

yearly Tribute both of Men and Mony, and to remain subject to the Empire. *Constantius*, who gave too great Credit to their gentle Behaviour, order'd 'em to come over to the hither Bank of the River, there to be inform'd of his Pleasure, which they did but rather to dispute his Commands than obey 'em, and to let him know they were not afraid to Face his Army. The Emperor observing their surly Temper, so dispos'd of his Men as to encompass them, and prevent their Designs should they attempt any Violence; then standing on an Eminence rais'd on purpose that he might be seen and heard, attended by some of his Principal Officers, and his Guards about him, he gently admonish'd them to be quiet. But they mixt their Desires of Peace with a sort of Stratagem, for they cast their Targets at a great distance from them, as in Jest, that going to take them up they might gain the more Ground, and give the better Onset. Night coming on, the Army with Banners display'd fell upon them, whereupon they made with great Fury towards the Throne; but the Soldiers speedily forming themselves into the shape of a Wedge, with great Violence remov'd them, and then slaughter'd them like so many Wild Beasts caught in the Toil; but they fell with invincible Constancy and Resolution, asking neither for Pardon nor Quarter, but avowing in Death they deserv'd a better Fortune. This Execution being over, the enrag'd Soldiers dragg'd the Relations of those who were Slain out of their Huts, and without regard to Sex or Age destroy'd all alike. Some that escap'd attempted to swim the River, but were either drown'd or kill'd by the Pursuers. The rest of these *Limigantes* upon Security of the Publick Faith came down from the Mountains, and flock'd with all their Relations to the *Roman* Camp, from whence they were remov'd by

their

their own Consent to other Places, where for some time they liv'd in Peace and Security, but at length return'd to their former Fierceness and Barbarity. After this the Emperor, for these his Atchievements call'd *Sarmaticus* by his Soldiers, return'd to *Sirmium* in Triumph; from thence he remov'd towards *Constantinople*, the better to prepare against *Sapor* the King of *Persia*, who for some time had laid Claim to *Armenia* and *Mesopotamia*, and was now resolv'd to make it good by force of Arms.

A. D. 359.

The King of Persia begins new Troubles.

VIII. He being now in perfect Peace with the Princes his Neighbours, and observing the Distractions of the Empire, thought it a proper time to pursue his Pretensions. *Constantius* was wholly guided by *Eusebius* the Eunuch, a proud, factious, intreaguing Courtier, who listen'd more to his own Avarice, Ambition or Revenge, than his Master's Honour or Profit. *Ursicinus* at that time commanded in the East, and was the fittest Man in the Empire for that Post in Case of a War. *Eusebius* had long been contriving his Ruin, as being the only Person who was either Independent of him, or else scorn'd his Support; and herein he succeeded so far that he was recall'd to Court under a Pretence of succeeding *Barbatio*, who had been lately Beheaded, and *Sabinianus* a decrepid old Man, every way unfit for such an Employment, was sent in his Place; who making what haste he could to be possess'd of his new Dignity, produc'd the Emperor's Letters to his Predecessor at *Cilicia*; the Substance of which being known abroad created great uneasiness in the People, who judg'd themselves expos'd to manifest Ruin, being depriv'd of their Guardian at so nice and dangerous a Conjuncture; on the other Hand the King of *Persia* was resolv'd not to omit so favourable an Opportunity, but march with all speed and

Ursicinus recall'd from his Command,

and Sabinianus sent in his room.

and seize on those Countries, which were now govern'd by so unfit a Commander; being prompted to it by the Advice of *Antoninus*, who had lately been a Servant to the Emperor, but being injur'd and opprefs'd by the great Officers had withdrawn with all his Family, and thrown himself into the Protection of *Sapor*; to whom he discover'd the whole State of the Army, of what Numbers the several Parties consisted, of what Strength, where Quarter'd, and who commanded them in times of Expedition; as likewise whence, where, and how they were furnish'd with Arms and Provision.

In the mean time *Ursicinus*, pursuant to his Orders, was returning into *Italy*, but in *Thrace* he receiv'd Letters from *Constantius*, requiring him to haste back into *Mesopotamia*, but without any Guard, for that the Power was now entrusted in another's Hand; and this was contriv'd on purpose by his Enemies, that the new Commander might have the Honour of the Action if the King of *Persia* miscarry'd, but if he succeeded in his Expedition, the Ignominy might be charg'd upon *Ursicinus* as a Traitor to his Country. However he return'd in Obedience to the Emperor's Command, and tho' he found *Sabinianus* a Man of a mean Spirit and narrow Soul, he took the best Care he cou'd, and diligently fortify'd *Nisibis*, left the Enemy should attack it unawares. Understanding the *Persians* had pass'd the *Tigris*, he with some Forces travers'd the Country, burnt up all the Forage, and fortified the Bank on this side *Euphrates*; so that the *Persians* cou'd neither find Subsistance for their Army, nor a Ford to pass the River, 'till *Antoninus* conducted 'em more towards the Right, where they found Grass and Corn enough, and a Place towards the Head of the River that was fordable. During these Marches and Counter-marches *Ursicinus* by chance met with *Antoninus*, whom he reviled

viled in very bitter Terms, calling him Villain and Traitor. *Antoninus* instead of endeavouring to conceal himself, leap'd from his Horse, took the *Tiara*, which as a Badge of the greatest Honour had been presented him, from his Head, bow'd himself to the Ground, call'd him Patron and Lord, and begg'd him to pardon him; confessing he had embrac'd a dishonourable Course, but was necessitated to it by the Avarice and Oppression of some, against whom neither your Power, said he, Virtue or Authority can protect you; and then withdrew to his Party with all the Signs of Submission and Respect.

King Sapor besieges Amida. Not long after this two *Roman* Castles were surrender'd to *Sapor*, who in prosecution of his Designs came the third Day after, and sate down before *Amida*, the Metropolis of *Mesopotamia*, much beautify'd and enlarg'd by *Constantius*; which he expected would have been deliver'd up to him immediately, and not have hinder'd him in the Pursuit of those Councils had been suggested to him by *Antoninus*, concluding those within would not dare to hold out, when once they beheld him in all his Pomp of Majesty at the Gate: But was highly incens'd when he found they were so far from receiving him with the Honour he expected, that they assaulted him with their Javelins from the Wall, one of which was directed so well that it cut off part of his Robe: Upon which he exclaim'd against them with as much Indignation as if they had sacrilegiously robb'd a Temple, in that they had presum'd to offer Violence to him that was Lord of so many Kings and Nations, and therefore finding upon a second Trial that they were inflexible, he resolv'd at once to destroy the Town and the Inhabitants, and accordingly prepar'd for a vigorous Attack; whilst they within, who thought of nothing but how to die with most Honour, prepar'd for as vigorous a De-

Defence. Never was Seige carry'd on with more Bravery, nor so many Men lost in so short a time. The Besieg'd, besides the Difficulties they met with from without, labour'd with as great within; for such a noisom Stench arose at that hot Season of the Year from the multitude of dead Bodies which cover'd the Streets, and which they had not time to bury, that it bred a devouring Pestilence, which swept away almost as many as the Sword. In the mean time *Ursicinus*, tho' much disdaining to be subjected to the Command of another Person, especially one so unworthy as *Sabinianus*, however sent and advis'd him to bring the *Velites* into the Field, that they might divert the Enemy, and force him to raise the Siege, or at least distress him in his Trenches, and intercept him by Stratagems as he removed from Place to Place. But *Sabinianus*, who had privately agreed with those who had promoted him never to give his Predecessor the Opportunity of doing any thing that would redound to his Honour, tho' the Provinces in the mean time lay at stake, absolutely deny'd him, alledging his Instructions were to do nothing that might endanger the Army. *Ursicinus desiring to relieve it, is oppos'd by Sabinianus.*

There were in *Amida* two Legions of *Gauls*, who had formerly serv'd under *Magnentius*. They, unused to the Fatigues of Sieges, were impatient to see themselves immured up, whilst their Enemies raged with so much Fury abroad; especially when they beheld from the Walls a multitude of miserable Wretches led into Slavery, whom *Sapor* had forc'd out of the several Forts in the Country, whither they had flock'd for Safety, many of whom spent with Travel, and unable to proceed any further, they hamstring'd, and left behind on the Roads: Whereupon grown too unruly for their Commanders, they took the Advantage of a dark misty Night, and issued *A desperate Attempt of some Gauls.*

sued out at a Postern, arm'd with Swords and Battle-Axes, having first fortified themselves by their Prayers, and then proceeded with so much Caution that they were in hopes of reaching the King's Quarters without Discovery; but falling of necessity upon the Guards, whom they cut in pieces, the Noise of the wounded quickly alarm'd the Body-Guard, which put these daring *Gauls* to a stand, who finding themselves frustrated of what they chiefly aim'd at, retir'd in the best order they cou'd out of the Lines, with their Faces still turn'd towards the Enemy, and by degrees recover'd the City with the Loss of 400 of their Company, besides those that were wounded, having narrowly miss'd killing the *Persian* King, tho' surrounded by an Army of 100000 fighting Men. The rising Sun discover'd to the *Persians* the mighty Loss they had sustain'd; several of the Principal Nobility were found among the Slain, which rais'd a general Lamentation throughout the Camp, the King himself having the greatest Reason to bewail the Loss of his nearest Friends and Relations. This made him push on the Siege with more vigour, and oblig'd the Besieg'd to defend themselves with more obstinate Resolution; and thus Rage combating with Despair occasion'd the Loss of many brave Men on both sides. But at length the very Instruments of their Defence reduced the Besieg'd to the last Extremity. One of the Mounts they had rais'd to oppose the *Persian* Towers remov'd as with an Earthquake, and fell upon the Wall bearing it down into the Ditch, where it serv'd as a Bridge to the Enemy, and gave 'em a large Entrance. The greatest Part of the Garrison were by this time kill'd or disabled, and yet they that were left flock'd in great Numbers to make good the Breach, tho' at the certain Hazard of their Lives. But the Vigour and Alacrity of the *Persi-*

Amida taken.

an

an King, who expos'd himself equally with the meanest Soldier, bore down all before him. The Ditch was fill'd with dead Bodies, which thereby afforded a larger Access to the Town. When no further Resistance could be made, the Defendants, half dead already with their Watching and Labour, were slaughter'd like Sheep without any Regard had to Sex or Age. Some of the most healthy got together, and made as resolute an Opposition as they were able, resolving to sell their Lives at as dear a rate as they cou'd. But *Ammianus* our Historian, with two or three more escap'd, and got safe to *Ursicinus*, who was then on his way to *Antioch*. *Sapor* having rased the City, as he threatned, return'd homeward in an outward Show of Triumph, but inwardly afflicted at the Loss of so many Men, for no less than 30000 are said to have perish'd on his side before the Town; which, considering it hinder'd him from pursuing those advantagious Designs suggested to him by *Antoninus*, gave him little Reason to brag of this Expedition.

and destroy'd.

Tho' *Ursicinus* had done all he could, without the Concurrence of the Commander in chief, who in ev'ry thing oppos'd him, to relieve the Town; yet the Loss of that, and several other heinous Matters, were with all Bitterness alledg'd against him at his Return to Court, whither he was sent for under the Pretence of succeeding *Barbatio*. The Emperor, whose Ears were always open to Accusations, tho' brought against his most faithful Servants, committed the hearing of the Matter to *Arbetio* and *Florentius*, with Charge to enquire into *Ursicinus* his Conduct, and how *Amida* came to be destroy'd.

Ursicinus *accus'd at Court.*

The Allegations brought against him were so notoriously false, that they cou'd not for Shame but reject 'em; and yet so much were they afraid of offending *Eusebius*, that they durst not lay the Load as they ought, upon the base Cowardise of *Sabinianus*, and therefore declining any farther Enquiry into that Affair, they insisted only on trifling Matters, that were foreign to the Purpose. *Ursicinus* worthily provok'd at such corrupt Proceedings told 'em boldly, that tho' they pass'd it over with so much Contempt, the thing was of too great a Consequence to be neglected: That it deserv'd the Emperor's own Examination, who could not but severely punish so foul a Miscarriage, in whomsoever he should find it; and foresaw that so long as he suffer'd himself thus to be govern'd by Eunuchs, tho' he should go himself in Person next Spring with an Army into the Field, yet should he not be able to protect *Mesopotamia*. This was told to *Constantius* with very malicious Aggravations, which so highly incens'd him, that he broke off the Inquisition, not permitting those things to be expos'd to the Light which had been industriously hid from his Knowledge; and turn'd *Ursicinus* out of his Place, confining him to a retir'd Life in the Country.

and confined to a private life

IX. In the mean time *Julian* proceeded with wonderful Success against the *Germans* inhabiting on both sides of the *Rhine*, and in the end forc'd 'em to accept of a Peace, upon such Conditions as he thought fit to prescribe. And hearing the *Picts* and *Scots* were making Incursions into the *Roman* Territories in *Great Britain*, he sent thither his Lieutenant *Lupicinus*, who drove 'em back into the Northern Parts of the Island, and settled the Subjects of the Empire in Peace and Tranquility.

These Exploits, which added much to *Cæsar*'s Reputation, were no way acceptable to the jealous Temper of *Constantius*, who thought those new Accessions to the Empire were no other than Diminutions to his Honour and Security. He remember'd

The Emperor jealous of Julian,

how

how dangerous *Gallus* had like to have proved to him, and look'd on him as still living in *Julian*; for which reason he greatly desir'd to weaken and oppress him, which could be done no way so effectually as by recalling part of his Army from him, for which he had now a fair Opportunity, and, outwardly at least, a very just Pretence.

   Sapor persisting still in his Resolution of conquering *Mesopotamia*, had pass'd the *Tigris*, and laid close Siege to *Singara*, which after a vigorous Defence he took by Assault, as he did likewise *Bezabde* a strong Fort situated on a Hill, the Walls of which he repair'd, and put into it a good Garrison, well knowing of what Consequence it was to either Party that were in Possession of it: And if his victorious Arms had not met with some Resistance at *Urta*, he had undoubtedly over-ran all *Mesopotamia*; which *Constantius* was in Interest and Duty bound if possible to prevent, and therefore sent to *Julian* for the best Soldiers and most experienc'd Commanders of his Army, together with all the Auxiliary Troops he had rais'd in *Gaul* and *Germany*, that by such an Accession of Strength he might be the better able to make head against the *Persians*. These Forces had been rais'd by *Julian*, upon a Promise that they should never be oblig'd to pass the *Alps*, nor be forc'd to serve in remote Parts, which their Officers in a submissive manner represented to him. He receiv'd 'em with wonderful Civility, inform'd 'em that he was as much dissatisfied as themselves, but that it was the Emperor's Pleasure, which by all means was to be obey'd. He highly commended such of them as were known to him, remember'd them of the glorious things they had perform'd under his Conduct, express'd a great Unwillingness to part with such worthy Fellow-Soldiers; however in the Conclusion gently advis'd them chearfully to sub-

margin: *Julian sends for part of his Army;*

submit to the Emperor's Command, and signalize their Valour in foreign Parts, for which they might be assured of very honourable Rewards: And when he had finish'd his Speech he invited them all to Supper, where he entertain'd 'em with much Tenderness and Affection, as well as Magnificence. This Condescension prevail'd so far with Men, who were before unwilling to be banish'd in a manner from their Native Country, and were now resolv'd never to part with so obliging a Commander, that they had not patience to stay 'till Morning, but after they were dismiss'd from Supper they communicated their Thoughts to one another, and return'd in a menacing manner to the Palace, which they surrounded, and with a rude tumultuous Noise saluted *Julian* by the Title of *Augustus*. He at first outwardly oppos'd the Honour they were bestowing upon him, and reminded 'em of their Duty; but when he found they were firm to their Purpose, and that all he could say made no Impression on 'em, he with much seeming Reluctancy was at length compell'd to accept of the *Imperial Title*.

who mutiny, and declare Julian Emperor.

A. D. 360.

For some time after this he kept himself retir'd, without any regard to the publick Affairs, as if he was displeas'd and uneasie at what was done; but when he found the Soldiers began to be in a Uproar, and how it was spread abroad in the Camp that he was secretly murder'd, which threw 'em all into a Flame, he show'd himself publickly amongst 'em like an Emperor, and from a Tribunal erected on purpose he address'd himself to 'em, as his manner was, in a very lively Speech, bidding 'em remember "With how much Virtue and Sobriety he "had liv'd among them; with how much Diligence, "Pain and Patience he had contributed to the many "Victories they had obtain'd over the Barbarians; "how he was ever a Sharer with them in all their "La-

"Labours, whilst in the depth of Winter, when others
"ceas'd from War, they push'd on their Fortunes
"against the *Germans*, and conquer'd those, who
"'till then had been invincible. But above all that
"glorious Day was never to be forgotten, which
"in a great measure bless'd the *Gauls* with a per-
"petual Liberty, purchas'd by their own Valour
"and the Merit of their Arms in that memorable Bat-
"tel near *Argentoratum*, where whole Torrents of
"their Enemies fell with Violence upon them, but
"were receiv'd with such a God-like Virtue, that
"to avoid the Terror of their Swords they com-
"mitted themselves to the Dangers of the Deep,
"and fled from Death into the Arms of Destructi-
"on: He appeal'd to 'em if his Example did not
"lead 'em on to Victory, for which he tugg'd there
"where Death was busiest, and Danger appear'd
"in every Shape: He assur'd 'em that these their
"great Deserts would live in the Mouth of Fame
"to late Posterity, especially if they took care to
"defend him they had rais'd, and vindicate that
"Authority which was of their own Creation; for
"his part he was resolv'd to rule with Justice and
"Moderation, that it never should be said Valour
"went unrewarded in his Days, or Ambition seiz'd
"on what was due to Merit.

A Speech consisting of such popular Topicks could not but be acceptable to the Soldier, who having hitherto receiv'd no Reward for all his Services, assur'd himself mighty Advantages from a Reign that promis'd such material Regulations.

After this *Julian* began again to apply himself to the Affairs of State, and Exercise of the Sovereign Authority, making such Alterations in the Court and the Army as he judg'd convenient; and knowing how much *Constantius* would be displea'd at what was done, he dispatch'd *Pentadius* and *Eutherius*,

therius, two of his Principal Officers, with Letters to him, in which he represented the great Labours and imminent Dangers he had undergone in the Execution of the Service he impos'd upon him, and with what readiness he had embrac'd it. How the Army, sensible of his high Deserts, and the Hardships they lay under in being forc'd to quit their Native Country, and serve in Foreign Parts, had compell'd him to accept of that, which he obstinately refus'd 'till they threaten'd him with Death, and had given him reason to think they would have vested the same Honour in some other when they had dispatch'd him. That he own'd he ow'd his Advancement entirely to him, and shou'd never make an ungrateful use of the Power which was now given him. However he gave him to understand that he could not approve of his last Orders, that *Gaul* was so far from being able to send any of her Natives against the *Persians*, that she stood rather in need of Assistance from the other Provinces, being continually harass'd either with Foreign Invasions or Domestick Tumults. He concluded all with an earnest Desire of his Friendship, and told him a mutual Love and good Understanding between Princes was the only certain Foundation of a mutual Prosperity. The Emperor was then upon his Expedition against the *Persians*, and was advanc'd as far as *Cæsarea*, where the Embassadors from *Julian* found him. Upon his first reading the Letters he fell into so great a Passion, that they who brought 'em were in fear of their Lives; he drove 'em out of his Presence, and commanded 'em no more to appear upon so Presumptuous a Message before him; then he consider'd with himself whether he had best proceed in his Expedition against the *Persians*, or turn back and chastise his Rebellious Kinsman; after some Deliberation cooler Coun-

At which Constantius is enrag'd.

Councils prevail'd, and he purfu'd his Expedition againft the *Perfians*. He difmifs'd *Julian*'s Meffengers without any Anfwer, but fent *Leonas* his Quæftor into *Gaul* prefently after with Letters to him. *Leonas* being arriv'd at *Paris* was kindly receiv'd by *Julian*, to whom he deliver'd the Emperor's Letters whilft he was upon the Tribunal in the Prefence of the Army, at which he was not a little pleas'd. He order'd 'em to be read openly to the whole Affembly, who for fome time liften'd with Patience, but when they came to that part wherein he admonifh'd and exhorted him, if he had any regard to his own Security, and that of his Friends, to humble himfelf and be fatisfy'd with the Dignity of *Cæfar*, which he permitted him ftill to enjoy, but difapprov'd and annull'd whatever elfe had been done, they cry'd out with one Voice, *Julian Auguftus*; alledging *it was unlawful in any to revoke what had been ratify'd by the Army and the People*; and that they were refolv'd to ftand by their Election. With this Anfwer *Leonas* return'd to the Emperor, to give him an Account of his Embaffy; and *Julian*, who was unwilling, as yet, to come to an open Rupture, difpatch'd other Embaffadors to *Conftantius*, by whom he affur'd him of his good Intentions and Zeal for his Service. After which, that he might keep himfelf and his Army ftill in Action, he march'd into *Germany*, and having pafs'd the *Rhine*, he fell fuddenly upon the *Atthuarii*, the Inhabitants of *Franconia*, a turbulent uneafie People, that had lately made feveral Incurfions into *Gaul*, who being not prepar'd for fo unexpected a Vifit were eafily fubdu'd, and forc'd to fubmit to fuch Laws as the Conqueror thought fit to impofe upon them, by which means he made a fufficient Provifion for the Peace of the Empire on that fide; from thence repaffing the River he reinforc'd the

Garrisons upon the Borders, came to the *Rauraci*, where he recover'd some Places out of the Enemy's Hands, fortify'd 'em, and return'd by the way of *Besançon* to *Vienna* upon the *Rhône*, where he continu'd a great part of the Winter. About this time his Wife *Helena* dy'd without leaving any Children behind her, which was imputed chiefly to the Practices of the Empress *Eusebia*, as has been before observ'd.

Helena, Julian's Wife, dies;

Nor did *Eusebia* her self long survive her, but dy'd whilst the Emperor lay at *Antioch*. She was a Woman of a great Capacity, and well acquainted with the Languages and Sciences. Her Wit and Conduct were so prevailing as to gain her an Absolute Power over her Husband, which she unfortunately abus'd in Defence of Arianism, a Heresie she had suck'd in with her Milk, and to which she gave her Protection during her whole Life. And here it will not be amiss to give the Reader a short Account of the State the Church was in during this Emperor's Reign.

and the Empress Eusebia.

Christianity had from the time of *Constantine* the Great met with wonderful Encouragement, and was propagated far and near; it was profess'd in *Persia*, *Armenia*, in *Georgia*, and among the *Iberi*, Inhabitants of Mount *Caucasus*, towards the *Caspian* Sea. It had been planted in *India*, where it had some Churches, a Bishop, and Multitudes of Professors, so that the Promise to the Son was already in a great measure accomplish'd, *That he should have the Heathen for his Inheritance, and the utmost Parts of the Earth for his Possession*; but among this good Seed which the Holy Spirit of Truth had Sown in so plentiful a measure, the Enemy had mingl'd some Tare, which multiply'd with a sudden Encrease, to the great Danger of Christianity, and Scandal of the Faithful; and the Church

The State of the Church under Constantius.

may be said to have suffer'd more in those Days from them, who profess'd themselves her Fathers Confessors and Defenders, than the open and avow'd Malice of her most implacable Persecuters.

 The Council of *Nice* had in a very solemn manner Condemn'd *Arius* his Heretical Doctrine; to which Condemnation, tho' some of the Bishops that were infected by him had craftily subscrib'd, yet did they privately favour his Opinions during *Constantine*'s Reign, and more openly maintain and profess 'em under his Son *Constantius*; who being himself tainted with that abominable Pestilence, suffer'd it to spread through *Constantinople* the Metropolis of the East, from whence it issu'd forth and poisoned the greatest part of the Western Empire, and grew up into a merciless Persecution against all the sound Believers, which was the more dangerous for that it was manag'd under the Pretence of Piety. Bishops that had been Canonically chosen, and regularly establish'd were tumultuously pull'd out of their Sees by the Authority, or Connivance of *Constantius*, and others substituted in their Places, for no other reason but because they violently adher'd to *Arius* his Tenets, denying the Divinity of the Eternal Son of God. One Council was summon'd to annul what another had done, and all things were manag'd with that Faction, Strife and Contention, as if they labour'd to quench the Spirit of Meekness and Brotherly Love, so often recommended in the Gospel. Some were banish'd, some imprison'd, and against others they proceeded with more Severity even to the loss of their Lives; notwithstanding which the Church had then her Confessors, that with a Divine Constancy preserv'd the Faith entire and uncorrupted.

X. *Julian*

X. *Julian* was all this Winter confidering with himfelf what Courfe he was to take, whether it was moft prudent to endeavour to bring Matters to an amicable Compofure with *Conftantius*, and perfuade him by fair means to admit him for his Collegue, or wreft a Compliance from him by open force, and by ftriking firft add the greater Terror to his Arms. He thought it dangerous to depend upon his Friendfhip, under the pretext of which he might the more eafily deftroy him, as he had done his Brother *Gallus* before. On the other Hand it was no lefs dangerous to provoke him to be his Enemy, he having always been too ftrong for thofe, who fet themfelves up in Oppofition againft him; befides it would be a piece of the higheft Ingratitude, to Rebel againft his great Friend and Benefactor. However, after fome Deliberation, he concluded it more fafe and honourable to ftand upon his Guard, and therefore openly affum'd the Imperial Diadem and Purple, and made all manner of Preparations to march againft *Conftantius*, being incited to it by his Magicians, in whom he had an entire Confidence, and the Encouragement he receiv'd from fome Dreams, by which he faid he knew *Conftantius* was near his End. He was a downright Heathen in his Heart, but by an Hypocrifie unworthy an honeft Man, much more a Prince, he conftantly frequented the Chriftian Affemblies, infomuch that upon the Feaft of the *Epiphany*, which us'd to be obferv'd with more than ordinary Solemnity in the Church, he publickly affifted at Divine Service, hoping by this means to fecure the Chriftians to his Party, who were more in number than the Heathens.

At the beginning of the Spring, whilft he was bufied in forming and perfecting his great Defigns,

he

he receiv'd Advice from the Borders, that the *Germans* were again flown out into Rebellion, and had committed exceffive Outrages in the Parts adjoining to *Rhætia*, now call'd the Country of the *Grifons*, which he imputed to *Conftantius* his Inftigation, who defign'd in it fo to embarafs the *German* Affairs, that *Julian* fhould have no time to look after him, who indeed had enough to do elfewhere. 'Tis certain he writ to *Vadomarius*, one of their Kings, upon that Subject, and the Letters by accident were intercepted and brought to *Julian*, who found what Pains the Emperor took to entangle him, and therefore was fo much the more provok'd to break out into open Rebellion; but refolv'd firft to punifh thefe Barbarians, and fent *Libino*, one of his Commanders, with a fufficient Force againft 'em; but he falling unadvifedly upon them, was kill'd in the beginning of the Engagement, and his Men routed. *Julian* advanc'd with all his Army to repair this Lofs, and was herein fo fuccefsful that he defeated the Enemy, took their King Prifoner, whom he fent under a Guard into *Spain*, conftrain'd 'em to ask Pardon, reftore the Booty they had lately taken, and give him all Affurances of a quiet and dutiful Behaviour for the future; which being done, he refolv'd to march directly againft *Conftantius* and attack him. So that as foon as he had facrific'd to *Bellona*, the Goddefs of War, and had by that means fecur'd her to his Party, he affembl'd the Army, and from his Tribunal addrefs'd himfelf to 'em with more open Authority than formerly. He reprefented to 'em "what great things they had already done under "his Conduct, how they had reftrain'd the *Ger-* "*mans*, and made the *Rhine* paffable to the *Roman* "Armies. He bid 'em remember in what a mifera- "ble Condition he found *Gaul*, and in what a

"flourifhing

"flourishing State he should leave it; and exhorted them to assist him with Chearfulness and Resolution to make himself own'd for Emperor, since they, his great Comerades, had thought him worthy so glorious a Title. He told 'em there were greater things behind, which if he succeeded in this Expedition he would undertake for their Honour, and the Welfare of the Empire. That as he had hitherto behav'd himself with all Care and Diligence, so would he proceed, constantly endeavouring to discharge a good Conscience, and aim at nothing but what regarded the Publick good. He desir'd 'em to confirm that Concord and Fidelity they had express'd towards him by a Military Oath, as it was usual, concluding with this Advice, That they should make haste to seize upon the Limits of *Dacia*, before the Provinces of *Illyricum* were secured by Garrisons, beseeching 'em not to sully the Fame they had already acquir'd by their Moderation, nor offer an Injury to any private Man whatsoever. When he had done, the whole Army with all possible Demonstrations of Joy took the accustomed Oath, promising to follow him where ever he thought fit to lead 'em, and to endure all Extremities for his sake. *Nebridius* was the only Man throughout the Army who refus'd the Oath; he alledg'd the great Obligations he had to *Constantius*, and his former Oath to him would not permit him to bind himself by a second to any other; notwithstanding which *Julian* dismiss'd him in safety, and having preferr'd *Germanianus* to his Place, he sent away *Salust* to be his Lieutenant in *Gaul*.

Julian openly professes himself a Heathen:

Julian thinking his Army well secured to him by this Oath, began to throw off the Mask, and publickly to declare himself a Heathen; he took upon on him the Title of *Pontifex Maximus*, as was cuſtomary with his Predeceſſors that were Heathens, and ſtrictly obſerv'd all their Idolatrous Ceremonies. After this he order'd his Army to march, diſtributing it into ſeveral Parties, ſending *Jovinus* and *Jovius* with ſome by the common Roads of *Italy*, and others under the Conduct of *Nevita* through *Rhætia*, and ſo into *Pannonia*, that marching in ſuch a Compaſs they might ſeem more numerous, and ſtrike a greater Terror into their Enemies. They met with nothing to oppoſe their March, but enter'd without the leaſt Reſiſtance into *Illyricum*; for the Inhabitants were perſuaded that he came aſſiſted by all the Kings of *Gaul*, in which Provinces he had perform'd ſuch brave Exploits. At *Sirmium* he was receiv'd with the general Joy and Applauſe of the Inhabitants and Soldiers, who with frequent Acclamations brought him to the Palace, where they proclaim'd him *Augustus*. This proſperous Beginning was a great Encouragement to him, for he hop'd that the Example of ſo great and populous a City would influence others to do the like. The third Day after he left *Sirmium*, and took in *Succi*, a Place famous for its Situation between the Mountains *Hæmus* and *Rhodope*, of which he made *Nevita* Governor; and then went forward to *Neſſus* a Town of Conſequence, where he reſided for ſome time, writing from thence a Letter to the Senate at *Rome*, in which he exclaim'd againſt *Conſtantius* his Government, loading it with all imaginable Reproaches. This Letter was read publickly in an Aſſembly of the People, by whom the Subſtance of it was in general approv'd. For *Conſtantius* was not much belov'd by the Orthodox Chriſtians, who had been perſecuted by him upon the account of *Arianiſm*, nor acceptable to the Heathens who were all for *Julian*.

And ſets out againſt the Emperor:

And is joyfully receiv'd at Sirmium.

Thus

Thus far *Julian*'s Affairs met with a succesful Progress; but whilst he lay at *Nessus* without the least Apprehension of an Enemy at his Back, he was inform'd that *Nigrinus* a Tribune of Horse had seiz'd on *Aquileia* in *Constantius* his Name, to whom he knew the Inhabitants were well affected, and put into it two Legions, and a Cohort of Archers. *Julian*, who knew of what Consequence this would be to his Proceedings, order'd some Troops to besiege it, who press'd it very hard, and attempted all Ways imaginable to reduce it; but the Besieged behav'd themselves so well, and defended it with so much Resolution, that they held out 'till they heard *Constantius* was dead, and then they surrender'd.

XI. The Emperor was about this time at *Edessa* in *Mesopotamia*, whither he had removed from *Antioch* at the beginning of the Campaign. He was continually alarm'd with the Account of *Julian*'s Behaviour in the West, and at a loss to find what Course the *Persian* intended to take in the East. His Indignation prompted him to go and chastise his Kinsman, but then it troubled him to think he should leave *Mesopotamia* expos'd to the Violence of the Enemy. He was willing to preserve his Army as entire as he could in case of a Civil War, which he look'd on as unavoidable; and therefore declining any farther Designs upon the *Persian* Garrisons, which he found by experience to be strongly fortify'd, he sent part of his Army under *Arbetio* to secure the Banks of the *Tigris*, and do the best they could to prevent the *Persians*, should they attempt to pass it. These Orders were so well perform'd, that the King of *Persia* was forced to return home without attempt-

The Emperor prepares to meet him. ing any thing; which when the Emperor was inform'd of he drew his Army together, and departed to *Hierapolis*, leaving only such behind as were
neces-

Chap. I.   XLII. Constantius.

necessary for the Defence of *Mesopotamia*. At *Hierapolis* he caus'd his Army to be drawn up in the Camp, and from a lofty Tribunal he told 'em with a serene and pleasant Countenance, "That having "through the whole Course of his Reign endea- "vour'd so to comport himself as to be free from "Reproach, he was now constrain'd to accuse him- "self before them of too much Humanity, which "he always thought conduc'd to the Publick Good. "That during the necessity of his Affairs he had "created *Gallus Cæsar*, who ingratefully abus'd the "Honour he had given him, and after the Commis- "sion of infinite Enormities had receiv'd the Pu- "nishment he deserv'd. That persisting still in his "Friendship and Affection to the Family he advan- "ced *Julian* to the same Honour, who intoxicated "with a few Advantages obtain'd over a weak un- "skilful Enemy, presumed to rebel against the "Common-wealth, which it was their Part to de- "fend and preserve from such monstrous Attempts. "That he made no doubt but when they came to "engage God would fight on their side, and turn "the Swords of their Enemies against them, in be- "half of those who drew not their Swords but to "revenge the foulest Treason, and most barbarous "Ingratitude. The Army answer'd his Speech with an universal Acclamation, desiring him to lead 'em where his Service requir'd, and promising to sacrifice their Lives and all in the Defence of so just and honourable a Cause. By this chearful Answer exceedingly encourag'd, he dispatch'd *Arbetio* with a good Part of the Army towards the Streights of *Succi*, where *Julian* then was waiting for the Accession of some more Forces, with which he intended to invade *Thrace*.

The Emperor after this return'd to *Antioch*, where finding himself a little indispos'd he receiv'd Baptism.

The Emperor indispos'd is Baptised at Antioch.

tism at the Hands of *Euzoius* the *Arian*. From *Antioch* he came to *Tarsus*, where he was seiz'd with a feavourish Fit; but believing that Motion and Exercise might do him good, he proceeded in his Expedition, and through many difficult Ways at length reach'd *Mopsuestia* or *Mopsuerence*, a small Town in *Cilicia*, situate at the Foot of the Mountain *Taurus*. Hence he intended to proceed the next Day, but was detained by the Violence of his Disease, which increased more and more upon him; so that when he found all the Means us'd for his Recovery ineffectual, he dy'd on the 5th of *October*, after he had reign'd near 38 Years, and lived 44, *An. Dom.* 361. *Taurus* and *Florentius* being Consuls. Some say that at his Death he named *Julian* for his Successor, for which they plead *Ammianus* his Authority; who however is not positive in the Matter, but delivers it in very uncertain Terms, and for fear so wild a Will should be call'd in question by Posterity, he takes care to tell the World the Emperor was in his right Senses when he made it. *Gregory Nazianzen*, and several others, are of a contrary Opinion; they say, that *Constantius* foreseeing what Calamities were like to befal the Church under *Julian*'s Administration, was very sorry he had made him *Cæsar*; after which its very improbable he should declare him his Successor. *Gregory* saith, he was likewise truly penitent for the many Murders he had caus'd to be committed upon his nearest Relations, and the Cruelties the *Arian* Hereticks had made him exercise upon the Faithful.

<small>Constantius's Death, A.D. 361.</small>

<small>Successorem statuisse dicitur Julianum.</small>

<small>His Character.</small>

It is not easie to determine whether his Virtues or Vices were more abundant in him, tho' in Charity we ought to give it for the former. He had a Capacity, both in Civil and Military Affairs, that was fit for an Emperor; and a Greatness of Mind which made him neglect and despise all manner of

Popularity, and taught him how to maintain the Grandure of Majesty and Authority. He always observ'd that useful Maxim among Princes, of conferring Honours upon his Subjects with a sparing Hand, by which he upheld the Reputation of the Nobility. The same Care did he use in preferring his Servants, advancing none to any Employment of Honour, or Profit, but those who for their Diligence and Integrity had been before eminent in some inferiour Office. He was chaste and temperate, and an utter Stranger to those Vices with which Courts too often abound, and are usually laid to the Charge of those in greatest Authority. He was a zealous Promoter of the Christian Religion, and establish'd several wholsome Laws for the Suppression of Idolatry, Magick, and ill Manners. On the other hand, he was so jealous of his Authority, that upon the least appearance of a design'd Usurpation there was no end of his Inquisitions. In his Foreign Wars he was generally unfortunate, and the least ill Success made him discompos'd and dejected; in his Civil Contests he was always prosperous, and upon every Advantage he grew proud and insolent. He suffer'd himself to be govern'd too much by his Wives, Eunuchs and designing Courtiers, who by their abominable Flatteries miss-led and infatuated him. He was not always constant in his Favours, but often recall'd what he had before bestow'd. Add to all this, the innocent Blood he caus'd to be spilt during his Reign, and the Protection he gave the *Arians*, in whose behalf he discountenanc'd and persecuted the Orthodox Christians, thrusts him out of the Company of good Princes, and seems to have drawn down the Vengeance of Heaven upon himself, his Family, and the Empire: Tho' he was out-done in this by his Successor, whom God thought fit to raise up on purpose to chastise and purge his Church. For he being a sworn Enemy to Christianity, which he carefully oppress'd, and preferring none but such as declar'd against it, he quickly distinguish'd those who were Christians indeed, from such as for some worldly End had formerly made an outward Profession of it.

Constantius his Complexion was brown, his Looks lofty, and his Sight quick and piercing; the Hair of his Head was soft; his Face, which he kept constantly shaved, smooth, and comely; from his Neck to his Groin he was very tall, but his Legs were short and bending, which made him excellent at Leaping and Running, Exercises in which he took much Delight.

XII. *Constantius* being dead the Corps were committed to the Care of *Jovian*, to be convey'd by him in Royal Pomp to *Constantinople*, there to be interr'd near his Progenitors: Whilst the chief Officers, both Civil and Military, after they had by their Tears and Lamentations testified the great Respect they had for the deceased Emperor, consulted together what Methods were to be taken in reference to a Successor, and after some time agreed to dispatch away *Theolaiphus* and *Aliguldus* to *Julian*, to desire his Presence in the East, where they were all ready to receive his Commands.

Julian was all this while employing himself in *Illyricum*, chiefly in a superstitious Enquiry into the Entrails of Beasts, sometimes promising himself the best, at others apprehending the worst Events; for the most part doubtful and uneasie, not daring to rely upon Conjectures, which too often fall out contrary to what they suggested. Whilst he was labouring under this Anxiety of Thought, *Theolaiphus* and *Aliguldus* arriv'd with the News of *Constantius* his Death, and that he had declared him his

Suc-

Successor: Upon which, deliver'd now from all his Doubts and Apprehensions, he gave Orders to march away into *Thrace* with all Expedition, moving directly towards *Constantinople*; where he was receiv'd with the universal Joy and Applause of the Inhabitants, who beheld him with Wonder, as one dropt down from Heaven; scarce believing it possible that a young Man as he was, little in Stature, but renown'd for his great Exploits, after an impetuous March from City to City, like a rising Flame devouring all that oppos'd him, should at length, as by Divine Appointment, obtain the peaceable Possession of the Imperial Seat, without any expence of Blood or Treasure to the Common-wealth.

Julian arrives at Constantinople.

Being thus settled in the Empire, his first Care was to punish such as had the Misfortune to have been his Enemies formerly, tho' now some of 'em submitted readily, and closed in with his Interest. Among these was *Nigrinus*, who had seiz'd on *Aquileia* in *Constantius* his Name, as we observ'd before, which he defended resolutely 'till the Besieg'd heard of the Emperor's Death, and then they surrender'd at Discretion, laying the Blame of their obstinate Resistance upon *Nigrinus*, who for his gallant Fidelity to his Prince was condemn'd to be burnt alive, which Sentence was executed upon him accordingly. *Apodemius*, who had so great a share in the Death of *Gallus* and *Sylvanus*, and *Paul* the Notary, that violent Prosecutor, were likewise burnt alive: Nor would the watchful Eye of Justice suffer *Eusebius*, that execrable Eunuch, to escape the Punishment he so well deserv'd. These Proceedings were just and equitable, and had *Julian* gone no farther he had not put his Friends to the Trouble of endeavouring to clear him from the Sin of Ingratitude; but the Death of *Ursulus* is a Stain all their Arts can't wash out. This Person was *Comes*

Largitionum, or Treasurer, and when *Julian* was created *Cæsar*, and sent into the West, he perceiving they had a Design to straighten him in Mony, that he might have nothing to bestow upon the Soldiers, who would thereupon grow bold and ungovernable, sent Orders to the Treasurer of *Gaul* to supply *Cæsar* with whatever his Occasions should require. When *Julian* perceiv'd his Death appear'd so heinous to the People, he endeavour'd to excuse a Crime he could not expiate, pretending he fell against his Will, and without his Knowledge, by the Fury of the Soldiers, whom a severe Reflection of his at *Amida* had incens'd against him. But this his best Friends and Followers allow to be a lame Excuse; and that herein he came short of that regard to Justice which at other times they say he usually observ'd. An Instance of which they give us in his Answer to *Delphidius*, who having accus'd *Numerius*, sometime before Governor of *Gallia Narbonensis*, of robbing the Publick Treasury; this bitter Orator finding *Numerius* give so good an Answer to all his Allegations, that there were no Proofs sufficient to convict him, turning to *Julian* ask'd him in some Passion, *If to deny be sufficient to be cleared, what Offender will ever be found guilty?* To whom *Julian* reply'd, *And if to accuse be enough to condemn, what innocent Man will ever be safe?*

Julian reforms the Court, and the Camp. From his Inquisitions upon these Persons *Julian* apply'd himself to a Reformation in the Court, the great Officers of which had from an Indigence of Fortune rais'd themselves up to vast Estates; they burthen'd the Common-wealth by their intollerable Exactions, and debauch'd it by their vicious Examples. They were in their Demands exorbitant, in their Gifts profuse, in their Expences luxurious; being grown so habituated to invade the Rights of others, that they stuck neither at Perjury nor Sacrilege.

crilege. Nor was the Camp less corrupt than the Court, where the Soldier exercis'd himself daily in Amorous Airs, slept on his Field Bed, was fed in Plate, and having enrich'd himself by his ambitious Courses, grew vainly fond of Jewels, the intrinsick value of which he pretended perfectly to understand, unlike the Ignorance of those who liv'd but in the Age before him; for it was reported of a common Soldier in the Reign of *Maximian*, that at the Plunder of the King of *Persia*'s Camp having found a Purse of precious Stones, and being taken with the fineness of it, he threw away the Jewels as things of no value, and went away highly satisfy'd with his good Fortune. These Corruptions and Disorders *Julian* took great Care to reform, either because they call'd aloud for such a Reformation, or to cast an *Odium* upon his Predecessor, under whose Reign they had gain'd so much Ground. He thoroughly purg'd the Court of all that were obnoxious in it, and made such Regulations in his Camp as he judg'd convenient.

He had in his Infancy been instructed in the Christian Religion, of which, for the most part, he made an outward Profession, 'till by the Death of *Constantius* his Fears were remov'd, and he found himself at Liberty to Act as he pleas'd; at which time he commanded all the Temples to be open'd, such as had been demolish'd to be re-built, advanc'd the Heathen Priests to their ancient Privileges and Immunities, order'd Sacrifices to be offer'd as formerly, and the Worship of the Pagan Deities to be restor'd. At the same time he recall'd all the Christian Bishops, whether Orthodox or Hereticks, that had been banish'd by *Constantius*; and having sent for 'em to Court, he advis'd 'em to lay all Dissentions aside, and gave 'em free Liberty to live and believe every one as he thought fit, *Opens the Heathen Temples*, *and deals craftily with the Christians.*

fit, intending by that Liberty to sow greater Dissentions among them, and so prevent the Dangers he apprehended if once they came to be united; for he knew by Experience, saith *Ammianus*, that Wild Beasts are not so enrag'd against Men, as Christians dissenting upon Points of Faith are enrag'd against each other. Being himself bred a Scholar, he ever had a great Esteem for Learned Men, with whom he familiarly convers'd, particularly *Oribasius Themistius*, and *Libanius* the Sophist, who had been his Tutor, and instill'd into him an abhorrence to the Christian Religion, which after he came to be Emperor he had a great Desire to exterminate; but observing that Persecution was so far from diminishing, that it rather encreas'd the number of its Professors, who glory'd in that they were thought worthy to suffer for the Name of Christ, he therefore sought another way to ruin them. He try'd by gentle Persuasions and glorious Promises to induce 'em to an Abjuration. He depriv'd all such as stood firm to the Faith of all their Offices and Employments, whether Civil or Military. He prohibited Christians from keeping any Publick Schools, or teaching the Sciences, unless they would first turn Heathens. And whereas 'twas Customary for the Emperors to present the Soldiers with a Donative upon the first Day of the Year, upon their Birth-days, or the like; *Julian* order'd, that whoever came into his Presence for that purpose, should first, according to an ancient *Roman* Custom, offer Incense upon an Altar adorn'd with the Images of the Gods intermix'd with several of his own. Several Christian Soldiers being better instructed, and more zealous than the rest, chose rather to lose the Present than pollute themselves with Idolatry: Some ignorant of what they were doing, and others either through Avarice or Fear, did as the

the rest of their Comerades that were Heathen. But some time after, when diverse of 'em, who invok'd the Name of Jesus before they sate down to Meat, were ask'd how they came to call upon him, whom they had deny'd, having offer'd Incense in Honour to his sworn Enemy; they, sensible of their Error, publickly protested to the whole World that they were Christians, and were resolv'd to live and die in the Faith of Jesus Christ; that they had err'd through Ignorance, and that their Consciences had no share in the Crime of which their Hands were guilty. After this they went to the Emperor, and return'd him his Donative, declaring they repented from their Souls the abominable Sin they had committed, to expiate which they were ready to suffer Death for the Name of Jesus Christ. *Thedoret* adds, that *Julian* was so enrag'd at this generous Action, that he commanded all their Heads to be chopp'd off; and that when they were brought to the Place of Execution, the eldest among 'em desir'd the Executioner to begin with the youngest, who was call'd *Romanus*, lest seeing so many of his Companions Executed before him he should, through the weakness of his Youth, lose his Courage, and relapse; and that whilst he was calling on the Name of God upon his Knees, in Expectation of the Fatal Stroke, an Order came from the Emperor to stop the Execution, and they were all banish'd to the remotest Parts of the Empire.

Whilst he continu'd at *Constantinople* he was courted by Embassadors from all Nations, among whom he was renown'd for his Fortitude, Sobriety, Military Skill, and other eminent Virtues. With these and his other Felicities he was much elevated, forming to himself Designs and Fancies that exceeded the Bounds of Human Nature. His Thoughts ran much upon the *Persian* War, which he was resolv'd to carry on with the greatest Vigour. Before he enter'd upon it he consulted the Heathen Oracles, who all promis'd him glorious Success; but none encourag'd him to this Expedition so much as *Maximus* the Philosopher and Magician, who promis'd him no less a Victory than that which *Alexander* obtain'd over the *Persians*, persuading him, according to the Doctrine of *Pythagoras*, that the Soul of that renown'd Conqueror was transmigrated into him. The gross Assurances and Flatteries of his Priests and Magicians had made him so secure and presumptuous, that he rejected the Assistance his Allies offer'd him by their Embassadors at *Antioch*, telling 'em it became the Greatness of the *Roman* Empire to succour and support her Friends, and not trust to the Assistance of Strangers.

A. D. 362.
He beautifies Constantinople.

Before he left *Constantinople* he much improv'd and enlarg'd it by the Addition of many beautiful Buildings; for being the Place of his Nativity, he always express'd a great Affection for that City. He order'd a very convenient Harbour to be built in the Shape of a *Greek Sigma*, where those Ships that Traded thither from the South might ride in great Safety; and in the Gallery of his own Palace he furnish'd a Library with the choicest and most valuable Books he could procure, after which he remov'd Eastward in his Progress to *Antioch*.

Begins his Expedition.

XIII. Having cross'd over into *Asia* he pass'd through *Chalcedon* and *Libyssa* (where *Hannibal* was bury'd) and thence came to *Nicomedia*, a City, which the Care and Indulgence of former Princes had so much enlarg'd and beautify'd, and which an Earth-quake had now reduc'd to so miserable a Condition, that *Julian* could not behold it without Tears, having himself resided here in his Youth under

der the Care of *Eusebius* the Bishop, the great Patron of Arianism. After he had given Orders for the Repair of the Place he proceeded on in his Journey, and arriv'd at *Antioch* about the latter end of *July*. As he drew nigh the City, that beautiful Head of the East, he was met and receiv'd like some Deity, the People following him with their Vows and Acclamations, and gazing on him as on some Propitious Star newly risen in their Hemisphere, which high Opinion of him he improv'd at his first coming by several Examples of his great Patience and Humility. There was one *Thalassius*, who had been a bitter Enemy to his Brother *Gallus*, and was therefore in no degree of Favour with him. This some Persons, with whom *Thalassius* was then at Law, having observ'd, came in a great Body and accus'd him to the Emperor, complaining that *Thalassius*, who had the Insolence to be at Enmity with him, had by Violence depriv'd 'em of their just Rights. *Julian*, sensible that this was done designedly to ruin the Man, answer'd, That the Person of whom they complain'd, had, he confess'd, highly offended him, and that therefore they ought in good Manners to suspend their Claim 'till he had given him, who was so much their Superiour, a suitable Satisfaction; and at the same time commanded the Præfect, assisting him as the Custom was upon the Bench, not to hear their Cause 'till he was reconciled to *Thalassius*, which was done a short time after; for *Thalassius* renouncing the Christian Religion, and embracing that which was then most in Fashion, recover'd the Emperor's Favour, and was afterwards very intimate with him.

Julian Winter'd, according to his first Intentions, at *Antioch*; where, averse to those Pleasures with which *Syria* too much abounded, he spent his time in hearing and determining Causes, with exquisite

He arrives at Antioch.

An Instance of Justice.

Care

Care and Dexterity adjudging to every one his due. And tho' fometimes, as our Hiftorian confeffes, he would ask improper and unfeafonable Queftions in a Debate, as what Religion this or that Party then at Law profefs'd; yet no Refpect to Religion, or any thing elfe made him deviate from Juftice, or inclin'd him to a partial Determination; for being fenfible of the Levity and Heat of his Temper, he permitted the Præfects and thofe about him by feafonable Hints to reftrain his Impetuofity, being pleas'd to be corrected by 'em, and afham'd of his Faults when they had made him fenfible of them.

Quarrels with the Inhabitants at Antioch. Thefe things highly ingratiated him with the Inhabitants, but the good Underftanding between 'em was of no long continuance; for whilft he lay at *Antioch*, and obferv'd the Multitudes of People that flock'd thither upon his own Account, and that of his Attendants, he concluded fo great a Concourfe muft in a fhort time create a Dearnefs of Provifions, which out of a Humour of Affectation and Popularity he had a great Ambition to prevent, by endeavouring to make things cheaper than they cou'd well bear to be, which being forc'd in an inconvenient way ferves rather to create a Scarcity than prevent it; this the Corporation of *Antioch* reprefented to him, yet was he obftinate to fee it accomplifh'd; for the Merchants, who found themfelves oblig'd to Trade to their own Lofs, chofe rather to fhut up their Ware-houfes than expofe their Goods; from whence enfu'd a great want of Neceffaries throughout the City, which highly provok'd the Inhabitants againft him, and expos'd him to their fevereft Reflections. They call'd him *Victimarius*, by reafon of his multitude of Sacrifices, to which he was fo extravagantly addicted; *Cercops* or Dwarf, and Goats-Beard, becaufe he took great Delight in a long picked Beard; at which he was so highly incens'd that he writ an Invective against 'em, which he call'd the *Antiochian* or *Beard-Hater*, in which he expos'd, with a deal of Virulence, the Vices and Defects of the Citizens, mixing with the Truth many things that were Foreign to it.

During his stay at *Antioch*, *Gaudentius*, who had been sent by *Constantius* into *Africk* to secure that Country to him, and *Julian* another of *Constantius*'s Favourites were apprehended and put to Death, as was likewise *Artemius* Governor of *Egypt*, upon the importunate Application of the Citizens of *Alexandria*, who accus'd him of many enormous Crimes, if *Ammianus* may be credited; for several Christian Writers affirm he dy'd a Martyr, that he lost his Head by *Julian*'s Order, because during *Constantius* his Reign he had destroy'd many of the Heathen Idols in *Egypt*. About the same time *George*, who had thrust himself into the Bishoprick of *Alexandria* when St. *Athanasius* was expell'd, was kill'd by the Multitude. He was a great Champion for the *Arians*, who charg'd *Athanasius* his Followers with his Death, and plac'd him in their Calender as a Martyr, from whence he crept insensibly into the *Latin* Church, by whom he is esteem'd as a Saint and Martyr, challenging the 23d of *April* for his Festival. His Legend is stuff'd with many ridiculous Absurdities, among which his fighting the Dragon on Horseback is not the least remarkable. If the Account the Authors of those Times, both Christian and Heathen, have left us of him be true, we have little reason to take him either for a Saint or Martyr.

George, the Arian Bishop.

All this while *Julian* was very intent upon the War; he consider'd how the *Persians* had for the last Sixty Years miserably harass'd the Eastern Provinces, and overthrown several Armies that were sent to restrain

restrain 'em; this kindl'd in him a Desire of Revenge, which together with an Ambition of gracing his former Exploits with the glorious Sirname of *Parthicus*, made him very zealous in his Preparations, but he was in nothing so assiduous as his Sacrifices, compassing Sea and Land for Victims which bled upon the Altars. Sometimes he would offer an hundred Bulls at a time, innumerable Droves of other Beasts, and white Birds procur'd at a vast Expence; so that almost every Soldier, and that almost every Day, was lead or born Home to his Quarters Drunk and Surfeited from the Temple wherein they feasted, and that contrary to the Discipline he is said to have establish'd so carefully in the Army. And as his Superstition encreas'd, so was there no end of Rites and Ceremonies in his Religion, which introduc'd an Expence that swell'd up to Sums vast and unusual. Whosoever pretended to the Art of Divination, which in his Predecessor's Days was esteem'd a Capital Crime, was receiv'd with all imaginable Encouragement; and so far was he addicted to Practices of this Nature, that he resolv'd to open the *Castilian* Fountain, consecrated heretofore to *Apollo*, in whose Name the Devil issu'd out his Famous Oracles. This Fountain had been long since choak'd up by *Adrian*, who being here foretold that he should one Day be Emperor, was unwilling any hereafter should meet with the same Encouragement. But whilst the Emperor was amusing himself with these Superstitious Vanities an Accident happen'd, from which he receiv'd no small Disturbance. On the 22d of *October* the spacious Temple of *Apollo* at *Daphne*, the Suburb of *Antioch*, built by *Antiochus Epiphanes*, took Fire, and was suddenly burnt to the Ground; this the Emperor charg'd upon the Christians, and commanded the great Church at *Antioch*

The Temple of Apollo burnt.

tioch to be shut up; tho' *Ammianus Marcellinus* gives another Account of it.

However this aggravated the great Aversion he had to the Christians, and made him more desirous to suppress 'em. He knew Christianity was supposed to succeed, and to be founded upon the Ruins of Judaism, and he thought if he could once restore the old Ceremonies and Sacrifices of that Religion, he should raise a great Argument against the Truth and Progress of the former; the readiest way to which was to rebuild the Temple of *Jerusalem*, which had been long since destroyed by *Titus Vespasian*: And therefore he was resolv'd to effect it, how great soever the Expence should be, and committed the Care of it to *Alypius* an *Antiochian*, who had formerly commanded here in *Britain*; at the same time he encourag'd the *Jews* to be assisting to so good a Work, desiring 'em to pray the Soveraign of the Universe to prosper him in his Expedition against the *Persians*, releas'd 'em from several Impositions with which they had been charged, and promis'd 'em all the Happiness they cou'd expect under his Administration. *Alypius* apply'd himself diligently to the Work, and was assisted in it by the Governor of the Province; but on a suddain dreadful Balls of Fire broke out from the Ground, where the Foundations were laid, and consuming the Works made the Place inaccessible. *Julian endeavours to re-build the Temple at Jerusalem, from which he is diverted by a Prodigy. Ammian. Marcell.*

The same Year there happen'd an Earthquake at *Jerusalem*, which rased the Foundations of the former Temple, and over-turn'd several publick Buildings, under which a great multitude of *Jews* lay buried; and another at *Constantinople*, which tho' not so violent, endanger'd a great part of the City. These Accidents, with several other unluckly Omens, as he term'd 'em, strangely terrified the superstitious Emperor. *Felix* and *Julian*, two Officers of great *A.D. 363.*

Au-

Authority, dy'd much about the same time; and the People, who usually saluted him with the Titles of *Julianus Felix Augustus*, look'd on it as ominous that he who was *Augustus* should be named in company with *Felix* and *Julian*, who were both dead. When he departed from *Antioch* a confus'd multitude of the Citizens attended him out of the City, wishing him a successful Journey, and a triumphant Return, and pray'd him for the future to be more mild and gracious to them: But he still nettled at their bitter and undutiful Reflections told 'em in great Anger, he would never visit 'em again, but winter at *Tarsus* in *Cilicia*; which he accordingly did, for he was privately buried in the Suburbs of that City. As he enter'd into *Hierapolis* on the 5th of *March* fifty Soldiers were kill'd by a Fall of some Buildings, and a great many more hurt. Having pass'd the *Euphrates* by a Bridge of Boats he came to *Batnæ* a Town of *Osdruena*, where fifty Soldiers more were overwhelm'd with a Stack of Straw. From *Batnæ* he proceeded to *Carhæ*, an ancient Town and a Frontier toward *Assyria*, famous for the Death of *Crassus* and the Overthrow of the *Roman* Army. Here he rested a while to furnish his Army with Provisions, and sacrificed to the Moon, the great Goddess of the Country; at whose Altar he is said secretly to have deliver'd his Purple Military Coat to his Kinsman *Procopius*, bidding him resolutely to seize on the Empire upon the first Intelligence of his Miscarriage in *Parthia*. The late unlucky Omens had made him irresolute and uneasie, so that being troubled with ill Dreams he foreboded some Mischief at hand, and both he and his Wizards declared that they must expect some signal Disaster the Day following, being the 19th of *March*, which brought nothing extraordinary with it notwithstanding their Predictions; tho' it appear'd afterwards that the Temple of *Apollo Palatinus*

¹ *His Progress.*

Chap. I.   XLIII. Julian.

latinus was burnt the very same Night at *Rome*. Whilst he was here employ'd in disposing the March of his Army, he was inform'd that a Party of the Enemies Horse had broken into the Empire, and were return'd with a considerable Booty. Provok'd at this he put a Design, he had before laid, in execution, and committed a Party of 30000 Men to *Procopius* and *Sebastian*, who had been Commander in *Egypt*, ordering 'em to keep a strict Watch within *Tigris*, the better to prevent any sudden Accident, and when they had join'd *Arsaces*, which they were to attempt, he commanded 'em to waste *Chiliocomus*, that fruitful Tract of *Media*, and meet him if possible in *Assyria*. After this he began his March, and arriv'd the second Day at *Callinisus*, where he celebrated the Feast of the Mother of the Gods. The Day following he directed his March by the River Side, where he was met by his Fleet, under the Conduct of *Constantianus* and *Lucillianus*. It consisted of a thousand Vessels of Burden, laden with Provisions, Arms and Engines, besides fifty Men of War, and as many design'd upon occasion to make Bridges for the Army. From hence he proceeded to *Circusium*, which he enter'd about the beginning of *April*. It was then a very strong and neat Town, fortified heretofore by *Dioclesian* the better to restrain the *Persians*, who by their frequent Incursions into *Syria* did great Mischief to the Provinces. Here whilst *Julian* was busied in passing his Army over the River *Avora*, which with the *Euphrates* encircled the Town in the manner of an Island, he receiv'd Letters from *Sallust*, Præfect of *Gaul*, earnestly pressing him to desist for the present from his intended Expedition, and not thrust himself upon inevitable Destruction before the Divine Powers were fully pacified. But he, in contempt of this wholesome Admonition, press'd on with greater Confidence;

dence; and having pass'd his Army over, caus'd the Bridge to be broken down, to cut off from his Men all Hopes of a Retreat. At *Dura* a Lion of vast Bigness presented it self to the Army, who with a shower of Darts dispatch'd it in a moment. This Spectacle rais'd his Hopes and redoubled his Courage; but upon what insufficient Ground the Event will demonstrate. His Philosophers persuaded him 'twas a lucky Omen, but the *Hetruscan Aruspices*, who were the better Artists, prov'd from their Books the contrary. The Day following a Soldier named *Jovian* was struck dead by a Flash of Lightning, which confirm'd the *Hetruscans* in their former Opinion, and made 'em advise him to quit the Country as dangerous and fatal, which the Philosophers oppos'd with Arguments more agreeable to *Julian*'s Temper; who in a chearful Speech addres'd himself to the Army, telling 'em what mighty Actions had been perform'd by former Commanders as well against the *Persians* as others, animated to it by their Affection to their Country, and assisted by the Love and Resolution of their Soldiers; that he was resolv'd to imitate such generous Examples, if they were willing to join with him in so glorious an Undertaking, wherein he had the Advantage of Justice on his side, in revenge of those many Injuries the *Roman* Provinces had of late Years receiv'd from 'em. The Soldiers animated with this Discourse resolv'd to obey him chearfully, and appear worthy so Noble a Commander; who thereupon immediately enters the *Assyrian* Borders, where fearing an Ambuscade he prudently divided his Army into four Bodies, appointing 1500 as a Forlorn, who marching sometimes before, sometimes on each side, were to prevent any suddain Irruption from the Enemy, and give warning upon all Occasions. In the middle he placed the Foot, consisting of the main Strength of his

His Order of Marching.

his Army, which he led himself; on the Right he order'd several Legions under the Conduct of *Nevita* to coast along the River *Euphrates,* and the Left Wing with some Troops of Horse he committed to *Arintheus,* and *Horsmisda* a *Persian,* who having been injur'd by the King his Brother fled for Refuge to *Constantine* the Great, and after several Proofs of his great Fidelity was preferr'd to considerable Commands. They were to march through the Plains and Marshes, whilst *Dagalaiphus, Victor* and *Secundinus* brought up the Rear. And to strike a greater Terror into the Enemy if they dar'd assault him, or view him at a Distance upon his March, he enlarged his Ranks, by which means the Front was almost ten Miles distant from the Rear, which made his Army appear much more numerous than it was. As for the Fleet, he order'd it to attend the Army as near as possibly it could, that upon occasion they might afford each other a mutual Assistance.

In this manner they march'd to a Fort call'd *Anathan,* which surrender'd upon the first Summons, and was burnt by the Emperor's Order. Here they found a *Roman* Soldier, who when *Maximian* made Irruptions into these Parts had been left behind very sick. Upon his Recovery, being then in the flower of his Age, he was marry'd to several Wives, according to the Custom of the Country, and was now grown extream old, and the Father of a numerous Issue. He with great Joy was brought to the Emperor, before whom he affirm'd that he knew and had formerly often foretold, that he should live 'till he was near an hundred Years of Age, and be bury'd at length in the *Roman* Territories; which was confirm'd by the Testimony of several of his Acquaintance. The Day following the Army suffer'd much by the violence of a tempestuous Wind, as likewise by the breaking out of the River, which

G whether

whether it proceeded from a natural Cause, or was the Effect of some Stratagem in the Enemy, is uncertain. From hence they march'd without meeting any opposition to a Town call'd *Ozogardana*, which they took, the Inhabitants having abandon'd it upon the Approach of the Army. From hence *Horsmisda* was sent out to make Discoveries, and had like to have fallen into the Enemies Hands, who lay ready to entrap him; but the River swelling higher than usual hinder'd their Passage, and being discover'd by a Party of *Roman* Soldiers they were forc'd to retire with some Loss. The first Difficulty of any moment they met with was at *Pirisabora*, a Town strongly fortify'd by Art and Nature, and no less secured by the Resolution of the Inhabitants, who gave Ear to no Treaties 'till they had try'd their utmost in a very vigorous Defence, and found it impossible to maintain the Place. The taking this City, being the greatest next to *Ctesiphon* in all *Assyria*, brought great Reputation to the Emperor's Arms, besides the great quantity of Provisions and Ammunition that were found in it prov'd very seasonable to the Army, who began to stand in need of both.

After he had set Fire to the Town, and in a set Speech pacify'd the Army, that began to grow mutinous, he proceeded forward, and after a March of fourteen Miles came to a low Ground, which the Enemy, who had notice they would pass that way, laid under Water, and thereby expos'd 'em to many Difficulties. But at length they arriv'd at *Maiozomalcha*, a large and well fortify'd Town, before which he encamp'd in order to besiege it. He drew a double Line round it, and with his battering Engines broke down a Tower, and part of the Wall: Notwithstanding which the Besieg'd defended themselves with great Galantry, trusting much to the

natural

Chap. I.   XLIII. Julian.

natural Strength of the Place; 'till at length the Soldiers by means of a Mine got into the City, and put all they found to the Sword, except the Governor and some few of the principal Officers. The City was given up to the Soldiers, who first plunder'd and then burnt it.

After this they pass'd further, and arriv'd at two Forts, where *Victor*, who conducted the Forlorn, was oppos'd by the King of *Persia*'s Son, who at the Head of a strong Detachment, and attended by several Noblemen of the Country, disputed his Passage over the River; but when they saw the whole Body of the Army advancing they retir'd, and left the *Romans* Masters of a pleasant Country full of delightful Groves, and enrich'd with all sorts of Fruits. Proceeding a little farther the *Romans* lost part of their Baggage and Carriages: For whilst the Front of the Army was entertain'd by a Party of *Persians* who were sent on purpose to amuse them, another Party fell in upon the Rear, and surpriz'd them. *Julian* enrag'd at this drew on towards *Ctesiphon*, and as he was viewing a Fort which lay in his Passage thither, he rid too near the Walls, and they plied him so warmly with their Darts from above, that he was carry'd off with great Hazard of his Life. *Julian in great Danger.* He was resolv'd to be reveng'd for this Insolence whatever it cost him, and for that Purpose laid close Siege to the Place, which they within defended with great Vigour, encouraged by Promises of a speedy Succour from the King, who lay with his Army not far off from them. But he thrusting himself forward into all Difficulties, and fighting in Person at the Head of his Men, who were encourag'd by his Example, and influenc'd by his Presence and Observation, obtain'd his Desire, and having burnt the Fort, allow'd his Army some time to refresh themselves. After which, through a Cut cleans'd for that Purpose, he pass'd his Fleet out of *Euphrates* into *Tigris*.

Hitherto Fortune for the most part seem'd to court and encourage him, but his Success made him *He grows* rash and inconsiderate, and rais'd him in Imagination *obstinate:* above all Difficulties to which he frequently expos'd himself and his Army, contrary to the repeated Advice and Petitions of his most experienc'd Officers. He totally gave himself up to the Direction of his own Fancies and improbable Chimæra's, suggested to him by his vast Ambition, which aim'd at nothing less than the entire Conquest of all *Persia*. And tho' at a Council of War held near *Ctesiphon* he was advis'd to the contrary, he obstinately persisted in his Resolution of proceeding farther up into the Country, induced to it by the Encouragement of some Guides, who undertook to conduct him. And left the Enemy should become Masters of his Fleet, or else for that no less than 20000 Men were constantly employ'd to man and govern it, he order'd *And burns* all his Ships to be set on Fire, except twelve small *his Fleet.* Rates, which were to be taken in pieces, and convey'd over Land in Waggons to build Bridges with if there should be occasion. This was put in execution accordingly, notwithstanding all the Arguments his Friends offer'd to oppose it, to which he was deaf 'till it was too late, and his Guides were forc'd by Torture to confess that they had offer'd him their Service with no other Design but to ruin him.

This unlucky Proceeding reduc'd the Army to the last Extremity, for now they had lost all Means of a Retreat, and were cut off from all Opportunities of a Supply either of Men or Provisions: And the *Persians*, perceiving the Disadvantages under which they labour'd, laid all the Country waste before 'em, and insulted 'em sometimes in the Front, sometimes

in

in the Flank, and at others in the Rear, and in a manner besieg'd 'em. This extreamly dispirited the *Roman* Army, which was very much weaken'd through the Inconveniences of the Country, and the Hardships to which they were expos'd; nor knew they what Course they were best to take in a strange Country, depriv'd of all manner of Provisions. After many Consultations they resolv'd at length to march towards *Corduena,* and on the 16th of *June* they set forward accordingly.

They had not march'd far before they were met by a strong Body of *Persians,* well provided in every respect, and commanded by *Merenes* General of the Horse, accompany'd by two of the King's Sons, and a great number of the Nobility; here an obstinate Fight began, which lasted for a considerable time, 'till the *Persians,* over-power'd by the *Roman* Legions, gave Ground, and retir'd in the most orderly manner they could. The *Romans* remain'd Masters of the Field, but found little Satisfaction in a Victory, which could not relieve their Wants in a Place where no Provisions were to be had, the Corn, and Grass, and every thing else proper for the Nourishment of Man or Horse being burnt up by the Enemy. *He engages with the Persians, whom he defeats.*

Both sides had agreed to a Truce for three Days, which time was employ'd in burying the Dead, and refreshing their Bodies tir'd with excessive Heat and Fatigues of the Battel. *Julian* all this while labour'd under great Perplexities, for he found the *Persians* resolv'd to oppose his March, and attempt all manner of ways to distress him, without coming to a formal Engagement. The Night before his Death, after a short and troublesome Sleep, he rose, as his Custom was, to Read or Write, and in the dead of Night he beheld the Publick Genius, which is said to have appear'd to him once before upon his being declar'd Emperor in *Gaul*, to move in a melancholy dejected Posture before him, and with a Countenance full of Sorrow forsake him. This suddain unexpected Accident surpriz'd him for the present, but being above the Weakness of Fear, he resign'd all, saith my Author, to the Determination of Providence; and rising early to his Devotions he saw an Exhalation shooting through the Skies, which having traverss'd a good part of the Air vanish'd in a Moment. This he violently suspected to be the Star of *Mars*, who not long since had rejected his many Sacrifices, and was now come in a menacing manner to tell him how little he was to expect from him. Hereupon he consulted his *Hetrurian Augurs*, who told him he was by that Omen advis'd to abstain from fighting; and when they perceiv'd that in spite of this their Interpretation he was resolv'd to proceed, they intreated him to defer his March but for a few Hours, to which he gave so little heed, that as soon as it was Light he order'd his Army to Decamp. The *Persians*, who made the best of every Advantage, sometimes assaulted him upon the Flank, and sometimes fell in upon the Rear, which occasion'd several Encounters between 'em, in all which the Emperor behav'd himself with an unexampled Bravery; but at length being too eager in Pursuit of the *Persians*, who now began to give Ground, a Horse-man's Javelin pierc'd through his Arm into his Side, from whence or by whom directed no one knew, with the Pain of which he sunk down upon the Neck of his Horse, and was with all speed convey'd into his Tent; where observing those about him to be dejected and sorrowful, he told 'em, "He was now call'd "upon to pay the Debt of Nature, which he did "with a willing and chearful Mind, being taught "by Philosophy how much happier the State of

He is wounded.

"the

"the Soul is than that of the Body, upon which
"Confideration he embrac'd Death as the greateſt
"Bleſſing, which exempted him from thoſe Dan-
"gers to which the Neceſſity of his Affairs muſt
"daily expoſe him, to the great Hazard of his
"Virtue and Reputation. That having liv'd at firſt
"in a private, and afterwards in an exalted State,
"he had ſo behav'd himſelf in both as to repent of
"no Action throughout his whole Life. That
"he had great reaſon to thank Divine Providence,
"for that he fell not by the Hand of Conſpirators,
"nor languiſh'd under a Diſeaſe, or ſuffer'd Death
"as a Criminal, but that he made a glorious Paſſage
"out of the World with his Honours freſh and
"blooming about him. That he who is fond of
"Life when he ought to Die, is as great a Coward
"as he who deſires Death when he ought to Live.
"That he declin'd naming a Succeſſor, leſt through
"Ignorance he ſhould paſs by a worthy Perſon, or
"in naming one fitly qualify'd he ſhould expoſe
"him to Danger upon the preference of another after
"his Death, but like a dutiful Son to the Common-
"wealth he wiſh'd her a worthy Governor to ſuc-
"ceed him.

After this, and a ſhort Diſcourſe with the Philo-
ſophers, *Maximus* and *Priſcus*, concerning the Sub-
limity of the Soul, the Wound began to gape, and *He Dies of*
the Tumour of the Veſſel intercepted his Breath; *his Wound.*
then calling for a Glaſs of cold Water, which he
drank up, he expir'd about Midnight. *Theodoret,*
and moſt Chriſtian Writers who have written of
him, ſay, when firſt he was wounded he fill'd his
Hand with Blood iſſuing from the Wound, and
threw it up into the Air with this dreadful Blaſ-
phemy, *Thou haſt Conquer'd,* O Galilean; tho' o-
thers maintain it was the Sun againſt which he thus
threw up his Blood, becauſe he was God of the

Persians, and was then come to their Succour against him; and being, according to the Astrologers, Lord of his Ascendant when he was Born, he had not taken due care to protect him. Sometime before his Death, *Libanius* the Sophist is said to have ask'd a Christian School-master at *Antioch*, by way of Derision, *What he thought the Carpenter's Son was then a doing?* To whom he reply'd, *Know thou Wretch, that that God who made both Heaven and Earth, and whom in Contempt thou call'st the Carpenter's Son, is preparing a Coffin for thy Disciple* Julian.

His Character. As to his Character, even our Christian Writers, who can't be expected inclinable to flatter him, own he enrich'd the Empire with a great many excellent Qualities, that he was Valiant, Chaste, Prudent, Patient of Labour, a great Lover of Learned Men, being himself Learn'd and Eloquent. His Exploits against the *Germans* were extraordinary, considering his Youth and his Education, which had prepar'd him more to the Gown than the Sword; on the other Hand his best Friends allow him to have been Superstitious to the highest Degree, hot, talkative and inconsiderate, that he was very much given to Vain-glory and Ostentation, that in many things he was guided more by his own Humour than the Advice of his ablest Counsellors. These Defects grew upon him with his Years, which Consideration has made some conceive that he ow'd the extent of his Fame to the shortness of his Life, and that had he liv'd longer, Time and Temptation might possibly have expos'd him to such Infirmities as would have sully'd the Reputation acquir'd in his Youth. *Julian* dy'd on the 26th of *June*, in the Second Year of his Reign, and Two and thirtieth of his Age, in his fourth Consulate, which he bore with *Sallust*, *A. D.* 363.

XV. Thus

XV. Thus fell *Julian* in the Flower of his Age, and full Pursuit of his mighty Designs, which as none but a Genius like his, bold and impetuous, could ever have suggested; so now there wanted an equal Resolution to pursue and direct 'em. In him the *Constantine* Family was extinct, under whose Government the Imperial Power seem'd still to retain its native Influence and Vigour. Justice was duly administer'd, and the Laws of the Empire regularly observ'd throughout the Provinces; and tho' in those Times we meet with frequent Usurpations, they serv'd rather to awaken than impair the Supream Authority; as all the Motions and Irruptions occasion'd by the barbarous Nations seem design'd to make a fatal Experience of the Strength of the Empire, rather than to insult or weaken it. But after this the *Roman* Eagle, that with extended Wings us'd to defend those Nations that fled to her for her Friendship and Protection, sicken'd as with Age, and lay expos'd to the Attempts of every Enemy that dar'd Assault her.

The Sorrow the Army conceiv'd at *Julian*'s Death is unexpressible: They were in a strange Country far from home, with a provok'd Enemy round about 'em, without a Head to direct, command and provide for 'em. The Common Soldiers were ready to Mutiny, and the Officers at Variance about a Successor. At last they unanimously pitch'd upon *Sallust* the Præfect, who being a Man of great Worth, and long Experience in Military Affairs, was acceptable to all Parties. But he excusing himself upon the Account of his Age, which had brought many Infirmities upon him, they were forc'd to make a new Election; and being hurry'd by the Distraction of their Affairs, and imminent Dangers to which they were expos'd, the Choice
fell

Jovian E-
lected.

fell upon *Jovian*, Son of *Varronian*, who from an Eminent Post in the Army, where he had behav'd himself like a Brave Commander, was lately retir'd to a private Life. *Jovian* was immediately saluted by his Electors with the Acclamation of *Jovianus Augustus*, which a great part of the Army extending four Miles in length mistook, and conceiving *Julian* to be miraculously recover'd, out of an ill grounded Hope, join'd in the common Cry, 'till upon a Discovery of their Mistake they turn'd their Joy into Tears and Lamentations. As soon as *Jovian* was advanc'd to the Imperial Dignity, an Officer in the Army, who had serv'd formerly under his Father, and had carry'd himself with much Insolence towards him, being afraid of his Son, who had it now in his Power to revenge his Father's Quarrel, deserted and fled over to the *Persians*; and being admitted into the King's Presence, acquainted him with the Death of *Julian*, and that the Army had in a tumultuous manner made Choice of *Jovian*, a mean spirited Man, for his Successor. This News was highly acceptable to the *Persian* King, who thereupon prepar'd his Men to fall vigorously upon the Rear of the *Roman* Army, who upon an Encouragement receiv'd from the Entrails of Beasts, were issuing out of their Camp, when they were attack'd by the *Persians* with their Elephants plac'd in the Front. After a resolute Engagement on both sides, which lasted for some time, the *Persians* gave Ground, leaving two of their Elephants, and a great number of Men dead upon the Place. The *Romans* lost three Principal Officers, and some Soldiers, and after they had given 'em as good a Burial as the Exigency of their Affairs would allow of, they proceeded to a Castle call'd *Suma*. Here they encamp'd the next Day, in the best manner they could, drawing

a

a Line round their Camp for their better Defence; but were however infested by the Enemy at a distance, a Party of whose Horse had the Confidence to break into the Camp, and had almost reach'd the Emperor's Tent, but were at last repulsed with a very great loss. The Night following they dislodg'd, and came to *Charcha,* from whence they remov'd to *Dura,* where they were forc'd to continue four Days through the Obstinacy of the *Persians,* who when ever they were in Motion press'd hard upon their Rear, but when they fac'd about to give 'em Battel retreated, and by this means very much retarded them in their March. Here they were inform'd by some, who pretended to be more knowing than the rest, that they were not now far from the *Roman* Borders, and therefore the whole Army demanded, in a peremptory manner, that they might be permitted to pass over the *Tigris,* which the Emperor and the Chief Officers very prudently oppos'd, assuring 'em the River at that Season of the Year was always swoln higher than usual, that the greatest part of 'em were ignorant of Swimming, and that the Enemy was ready on the other side to reward such desperate Adventures with Death. But they were impatient of Contradiction, and insisted with great Insolence upon their Demands, which they mingl'd with Menaces, and thereby forc'd the Emperor in some measure to comply. He order'd the *Germans* and the *Gauls* to take the River first, hoping, if they perish'd in the Attempt, the rest would learn to be more tractable, and if they got safe a Shore the whole Army might venture after 'em with more Confidence. Hereupon some of the greatest Artists among 'em, who from their Childhood had learnt to Swim over vast Rivers in their own Country, were alotted out for this Expedition; they taking the Advantage of the Night reach'd the opposite

A Mutiny in the Army.

posite Shore sooner than was imagin'd, and having kill'd the *Persians* that were plac'd there for a Guard, by a Signal gave the Army notice of their Success, who were so impatient to follow 'em, that they would hardly allow time for the making a Bridge, which some had undertaken to compose of Bladders for their more convenient Transportation.

Whilst the *Romans* were busied in this extravagant Project, the King of *Persia*, who during his Absence, and now upon his Return to his Army, had by repeated Messengers been inform'd of the desperate Valour of the *Romans*, who instead of being dispirited at the loss of *Julian*, were grown more hardy by continual Labours and Dangers, and had kill'd him a great many brave Men, and an unusual number of Elephants, began to listen to Thoughts of an Accommodation. He was unwilling to enrage 'em too much, not knowing how far the Thirst of Revenge, and Fury of Despair might thrust 'em. He knew fresh Supplies might be rais'd out of the Neighbouring Provinces, and that an Army lay ready in *Mesopotamia* little inferior to this. He was sensible how his own Men were continually harass'd, his Country wasted, the Strength of his Army impair'd, and his Subjects in general desirous of a Peace. The Author of the *Alexandrine* Chronicle saith, the first Overtures of Peace were made by him before he had heard of *Julian*'s Death. Others, that he made mention of it at first only to try the Temper of the *Roman* Army, and the Inclinations of their new Prince; and when he found 'em both a like eagerly desirous of a Peace, he prolong'd the Negotiations from time to time, that the *Romans*, whilst they stood expecting the Result of the Treaty, might spend the small Remainder of their Provisions, and so be forc'd through Famine to comply with his Exorbitant

tant Demands. This is not unlikely, if we consider the Condition the *Roman* Army was then in, and the Articles upon which the Peace was concluded. The Famine rag'd so dismally in their Camp, that they were ready to end their Days by the Sword, rather than wait a painful lingring Death. And *Sapor*, who pretended he permitted the Remnant of *Julian*'s Army to retreat out of mere Pity, made a Demand of no less than five Provinces, together with fifteen Castles, besides *Nisibis, Singara*, and *Castra Maurorum*, a Fort of very great Consequence, before he wou'd hearken to any Terms of Accommodation. This the Emperor was forc'd shamefully to condescend to by a Company of Flatterers, who terrify'd him with the Name of *Procopius*, as if he hearing of *Julian*'s Death would take the Advantage of the Army under his Command, and set up for himself, unless *Jovian* speedily return'd to prevent him. Which indeed was no unlikely Presumption, and was therefore more readily listen'd to by the Emperor, who with much ado prevail'd with the King of *Persia* to permit the Inhabitants of *Nisibis* and *Singara* to be remov'd into the *Roman* Territories; and shamefully engag'd himself never to assist *Arsaces* King *Armenia* against the *Persians*, tho' *Arsaces* was a Christian, and a faithful Friend to the Empire. By which Means *Sapor* had his Revenge upon *Arsaces*, who at the Emperor's Instance had wasted *Chiliocomus*, for he took him Prisoner some time after, and the *Parthians* seiz'd on the greatest Part of *Armenia* bordering on the *Medes*, together with *Artaxata*. The Peace being concluded, Hostages were exchanged on both Sides, for Performance of Conditions; On the *Roman* Part, *Nevitta, Victor*, and *Mellobandes*; on the *Persian, Binefes*, and three other of the Principal among the Nobility.

A Peace concluded.

The

The Conclusion of this Peace, which was to last for thirty Years, was as remarkable a Passage as any of those Times, and occasion'd various Reflections upon it, manag'd variously according to the different Temper of those Writers who have written of it. All allow it to have been shameful and ignominious, forasmuch as the *Romans*, tho' they often receiv'd notable Defeats, could never be prevail'd with to relinquish any of their Territories before. Some say *Jovian* ought not to have submitted to it; others, that he did well in accepting of it, but was bound to observe it no longer than 'till he found himself in a capacity of breaking it. *Ammianus* saith, that during the Treaty he might easily have marched into *Corduena* a fertile Country within his own Dominions, and distant but an hundred Miles from the Place where the Army lay. If they cou'd have made so safe a Retreat without a Truce they would certainly have done it, and not have hazarded themselves in that dangerous Passage over the River, an account of which we have in express Words from him. *Julian*, who to give every one his due had by his obstinate Proceedings made the Retreat necessary, is condemn'd by him and several other Authors for burning his Ships, and thereby cutting off all security of a Return into his own Dominions; which wou'd not have been, had the Retreat been now so easie and possible as he would have it. The Army, as we shall find hereafter, arriv'd at *Nisibis* with great Toil and Labour after the Conclusion of the Peace, which permitted 'em to return at their ease: How then must they have broke through those Multitudes of *Persians* which surrounded 'em on every side before the Conclusion of the Treaty? And yet did they not appear half so terrible as the Famine. These Considerations seem to make the Truce necessary, which was the only Means the Emperor had left

to

to preserve the Remainder of the Army: And as he was forc'd to conclude it for the Safety of his Men, so was he oblig'd by his own Honour after it was concluded to observe it, and not have made an ignominious Breach of Faith, and violated the Laws of Nations. He was not acquainted with that Maxim so prevalent in our Days with the Most Christian Princes, That no Treaties, how solemnly soever enter'd into and religiously ratify'd, ought to be in force, when they grow disadvantageous in the Observance, and are a Curb to any aspiring ambitious Designs.

The Peace being confirm'd on both sides, the *Romans* pass'd the River and came by long Marches to *Hatra*, an old Town in the Middle of the Desart: Here being inform'd that they were to march for seventy Miles together through a dry barren Country, where no Water was to be had but such as was salt or stunk, nor any thing to feed on but bitter unwholesome Herbs, the Emperor took care to provide the Army with sweet Water, and order'd some Camels to be kill'd, to make the best Provision they cou'd. Which being done they prosecuted their Retreat, and after a tiresome dangerous March of six Days they arriv'd at *Ur* a *Persian* Fortress, where *Cassianus* Governor of *Mesopotamia*, and *Mauritius* a Tribune, who had been sent before for that Purpose, met 'em with such Provisions as the Frugality of the Army commanded by *Procopius* and *Sebastian* had been able to spare 'em. From hence the Emperor dispatch'd some in whom he could most confide into the West, there to improve and strengthen his Interest the best they cou'd, sending secret Commissions by 'em, by vertue of which he remov'd some whom he had reason to suspect, and substituted others in their Places, who he judged would be more faithful to him, He order'd these his Agents

to

to report every thing to the best Advantage, to sound how the Generality of the People approv'd of his Advancement, and in what degree they stood affected to him; after which they were speedily to return with the best Intelligence they could get, that the Emperor might take such measures in his Council, as should be judg'd most proper for his Service. Tho' these Messengers set forward with all Expedition, Fame had got the start of 'em, and had alarm'd the Provinces with a melancholy Account of the *Persian* Affairs; especially they at *Nisibis* receiv'd it with the greatest Confusion, when they were inform'd their City was to be surrender'd up to *Sapor*, from whom they cou'd expect no Mercy, having so often withstood him with so much Resolution, and destroy'd so many of his Men.

In the mean time the Army was again in want of all manner of Provisions, which was once more supply'd with the Flesh of their Carriage-Beasts, the only Means left to save that of one another, with so much Fury did the Famine rage among 'em. At *Thilsaphata*, *Procopius* and the general Officers of his Army came to wait upon the Emperor, who receiv'd 'em very graciously. From thence they march'd on to *Nisibis*, in sight of which when they were arriv'd, they pitch'd their Tents without the City. The Emperor, tho' earnestly importun'd by the Inhabitants to lodge in the Palace, as his Predecessors used to do, refus'd it with great Obstinacy, out of Shame to suffer a City so strong and impregnable to be deliver'd up to an enraged Enemy, whilst he was residing in it. The next Day *Binefes*, according to his Master's Orders, and in pursuance of the Conditions of Peace, demanded the City to be deliver'd up to him, and accordingly enter'd by the Emperor's Permission, and took Possession of it in the King of *Persia*'s Name. He had no sooner seiz'd on
the

the Place, but by a Signal from the Castle he commanded the Citizens to quit their Habitations; who in a most passionate manner earnestly besought the Emperor not to be forc'd into foreign Parts, but have liberty to defend the Place of their Nativity, which they undertook to do without putting the Publick to any Charge in their Assistance, affirming they were well acquainted with the Fatigues of a Siege, and knew how to withstand the enraged *Persians*. But all this was to no purpose, the Emperor insisting still upon his Promise, and how perjur'd he must be if he broke it.

Hereupon *Sabinus*, an eminent Man in the Town, said boldly, That *Constantius*, in the whole Course of his Wars against the *Persians*, tho' once driven to such great Straits in his Flight, as to satisfie his Hunger with a Crust of Bread, which he had begg'd from an old Woman, yet to his dying Day would not suffer a Foot of his Territories to be alienated; but *Jovian*, before he was scarce saluted Emperor, tore from the Empire the very Bulwark of his Provinces, which had hitherto been protected by the vigorous opposition of this Town. But when all was to no purpose, the Emperor still urging the Sanctity of his Oath, and they had presented him with a Crown, which after much Entreaty he was prevail'd upon to accept of, one *Sylvanus* an Advocate with great Confidence cry'd out, *So, O Emperor, may'st thou be crown'd by the rest of the Cities.*

This so highly incens'd him, that he strictly commanded the Town to be evacuated within three days, and order'd a Party of Soldiers to drive 'em out, who threaten'd those that were the most unwilling to kill 'em if they loiter'd. The Sun never beheld a more melancholy Sight than was then at *Nisibis*, every Corner of the City was fill'd with Groans and Lamentations, in which all Ages and Conditions

H join'd;

join'd; the Walls and Streets were crowded with miserable Multitudes, that wept and exclaim'd as if they were then to be deliver'd into the Hands of Death, and were all to be Executioners to each other; the helpless Women embrac'd the Doors and Posts of the Houses at their Farewel, with as much real Passion, as if they were going to be torn from what was dearest to 'em, their Husbands or their Children, who stood by and help'd to fill up that measure of Grief in which they had so large a share; whilst the Men, who at the Expence of their Lives had so often defended the Walls, and repell'd the Enemy, curs'd a Peace, that was now depriving 'em of that which their Valour had made good against the most violent Attacks of a bloody and obstinate War. The Roads were fill'd with these desolate Exiles, loaden with what they could most conveniently bear away themselves, but being expell'd in haste, and for want of the Convenience of Carriages, they left several Things more in Quantity and of greater Value behind 'em. The greatest Part of 'em in this forlorn Condition were conducted to *Amida*, the Suburbs of which City were given them by the Emperor to inhabit; the rest were dispers'd into other Parts, where such Care as the Necessity of the Publick Affairs would admit of, was taken for 'em.

After this *Procopius* was sent to attend *Julian*'s Corps to *Tarsus*, in the Suburbs of which City he was bury'd, according to the Orders he had given in his Life-time. After the Funeral Ceremonies were over *Procopius* privately withdrew from *Tarsus*, and tho' diligent Enquiry was made in all Parts for him, he never could be heard of, 'till he appear'd publickly at *Constantinople* a long time after, where he assum'd the Imperial Purple, as shall be shown in its proper Place.

From

Chap. I.   XLIV. Jovian.

From *Nisibis* the Emperor went directly to *Antioch*, where several Prodigies are said to appear, denouncing the Wrath of Heaven, which hasten'd *Jovian*'s Departure from thence, so that he spared neither Man nor Beast 'till he arriv'd at *Tarsus* in *Cilicia*; at which Place the Messengers he had before dispatch'd into the West met him, and were some of 'em sent back with fresh Instructions, for the better settlement of Affairs in those Parts. From *Tarsus* he proceeded on to *Ancyra*, where in as solemn a manner as the Time would permit, he enter'd into the Consulship, assuming for Collegue his Son *Varronian*, a very Infant, who by his crying and struggling, not suffering himself to be carry'd in the Consular Chair, as Custom requir'd, seem'd to portend what happen'd in a very short time after. For proceeding on towards *Constantinople* he arriv'd at *Badastana*, a Town situate upon the Borders of *Bithynia* and *Galatia*, where he was found dead in the Night. His Death gave occasion to many Conjectures; some say he was stifled by the Dampness of his Chamber, which had been newly plaister'd; others, that he was choak'd by the Vapours of Charcoal, plac'd there to dry the Room; and some impute his suddain Death to a Surfeit. *Zonaras* saith he was poison'd with Mushrooms, and *Ammianus* himself seems to be of Opinion, that he came to a violent End, when he compares the Manner of his Death to that of *Scipio Æmilianus*, who according to *Cicero* was murder'd by Night in his Bed.

He is said in many things to have imitated *Constantius*; for he usually dispatch'd Business after Dinner, and lov'd to discourse merrily with those about him. He was a great Friend to the Christian Religion, protecting the Christians from the Malice of the Heathens, and defending the Orthodox Believers against the *Arian* Hereticks; tho' he often declar'd

Ammian.

A. D. 364.

Jovian *Dies.*

His Character.

declar'd he hated all Disputes, and had a great Esteem for those who promoted a Union in the Church. He had so great a Veneration for *Athanasius*, that he desir'd him to send him a Form of Faith, which as a Rule might preserve him from falling into Error: Whereupon *Athanasius* summoned a Synod at *Alexandria*, where they unanimously agreed upon a Creed, conformable to that of *Nice*, to which they all subscribed, and transmitted it to the Emperor. He was sometimes magnificent, tolerably well learn'd, affable and courteous. By the few Officers he preferr'd during his short Reign, we may judge how careful he would have been in his Promotions, had he lived longer. The unlucky Peace he made with the *Persians*, is the only Instance the Writers of that Age have given us of his Cowardice or Imprudence, in other Respects he behav'd himself like a Man of Courage and Experience. He was a great Eater, and given much to Wine and Women, which Faults *Ammianus* thinks the sense of his high Condition would in time have corrected. His Father is said to have foreseen in a Dream his Son's future Advancement, which he discover'd to two of his intimate Friends; adding, that he himself should in time attain the Honour of the Consulate. In this last he was deceiv'd, for he heard indeed of his Son's exalted Fortune, but never liv'd to see him afterwards, or enjoy the Honour the Emperor had design'd him, which was therefore transferr'd to his Grandson *Verronianus*, as we observ'd before. *Jovian* dy'd on the 17th of *February*, in the 33d Year of his Age, after he had Reign'd seven Months and twenty Days, *A. D.* 364.

XVI. The Body of the deceas'd Emperor being prepar'd with the accustomed Rites, was in a solemn Manner convey'd to *Constantinople*, there to be Interr'd

Chap. I.   XLV. Valentinian.

terr'd with his Predecessors. His Reign had been so very short, and consequently his Subjects so little acquainted either with his Virtues or Vices, that they had no reason to lament much, or rejoice at his Death. The Army sometime after dislodg'd from *Badastana*, and proceeded to *Nice*, the Metropolis of *Bithynia*, where all the Officers, both Civil and Military, enter'd into a serious Debate about the Election of a new Prince, some of 'em not despairing of that high Dignity themselves. The first that was whisper'd, rather than nam'd, was *Equitius* a Tribune, but he being of a surly rustick Temper was immediately rejected. Then was *Januarius*, a Relation of *Jovian*'s, propos'd by a few, but they who disapprov'd of the Election had a ready Reason for it, for he being then Commander in *Illyria* was too far off. At length *Valentinian*, a Tribune in the Army, was by Universal Consent chosen Emperor; he was at that time at *Ancyra*, where he had been left with Orders to follow *Jovian*. Immediately upon the Election Messengers were dispatch'd away for him, but being at such a distance there was an *Interregnum* for ten Days together. However *Equitius* and *Leo* had Orders from the rest of the Officers to take care of his Interest 'till his Arrival, and prevent any Innovations in the Army. *Valentinian* was Born at *Cibale* in *Pannonia*, and was Sirnam'd *Funacius*, for that Five Soldiers together were not able to wrest a Rope from him, which he held in his Hand. He arriv'd at *Nice* so soon as he was inform'd of his Advancement, but would not appear abroad the Day after his Arrival, because it was the *Bissextile*, a Day for the most part unlucky to the *Romans*, and therefore they generally declin'd ent'ring on any great Business upon it. Towards the Evening Orders were given by the Advice of *Sallust* the Præfect, that

Valentinian chosen Emperor.

no Person whatsoever of the first Rank, or who was suspected to aim at the Empire, should on Pain of Death be seen abroad the next Morning; but as soon as it was Light the whole Army was drawn up together, and *Valentinian* adorn'd with the Imperial Robes, and saluted *Augustus*, ascended the Tribunal, from whence as he was going to address himself in a Speech to the Army, and stretch'd forth his Hand the better to gain their Attention, the ordinary Soldiers requir'd him in Seditious Murmurs to chuse a Collegue. This at first was thought to have been done at the Instigation of some who had been defeated in their Pretentions to the Empire; but the Noise continuing, and the Soldiers appearing more Bold and Violent, there was great reason to apprehend an Universal Tumult; which *Valentinian* having greater Motives than any else to fear, and if possible to prevent, with Looks full of Authority he again extended his Hand, boldly reprov'd those who appear'd the most forward and seditious, and then without any Interruption deliver'd himself in these Terms to the Army.

His Speech to the Army. "Some Days since it was in your Power to chuse "whom you thought fit to be your Emperor, but "since your Knowledge of me, and my Method "of Life has encourag'd you to raise me up to "that high Dignity, I must tell you, you have "pass'd the Power out of your own Hands; nor "are you to prescribe Laws to your Soveraign: 'Tis "now my Business to Command, and your Duty "to Obey. I know as well as you, that the State "of Affairs, and the Condition of the Empire re- "quires an Associate, whom, as soon as I find it "convenient, I intend to chuse and nominate. In "the mean time you may expect to find me a "tender and careful Prince, as I shall expect from "you all Offices of Submission and Obedience; come "there-

"therefore and receive the Donative, which Cu-
"ſtom and my Love towards you has made your
"due.

 By this reſolute Speech *Valentinian* gain'd his Ends upon the whole Army, not one among 'em dar'd appear ſo hardy as to oppoſe a Man who ſeem'd Born to Command; with a general Acclamation they ſaluted him *Auguſtus,* and conducted him in Royal Pomp to the Imperial Palace, where he ſummon'd together the general Officers, reſolving to be guided by ſuch Councils as appear'd moſt beneficial to the Empire, and not be influenc'd by ſuch as were more agreeable to himſelf. When they were all met he ask'd 'em whom they thought fitteſt to be his Aſſociate in the Empire. After a general Silence for ſome time, *Dagalaiphus* boldly anſwer'd, *If, Sir, you are partial to your own Family, you will make Choice of your Brother; but if you have any Regard to the Publick Good, you will fix on ſome other.* *Valentinian* was inwardly nettled at the Liberty of this Speech, however he conceal'd his Reſentments, and ſet out for *Nicomedia,* which he enter'd on the Firſt of *March*; from thence he remov'd to *Conſtantinople,* where reflecting on the Weight of his Affairs, and how unable he was to ſuſtain ſo vaſt a Burden without an Aſſiſtant, he reſolv'd no longer to defer it; ſo on the Firſt of *March,* without any Oppoſition, he declar'd his Brother *Valens Auguſtus,* who was receiv'd as ſuch with an Univerſal Approbation. Some time after this both Emperors were ſeiz'd with a violent Feavour, which according to *Ammianus* made 'em apprehend ſome foul Play, as if they had been bewitch'd by *Julian*'s Friends; but upon a diligent Enquiry the thing came to nothing, for they could not diſcover the leaſt Grounds for ſuch a Suſpicion.

Makes his Brother his Aſſociate in the Empire.

They were scarce recover'd before the whole Empire was in a manner alarm'd with a general Invasion from the barbarous Nations; the *Germans* were in a cruel manner wasting *Gaul* and *Rhætia*; the *Sarmatæ* and *Quadi, Pannonia*; the *Picts, Scots* and *Saxons* miserably infested *Britain*; the *Moors* grew more Outragious in *Africk* than ever, and the *Goths* as cruelly behav'd themselves in *Thrace*; nor could the late Peace restrain the King of *Persia*, who again laid Claim to *Armenia*, pretending the Truce was made with *Jovian*, whose Death unbound his Hands, and left him at Liberty to recover what he said had formerly been wrested from his Predecessors.

The two Emperors continu'd Thirty Days at *Constantinople*, where they provided for the better Victualling that City and *Rome*, by regulating the Officers who had the Management of the publick Corn. From thence, when the Winter was over, they pass'd through *Thrace* to *Naissus*, in the Suburbs of which, distant three Miles from the City, and call'd *Mediana*, being upon the Point of separating, they made a Partition of their Officers. *Valentinian* made Choice of *Jovinus* and *Dagalaiphus*. *Victor, Arintheus* and *Seronianus* were to attend *Valens* into the East; and at *Sirmium* they parted, *Valentinian* for *Milan*, and *Valens* for *Constantinople*; upon their Arrival at which Cities they both took the Consular Ornaments. All this Year the Empire was grievously burden'd and insulted. The *German* Embassadors, sent as the Custom was once a Year to Court, were roughly treated by *Ursatius*, who by his Office was to receive and answer all Embassadors, and being an obstinate angry Man sent them back with less Presents than were usually given; which upon their Return their Principals threw away in Indignation, and provok'd by the Usage

A. D. 365.

Chap. I. XLV. Valentinian, Valens.

Usage of their Embassadors in great Rage took Arms, and broke through the Borders. At the same time, or not much after, *Procopius* began to set up for himself in the East; of all which *Valentinian* was inform'd, as he was travelling towards *Paris*, about the beginning of *November*. *Dagalaiphus* was sent with a powerful Army against the *Germans*, who, after they had done what Mischief they could, retreated, not waiting for *Dagalaiphus* his Arrival. The Rebellion of *Procopius* was of a more difficult Nature, whom *Valentinian* was willing, if possible, to crush in the beginning, but knew not whether his Brother was alive, or *Procopius* had assum'd the Imperial Title upon his Death; so lame was the Account *Equitius* sent him of this Matter, who had receiv'd his Information from one *Anthony*, commanding in the Mid-land *Dacia*. He had a Mind to march into *Illyricum* with all Expedition, and prevent the Usurper, if he had any Designs upon *Pannonia*; for he well remember'd with what speed *Julian* over-ran all those Parts, when he had declar'd himself against *Constantius*, and usurp'd the Imperial Title, and how serviceable his extraordinary and unexpected Diligence prov'd to him: But his Friends about him dissuaded him all they could from that Resolution; they remonstrated to him, how by leaving the West, *Gaul* would unavoidably be expos'd to the Inroads of the Barbarians; in this they were assisted by Deputies from the Cities, who earnestly besought him not to forsake 'em in so great an Extremity, but awe the *Germans* by his Presence, and restrain 'em by the Terror of his Name. These Arguments made him change his Mind, and prevail'd upon him to comply with their Requests. He consider'd *Procopius* was an Enemy to no more than himself and his Brother, whereas the *Germans* were declar'd

margin: Procopius sets up for himself.

clar'd Enemies to the whole *Roman* Empire. He resolv'd therefore not to stir out of *Gaul,* but went and resided at *Rheims*; where taking the Affairs of *Africk* into Consideration, and to prevent any sudden Attempt that might be made upon those Parts, he sent away *Neotherius* and others, whose Care it was to keep all quiet there.

In the mean time *Procopius* was very busie at *Constantinople,* where his Affairs seem'd to be in a tolerable Condition. He was Born of a great Family in *Cilicia,* where he had been educated; and being nearly related to *Julian,* he from his Youth met with more than common Esteem. He was a Man of few Words, for the most part very close and reserv'd; tho' he had been bred a Heathen, yet in *Constantius* his Time he was made first a *Notary,* after that a *Tribune* in respect to his Integrity, being reputed a good Moral Man. When *Julian* came to be Emperor he was preferr'd to higher Dignities, and gave some, who more narrowly enquir'd into him, occasion to think he would be ready, if ever it came into his Power, to disturb the Publick Peace. Being sent to attend *Julian*'s Corps to *Tarsus,* as we observ'd before, he privately withdrew from thence for fear of *Jovian,* whose Jealousie he had great reason to suspect, for that it was whisper'd abroad that *Julian* had nam'd him for his Successor at his Death; and he knew that *Jovian* had upon his Advancement put one of his own Name to Death, for no other reason but because a few Soldiers had propos'd him as worthy the Empire. For a long time he led a melancholy Life in solitary remote Places, with great Care avoiding the Industry of those whom *Jovian* had sent to enquire strictly after him, without Company or Sustenance labouring under the utmost Penury; but grown weary of so desolate a Condition,

Chap. I. XLV. Valentinian, Valens.

he ſtole ſecretly into the Parts adjacent to *Chalcedon*, and concealing himſelf in the Houſe of *Strategius*, a truſty Friend, he went often to *Conſtantinople*, where his mean Habit and meagre Countenance made him unknown to the moſt curious Eye. Here, like a cunning Spy, he enquir'd diligently after News, and was well pleas'd to hear how the People generally complain'd of *Valens* for Injuſtice and Oppreſſion, to which he was continually prompted by his Father-in-Law *Petronius*, a Man deform'd both in Body and Mind, ſo Cruel, Covetous and Inexorable, that like a Wild Beaſt he rag'd equally againſt the Innocent and the Guilty. Theſe his violent Proceedings, by which he had ruin'd many Perſons of all ſorts in his ſevere Inquiſitions after Debts that had been owing to the Publick ever ſince the Reign of *Aurelian*, created a general Diſlike to the preſent Government, and a Deſire of a Change, which highly pleas'd *Procopius*, who did not deſpair of improving it one Day to his own Advantage. *Valens* was about this time preparing for his Expedition into *Syria*, the better to oppoſe the King of *Perſia*, who ſeem'd to have a Deſign upon *Armenia*; and about the beginning of the Spring the Emperor ſet forward with a very good Army, whoſe Abſence ſeem'd much to contribute to *Procopius* his Ambition, who at length grown weary of his private Neceſſities, and preferring Death to ſo forlorn, uncomfortable a Life, raſhly ventur'd upon a bold and deſperate Undertaking. The Emperor at his Departure out of *Bithynia* had detatch'd a ſtrong Party of Horſe and Foot from his Army to defend *Thrace* from the Incurſions of the *Goths*, who he was inform'd deſign'd to Invade it. Part of this Detachment was in their March Quarter'd at *Conſtantinople*, and to ſome of the Officers *Procopius* had the Courage to diſcover himſelf and his

Valens in no Favour with the People.

Inten-

Intentions, and after many Promises of mighty Rewards they undertook to secure all that Party to his Interest; accordingly the next Day they were drawn up at the *Anastatian* Baths, where *Procopius* was presented to 'em, and appear'd more like a Ghost than one fit for any noble or dangerous Undertaking. He was Cloath'd in an Embroider'd Coat like a Courtier, having nothing of a Soldier about him but a Pike, which he bore in his Right Hand, having thrown a Purple Coat over his Left Arm, and indeed appear'd like a Player, representing that Dignity he was going to Usurp. In this ridiculous Figure he address'd himself in a fawning Speech to the Soldiers, and implor'd their Assistance, who receiv'd him with Promises of Protection, and a Show of Honour, conducting him publickly into the City, where he was neither oppos'd nor encourag'd by the Inhabitants, either for that they were fond of a Change, or out of a Detestation to *Petronius* his Extortions. Having ascended the Tribunal, he observ'd a deep Amazement in the Face of the People, which was attended with as extraordinary a Silence; this threw him into a great Perplexity, for he now thought he was arriv'd at the end of his former Wishes, Death rather than so miserable a Life, and therefore stood Speechless for some time. Recovering by degrees a little Courage, he made the Multitude a confus'd Speech, more agreeable to the Distractions of his Mind than the Exigencies of his Affairs, and was answer'd first by the Applause of a few among 'em hired for that purpose, and afterwards by the Acclamations of the rest, who in a tumultuous manner gave him the Title of Emperor. This Ceremony being over they hurry'd him away to the Palace, attended by none but the meaner sort, and most profligate of the People. From so contemptible a Beginning

Procopius Usurps.

Beginning did he by Degrees raise himself up to so great a height, as to be able for some time to maintain his Usurpation, to the no small Expence and Hazard of the State. Some Days after he was join'd by others of the better Sort, invited to it either by their own Inclinations, or the Prospect of great **Advantages.** And that no Artifices might be wanting to support his Designs, several Persons at the Procurement of *Procopius* impudently affirm'd they were come out of *Gaul*; that *Valentinian* was dead in that Province, and the People were generally willing to submit to the new Prince. The better to colour this Imposture, *Nebridius*, whom *Petronius* his Intrigues had got to be made *Præfectus Prætorio* in the room of *Sallust*, and *Cæsarius*, Præfect of *Constantinople*, were both imprisoned; and lest *Julius*, who commanded in *Thrace*, should be able with the Forces under him to crush the Rebellion in its Birth, *Nebridius* was with great Menaces forc'd to write to him in *Valens* his Name to hasten to *Constantinople*, there to assist the Emperor with his Advice upon very weighty Affairs; whither he was no sooner come, but he was likewise thrown into Prison. Things proceeding thus far according to his Wishes, *Procopius* began to alter and new-model the Officers of the Court, some courting and purchasing at a great Expence Employments under this mock Emperor; others, who beheld 'em as no other than transitory Pageants, were compell'd by Force to accept of 'em; and as it is usual in such intestine Confusions, some from the very Dregs of the People were advanc'd to Offices of Honour and Profit, whilst others of Noble Birth, great Possessions, and large Endowments, were either Banish'd or put to Death.

By these Arts *Procopius* imagin'd he had settled his Affairs upon a reasonable Foundation, and began to think of an Army, whereby he might defend the Dignity he had thus happily acquir'd; and in this he succeeded according to his Wish, for all the Troops which were design'd for *Thrace* readily swore Allegiance to him, and bound themselves under the severest Execrations to be firm and faithful; this they did with more Chearfulness upon sight of *Constantius* his little Daughter, whom *Procopius* brought forth in his Arms to 'em, for this reminded 'em of their Affections to that Prince, and *Procopius* his Relation to *Julian*; nor were they a little animated when they beheld *Faustina*, the Child's Mother, who either designedly, or else upon some other accidental Occasion, had that Day put on the Imperial Habit. After this he dispatch'd several Persons to make sure of *Illyricum*, who went arm'd with nothing fit for so great an Enterprize, but a groundless Impudence, and a few of this new Emperor's Medals, and were therefore seiz'd by *Æquitius* who commanded in those Parts, and tortur'd to death These Proceedings made *Æquitius* apprehend the like Treatment from the Enemy, if ever he should fall into their Hands; whereupon he fortify'd all the Northern Passages, and thereby defeated the Usurper's Designs upon *Illyricum*, wherein he did the Emperor a very great piece of Service.

Valens upon the first Account of these Commotions resolv'd to return, and ruin *Procopius*, e'er he was able to make too great a Head against him; and was now in *Galatia*, where he heard of the Usurper's unexpected Progress; the News of which distracted him to that Degree, that in great Consternation he resolv'd to quit the Imperial Purple, but was prevented by those about him, who with powerful Arguments encourag'd him to the contrary, and persuaded him to detach two Parties, who were to march before, and break into the Camp of the Rebels

bels. At *Mygdus,* a Town in *Phrygia,* situate on the River *Singarius,* they met *Procopius,* who had been at *Nice,* and to those who before had sworn Allegiance to him had added such a promiscuous number of Fugitives and Deserters, as were willing to try their Fortunes with him; and when both Armies were ready to engage, stepping boldly forward, as if he was going to challenge one of the adverse Party to a single Combat, he took *Vitalianus,* one of the Officers, by the Hand, accosted him with a familiar and gentle Salutation in *Latin,* and whilst all on each side were in a suspence, he mildly upbraided him and his Fellow-Soldiers, for drawing their Swords in the behalf of a *Pannonian* Thief, against one ally'd to the Family of *Constantine* the Great, who desir'd nothing but to be restor'd to the Rights of his Royal Progenitors. By this Speech he so effectually insinuated himself into 'em, that they who came arm'd with Resolutions to fight and destroy him, were mollify'd in a moment, and vailing their Ensigns, in token of their Defection, passed over to his Party; where with loud Acclamations they saluted him Emperor, conducting him with general Approbation to the Imperial Pavilion; and affirming, as the Custom was among the Soldiers in those Cases, that *Procopius* was invincible.

A Party sent against Procopius desert to him.

This Defection brought a very seasonable Accession to the Strength of *Procopius,* who sent *Rumitalca* a Tribune, and one of the Deserters, with Orders to seize on *Nice,* which he did with all Expedition. *Valens* detach'd *Vadomarius* with a strong Party to recover it, whilst he went and laid close Siege to *Chalcedon,* where he met with a very obstinate Resistance, and beginning to grow in great want of Provisions he was forced to decamp; of which they in *Nice* having Notice, made a bold Sally under the Conduct of *Rumitalca,* and bearing

down

Valens in Danger. down all before 'em had certainly surprized the Emperor, had he not upon timely Notice of their Design saved himself by the Lake of *Sunona*, and the Windings of the River *Gallio*. By this means all *Bithynia* fell into the Hands of *Procopius*, and *Valens* removed with all Expedition to *Ancyra*, where he was inform'd that *Lupicinus* was marching with considerable Forces out of the East to his Assistance. Upon this Encouragement he sent *Arintheus*, an experienc'd Commander, against the Rebels; who proceeded as far as *Dadastana* before he met with any Resistance, but was there oppos'd by one *Hyperechius*, with whom as a despicable Fellow disdaining to fight, he sent Orders to his own Men to lay hold on their Leader and bind him, which they did accordingly. In the mean time *Procopius* had laid Siege to *Cyzicus*, in which the Treasure, brought formerly out of *Nicomedia* to pay the Army that had served in the East, was at present lodged; upon which account the Usurper had great reason to have an Eye upon that City, by which, if he could take it, he might join the *Hellespont* to *Bithynia*. *Seronianus* was then in the Town, and made the best Defence he could. He chain'd up the Haven and so kept out the Enemies Ships, and very much gall'd the Assailants from the Walls. This Resolution in the Defendants was a very great Obstacle to *Procopius* his Proceedings, and he had rais'd the Siege but for the couragious Attempt of one *Aliso* a Tribune, who with much Danger and an undaunted Resolution contriv'd a way to cut the Chain; in consideration of which bold Exploit he had afterwards his Pardon, and was continu'd in his Employment, tho' they proceeded with great Severity against the rest of the Rebels. *Procopius* being by this means become Master of *Cyzicus*, pardon'd all the Besieg'd, except *Serenianus*, whom he sent bound to *Nice*, with

with Orders that he should be kept in safe Custody.

Hitherto he had behav'd himself with much Moderation and Humanity: He had lately narrowly escap'd a Party sent out by *Valens* to entrap him, and with much Diligence saved himself and his Wife in a Ship prepared for the Purpose, against any sinister Accidents, or unexpected Attempts. But puffed up now with the glorious Progress of his Affairs, he began to grow proud and tyrannical, and not regarding the Vicissitude of Fortune, he commanded *Arbetio*'s House, full of Moveables of an inestimable Value, to be rifled. He had hitherto spared it in confidence of *Arbetio*'s Friendship, but when he found that upon repeated Messages he had pretended Sickness, and the Inconveniencies of old Age, and for that reason declin'd waiting upon him, he gave him this unseasonable Proof of his Indignation. He could not but think this improvident Act would draw great Inconveniencies upon him, however he pleas'd himself with the Thoughts of being able to pass into the East at his Pleasure, where the Provinces grew weary of the present Government, and were desirous of a Change; upon which Account he attempted to draw the Cities of *Asia* over to his Party, and listen'd diligently to those who propos'd to him the readiest Ways to raise Mony, whereby he might be the better able to raise Recruits upon occasion, and supply his Army.

The Year following, in which *Gratian* the Son of *Valentinian* and *Dagalaiphus* were Consuls, *Valens* having joined *Lupicinus*, march'd with a strong Army to *Pessinus*, a Town belonging to *Galatia*, which he reinforced, and proceeded into *Lycia* with a Design to surprize *Goamoarius*, who lay little expecting him. *Valens* found by Experience the adverse Party were much animated against him by

A.D. 366.

Fau-

Fauſtina, Conſtantius his Widow, and her little Daughter *Conſtantina,* who by *Procopius* his Order were expos'd to the Army, the better to encourage 'em to fight for ſo tender a Branch of that Imperial Stock, to which he himſelf pleaded a Relation's Right. To obviate theſe Artifices, the Emperor prevail'd with *Arbetio,* who was now retir'd to a private Life, to come to him, hoping by the Preſence and Intereſt of one of *Conſtantine*'s Commanders, the Soldiers Minds would be mollify'd; he was not deceiv'd in his Conjectures, for *Arbetio* being provok'd at *Procopius* his late Proceedings againſt him, came as ſoon as ſent for, and being reverenc'd by all for his Age and Dignity, he eaſily perſuaded 'em to their Duty. He told 'em *Procopius* was no better than a Highway-man; but call'd thoſe who had been ſeduced by him, his Sons and Fellow-Soldiers, who had formerly drawn their Swords with Honour, in Defence of the Empire, and Vindication of the Legal Authority, tho' they were now miſs-led by a deſperate Rebel, whom he advis'd them to quit, and reſign up to the Puniſhment his Uſurpation had deſerv'd. This wrought ſo effectually, that *Goamoarius,* whom, with *Agilo, Procopius* had advanc'd to the chiefeſt Command in the Army, ſurrender'd himſelf at *Thyatira* in *Lydia,* as did likewiſe *Agilo* at *Nacolia* in *Phrygia,* whither the Emperor was advanc'd to give the Rebels Battel. Here moſt of the Army follow'd the Example of their General, and went over to *Valens*; at which unexpected Accident *Procopius* was ſo amaz'd, that he forſook his Horſe and fled into the adjoining Woods, whither he was attended by *Florentius* and *Barchalbas* a Tribune, who having been acquainted with him ever ſince the Days of *Conſtantius,* had follow'd him out of Neceſſity rather than good Will. There, having ſpent the greateſt Part of the Night in diſtracted

stracted Thoughts and doubtful Apprehensions, 'till the Moon began to shine so bright that they were in fear of a Discovery, they seiz'd on the dejected *Procopius*, and led him bound to the Emperor, who immediately commanded his Head to be struck off, and *Florentius* and *Barchalbas* to be put to Death, contrary (in *Ammianus* his Opinion) to the Rules of Justice and Reason: If they had betray'd a lawful Prince, Death had been no more than what their Treason had deserv'd; but if he was a Rebel and Usurper, they might reasonably have expected another sort of Reward for their seasonable Service. However this was the End of *Procopius* his Usurpation, who suffer'd Death in the fortieth Year and tenth Month of his Age. He was a Man of no mean Presence, tho' he went something stooping, with his Eyes ever fix'd upon the Ground, which proceeded from his melancholy Temper, not much unlike *Crassus*, who is reported never to have laught but once in his Life. Yet was he always averse to the shedding of Blood, which, considering the Morosenefs of his Temper, is a thing to be wonder'd at, in *Ammianus* his Opinion.

Procopius taken, and beheaded.

Marcellus, Governor of *Nice*, and Kinsman to *Procopius*, hearing of his Death, commanded *Serenianus* in the dead of Night to be slain, in which he luckily provided for the Safety of a great many Persons; for being an ill-natur'd cruel Man, and of great Power with *Valens*, whose Country-man he was, it is not unlikely but, had he out-lived the Defeat of *Procopius* his Party, he would have exasperated the Emperor, too much of himself inclin'd to Revenge, and procur'd the Destruction of many as well innocent as guilty. After this *Marcellus* seiz'd on *Chalcedon*, where being assisted by a few, whom Poverty or Despair had thrust into Rebellion, he assum'd the Imperial Robe; but was shortly after surpriz'd by a Party of stout Soldiers sent for that purpose, who threw him into Prison, from whence he was taken out the next Day, and together with his Accomplices was tortur'd to Death. Tho' *Serenianus* his Death is thought to have abated something of the Rigour in the Prosecutions of the Rebels, yet *Valens* proceeded with the utmost Severity against those who really were, or who were but barely suspected to have been in *Procopius* his Interest. His Ears lay open to all Complaints and Informations, and the least Presumption made him use the suspected Person with the greatest Barbarity; so that this which appear'd like a Peace, was more cruel, bloody and inexorable than the most raging War: Death Banishment, and Confiscations, were the ordinary Methods of Proceeding, and no Man that had the Misfortune to be accused was so happy to escape one of those three Punishments, 'till the Emperor by degrees grew weary of Blood, and he had fill'd his own Coffers and those of his Followers.

Valens his Severity.

During *Procopius* his Usurpation there happen'd such horrible Earthquakes throughout the World, the like of which were so far from being met with in ancient History, that they exceeded the most extravagant Fables. About Break of Day, on the 21st of *July*, a violent Storm of Thunder and Lightning arose, which was attended with so dreadful a Motion of the Earth, that the Sea deserted its ancient Bounds, exposing Multitudes of its Inhabitants, that were seen sticking on the Mud, and the Sun now, first since the Creation, beheld the naked Bosom of the Deep, swelling up here into vast Mountains, and stretching forth there into continu'd Vallies; which whilst Swarms of People came to contemplate, and to behold the Ships that under Sail were left as it were on dry Ground, the Sea on a sudden, disdaining a Repulse, return'd with redoubl'd

Horrible Earthquakes.

doubl'd Fury, and bounding over its former Limits, broke with irresistible Rage over Islands into the Continent, where it bore down all before it, private Habitations, publick Buildings, Men and Beasts. No less than fifty thousand are said to have perish'd upon this Occasion, great Multitudes of Ships were found stranded after the Recess of the Waters, and some by the Violence of the Winds had been born up on the Tops of Houses, as it happen'd at *Alexandria*, and some at two Miles distant from the Shore, as *Ammianus* saith he saw one himself near *Methone*, a Town in *Laconia*. These Prodigies he seems to relate as if they portended *Procopius* his Rebellion, tho' they ought rather to be consider'd as Introductions to that Fatal Inundation of the Northern Nations, which happen'd not long after, and the Total Ruin of the Western Provinces, which follow'd thereupon.

During these Transactions in the East, the *Germans* having recover'd their Strength, which had been so much impair'd under the Conduct of *Julian*, began again to give the Empire some Trouble, and renew'd their Incursions into *Gaul*, piercing in the midst of Winter a great way up into the Country; against whom *Charietto* and *Severianus* were first dispatch'd, who being overthrown and kill'd in a obstinate Engagement with the Enemy, *Dagalaiphus* is made choice of at *Paris*, where *Valentinian* then kept his Court, to restore the Honour of the *Roman* Arms; but he delaying the Expedition, and pretending he had not Strength sufficient to restrain the Barbarians, who in several Bodies were roving about the Country, and being sent for sometime after to receive the Consular Ornaments, and share that Honour with *Gratian*, *Valentinian*'s Son, *Jovinus*, Master of the Horse, was dispatch'd away with convenient Forces in his room; he in-

New Troubles in the West.

Jovinus Defeats the Germans. forming himfelf of the Condition the Barbarian Army was in, and ordering his Marches with great Warinefs and Circumfpection, fell upon a great Party of the Enemy near a Place call'd *Scarponna*, about Twelve Miles from *Mets*, and cut 'em all off before they were able to Arm and put themfelves upon their Guard, without lofing one Man on his own fide; from hence he march'd his Army, animated with fo good Succefs, in queft of another Party, and ufing the fame Care as before, he was inform'd by fome Scouts he had fent out for that purpofe, that he was not far from the Enemy, who lay in a carelefs manner upon the Bank of the River. As he drew near he refrefh'd his Men in an adjacent Vally, and then upon a Signal given they broke violently into the Camp of the Barbarians, who had neither time to draw themfelves into a Body, or take to their Arms, or make the leaft Refiftance, but were all kill'd bitterly curfing and threatning the *Romans*, who were come thus unexpectedly upon 'em. This continu'd Succefs, with which Fortune in Juftice to his Virtue had crown'd his Arms, encourag'd him to proceed againft a third Party, whom he found in the *Catalaunian* Plains, but in a better manner prepar'd to receive him. Here he entrench'd himfelf, and having allow'd his Men time for Sleep and Refrefhment, he drew out his Army early in the Morning, and fo difpos'd it, that it made an appearance of a good Body, and feem'd to equal that of the Enemy, tho' they far exceeded him in Numbers of Men, but not in Courage and Difcipline. Upon a Signal given the Fight began, which continu'd all the Day, tho' the *Romans* had vifibly the Advantage during the whole Engagement, 'till *Balchobaudes*, a Tribune of the *Armatura*, a great Boafter, but a downright Coward, ran away towards the Evening, and endanger'd danger'd the loss of the whole Army, which began to be in a Confusion; 'till the General by his extraordinary Diligence encourag'd the Soldiers afresh, who press'd with such Resolution upon the Enemy, that they kill'd six thousand upon the Place, and wounded four thousand, and that with the loss of no more than two hundred on the *Roman* side, and as many wounded. The Night having put an end to the Dispute, *Jovinus* appear'd again next Morning at the Head of his Troops in the Field, but found the Enemy had taken the Advantage of the Night, and were fled, whom he pursu'd as far as he thought he might with Safety; but finding they were too far gone to be overtaken he return'd to the Camp, where he was inform'd that their King, who with a few others had been taken by some whom *Jovinus* had sent to Plunder the Camp, was in his Absence hang'd; at which he was so highly enrag'd, that he had punish'd the Commanding Officer with Death, had it not been made appear to him that it was done by the ungovernable Rage of the Soldiers, who in the Heat of the Service were not to be restrain'd. After this compleat Victory he march'd back to *Paris*, and was met without the City by the Emperor, who in respect to his eminent Services design'd him Consul for the ensuing Year. The Joy they conceiv'd for so prosperous a conclusion of the Campaign, was improv'd by the arrival of Messengers from *Valens*, who about the same time sent his Brother *Valentinian* the Head of the Usurper *Procopius*.

Whilst the Empire was thus assaulted on all sides, the Church was no less distracted by Heresie and Schism; the *Arians* had receiv'd so small a Check during the short Reign of *Jovian*, who espous'd the Orthodox Interest, that they still continu'd their Arti-

The State of the Church.

Artifices, Oppressions and Cruelties; tho' *Valentinian* was an utter Enemy to their abominable Opinions, yet desiring, if possible, to Unite the Minds of the People, he chose rather to wink at than openly oppose 'em; but *Valens*, whose Wife *Domitia* was an *Arian*, and who had been this Year Baptiz'd by the Hands of *Eudoxius*, Bishop of *Constantinople*, the Grand Patron of Arianism, declar'd himself openly for that Heresie, omitting no Opportunities for its Encouragement and Support, and doing all he could to drive those Pastors out of the Church, who had the Courage to oppose it, so that the *Arians* govern'd as they pleas'd in the Spiritual Affairs throughout the East; nor were they much inferior in Power in the West, obtaining that by force of Arms which they could not procure by the Favour and Indulgence of the Emperor. This Year *Liberius*, Bishop of *Rome*, dy'd, upon which ensu'd a Scandalous Sedition in the City, occasion'd by the different Parties contending for the Succession, in which the *Partisans* of *Damasus*, who had been Elected by the *Arians*, disputed it so warmly with the Catholicks, for whom they were too strong, that *Ammianus* said no less than 137 Persons were found dead in a Church, where they us'd to assemble to perform their Publick Worship; and that *Juventius*, Præfect of the City, finding himself unable to quell the Tumult, was forc'd to retire into the Suburbs. He adds, *That it's no wonder to see those, who are ambitious of Human Greatness, contending with so much Heat and Animosity for that Dignity, which when they have obtain'd they are sure of being enrich'd by the Oblations of the People, of appearing in great Splendor abroad, conspicuous in their costly Coaches, sumptuous in their Feasts, out-doing Soveraign Princes in the Expences of the Table.* For which reason *Prætextatus*, a Heathen,
who

who was Præfect of the City the Year following, was in the right when he said, *Make me Bishop of Rome, and I'll be a Christian too.*

Whilst the *Roman* Arms were busied, as we observ'd before in the West, *Thrace* began to be threatned with new Commotions; for the *Goths* having assisted *Procopius* in his Designs upon the Empire, and supply'd him with a good number of Soldiers, *Valens* thought he had just reason to call 'em to an Account for so bold an Affront; and therefore first sent *Victor*, Master of the Horse, to demand of 'em why they who were at Peace, and in League with the *Romans*, presum'd to join with a Rebel, who had rais'd War against his lawful Soveraign. They alledg'd in Excuse, and produc'd *Procopius* his Letters, wherein he affirm'd himself the Heir of *Constantine*'s Family, and upon that Grounds had a right to the Imperial Title, which he had assum'd; this they said ought to excuse their Proceedings, which were influenc'd by what appear'd to them just and equitable. *Valens* in no manner satisfy'd with this frivolous Answer, march'd towards the latter end of the Spring with a good Army against them, and having muster'd his Men near *Daphne*, a Fort built by *Constantine* the Great in *Mœsia Secunda*, the better to restrain the Inroads of the *Goths*, he pass'd 'em over the *Ister* by Bridges built for that purpose, and got safe on the other side without the least Resistance, where he found little to do; for upon the approach of the *Roman* Army the *Goths* were all fled into the Neighbouring Mountains of *Serri*, inaccessible to any but those who were well acquainted with the Country. But that he might be said to have done something in this Summers Expedition, he sent out *Arintheus* to surprize some who were wand'ring o'er the Plains, and had not yet reach'd their Companions, and so

Commotions in Thrace.

without

without receiving any harm, or doing much damage he return'd. The Year following he prepar'd with the same Application for a second Invasion, but was stopp'd in his Expedition by the immoderate Overflowings of the *Danube*, and forc'd to encamp near a Village call'd *Carporus*, 'till Winter coming on he remov'd to *Marcianopolis*, where he continu'd the rest of the Year. The next Summer he renew'd his Design, and having laid a Bridge of Boats over the River at *Novidunum*, he pierc'd far into the Country, and fell upon the *Gruthungi*, a very Warlike Nation, and after several Encounters forc'd *Athanaric*, their Chief Commander, and a Brave Soldier, to fly; after which Exploits he return'd again to Winter in *Marcianopolis*, where some Overtures were made of a Peace, which both sides seem'd inclinable to listen to. By reason of the Prince's Absence the East was expos'd to great Danger, and the Barbarians, who us'd to drive a great Trade with the Subjects of the Empire, began to be in great Distress from so long an Interruption, so that they sent their Embassadors sufficiently instructed to offer their Proposals for a Peace: And the Emperor, who as yet had a regard to Justice, and study'd the Welfare of his Subjects, tho' he was afterwards miss-led by his gross Flatterers, and overwhelm'd the Empire in unspeakable Misfortunes, gave Ear to the Embassadors, so that he immediately sent away *Victor* and *Arinthæus*, who finding the *Goths* to be in good earnest, agreed upon the Preliminaries, and the Place of Treaty. *Athanaric* affirm'd his Father had made him swear solemnly never to tread on *Roman* Ground; and because it was below the Majesty of the Emperor to go to him, they met by consent in Boats in the

Peace with the Goths. middle of the River, where the Peace was ratify'd to their mutual Satisfaction, and Hostages deliver'd on both

both sides; after which *Valens* return'd to *Constantinople*, whither *Athanaric* likewise fled in the Reign of *Theodosius*, being driven out of his own Country by a Faction rais'd against him, and was there very magnificently bury'd after the *Roman* manner.

All this while the *Germans* seem'd to be very quiet in the West, so that *Valentinian* was at leisure to look after the Affairs of *Britain*, where the *Picts* and *Scots* committed great Outrages, but were by his extraordinary Care and Management repress'd for the present; but as he was returning from *Amiens* towards *Triers*, the Year following, he was inform'd that the Barbarians were again up in Arms, and had reduc'd this Island to a miserable Condition, having kill'd *Nectaridus*, and circumvented another Principal Commander of the *Romans*; whereupon *Jovinus* is sent with great Expedition to reinforce the Army in *Britain*, but receiving still worse News of the State of Affairs in this Island, the Emperor made Choice of *Theodosius*, a Man of great Experience and exemplary Courage, who at the Head of a gallant Army, both of Horse and Foot, chearfully undertook the Service. The *Picts* at that time were divided into two Nations, the *Deucalidonii* and *Vecturiones*, besides whom there were the *Attacotti* and the *Scots*, who rov'd up and down, and committed a great deal of Mischief. *Theodosius* embark'd at *Bulloign*, and landed safely at *Rutupiæ*, or *Richborough* in *Kent*, where, as soon as he was join'd by his whole Army, he march'd directly to *London*, call'd *Londonium* by *Ammianus*, but afterwards *Augusta*, accounted a City of great Antiquity in his Days; and dividing his Forces into several Parties, fell upon the Rovers whilst they lay scatter'd up and down loaden with their Booty, which together with their Captives he quickly recover'd out of their Hands, restoring all to the right

The Affairs of Britain.

A. D. 367.

Theodosius sent thither.

Pro-

Proprietors, except a small Portion which he distributed among his weary Soldiers. After this he return'd in a triumphant manner to the City, oppress'd before with great Difficulties, but by his means restor'd to its ancient Freedom. Here whilst in the secret Satisfaction of his present Success, and an Uncertainty of the future, he lay considering what further Course he was best to take, he was inform'd by the Prisoners and Deserters, that his Enemies consisted of many Nations fierce and intractable, not to be master'd but by Stratagems and sudden Onsets. First therefore upon Promise of a general Pardon he encourag'd those, who had forsaken their Colours, to return; and still intent upon the better Management of the Affairs in the Island, he sent for *Civilis* to govern *Britain* as Vice-Præfect under him, joining *Dulcilius* in Commission with him. Here he continu'd 'till the Year 370.

His Prudent Management. during which time he acted the Part of a hardy couragious Soldier, as well as an experienc'd and vigilant Captain. By his great Care and excellent Management he laid the Foundations of Peace and Security, which continu'd for a long time after, restoring both the Cities and Garrisons, into which great Disorders had crept, to as good a Condition as they had formerly been in. After he had recover'd a Province the Enemy had over-run, fortify'd the Borders, and settled all things that were amiss in the Island; he was with much Commendation recall'd to Court, and left his Charge with no less Honour, than formerly had waited on the Industry and Fortunes of *Furius Camillus*, or *Papirius Cursor*. Tho' these Exploits were the Work of several Years, I thought fit to touch upon 'em once for all, that I might with less Interruption attend such Transactions as more immediately relate to the Empire.

But

But to return to *Valentinian*, who whilſt he lay at *Amiens* fell dangerouſly ill, inſomuch that his Life was deſpair'd of: Whereupon *Ruſticus Julianus*, a Man of a moſt cruel and implacable Nature, was at a private Meeting propos'd by ſome *Gauls* for his Succeſſor; but was for good reaſons oppos'd by others, who were more inclinable to *Severus*, a Man indeed of an auſtere ſurly Temper, but in all Reſpects to be preferr'd before him. In the mean time the Emperor's unexpected Recovery put an end to the Hopes and Contentions of both Parties; who perhaps not ignorant of what had been tranſacting, reſolv'd to prevent any further Diſputes, and veſt his Son *Gratian* with the Purple. Having prepared the Minds of the Soldiers to ratifie his Choice, he led *Gratian* into the Camp, where attended by a great Concourſe of the Nobility, he plac'd his Son on his right Hand, and in a ſet Speech recommended him to the Army for their future Emperor. The Sight of the Emperor, the Joy for his Recovery, the Preſence of the Young Prince, under whoſe Reign they promis'd themſelves mighty Advantages, eaſily perſuaded 'em to concur with the Emperor in his Requeſt; whereupon they receiv'd and proclaim'd *Gratian* Emperor, giving all poſſible Demonſtrations of their Joy and Satisfaction.

Valentinian falls ſick and upon his Recovery makes his Son Gratian Auguſtus.

This great Work being over, the Emperor could no longer conceal the Cruelty of his Nature, which he had hitherto for private Ends with great Care and Induſtry conceal'd. He commanded *Diocles*, who had been *Comes Largitionum* in *Illyricum*, to be burnt alive, upon very inconſiderable Crimes objected againſt him; as he did likewiſe *Diodorus* and ſeveral others, and that only for flying to the Protection of the Law, againſt the Oppreſſions of a great Man in favour. Theſe Executions were done at *Milain*, where the Chriſtians ſolemniſed the Memory

mory of those who suffer'd, calling the Place where they were bury'd *The Innocents*. His Fury extended it self to the Corporations, many in whom he had put to death, had he not been restrain'd by the seasonable Interposition of *Euphraxius* the Quæstor, and *Florentius* the Præfect. If any one declin'd the Jurisdiction of a Judge, whose Malice he had reason to think would make him partial in his Cause, and from whom upon such an account he might in Equity appeal, he certainly remitted the Cause to the same Judge, notwithstanding all the Exceptions the Appealant could make: And if any Man was found to owe the Publick more than it appear'd he was able to pay, *Valentinian*, according to the Severity of an old Law, which the Gentleness of milder Administrations had long since abrogated, adjudg'd him to die.

<small>Great Troubles in Africk.</small> We observ'd before how much *Britain* was afflicted by the *Scots* and *Picts*, at the same time *Africk* groan'd under the Rage and Cruelty of the Barbarians, having hardly been at ease ever since the Beginning of this Emperor's Reign, which may well be imputed to the great want of Discipline in the Army. One *Romanus* had been sent to govern in those Parts, a Man of so covetous and insatiable a Temper, that he exceeded the very Barbarians in oppressing and pillaging the Provinces; but still took care to have a Friend at Court, who blinded the Emperor with a plausible Representation of *Romanus* his Conduct, and kept him in Ignorance of the miserable Condition the Country was in. The *Asturiani*, a barbarous Nation, had for a long time harrass'd the Province by their frequent Inroads, but either upon Compulsion or through Fear had sate still for some time in *Jovian*'s Reign, 'till a little before his Death they renew'd their Hostilities, and grew more outragious than ever; and that upon this Occasion.

One

One *Stachao* their Country-man had been guilty of many abominable Practices within the *Roman* Pale, and had proceeded so far as to attempt the betraying of the Province, upon which he was apprehended, convicted, and burnt alive. This so enrag'd the Barbarians, that like wild Beasts they broke out and laid all the Country waste before 'em. They had not the Confidence to attempt *Leptis*, a strong City, well fortify'd and inhabited, but continu'd for three Days together in the fruitful Country about it, kill'd all they met, burnt what they could not bear off, and took *Silva* Prisoner, who was one of the chief Men of the Town, and happen'd to be then with his Family in the Country. The *Leptines* had great reason to be concern'd at this Affront, and therefore apply'd themselves to *Romanus* for Redress; but he refus'd to concern himself in the Matter, unless they would make very large Provisions for him, and furnish him with no less than 4000 Camels for his Expedition. These Demands were too high and exorbitant to be comply'd with by People, who had been exhausted by so many Depredations; so that after he had amuz'd 'em with a pretended Negotiation for 40 Days together, he left 'em to follow other Measures. They seeing they could have no Protection from him, dispatch'd away *Severus* and *Flaccianus* to *Valentinian*, who were to give him a true Account of the miserable State of their Affairs. Of this when *Romanus* was inform'd he sent a Messenger away Post to *Remigius*, his Kinsman and Confident, who was great Steward of the Houshold, desiring him to persuade the Emperor to defer the Business to the Vicar of *Africk* and himself. When the Messengers were arriv'd at Court, and had presented their Petition, offering to prove the Particulars contain'd in it, *Remigius* managed his Friend's Cause with so much Cunning, that the Emperor

peror was at a loss which to believe; and so the Matter slept for the present, as is usual in Courts where there is a hurry of Business.

Whilst the People of *Tripolis* waited in expectation of their desir'd Relief, the Barbarians encourag'd by these sinister Practices came down in greater Numbers, and wasted all the Territories of *Leptis*, and *Oea*, a Town situated between that and *Sebrata*, from which three Cities the Province of *Tripolis* is said to have its Name. They kill'd several Officers, and an infinite number of inferior Rank; *Romanus*, to whom the Charge of the Militia was lately transferr'd, sitting all this while idle and unconcern'd. The Noise of these Devastations at last reach'd the Emperor's Ears in *Gaul*, at which he was so concern'd, that he immediately sent away *Palladius* with Mony to pay the Army their Arrears, and Orders to bring him a true Information of the State of the Province. In the mean time the *Asturiani* encouraged by these Delays continu'd their Incursions, raging like ravenous Wolves, whom the Taste of Human Blood had made more thirsty and implacable. *Mychon*, a substantial Citizen and a Man of great Interest, was surpriz'd near the Town, and endeavouring to make his Escape he fell into an empty Pit, breaking one of his Ribs in the Fall; from hence he was taken up by the Barbarians and led to the Gates, where he was ransom'd by his Wife, and drawn up by a Cord to the Top of the Wall, but dy'd of his Wound two Days after. This Privilege of doing what they pleas'd, made the Barbarians more insolent and presuming: They attack'd *Leptis* it self, and continu'd before the Walls for eight Days together; but finding the Inhabitants resolv'd to defend the Town, and having some of their own Men wounded, they return'd something discourag'd. The *Leptines* all this while hearing no News of their

former

former Messengers, and reduc'd to the last Extremities; sent *Jovinus* and *Pancratius* with fresh Instructions to the Emperor, whom they were to inform of what they had both seen and suffer'd. At *Carthage* these Messengers met with *Severus* and *Flaccianus*, from whom they understood the Emperor's Will, but however proceeded with great Diligence to Court. *Severus* dy'd at *Carthage*, but *Flaccianus* return'd to give the *Leptines* an Account of his Embassy.

By this time *Romanus* was inform'd of *Palladius* his Approach, and the Substance of his Commission, and therefore consider'd what Methods were to be taken for his own Security. He dealt under-hand with the Principal Officers of the Army, with whom he maintain'd a good Intelligence, to present *Palladius* with the greatest Share of the Mony he had brought to pay their Arrears, which they readily consented to; and *Palladius*, being of a mean mercenary Temper, as readily accepted. Being arriv'd at *Leptis*, he receiv'd from *Erecthius* and *Aristomenes*, two of the chief Men in the Town, the dismal Complaints of the Inhabitants, by whom he was conducted to view the lamentable Condition of the Country, and the miserable Havock the Barbarians had made. Which when he had diligently survey'd he return'd with bitter Exclamations against *Romanus*, threatning to give the Emperor a full Account of the Condition to which he saw the Province was reduced by his Means. But *Romanus*, provok'd at his Reproof, and conscious of his Mismanagement, told *Palladius* he would turn Informer too, and let the Emperor know how faithfully he had discharged his Trust, having perverted the greatest share of the Soldiers Donative to his own private Use; which put *Palladius* into such a Fright, that he agreed with *Romanus* to conceal all from the Emperor; and accordingly assured him at his Return, that the Provincials complain'd without any reason: And being sent back a second time into *Africk*, he and *Romanus* tamper'd so cunningly with the *Leptines* that they deny'd they had given *Jovinus* any Commission to say what he did to the Emperor; who thereupon order'd *Erecthius* and *Aristomenes* to have their Tongues cut out, and *Jovinus* to be put to Death, and proceeded with the like Severity against all the rest, who had been industrious in exposing the Villany of *Romanus*. *Jovinus* was executed at *Utica*, but *Erecthius* and *Aristomenes* made their Escape, and lay conceal'd 'till after the Death of *Valentinian*; when the whole Intrigue was discover'd, and the Complotters suffer'd as they deserv'd.

The King of Persia begins new Troubles. As these Commotions in *Africk* seem'd an Instance of the Declension of the Empire, so did *Sapor*, the old King of *Persia*, by his Practices in the East bid open Defiance to it. He had, since that infamous Peace made with *Jovian*, been frequently tampering with the Nobility of *Armenia*, trying by fair Promises to allure them over to his Party, and to force the ordinary sort by Menaces: But being now no longer able to conceal his Designs, he openly Invaded it; and having by abominable Treachery got *Arsaces* King of the Country into his Hands, he first put out his Eyes, and then murder'd him at a Castle call'd *Agabana*: Then driving out *Sauromaces*, whom the *Romans* had set over *Iberia*, he insolently put one *Aspacuras* in his Place, and in Defiance of the *Roman* Authority honour'd him with a Diadem. Encourag'd by this Success in his Arbitrary Proceedings, he committed *Armenia* to the Care of *Cylaces* the Eunuch, and *Artabanes*, two Fugitives whom he had long entertain'd in his Court; and at the same time gave 'em Orders to take and

raze

raze *Artogeraffa*, a very strong Town, in which the Queen lay with her Son and the Treasure of *Arsaces*. They, as they had been commanded, laid Siege to the Place; but forasmuch as the Town stood very advantagiously, and the Severity of the Winter hinder'd the Besiegers from advancing their Works, *Cylaces* and *Artabanes* upon Promise of a safe Conduct were admitted into the Place, where they endeavour'd in high Terms to persuade the Queen to surrender, and by a speedy Compliance make the King of *Persia* her Friend. She in a very pathetical manner bewail'd her Husband's Death, and her own Misfortunes, and wrought so effectually with her Tears upon those two Captains, that from Enemies they began first to pity her Condition, and then to embrace her Interest; upon which entering into a more secret Consultation, it was concluded that the Besieg'd should, at a set Hour in the Night, sally out with an unexpected Force upon the Enemy, and attack 'em in their Trenches, and that *Cylaces* and *Artabanes* should favour the Attempt. These Things being agreed upon, and both Sides having solemnly sworn to the Performance of 'em, the two Commanders return'd to the Camp, telling the *Persians* the Besieg'd had desir'd two Days to consider of their Proposals. This threw the Besiegers into a stupid Security, so that in the dead of Night, whilst the Guards themselves were asleep, those from the City came suddenly upon 'em, and fell on 'em with so much Fury, that they suffer'd few or none to escape. *Sapor* was so exasperated at this Accident, that he breath'd nothing but Revenge; especially when he found that *Para* the Son of *Arsaces*, whom the Queen, after the late Advantage obtain'd over the *Persians*, had sent into the *Roman* Territories, was kindly receiv'd by *Valens* his Order, and appointed to reside at *Neocæsarea*. This

Generosity of the Emperor towards *Arsaces* his Son, encourag'd *Cylaces* and *Artabanes* to desire his Assistance against *Sapor*, and that he would send young *Para* to be their King. For some time the Emperor deny'd their Request, but at length commanded *Terentius* his Governor in those Parts to conduct *Para* into *Armenia*, where he suffer'd him to command, but without any of the Ensigns of Royal Authority; proceeding thus cautiously, lest *Sapor*, who was already highly provok'd, should have just Cause to object to the *Romans* the Breach of the Peace.

Sapor, when he was inform'd of what *Valens* had done, was enraged to the highest Degree, and fell violently upon *Armenia*, which he ravaged, and laid all waste before him, whilst *Para*, seeing no possibility of Relief, fled with *Cylaces* and *Artabanes* into the strong Holds of the Mountains, which lay between the *Roman* Borders and *Lazica*, where they lay lurking five Months together, in spite of all the Means made use of by *Sapor* to take 'em: Who seeing it to no purpose to hunt any longer after 'em, burnt all the Forts and Castles he had taken either by Fraud or Force, and sate down with a numerous Army before *Artogerassa*, which after several Sallies and Attacks he took and destroy'd, carrying away the Wife and Treasure of *Arsaces*. These Proceedings seem'd to give the *Romans* a just Occasion to begin the War, and therefore *Arintheus* is sent with a good Army to assist the *Armenians* upon all Occasions; which *Sapor* no sooner understood, but he betook himself to his usual Artifices, in which he seldom miscarry'd. By private Messengers he proffer'd *Para* his Friendship and Assistance, and seem'd to blame the Baseness of his Spirit, that could suffer himself to be cheated with the Shadow of Authority, whilst *Cylaces* and *Artabanes* assum'd all the Power,

Power, and were in Effect no other than his Governors; by these cunning Insinuations he so far impos'd upon the Ignorance of the Young Prince that he kill'd 'em both, and sent their Heads to *Sapor*, to let him know how tractable he should find him for the future. By this means he had unavoidably got all *Armenia* into his Hands, had not *Arintheus* by his timely Approach prevented him; so that finding himself likely to be over-power'd he requir'd by his Embassadors to the Emperor, that according to the Articles of Peace between him and *Jovian*, the *Armenians* might receive no Assistance from the *Romans*. This the Emperor was so far from condescending to, that he order'd *Terentius* with Twelve Legions to restore *Sauromaces* by force to his Principality of *Iberia*; but *Aspacuras* desir'd of *Sauromaces*, as he drew near with the *Roman* Army to the River *Cyrus*, that being Kinsmen they might govern conjointly, alledging that he could neither give up the Country, or take part with the *Romans*, because his Son was detain'd as an Hostage in the *Persian* Court. The Emperor being acquainted with these Proposals, and willing to settle the Affairs of *Iberia* in as peaceable a manner as he could, consented to a Partition of the Country, assigning that part which lay next to *Armenia* and *Larica* to *Sauromaces*, and to *Aspacuras* the Residue bordering upon *Albania* and *Persia*. This Agreement highly incens'd *Sapor*, who loudly complain'd that the *Romans*, contrary to the Treaty of Peace, had reliev'd *Armenia*, despis'd his Embassy, and without his Knowledge or Consent had divided *Iberia*, for which Indignities he vow'd to be reveng'd, making all Preparations accordingly both at home and abroad to undo what had been concerted without his Concurrence. These things happen'd in the Years 368. and 369. in the last of which *Valentinian*,

A.D. 369.

lentinian, the Son of *Valens*, and *Aur. Victor*, were Consuls.

Valentinian's Exploits in Germany.

About the same time one *Rhando*, a *German* of Royal Birth, seiz'd suddenly upon the City of *Ments*, a Design he had been long contriving, and could the easier execute by reason there was no Garrison in it; and it happening to be upon some Solemn Festival, the Inhabitants, who were all Christians, were busie at their Devotion, and therefore little able to defend themselves; after he had made himself Master of the Place he plunder'd it, and went off with a great Booty, and a great many Prisoners of both Sexes. Not long after, as if Fortune had a Mind to make the *Romans* some amends, *Vithicabius*, a Prince of that Nation, was murder'd by one of his own Servants at the Instigation of some *Roman* Emissaries. He was an active, vigilant Prince, tho' he outwardly appear'd weak and infirm, and had been both by his Arms and in his Councils a great Stickler against the *Romans*, whose open Attempts against him he had often evaded, and therefore they had no other means left to remove him but by Treachery. The Traitor, as soon as the Fact was committed, fled his Country to avoid the Punishment he too justly deserv'd, and was kindly receiv'd by the *Romans*. *Valentinian* could not but think the *Germans* would revenge so foul a Treason with all the Acts of Hostility imaginable, and therefore made more than ordinary Preparations to prevent them. He rais'd a very powerful Army, supply'd it with all manner of Provisions, and as soon as the time of the Year would permit pass'd the *Rhine* without any resistance, taking his Son *Gratian* along with him. After a long March of several Days into the Country, without meeting any Enemy to oppose 'em, they came to a Place call'd *Solicinium*, where he was inform'd by his Spies that the

the Enemy were near at Hand, who finding it impossible to avoid coming to an Engagement, possess'd themselves of a very advantagious piece of Ground, which they resolv'd to defend against the *Roman* Legions, and out of which the Emperor resolv'd to remove 'em. The Place was a high and scraggy Mountain, almost inaccessible on every side, except that which look'd towards the North; thither he sent *Sebastianus*, with part of the Forces under his Command, to intercept the *Germans* in their Flight, if he should have the good Fortune to gain the better of 'em from any other Quarter: He himself went attended with some in whom he could best confide, to see on what other part he might most commodiously attempt 'em, in which Enterprize he very narrowly escap'd an Ambuscade of the Enemy, and with much difficulty got safe to his own Men; who after they had refresh'd themselves prepar'd for the Engagement, and attack'd the Enemy with so true a *Roman* Courage, that notwithstanding all the Opposition the *Germans* could make, who fought with more Resolution than Conduct, they gain'd the Top of the Mountain, and surrounded them. However the *Germans* maintain'd the Fight for a long time with a desperate Bravery, 'till at length over-power'd by fresh Supplies they were first put into Disorder, and after that to Flight, in which more Men fell than in the Battel; those few that escaped fled into the Woods, leaving to the *Romans* the Honour of the Field, and the Advantage of a very great Victory, purchas'd at the Expence of a few common Soldiers, and the Loss of two or three brave Commanders. After this the Soldiers were sent into Winter Quarters, and the two Emperors return'd to *Triers*.

Great Cruelties exercis'd at Rome. About this time there were extraordinary Outrages committed in *Rome* by the means of one *Maximinus*, who from an obscure Beginning rose to a Principal Command in the City. He was of a cruel inexorable Temper, and being a Man of great Interest with *Valentinian*, who was almost as cruel as himself, he rag'd without Distinction against all Ages and Conditions, varnishing over his barbarous Proceedings with the specious Colour of Justice. Never did Tyrant with more Implacableness afflict a People he was sent to Govern, or more notoriously pervert the Laws to the Ruin of those they were design'd to Protect; from being Intendant of the Publick Corn, he at length, by his Impudence and Flattery, arriv'd at the Dignity of *Præfectus Prætorio* it self, bearing himself with equal Insolence, Pride and Corruption in all his Offices, 'till at last, under *Gratian*, he suffer'd Death by the Hands of the Common Hangman, together with several of his Instruments and Accomplices.

Valens his Tyrannical Proceedings in the East. About the same time *Valens* rag'd with equal Fury in the East, to which an appearance of Danger, and the evil Practices of some of his own Servants, had justly provok'd him. *Anatolius* and *Spudasius*, two Persons employ'd in the Revenue, were accus'd of having attempted the Life of *Fortunatianus*, who had the Principal Management of the Emperor's Private Estate, and who being a troublesom inquisitive Man, was calling them to a very severe Account for Matters relating to their Office. The Matter is brought before *Modestus* the *Præfectus Prætorio*, and one *Palladius* and *Heliodorus* are put to the Rack. *Palladius*, unable to endure the Torture, cry'd out, That these were slight inconsiderable Matters compar'd to others in Agitation, which were of that Consequence, as to bring all things into Confusion, without a timely Prevention; being urg'd to a Discovery of what he meant, he accus'd *Fiduftius*, who had formerly been Prefident, and *Irenæus*, and *Pergamius*, of learning, by fecret Practices and forbidden Arts, the Name of him who was to fucceed *Valens* in the Empire. *Fiduftius* was by chance then prefent, and was too much furpriz'd at fo peremptory and unexpected a Charge to deny the Fact. He confefs'd that he, together with one *Hilarius* and *Patritius*, two Perfons well skill'd in the Art of Divination, enquir'd into that Matter, and found, upon trial, that an excellent Prince was to fucceed *Valens*, but that they themfelves fhould come to untimely Ends for their fatal Curiofity; that examining farther between themfelves, who was moft likely to be the Man, they concluded it could be no Body but *Theodorus*, whofe great Accomplifhments made him worthy the Sovereign Command. And indeed they were not much deceiv'd in their Conjecture, for *Theodorus* was defcended of an Ancient and Noble Family in *Gaul*, tho' a *Sicilian* by Birth, and acceptable to all Men of all Conditions, who highly efteem'd him for his Modefty, Prudence, Learning and Humanity, Virtues that deferv'd a more exalted Fortune than that to which he was arriv'd, tho' he then had great Preferments at Court. *Fiduftius* confefs'd farther, being almoft tortur'd to Death, that he had inform'd *Theodorus* of thefe Predictions by the Intervention of *Euferius*, a Man of great Learning and eminent Quality, haivng formerly commanded as Vicar in *Afia*. *Euferius* was immediately committed to Prifon, and the Emperor inform'd of all that had pafs'd, which enrag'd him to the higheft degree. Orders were immediately iffu'd out for the apprehending *Theodorus* at *Conftantinople*, as were likewife feveral others, eminent for their Birth and Employments, feiz'd in more

remote

remote Parts of the Empire, and brought up in Custody. The Publick Prisons could not contain those that were apprehended, nor were private Dwellings sufficient for the Reception of such Multitudes of People, abundance of whom were committed upon bare Suspicion. For *Valens* was naturally of a jealous, distrustful Temper, which his Flatterers that were constantly about him labour'd to improve, and some late Practices against his Life had abundantly exasperated, which however can in no measure excuse the unexampled Rigour of his Inquisitions; he proceeded with equal Severity against the Innocent and the Guilty, and frequently resolv'd upon the Punishment before he was acquainted with the Crime, so that a great many were commanded to prepare for Death before they knew they were in the least suspected. He was too Proud and Imperious to submit himself to the Coolness of a sober Enquiry, too Covetous to suffer any to escape who had been once accus'd, and too much abus'd by his Parasites to give Ear in the Course of his Proceedings to the Advice of Men of Honour and Conscience: In a Word, he was grown so severely terrible that one *Salia*, who had a little before been Intendant of the Treasury in *Thrace*, fell down dead at the Officer's Feet the Morning he was to be examin'd, under an apprehension of the great Torture he was that Day to undergo.

The first that was brought upon the Stage was *Pergamius*, who being a Man full of Words, in a very large Discourse accus'd some thousands as Accessary, many of whom were then living in the remotest Parts of the Empire; but whereas the Judges were before at a loss in what Method to proceed, his indigested Allegations made it more confus'd and intricate, and so he was put to Death. After
several

several had been examin'd, who vary'd in some Particulars, but agreed in the main, *Theodorus* was commanded to speak, who at first made use of Intreaties, and earnestly begg'd of the Inquisitors to interceed with the Emperor in his Behalf; but being compell'd to speak more to the purpose, he declar'd that he once intended to discover the whole Practice to *Valens*, but was prevented by *Euserius*, who persuaded him that what had been foretold was not to be the Effect of any predominant, ambitious Passion, but to proceed from the absolute Necessity of Fate; the same was confess'd by *Euserius* upon the Rack, and some Letters written by *Theodorus* to *Hilarius* were produc'd against him, in which Letters he profess'd he did not doubt of the Truth of the Prediction, but waited for a convenient Opportunity to put the Design in Execution. After this they were remov'd, and *Eutropius*, who then govern'd *Asia* as Proconsul, and is thought to be the Author of the Abridgement of the *Roman* History, which he Dedicated to *Valens*, was produc'd as privy to the Crime, but when all their Endeavours and Tortures to make *Pasiphithus* the Philosopher accuse him were ineffectual, he was dismiss'd. The Examination being over, and the whole Discovery made and reported to the Emperor, he with one general Sentence commanded 'em all to be put to Death, which Sentence was executed accordingly without Mercy or Distinction, 'till the Hangmen were quite weary of their Employment. Among those that suffer'd was *Maximus* the Philosopher, and famous Master of *Julian*. He confess'd he had been inform'd of what the Oracle had predicted, but out of Respect to his Profession had conceal'd it, tho' he had foretold that they, who were concern'd in the Consultation, would lose their Lives. He was Beheaded at *Ephesus*, the Place of

his

his Nativity, by *Festus* Proconsul of *Asia,* sent thither by *Valens* for that purpose, tho' he then lay sick of an incurable Distemper, which in a few Days would have ended his Life without the Intervention of the Hangman's Ax. In this publick Massacre fell likewise *Diogenes,* a great Lawyer, who not long before had been Governor in *Bithynia,* who was guilty of no other Crime but the Possession of a large Estate. He was a Man of noble Birth, an excellent Wit, and profound Eloquence, and fell universally lamented for his Candor, Magnificence and Integrity.

These violent Proceedings, which seem'd to exceed the rigour of former Proscriptions, were highly distasteful to the People, for which reason the Emperor caus'd an infinite number of Books to be burnt, as if they contain'd dangerous Doctrines, and treated of forbidden Arts, thinking thereby to allay his Subjects Displeasure, whereas they treated of nothing but what related either to the Liberal Sciences or the Civil Law. In the mean time the Provinces were fill'd with general Lamentations, the Fury of the Inquisition sweeping away whole Families at once; for the Husband was no sooner dead, and the House by Publick Order seiz'd, but the Officers, appointed to examine the Goods, privately convey'd among the Writings some pretended Charm or ridiculous Enchantment, which being preferr'd in Court against 'em, they were all seiz'd by Order of the Judges, who had no regard to Law, Religion or Conscience; and after all their Limbs were broken upon the Rack, they were, both young and old, without any Defence made, convey'd forth in Chairs to be Executed. Hereupon so great a Terror seiz'd upon all sorts of Persons, that they burnt their Libraries, renounc'd their Learning, and chose rather to be reputed ignorant

and

and unskilful, than make the leaſt Profeſſion of Philoſophy at ſo certain a Hazard of their Lives.

This is the Account *Ammianus* gives us of this Matter; others ſay, the Oracle foretold that the firſt Part of the Perſon's Name who was to ſucceed *Valens* was *Theod.* for which reaſon he not only diſpatch'd *Theodorus*, but to make void the Prediction put a great many to Death, whoſe Names began with thoſe Syllables, ſuch as *Theodulus*, *Theodoſius*, and the like, without ever reflecting on that receiv'd Maxim, *That never any Prince can put his Succeſſor to death.*

Whilſt *Valens* was raging thus with more than Savage Fury at *Antioch*, *Valentinian*, whoſe greateſt Fault was his Cruelty, was carefully concern'd for the Borders of the Empire in the Weſt, which he diligently ſecur'd againſt the Incurſions of the Barbarous Nations; and had ſeiz'd on *Macrianus* a King of the *Germans*, a reſolute and troubleſome Prince, had not the Intemperance of his Soldiers, who contrary to his expreſs Orders burnt and deſtroy'd all that came in their way, given the King notice of his Approach, which he took all the Meaſures imaginable to conceal. He was ſcarce return'd to *Triers* from this Expedition, before he was inform'd of new Troubles in *Africk*.

Nubel, a petty Prince, but a Man of the greateſt Power in *Mauritania*, dying, left ſeveral Sons behind him; one of which, call'd *Zamma*, being privately made away by his Brother *Firmus*, gave a Beginning to a War, which enſu'd thereupon: For *Zamma* was a Man for whom *Romanus*, of whom we had occaſion to ſpeak before, had a great Eſteem, and for whoſe Death he was reſolv'd to have a full Revenge. To which purpoſe he had the Matter very earneſtly ſollicited by his Friends in *Valentinian*'s Court, and *Remigius* ſo managed it in his Behalf,

half, that *Firmus* was not allow'd by his Agents to offer any thing in his own Defence; which made the *Moor* afraid of being condemn'd unheard, and, for fear of a Surprize, put him upon his Defence;

The Moors revolt in Africk.
he therefore Revolted from the *Romans*, and assuming the Title of King set up for himself.

Theodosius sent against 'em.
This News was no sooner brought to Court, but *Theodosius* was sent immediately away to reduce him if possible, before he had time to strengthen himself too much. *Zosimus* saith, not only *Firmus* and his Adherents revolted, but the *Moors* in general, provoked to it by *Romanus* his Tyranny, who had so miserably harrass'd and impoverish'd 'em; so that the Emperor had great reason to be diligent in a matter which might turn to so ill a Consequence: And there was great need of so expert a Commander as *Theodosius*, who was forc'd to make use of all his Skill, to new model and regulate an Army, part of which for want of Discipline were grown headstrong and licentious; and the rest, newly arriv'd with himself from cold Climates, were unused to the Heat of the Country, and the less fit for Service. Besides there was no good Correspondence at first between 'em, which with great Industry he endeavour'd to procure, before he thought fit to enter upon Action. His first Care upon his Arrival in *Africk* was to secure *Vincentius*, who having been *Romanus* his Deputy, had concurr'd with him in all his Insolence and Extortion: To this Service he deputed *Gildo*, the Brother of *Firmus*, who continu'd then firm in his Obedience to the *Romans*; tho' he afterwards revolted from them in the Days of *Honorius*. At *Igilgitanum*, where he first landed, he by chance met with *Romanus*, whom for the present he dismiss'd without any Reproach, to take care of the advanc'd Guards, but not long after, upon his Arrival at *Sitifis*, gave Orders for his Apprehension.

Firmus

Firmus hearing so renown'd a Commander was sent against him, began to doubt of his Success, and therefore submitted himself by Messengers sent on purpose to him, and ask'd Pardon for what was past, affirming he was forc'd upon it, not by his own Will, but the Injuries and Indignities he had receiv'd from others, who provok'd him to that which he own'd he could no ways justifie. *Theodosius* thought it prudent to admit of his Submission and Excuse, and promis'd to pardon him upon Receipt of Hostages for his good Behaviour for the future: After which he march'd to *Panchariana*, where he had appointed the general Rendevouz, and muster'd his Army. Having establish'd a good Understanding between 'em, and by his generous Carriage procur'd the Love of the Inhabitants, he march'd to a Place called *Tubusuptius*, adjoining to the Mountain *Ferratus*, where he refus'd to admit of *Firmus* his second Embassy, because he had not sent the Hostages he had promis'd, and were agreed upon. After which in several Encounters he defeated *Mascizel* and *Dius*, two other of *Firmus* his Brethren, having wasted the Country round about, and possess'd himself of a strong Town, which he made choice of for a Magazine, in case he should think fit to penetrate farther into the Country. These Proceedings very much dishearten'd *Firmus*, who thereupon sent some Christian Bishops, with the Hostages he had promis'd, to interceed with *Theodosius* in his Behalf. *Theodosius* receiv'd 'em with much Civility, and, upon a Promise that his Army should be supply'd with Provisions, dismiss'd 'em with a favourable Answer to *Firmus*; which encourag'd the *Moor* to make the General a Visit, having first sent some Presents before hand to make way for his Reception. As he drew near he leap'd from his Horse, being surprized at the Lustre of the *Roman* Ensigns, and the awful Appearance of the Commander. He bow'd himself to the Ground, and with Looks full of Contrition bewail'd his Folly and Rashness, and begg'd Pardon for his Offence. *Theodosius* receiv'd him very graciously, and having given him all the Encouragement he expected or desir'd, dismiss'd him well pleas'd with his Entertainment. At his Departure he left some of his near Relations behind him for Hostages, and promis'd to restore the Prisoners he had taken when he first revolted. Accordingly two Days after he surrender'd *Icosium*, together with the military Ensigns, and whatever else he had seiz'd, delivering all up into the Hands of the *Romans*.

At a Place call'd *Tipasa*, *Theodosius* met with the Embassadors of the *Mazices*, a Nation inhabiting the Eastern Parts of *Mauritania Cæsariensis*, who had join'd with *Firmus* in the Revolt: They came to submit themselves in the Name of the whole Nation, and to beg Pardon for their Offence. *Theodosius* return'd 'em a very surly Answer, telling 'em he was resolv'd to chastise their Insolence, and punish 'em for their Perfidy to the *Romans*. With this Message he dismiss'd 'em, and proceeded to *Cæsarea*, a City *Firmus* had seiz'd upon by Stratagem in the Beginning of the Rebellion, and after he had almost ruin'd it with Fire and Sword, deliver'd it up as a Prey to the Barbarians. Here *Theodosius* for the present dispos'd of the first and second Legion, who were to secure it in the best manner they could against any farther Attempts of the Enemy. Whilst he continu'd here he found, upon a more narrow Enquiry, that *Firmus* mean'd nothing less than Peace, that he only watch'd an Opportunity of attacking him at the best Advantage, and destroying him and his Army. Whereupon removing to *Sugabarri*, a Town of *Mauritania Cæsariensis*, he punish'd a *Roman* Cohort, whom he had seiz'd there, and who had

Firmus his treacherous Dealings.

had formerly revolted to the Enemy. From thence he march'd farther up into the Country, and fell upon the *Mazices*, who having collected themselves into one Body, made at first a very vigorous Resistance, but were at length overthrown, and put all to the Sword, except some few who cry'd for Quarter. After this he detach'd part of his Forces to secure some Places that lay too much expos'd to the Barbarians, and proceeded on towards some other Nations that had favour'd the Revolt. In his March he was met by the *Moors*, who were pouring down upon him in great Multitudes from all Quarters, breathing nothing but Fury and Destruction. These People had been rais'd by *Cyria*, *Firmus* his Sister, who being a Woman of great Wealth and extraordinary Conduct had encourag'd 'em with the Promise of mighty Rewards. *Theodosius*, who was then but Three Thousand Five Hundred strong, declin'd Fighting upon such great Odds, for fear of losing his whole Army, and therefore preserving a Medium betwixt a Fight and a Flight, he gave Ground, and retir'd by Degrees. With this the Enemy were so encourag'd, that they stopp'd up all the Passages in order to cut off his Retreat; and had certainly destroy'd the whole Army, had not the unwary *Moors* mistook some of their own Countrymen for a fresh Supply coming to *Theodosius*, who indeed were marching to join them with some *Romans* at the Head, which gave ground to the Mistake: Affrighted at this they fled in great Precipitation, and left the *Romans* at liberty to make their Escape. *Theodosius* made a safe Retreat with the Army to a Place call'd *Muzucanum*, where having punish'd some Deserters, as a Warning to the rest, he came in *February* to *Tipata*; where reflecting upon the Posture of his Affairs, he began to manage the War after another Method, and without entring into the Field, he re-

L

solv'd

solv'd to tire out the Enemy, like *Fabius* of old, by Arts and Stratagems. He dispatch'd some, who were skilful in the Art of Persuasion, to the neighbouring Nations, to endeavour by Threats and Promises to draw 'em into an Association with him. Of this his politick Proceeding *Firmus* was quickly sensible, and knowing it the only way to ruin him, tho' he had a sufficient Guard about his Person, and an Army at Command, rais'd with great Industry and no less Expence, he took the Advantage of a dark Night, and retir'd with great Secresie to the Mountains, which by reason of the Rocks and Precipices were in a great measure inaccessible. The Multitude, now without a Head, were so dishearten'd at his sudden Departure, that they quickly dispers'd themselves, leaving their Camp to the *Romans*; upon which when *Theodosius* had seiz'd, he wasted the Country at his Pleasure, killing all who had the Courage to make any Resistance, and plac'd such Governors over the Nations through which he pass'd as he had great Reason to confide in. *Firmus* found the General pursu'd him very close, and therefore made all the Haste he could from him, attended only with a few Servants in whom he could trust, throwing away whatever things of Value he had with him, which might retard him in his Flight. He never rested 'till he was got into the Country of the *Isaflenses*, who very chearfully undertook his Protection; by whose Assistance he often reduced the *Romans* to great Straights, overpowering 'em with superior Numbers, falling upon 'em in advantagious Places, and at times they little expected 'em. However *Theodosius* his Fortune at length prevail'd; he overthrew the Enemy in two or three Battels, in one of which *Mazaca*, *Firmus* his Brother, was taken Prisoner, and dy'd presently of his Wounds. *Evasius*, a Person of great Authority among 'em, and

Florus

Florus his Son, were burnt alive for assisting the Rebels, and *Firmus* himself with great Difficulty escaped. These Disadvantages by degrees tired the *Isaflenses*, who at last grew weary of espousing the Interest of an unfortunate Man, and having been weary'd out by the frequent Alarms *Theodosius* gave 'em, dropp'd off from him one by one, and left him almost alone. In this Condition, whilst he was considering of an Escape, he was seiz'd by *Igmazen*, Prince of that Country, and clapp'd into Prison; where, to avoid the Terror and Disgrace of the Punishment he apprehended from the *Romans*, he hang'd himself. *Theodosius* receiv'd the News of his Death with a great deal of Satisfaction, and having order'd *Castor* and *Martinianus*, two of *Romanus* his Accomplices to be burnt alive, he return'd to *Sitifis*, where he was receiv'd with much Solemnity, to the universal Joy of the Inhabitants.

<small>Firmus *seiz'd, hangs himself.*</small>

Thus were the Troubles in *Africk* compos'd by the great Prudence and Industry of *Theodosius*, who after all his great Exploits, and the mighty Services he had render'd the Empire, was by an Order from Court beheaded at *Carthage*. We can't learn from History the Reasons for which he was put to death: They who are the least inclin'd to *Valens*, say it was done by his Procurement; and that for fear he should be the Man design'd by the Oracle for his Successor, in regard of his extraordinary Merit and great Atchievements. Others say he ow'd his Death to the malicious Suggestions of certain Courtiers, who envy'd him the Honours he had worthily acquir'd, and could not endure any Man should be better than themselves. According to his own earnest Desire he was Baptiz'd at *Carthage* just before he dy'd, and was as exemplary in his Death as he had been glorious in his Life.

<small>Theodosius, *after all his Services, put to Death.*</small>

The Fall of this great Man, as it was a Scandal to *Valentinian*'s Government, so was it contrary to a receiv'd Maxim he usually follow'd, which was, severely to punish the Common Soldiers upon the least Misdemeanour, but not so much as listen to any Complaints offer'd against the Superior Officers; which Remissness made 'em proud, insolent and tyrannical in the several Provinces, and gave Occasion to a great many Disorders: As about this time the Commander in chief in *Illyricum* had, contrary to all Laws of Hospitality, perfidiously murder'd *Gabinius* King of the *Quadi* at a Feast, to which *Gabinius* had in civil Terms been invited by him; upon which the *Quadi*, and other Nations, broke with great Violence into the *Roman* Territories. I know some are of Opinion, that *Gabinius* was a *Roman*, and Governor of the Province, and that by his Order the King was Assassinated; but *Ammianus*, whose Authority must be of greater Weight in this Case, tells us, *Gabinius* was the King, and that *Marcellianus*, Son to *Maximinus*, that cruel Incendiary, was then Governor of the Province; that *Valentinian*, who from the first time of his Advancement had been over sedulous in fortifying the Borders of the Empire, had built Forts over the *Ister* upon the Territories of the *Quadi*, as if their Country had been within the *Roman* Pale; that the Inhabitants, who were justly alarm'd at it, endeavour'd by their Messengers to hinder the Prosecution of the Design; that *Marcellianus*, who was sent to command the Army in those Parts by his Father's Procurement, return'd a very civil Answer, and invited *Gabinius* the King, and some others to a Banquet; and as he was taking his Leave, without the least suspicion of Treachery, got him to be murder'd.

New Troubles in Illyricum.

A.D. 374.

At this not only the *Quadi*, but the neighbouring Nations, who made the Case their own, were highly

highly incens'd, and uniting themselves in one Body, they pass'd the *Danube* with great Fury, fell in the time of Harvest upon the Reapers, whom they massacred in a cruel manner, and return'd loaden with a very great Booty; in this confusion *Constantina*, the Daughter of *Constantius*, whom they were then conducting through those Parts in order to be marry'd to *Gratian*, had fallen into their Hands, had not *Messala*, Governor of the Province attending her, put her into a Chariot in great haste, and convey'd her with speed to *Sirmium*, twenty six Miles distant from thence. In the mean time the Barbarians renew'd their Incursions to the utter Ruin of several of the Inhabitants, whom in a cruel manner they led away Captive, having first burnt their Houses and wasted their Possessions. *Sirmium* it self, the Capital of those Parts, seem'd to be in great Danger. *Probus*, the *Præfectus Prætorio*, who the Year before had born the Consulship with *Gratian*, was then Resident in it; a Man, tho' of Noble Birth, so little acquainted with the Terrors of War, that he was amaz'd at the Report of the bloody Slaughters and barbarous Cruelties they had committed; the Noise of which encreasing every Day more, he provided himself with swift Horses in order to a secret and shameful Flight; from this he was, with much ado, dissuaded by those about him, who represented to him how the Soldiers, whose Duty it was to defend the Place, would by his Example provide for their own Safety, and so quit the City, which must unavoidably fall into the Enemy's Hands. After this so reasonable a Remonstrance he was compell'd by Shame to stay, and so out of regard to his own Safety, rather than the Publick Good, he took all imaginable Care to put the City in a Posture of Defence, and was so industrious therein,

therein, that the Barbarians thought not fit to Attack it, but diverted their Course in Pursuit of *Æquitius*, whom they conceiv'd to have been the Contriver of *Gabinius* his Death; and hearing he was retir'd into the remotest Parts of *Valeria*, they resolv'd to follow him; in their Way they met with two Legions, the *Pannonia* and *Mæsiaca*, who were sent to oppose 'em, and were of Strength sufficient to have restrain'd their Fury, had they not fell into an unseasonable Contention between themselves for the Honour of Precedency; this Dispute ruin'd those, who had they been united would have been invincible; for the Barbarians, who were too cunning not to be sensible of their Advantage, without waiting for the Signal of Battel, fell first with great Fury upon the *Mæsiacan* Legion, who little expecting so sudden an Onset, fell in great Numbers before they had time to take to their Arms; this encourag'd the Enemy to break in upon the *Pannonian*, which they quickly routed, killing all those whom the Sense of their Danger had not by a speedy Flight secur'd.

Two Legions cut off by the Barbarians.

The loss of so many Men, which was entirely owing to their own Folly, was in some measure repair'd by the Success of the Army, which fought under the Conduct of *Theodosius*, Son of him we lately mention'd, and Governor of *Mæsia*, who with a Courage and Conduct exceeding his Years, defended it against the Incursions of the Barbarians, and worsted 'em so often, tho' they thought with Numbers to over-power him, that in Despair of any farther Success they begg'd Pardon for what was pass'd, and Peace for the future; which having obtain'd, they for some time religiously observ'd it, being kept in awe by a Supply of Soldiers sent out of *Gaul* for the Defence of *Illyricum*. During these Disorders in the North the *Tiber*, through excessive

Rains,

Rains, overflow'd its Banks to that degree, that all the lower Parts of *Rome* were laid under Water, and the Inhabitants forc'd to secure themselves upon the Hills, where they had perish'd with Hunger, had not *Claudius*, Præfect of the City, taken Care to have a seasonable Supply sent 'em in Boats from the Parts adjacent. These Overflowings of the *Tiber* were usually the Forerunners of some Publick Calamity, to which the Empire was now so generally accustom'd, that the present Danger being remov'd the People had no Apprehensions of the future.

This treacherous peice of Cruelty, exercis'd upon the Person of *Gabinius* in the North, was follow'd by an Act equally detestable in the East, where some Persons, who reap'd an Advantage to themselves from the Publick Confusions, among whom was *Terentius*, a Commander in the adjacent Parts, continually by their Letters alarm'd the Emperor with the sinister Practices and ambitious Designs of *Para* King of *Armenia*, constantly reproaching him for the Death of *Cylax* and *Artabanes*, and reviling him as an insolent Oppressor of the People. Hereupon he was invited in a Royal manner to *Tarsus* in *Cilicia*, where when he was arriv'd he was detain'd Prisoner, without Permission to go to the Emperor, or learn the reason of his Restraint. This unaccountable Proceeding made him more inquisitive and sollicitous, especially when by secret Intelligence he understood that *Terentius* had endeavour'd by Letters to persuade the *Roman* Governor to send some other Person immediately to be King of *Armenia* in his stead, lest upon his Return into his own Country he should, in Revenge of his ill Usage, persuade his Subjects no longer to adhere to the *Roman* Empire, but submit themselves to the *Persians*, who stood ready upon any Conditions

tions to receive them. This made him conclude, that without timely Care he should be inevitably destroy'd, and therefore he resolv'd upon a speedy Flight, which he attempted with the Assistance of three hunder'd of his own Subjects in whom he could rely, and who very earnestly persuaded him to it. They took care to supply him with Horses fit for his purpose, and towards the Evening watching their Opportunity they set forward together, guided more by their Courage than Conduct, as it is usual with Men in any hazardous or emergent Exigency. They were not got clear of the Suburbs before the Governor of the Province overtook 'em, and finding it impossible to stop him by Force, he endeavour'd by Persuasions to detain him; but he found him too resolute to be prevail'd upon, and therefore desisted for fear of drawing his own Life into Danger by too obstinate an Entreaty. Presently after he was overtaken by a whole Legion, sent on purpose to hinder his Escape, but he fac'd about with so much Resolution, and charg'd 'em with so desperate a Courage, that they made more haste to fly from him, than they had done to approach him; after this he proceeded without any Disturbance, and travelling Night and Day for two Days together he at last reach'd the *Euphrates*, which he pass'd with much Difficulty, and after a short Repose pursu'd his Journey with extraordinary Diligence. *Valens* having notice of his Escape concluded he would infallibly fall off from him, and therefore sent a thousand Archers under the Command of two Principal Officers to Waylay him, and bring him back: They being well acquainted with the Country, through which he wander'd an utter Stranger, travell'd through more compendious Roads and overtook him: Having divided their Forces they seiz'd on two Passes three

Miles

Miles distant from each other, at one of which they thought themselves certain of surprising him. But being inform'd of his Danger by a Traveller, who was coming that Way, he took a by Path, and piercing through a thick Wood he escap'd the Ambuscade, and got safe into his own Kingdom, whilst the *Romans*, who waited a long time for their Prey, were sufficiently laugh'd at for their Pains. This Disappointment was a great Vexation to *Valens*, who grew every Day more and more resolv'd upon his Destruction, and sent private Orders to *Trajan*, who commanded the *Roman* Forces Quarter'd in *Armenia*, by all means to effect it. *Trajan*, in Obedience to his Instructions, readily undertook it, and by degrees wrought himself into so much Credit with the King, by frequenting his Table, and producing Letters from *Valens* full of Expressions of Kindness to *Para*, that he made no scruple of accepting of a Dinner at his House, to which *Trajan* had in a solemn manner invited him. He was receiv'd with the highest Respect, and enentertain'd in a Royal manner, and after he had drunk him up to a high pitch, *Trajan*, pretending some necessary Occasions, withdrew, and immediately sent in a Villain provided for the purpose, who cut the young Prince in pieces as he vainly endeavour'd to defend himself, the rest of the Guests flying in great Consternation from so bloody a Banquet.

Para, King of Armenia, treacherously murder'd.

This inhospitable Proceeding was a great Affliction to *Sapor* King of *Persia*, who conceiv'd he had lost in *Para* a firm Friend and faithful Ally, for such he made no doubt but in time he should have found him; on the other side the *Romans* gather'd Courage, at which he was not a little dismay'd, and therefore he thought it the safest way to propose by his Embassadors to *Valens*, that *Armenia*,

menia, which had been the Cause of so many Confusions, might be entirely ruin'd, or at least, that the *Roman* Garrisons might be recall'd out of *Iberia*, and *Aspacures*, whom he had advanc'd, might be permitted to Reign there without any Disturbance. To this *Valens* answer'd, That he was resolv'd to stand to the late Division of *Iberia*, and see the Treaty punctually observ'd; and after several Messages and Remonstrances on one side and the other, the Emperor sent away *Victor* General of the Horse, and *Urbicius* Governor of *Mesopotamia*, to *Sapor*; who were to assure him, that unless he suffer'd the *Armenians* to be at their own Liberty, and forbore molesting the *Roman* Garrison in a Fort call'd *Sauromaces*, he should be forc'd upon such Measures as would be no ways agreeable to him. These Instructions were just and prudent, but the Embassadors went beyond their Commission, and imprudently accepted of some small Territories that had been offer'd 'em in *Armenia*, and without effecting any thing else they return'd home. They were follow'd by another Embassador from *Persia*, whom the Emperor kindly receiv'd, and entertain'd him with much Magnificence, tho' all his Offers were rejected, and *Valens* prepar'd to assault *Persia* with three Armies at once in the beginning of the Spring. *Sapor*, thus disappointed of his Expectation, was highly exasperated, but concealing his Indignation, he gave Orders to his Chief Officers by force to recover those Territories the *Roman* Embassadors had lately possess'd themselves of in the Name of the Emperor, and cut off, if possible, the Garrison in *Sauromaces*, which Orders they executed accordingly. Of all this *Valens* was inform'd, but found himself unable to resent it as he ought; the Empire being threatned by a general Invasion of the *Gothish* Nation, to a Narration of which

which the Course of the History will in a short time conduct us.

All this while *Valentinian* was employ'd in Building Forts upon the *Rhine*, and wasting the *German* Territories, in which he was often oppos'd with great Vigour by *Macrianus*, King of the Country, a haughty resolute Prince, but was this Year diverted upon an Information that the Barbarians were in great Numbers Invading *Illyricum*, whose Insolence he was resolv'd to chastise, and therefore at an Enterview between him and *Macrianus* upon the *Rhine* near *Mentz*, he concluded a Peace, which the latter kept inviolable 'till his Death. After this he return'd to *Triers*, where he spent the Winter in concerting the Measures he was to take in order to his Expedition early in the Spring into *Illyricum*, which had been this Year miserably wasted by the *Sarmatæ* and the *Quadi*; accordingly he advanc'd thither as soon as the Winter was over, and was met in the Way by Embassadors from the *Sarmatæ*, who in a very submissive manner throwing themselves at his Feet, desir'd him to entertain a more favourable Opinion of their Nation, who he would find upon Examination were guilty of none of those heavy Accusations that were urg'd against them. After they had often affirm'd the same thing he told 'em, that as yet he would determine nothing, but suspend his Judgment 'till his Arrival into those Parts, that were said to have been so highly injur'd by 'em. After this he proceeded on to *Cornuntum*, at this Day call'd *Haimberg*, an old decay'd Town of *Illyricum*, seated upon the *Danube*, and very convenient for the Defence of the Country. From hence he detach'd *Merobaudes* and *Sebastian* with a Party of Foot to waste the Enemy's Borders, and he himself remov'd with great Expedition to a Place call'd *Acincum*, from whence

he

he pafs'd his Men over the River, and enter'd into the Territories of the *Quadi*, who from the Mountains, whither they had retir'd with their Wives and Children upon the firſt notice of his Approach, in great Conſternation beheld the Motion of his Army. After his detach'd Parties had ſcower'd the Plains, killing all they met ſtraggling behind, and burnt their Houſes, he return'd in ſafety with his whole Army to *Acincum*, where he continu'd 'till the Year was almoſt ſpent, deſiring to find out ſome convenient Winter Quarters in thoſe frozen Tracts, but could meet with none ſo proper as *Sabaria*, call'd at preſent *Sarvar*, tho' he found that far from being convenient, or ſuitable to his Wiſhes, and therefore he continu'd his March along the River ſide 'till he came to *Bregetio*, where he was admoniſh'd of his approaching End by ſeveral O-

Several O-mens preceeding the Death of Valentinian.

mens; for a few Days before Blazing Stars were ſeen, which in *Ammianus* his Opinion forerun the Downfal of great Perſons. At *Sirmium*, the Palace, Court and Forum were burnt by Lightning; and whilſt he was at *Sabaria* an Owl Perch'd upon the top of his Bath, ſinging a melancholy Dirge, and was not to be frighted or forc'd away by the Multitude, who aſſaulted it very earneſtly with Darts and Stones. As he was marching from that Place, he reſolv'd to paſs out at the ſame Gate he enter'd, intending to ſignifie by it that he ſhould quickly return in Safety to *Gaul*; but as they were clearing it of ſome Rubbiſh, which through a long Neglect it had contracted, the *Portcullis* fell, nor could all the Endeavours they us'd raiſe it again, ſo that after they had loſt much time about it, he was forc'd to go out at another Gate. The Night before he dy'd he thought he ſaw his Wife, who was then abſent, ſitting by him in a melancholy Poſture, with her Hair diſhevell'd, and in a mournful Habit,

which

which *Ammianus* fancies was his Genius, then in that disconsolate manner forsaking him. In the Morning he appear'd with a heavy dejected Countenance, and his Horse, whilst he was going to mount, bounding with ungovernable Fury, as if it disdain'd to receive him, he commanded his Querry's right Hand to be cut off, because he unwillingly gave him a Blow as he was struggling to place him in the Saddle; this was agreeable to the Cruelty of his Nature, and had been undoubtedly executed upon his faithful Servant, had not *Cerealis*, Master of the Horse, at the Hazard of his own Life deferr'd the Execution.

After this came the Embassadors from the *Quadi*, humbly suing for a Peace, and an Act of Oblivion for what was past; which that they might in some measure deserve, they offer'd a Supply of Soldiers, and such other Matters as they thought at that time agreeable to the Emperor's Affairs. *Valentinian* having consider'd of the Motion thought it reasonable to give 'em Audience, and they were thereupon admitted into the Consistory, where they were commanded to declare what they had to say. They with their Bodies bent to the Ground in token of Submission, declared upon Oath, that the late Devastations were not to be consider'd as a publick Act of the whole Nation, but committed by some Free-Booters living upon the Borders, without the Knowledge or Consent of the chief Men in the Country; and that they had been provok'd to it by the Fort lately built upon their Territories by the Emperor's Order, contrary to the Rules of Justice and the *Roman* Interest. *Valentinian* was extremely incens'd at this Discourse, and in a high Passion upbraided their whole Nation as thankless and ungrateful, vowing to be severely reveng'd upon 'em; but in the midst of his Discourse sunk down upon
his

his Seat like one ſtruck from Heaven, and ſeem'd to have loſt both Life and Voice together. They about him convey'd him carefully into his Chamber, and laid him on his Bed, where he was ſeiz'd with Convulſion Fits, and violent Contorſions of his Limbs, in the Agonies of which he breath'd out his laſt, in the Five and Fiftieth Year of his Age, and Twelfth of his Reign, *A.D.* 375. after the Third Conſulſhip of *Gratian* and of *Æquitius:* For tho' *Auſonius* has aſſign'd *Pontius Paulinus* for Conſul this Year, yet it is agreed on all Hands, that the Wars with which the Empire was attack'd or threaten'd on every ſide, prevented that Annual Deſignation.

The Death of Valentinian.

Various are the Accounts of this Emperor's Death; even *Ammianus* is inconſiſtent with himſelf, or at leaſt his Interpreters have made him ſo. Some will have it, that he imputes his Death to the ſudden Stoppage of the Blood, others to the violent Guſhing of it forth, which agrees better with the reſt of the Text, and other Authors who have written of the ſame Subject; who have left us this Account of it: That after he had given the Embaſſadors Audience, he was affronted at the Meanneſs of their Equipage and their beggarly Appearance, demanding with ſome Heat, if their Country afforded Men of no better Quality, that were more fit to appear before him. He was anſwer'd, that he had now in his Preſence the very beſt of the Nation; whereupon he fell into a violent Paſſion, vehemently lamenting his own and the Misfortune of the *Roman* People, who had to do with ſo beggarly a Nation, that not content to live within their own Bounds, had the Arrogance to riſe up in Arms, and affront the Majeſty of the Empire. This he deliver'd with ſo much Violence, that, according to *Socrates,* he open'd every Vein in his Body, and brake the Arteries aſunder, out of of which iffu'd fo large a Flux of Blood, that he inftantly dy'd, in the Caftle call'd at that time *Bergetio*, fuppos'd to be what we now call *Gran*.

Thus dy'd *Valentinian*, after a Reign of Twelve Years wanting an Hundred Days, during which he apply'd himfelf diligently to the Defence of the Borders, the reinforcing of his Army, building of new Forts where any were wanting, and repairing the old ones upon the *Rhine*, fo that not an Enemy could pafs undifcover'd into the *Roman* Territories. He was generally fuccefsful againft the *Germans*, and put a ftop to the Devaftations made by the *Saxons*, a People no lefs greedy of Blood than Plunder, whom he forc'd firft to fue for Peace, and afterwards by a Stratagem that had more of Profit than Honour in it, procur'd them all to be cut off. By his Lieutenants in this Ifland he fettled the Affairs of *Britain*; he fupprefs'd *Valentine* a *Pannonian* Exile, who was defigning to difturb the Publick Tranquility, before it was well known what he was attempting: He reftor'd the Peace of *Africk*, after it had been violently fhock'd by the Infurrection of *Firmus* and the Barbarians, and he was in a fair way of effecting the fame in *Illyricum*, had he not been fuddenly fnatch'd off by Death.

From what hath been faid, the Reader will eafily form to himfelf a Character of this Prince, and muft own that his greateft Fault was Cruelty; which was attended by another of no lefs Confequence, and to which Men of his implacable, vindicative Temper are feldom fubject, an over Credulity, which expos'd him to the Artifices of his mercenary Courtiers, who miferably impos'd on his Underftanding, barring him up from the Accefs of Perfons of Learning and Fidelity. He was covetous to a high degree, a Vice fome Excufe in him from the Neceffity the State lay under by reafon of the Wars in *Perfia*,

His Character.

Persia, which had very much exhausted the Publick Treasury, and put him upon many violent and illegal ways of raising Mony. He had so high an Opinion of his own Accomplishments, that he hated all who were eminent for Learning, Riches, Nobility, Valour, or so much as a genteel Fancy in their Dress. He pretended himself a great Enemy to all Cowards, and yet appeared timorous and dejected upon every trivial Occasion or groundless Report. In the Choice of his Judges he generally had regard to Men of Temper and Æquanimity, but if he accidentally promoted any of a cruel relentless Disposition, he would presently cry out they were so many *Cassii* or *Lycurgi*, and encouraged them in their rigorous Proceedings. These are the greatest Vices and Imperfections with which this Emperor is charged, and are abundantly out-weigh'd by his Virtues, which seem'd to render him worthy that high Sphere in which he moved. He may be said to have been a Father to the Provinces, for whose Safety he provided in the many Forts and Castles he built upon the Borders, at the same time easing them as much as he could in the Abatement of their Taxes. He might have pass'd for an exact Observer of Military Discipline, had he not been too partial to the General Officers, who abus'd his Favours, and gave a Beginning to those Commotions in *Britain*, *Africk*, and *Illyricum*. Tho' he had many Relations, who upon his Advancement expected mighty Preferments, yet he indulg'd none of 'em any farther than consisted with the publick Interest, preferring none to any considerable Posts, his Brother *Valens* except, whom in a time of Danger he assum'd for his Collegue, and with whom he reign'd in perfect Concord. He was excellent at the Invention of new sorts of Arms; and having from his Youth been inur'd to Hardship, he knew admirably

well

well how to manage, govern and conduct an Army. He was very careful in the Difpofal of the greateft Offices, fuffering no Places to be bought or fold during his Government, or any to be preferr'd to the Command of a Province, who were concern'd in the Management of the publick Mony. In his Entertainments he was fplendid but not profufe, in his Perfon comely; in his Converfation agreeable, of a vaft Memory and ready Elocution, knowing well how to accommodate himfelf to all Times and Occafions. As he was very chafte himfelf, fo he endeavour'd by his Example to propagate that Virtue throughout his Court, and wherever he came. As to his Religion, he conftantly adher'd to the Orthodox Faith, in that Diverfity of Opinions which at that time divided the World: But avoiding all Difputes, he fuffer'd the reft of his Subjects to follow their own Perfuafions without any Moleftation. He is blamed by the Ecclefiaftical Writers, for permitting his Brother to perfecute with fo much Rigour the Catholick Believers; but we may fay in his behalf, that the Condition of his Affairs would not allow him in Prudence openly to oppofe *Valens*, left the Heat of their Difputes had kindled up a Civil War in the Empire, which at that time would infallibly have deftroy'd it.

XVII. *Valentinian* being dead, his Body with due Care was prepar'd to be fent to *Conftantinople*, there to be depofited among his Imperial Predeceffors, whilft the great Officers of the Court were under uneafie Apprehenfions, and uncertain what an Accident fo extraordinary might produce, efpecially they who knew the inconftant and haughty Temper of the *Gallick* Soldiers, had great reafon to be afraid of fome unfeafonable Commotions; and the rather becaufe *Gratian*, who knew nothing of what had

had happen'd was then absent at *Triers*, where his Father had order'd him to reside during this Expedition. After some Consultation between themselves, they agreed to send for *Merobaudes* in the Emperor's Name, who had the Command of those Soldiers, to come to him, as if he had been still living; *Merobaudes* either suspecting what had happen'd, or being inform'd of it by the Messenger who was sent to him, pretended to the Soldiers that Orders were come from the Emperor to lead 'em back to the *Rhine*; where the Barbarians began again to be up in Arms; and pursuant to his Instructions he sent *Sebastian* far out of the way, who was a Man of a quiet easie Temper, but in great Esteem with the Army, and therefore the more to be fear'd in so dangerous a Conjuncture. When he arriv'd at the Camp it was resolv'd in Council, that *Valentinian*, the Son of the Deceas'd, should be declared Emperor. He was then at an hundred Miles distance, living in a Village call'd *Murocincta* with his Mother *Justina*, *Valentinian*'s second Wife, whom he marry'd after the Decease of the Empress *Severa*; so that *Socrates* his Story must fall to the Ground, who accuses *Valentinian* of Polygamy, and makes him Author of a Law, whereby every Man had the Liberty of having two Wives at a time if he was so inclined. He tells us *Justina*, whilst she was a Virgin, became acquainted with the Empress *Severa*, who admitted her into the same Bath with her self, where she could not but see and admire her extraordinary Beauty, which she extoll'd in a high measure to her Husband *Valentinian*, who immediately marry'd her, without divorcing *Severa* the Mother of *Gratian*, whom he had associated with him in the Imperial Dignity but just before. As he is mistaken in the matter of Fact, so is he in the Quality of *Justina*, who was no Virgin, but *Magnentius*

the

the Tyrant's Widow. Besides this *Valentinian* she had three Daughters by the Emperor, two of which dy'd Virgins, but the third, call'd *Galla*, was afterwards marry'd to *Theodosius* the Great.

Valentinian was then a Child, not above four Years of Age, faith *Ammianus*, tho' others affirm he was nine, and that he was born in *Febr.* 366. *Gratian* and *Dagalaiphus* being Consuls; in which *Idatius*, the Author of the *Alexandrine* Chronicle, *Themistius*, and most of our Modern Writers after 'em, agree: But if *Ammianus* is right in his Account, we must allow that there were two young Princes of the same Name, and that he who was born in 366, was not the same with him who was created *Augustus* in 375. This will appear more than probable, if we consider that not only *Ammianus*, but *Victor*, *Zonaras* and *Zozimus* affirm, that *Valentinian*, who was made Emperor at his Father's Death was but four Years old, or thereabouts: *Nicephorus* saith he dy'd when he was twenty, and it's agreed on all Hands that he was kill'd, *An. Dom.* 392. which could not possibly be, if he had been born in 366. In a word, *Valentinian Junior*, who was born in 366, was Consul together with *Aurelius Victor* in 369. Now had he been the same with him who succeeded his Father in the Empire, and was created Consul with *Valens* three Years after, the Year had been distinguish'd in the Tables by his *Second Consulship*, which it is not, tho' *Helvicus* in his Chronology has follow'd the general Opinion. From all which it appears, as was observ'd before, that there were two of the same Name, one the Son of *Valens*, the other of *Valentinian*.

But to return to the Course of the History: According to the Resolution taken in Council, *Cerealis*, Uncle to this young Prince, was sent with all Expedition for him; who conducted him to the Camp,

Valentinian, Son to the late Emperor, declared Augustus. Camp, where in a solemn manner he was declared Emperor, the sixth Day after his Father's Death. Most Men concluded *Gratian* would be highly offended at a Promotion confirm'd without his Knowledge or Consent, who notwithstanding lived ever after in a very peaceable manner with him; behaving himself in this matter like a prudent Man, or rather cherishing his Brother with too much Fondness and Respect.

The Hunns *invade the Empire.* In the mean time a cruel Storm began to gather to an head in the East, which not only occasion'd the Death of *Valens*, but fell in a violent manner upon the whole Empire. It was first rais'd by the *Hunns*, a Nation almost unknown to the *Romans* 'till then, inhabiting that part of *Scythia* which lay upon the Ocean beyond the Fenns of *Mœotis*, call'd at present *Tartary*. They were a fierce savage People, ignorant of the Use of Fire, feeding altogether on Roots of Herbs, or such Flesh as was chafed betwixt their Thighs and their Horses Sides; without Houses, wand'ring from Place to Place, spreading themselves sometimes on the Mountains, at others descending into the Vallies, and living like Brutes, on whom Nature through a Mistake had conferr'd Human Shapes; from their Infancy accustomed to endure the Inconveniencies of Cold and Hunger, having their Cheeks mangled as soon as they were born to prevent Beards, in the want of which they resembled Eunuchs, but in appearance were most terrible and ghastly. Their Cloaths were either Linnen, or the Skins of a sort of Mice, which they tack'd together, and wore at home and abroad, awake and asleep, without any Change, 'till they dropp'd asunder. Their Legs were cover'd with Goat-skins, and their Feet with an ill-shapen unfashionable Shoo, which cramp'd 'em up when they walk'd, and render'd 'em unfit for Foot-Service,

their

their Genius inclining 'em more to the Horse, in which manner of Engagements they excell'd, fighting usually in Parties drawn up like Wedges; quick in their Onsets, disorderly in their Retreats, furious and discompos'd in their Pursuits, tho' they always avoided attacking the Camp of the Enemy. Having no King they liv'd under no Government, following the Conduct of their Nobility (if they had any such among 'em) whom they obey'd no longer than they thought fit. They were no more to be trusted in Times of Peace than in War, beginning the one without any Provocation, and concluding the other without any Forecast. They had no Sense of Religion, nor that Child of Ignorance, Superstition, but liv'd in common with a promiscuous use of Women, with whom they for the most part coupl'd openly, or if at any time they retir'd, their Quivers were hung out to let their Neighbours know what they were doing, that they might meet with no Disturbance.

These *Hunns* were near Neighbours to the *Alani*, who inhabited *Scythia* beyond *Tanais*, a River by which *Europe* is separated from *Asia*; like the *Hunns*, and the rest of the *Scythians*, they wander'd up and down in their Waggons, never Tilling their Ground, but feeding on raw Flesh and Milk; they drove their Cattle in great Herds before 'em, and when they were arriv'd at any pleasant Pasturage, with which the Country abounded, there they continu'd 'till it was all consum'd, and then they went forward with their moveable Cities, 'till they met with fresh Forage, accounting every Place they came at their Native Home. A People impatient of Ease, continually busied in Wars and Dangers, esteeming him only happy who dy'd in the Field, and reviling them as idle and degenerate Persons whom any Accident had destroy'd, or Age led down

down in peace to the Grave. All their Religion consisted in a naked Sword, which they stuck fast into the Ground, and worshipp'd under the Name of *Mars*, the Great Protector of the Regions they inhabited; in most respects they resembl'd the *Hunns*, only they appear'd to have been of a more civiliz'd Conversation. They were said to have a strange way of foretelling things to come; they lopt a Bough from off a bearing Tree, which they cut into several peices; these peices they distinguish'd by certain Marks, throwing 'em at random upon a White Linnen Garment; after which the Priest, if it was a Publick Concern, if not, the Master of the Houshold, invoking the Deity they worshipp'd, took each peice up in a solemn manner thrice together, and from the Coherence the Marks before imprinted bore each to the other, they collected their Divination. The name of Slavery was not known among 'em, being all accounted of Noble Birth; and those Persons had the Administration of their Affairs as their Officers and Judges, who were of most Experience in the Wars.

Into the Territories of these People did the *Hunns* break with great Violence, and having spoil'd the Country, and laid all waste before 'em, they forc'd those of the Nation, who had out-liv'd their Cruelty, to enter into an Alliance with 'em, by which means having reinforc'd themselves, they fell with incredible Impetuosity upon the *Gothick* Nations, assaulting first the Dominions of *Ermenrich* or *Ermanaric*, who tho' a Martial Prince, yet struck with Consternation at so unexpected an Attempt, put an end to his Troubles by a voluntary Death; after this they fell upon *Athanaric*, he who had assisted *Procopius* in his late Usurpation, who had resolv'd to stand upon his Guard, and was prepar'd for a vigorous Resistance; but the *Hunns* falling

falling upon him unawares, he was forc'd to fly to the Mountains, after he had loft some of his Men; from whence he pass'd in great Consternation down to the *Danube*, where he rais'd Fortifications to defend himself from any farther Attempts. The *Hunns*, whose great Booty had render'd 'em incapable of any hasty Pursuit, were in the mean time grown so terrible to the rest of the *Goths*, that they thought of removing from a Storm which they saw rolling irresistibly upon 'em, and resolv'd upon *Thrace*, both for that it was a fertile Country, and was separated by the *Ister* from those Tracts which lay expos'd to the Fury of the *Hunns*. Having therefore seiz'd on the Banks of the *Danube*, under the Conduct of *Alavivus*, they sent their Orators to *Valens*, by whom, in a most submissive manner, they begg'd leave to be admitted into *Thrace*, where they promis'd to live peaceably in Subjection to the Empire, to whom they would be ready to send Aid upon all Occasions.

Tho' the Rumour of these strange Commotions in the Northern Parts ought to have struck all Men with Admiration, as well as Terror, yet they were at first but little regarded at Court, which hitherto the Report of any Wars in those remote Regions could hardly reach before they had been finish'd, and the Fear of 'em was over; but when they saw the Embassadors from the *Goths*, and knew the Substance of their Embassy, all Wise Men were surpriz'd to hear such vast Multitudes of Barbarians should hover about the Banks of the *Ister*, driven out of the Country by People more barbarous than themselves. And yet there were not wanting some Sycophants about the Person of the Emperor, who had the Impudence to flatter him, and Extol his good Fortune upon this Occasion, which had un-

expectedly

expectedly brought him a perpetual Supply of Soldiers, with which he could be furnish'd at his Pleasure out of *Thrace*, and thereby save the Expence of new Levies, to the no small Benefit of his Treasury: The imaginary Prospect of this Advantage made him, without any farther Consideration, give Order for their immediate Transportation, which was done with so much Care and Diligence, as if it had been a Sin to leave any Person, who was to be concern'd in the Subversion of the *Roman* Empire, behind: For several Nights and Days together, without any Intermission, did they come over in such Multitudes, that they, who were appointed to see the Business effected, were in no manner able to compute their Numbers, exceeding, saith *Ammianus*, the Sands upon the *Libyan* Shore. Destruction follow'd close upon their Heels, and spread it self like a Contagion, infecting what it fed on. But what contributed as much as any thing to the Desolations that follow'd soon after, was the Corruption and Insufficiency of the Governors Commanding then in the Provinces, who by their Covetousness basely eluded the Emperor's Orders, who had ordain'd that none should be admitted 'till they had been first disarm'd; but these Officers, more intent upon their own private Gain and Satisfaction, suffer'd themselves to be impos'd upon by the Barbarians, who corrupted 'em with Presents of their finest Women, most beautiful Boys, and stoutest Slaves, and so were permitted to come over arm'd as they thought fit themselves. *Eunapius* saith likewise, that the Emperor's Intent was to have the Children of both Sexes first transported, who were to be dispos'd as Hostages throughout the Provinces of the Empire, and Pledges of their good Behaviour, which prudent Design was unhappily

The Goths admitted into Thrace

happily fruftrated by the mercenary Conduct of thofe treacherous Officers. This memorable Paffage, which fo largely contributed to the Downfal of the Empire, happen'd when *Valens*, the Fifth time, and *Valentinian* were Confuls, in the laft Year of the 288th *Olympiad*, the 1128th Year of *Rome*, and 28 Years after the firft Divifion of the Empire, *An. Dom.* 376.

CHAP.

CHAP. II.

From the Admission of the Goths *into* Thrace, *to the Death of* Theodosius *the Great.*

Containing about the Space of 19 *Years.*

I. IT's observable that a State subsists and flourishes no longer, than whilst it cultivates and improves the Means to which it ow'd its Rise and Progress. The first *Romans* were plain, hearty and sincere, they went to the Wars with Honour, and return'd with Success, and their very Enemies reap'd the Benefit of their Victories as well as themselves; for their Virtue always protected those whom their Valour had subdu'd. They fought for Dominion, but not for Tyranny, and chose rather to be Lov'd than Fear'd; this made the Provinces chearful in their Submission, hearty in their Contributions, and unwavering in their Obedience. In a Word, it is not so much to be admir'd, that from so small a Beginning they should rise to such a stupendious Height, as that so many Qualities productive of a real Greatness should be found united in one People, diffusing themselves with so exact a Tenor throughout every Part, as to make up the very Life and Being of the whole. How much the *Romans*, who liv'd in the Age we are now writing of, were fallen off from that Original Perfection, I leave the Reader to imagine; they were grown Effeminate, Factious, Proud and Inconsiderate; the Court was become debauch'd, the Camp licentious, and the Commonalty obstinate and mutinous;

tinous; they were so far from pushing on to new Conquests, that they were not able to maintain and defend their Hereditary Acquisitions; the Constitution was grown old and crazy, and had lost so much of its natural Vigor, that it must in course have dropp'd of it self without receiving an Enemy into its Bowels, that cruelly shook and tore it into pieces; but as some of her ancient Citizens chose to provoke Death by a Sword or Poison, rather than wait its leisure under the Fatigues of a painful lingring Distemper; so that State, grown old and infirm, may be said to have chosen a violent Subversion, rather than a natural Dissolution.

As it was the greatest piece of madness to receive so many Barbarians into the Heart of the Empire, so was it an equal madness to provoke and exasperate 'em after they had been admitted. *Lupicinus* and *Maximus* were at this time Commanders in Chief throughout *Thrace*, and by their pernicious Practices hasten'd the Ruin of their Country. The Barbarians stood in want of all manner of Provisions, and being bitterly pinch'd with Hunger made their Applications to these Officers, who got all the Dogs they could together, and exchang'd 'em for so many Men, amongst whom were the Sons of the first Nobility, whom with the rest they took for their Slaves; besides *Lupicinus* had dealt treacherously with them in several Respects, betraying his Trust, and oppressing 'em upon every Occasion. These Practices irritated a People, easie enough to be provok'd, and made 'em catch at the first Opportunity they met with to be reveng'd, with which *Lupicinus* himself presented 'em not long after. The Chief Captains of these People were *Alavivus* and *Fritigern*, Men of Courage and Resolution, who had formerly acted with much Vigour and Animosity against the Empire: These Commanders *Lupicinus*

cinus invited to Dinner at *Marcianopolis*, where he then resided; and lest the ordinary sort at the same time should press upon him for Provisions, of which they stood in great need, he order'd the Guard to keep 'em off from the Gates of the City, whither they desir'd to be admitted as Friends, to buy them Necessaries; betwixt these People and the *Romans* there happen'd a sharp Dispute, in which the *Romans* were slain and stripp'd by the Barbarians. *Lupicinus* was no sooner acquainted with it, but he caus'd all the Attendants, waiting upon the two Princes, in the midst of their Mirth to be murder'd, of which when they without the Walls were inform'd, they fell into a great Rage, vowing all manner of Revenge, concluding their Kings would be detain'd Prisoners by the Governor. Of this *Fritigern*, who indeed was afraid he should be secur'd as an Hostage, made a good use; for he earnestly press'd to be dismiss'd, that he might compose and pacifie his Soldiers, whereupon he was discharg'd together with *Alavivus*; for by this time *Lupicinus* was got so Drunk that he knew not what he did; whilst they made haste to their Countrymen, to whom they came unexpected, and were receiv'd with great Joy and Satisfaction. This Advantage they all agreed to improve, and consulted together how they might best raise a War, and be reveng'd upon the *Romans*. They were presently join'd by all the *Gothick* Nations, who fell with great Fury upon the Country, wasting all with Fire and Sword. *Lupicinus*, alarm'd at so dangerous an Insurrection, march'd out against 'em with more Fury than Discretion, and drew up his Army with a Resolution to engage the Barbarians, who watching their Op-

The Romans defeated by the Goths. portunity attack'd the *Romans* with much Bravery, cutting most of them off together with their Commanders, whilst the General with great Precipitation

ion fled back into the City. This Defeat was atended with a greater Mischief, for the Barbarians were hereby supply'd with *Roman* Arms, and ravag'd the Country round about without any Opposition. And as great Armies very often occasion a Famine and Pestilence, so at this time both the one and the other raged very violently in many Parts of the Empire.

These Advantages made the *Goths* more bold and outragious; for not content to be Masters of the Field, they went and laid Siege to *Adrianople*, being sometime before join'd by a Body of Forces under the Conduct of *Sueridus* and *Colias*, two Princes of their own Nation, who with their Troops had been long since admitted by the Emperor, and appointed to quarter near that City; and laying hold of this Opportunity, were, upon some small Provocations receiv'd from the Townsmen, resolv'd to run the Fortune of their Countrymen. They had not been long before the Town, before they found the Difficulty of their Undertaking, and were advis'd by *Fritigern* to quit the Siege, and content themselves with the Plunder of the wealthy Province, where they were like to meet with no Opposition, and which would turn more to their Advantage than a War with Walls. Leaving therefore a sufficient Force to block up the Town, they ranged all over *Thrace*, growing daily stronger by the Accession of fresh Numbers that came in to 'em. By this means the Province was reduced to a most miserable Condition, for they spared neither Sex nor Age, plucking the Infants from their Mothers Breasts, who whilst they were lamenting the Death of their Husbands saw their Children murder'd before their Faces. What the Sword had spar'd the Fire destroy'd, and they seem'd the most miserable, whom Fortune, not the

A. D. 377.
They besieging Adrianople.

the Mercy of the Barbarians, had permitted to di[e at] laſt.

All this while *Valens* was at *Antioch*, intent upo[n] the King of *Perſia*'s Deſigns, and as narrowly ob[ſerv]'d by him. Upon his firſt Notice of theſe dan[ger]ous Commotions, he was at a loſs what Courſ[e] to take; he ſent away *Victor*, General of the Horſe to compoſe Matters in the beſt manner he could wit[h] the *Perſians*; and reſolving to remove to *Conſtantino*[*ple*,] he ſent *Profuturus* and *Trajan*, two of his Ge[nera]ls, before him. They were Men of more Am[bi]tion than Conduct, for inſtead of endeavourin[g] by Stratagem to cut off and ſtarve ſuch Multitude[s] of Men that fill'd the Mountains and cover'd all th[e] Vallies, they inconſiderately engag'd 'em to thei[r] own Coſt, depending too much upon the Legion[s] drawn out of *Armenia*, who indeed were good Sol[diers,] but unable to make Head againſt ſuch Swarm[s] of the Enemy; at length they drove 'em up beyon[d] the Mountain of *Hæmus*, where they ſeiz'd upo[n] all the Paſſes, hoping to block 'em up, and deſtro[y] 'em by Famine, at leaſt 'till the *Pannonian* and *Tranſ*[*alpine*] Auxiliaries could join 'em, who had Order[s] from *Gratian* to march, under the Conduct of *Fri*[*geride*], to their Aſſiſtance. *Gratian* at the ſame tim[e] ſent *Richomeres* with ſome Forces out of *Gaul*, bu[t] the Soldiers deſerted in great Numbers as they wer[e] upon the March, ſollicited to it, as it was reported by *Merobaudes*, who was afraid ſo ſtrong a Detach[ment] would leave the Borders too much expos'd[.] So that *Richomeres* join'd with *Profuturus* and *Tra*[*jan*,] but to little or no effect; for *Frigeride* was ſeiz'd with the Gout, or, as his Enemies would have i[t] believ'd, pretended Sickneſs, and kept himſelf out o[f] Danger; tho' his eminent Services not long after leav[e] little room for ſuch a Suſpicion.

Richo-

Richomeres having join'd *Profuturus* and *Trajan*, the Army march'd to a Place call'd *Salices*, where the Enemy then lay. Here both Parties engaged, and fought with so much Obstinacy, that Night alone put an end to the Controversie, and the *Romans* retir'd, after the Loss of a great many Men, to *Marcianople*; tho' it is not easie to determine who had the better of the Day; for the Enemy kept themselves close seven Days together among the Carriages, not daring to stir out, or pursue the *Romans* in their Retreat; 'till they had allur'd the *Hunns* and *Alans* to join with them; and then like a mighty Flood they bore down all before them, spreading themselves over all the Coast of *Thrace*, as far as from the *Ister* to the Mountain *Rhodope*, devouring like a Plague all they met, and scattering Destruction on every side. At a Place call'd *Dibaltum* they fell upon *Barzimeres*, Tribune of the *Scutarii*, who was encamp'd there with his own Legion, and several other Parties of Foot. *Barzimeres* was an old experienc'd Commander, and knew well enough the Danger he was in; and therefore drawing his Men up into a close Body, he endeavour'd to force his Way through the Enemies Squadrons, and maintain'd the Fight so long that he destroy'd a great Number of the Barbarians, but was at length overpower'd with fresh Supplies, and cut in pieces together with the whole Party. Animated by this Advantage, which had cost 'em very dear, they went in quest of *Frigeride*, who was now come by the Emperor's Order into *Thrace*, and was posted near *Berea*. He was too cautious to hazard his Army against an Enemy that exceeded him so much in Numbers of Men, and therefore drew over the Mountains into *Illyricum*; but in his Retreat met with an Adventure with which he was much elevated. He fell in with *Farnobius*, one of the *Gothick*

A Roman Legion cut off.

Cap-

A Party of the Goths defeated. Captains, who was at the Head of a confiderable Body of Troops, whom he engaged and defeated, killing the Commander upon the Spot, together with the reft of his Army, except fome who cry'd out for Quarter; them in pity he fpared, difpofing of 'em about *Mutina Rhegium,* and *Parma* in *Italy,* where they were employ'd in the Tillage of the Ground.

A. D. 378.

Whilft *Thrace* was thus cruelly infefted by the *Goths,* other Parts of the Empire labour'd under the fame Calamities; for the whole Body of the *German* Nation, knowing the greateft part of the Imperial Forces were march'd into *Illyricum,* whither the Emperor *Gratian* was preparing to follow, they, *The Germans up in Arms,* to the number of Forty Thoufand, or upwards, pafs'd over the *Rhine* upon the Ice, and broke into the Borders of *Gaul. Gratian* hereupon recall'd the Troops he had order'd to march into *Pannonia,* and at *Argentaria,* call'd at prefent *Colmar* in *Alface, are defeated.* gave the *Germans* fo entire a Defeat, that not above Five Thoufand efcap'd; among the reft, *Priarius,* or *Priamus,* their King, the chief Promoter of the War, was flain.

Gratian was highly pleas'd with this Succefs, which redounded much to his Reputation; and now his Thoughts were bent towards the Eaft, whither he was refolv'd to march in Perfon to the Affiftance of his Uncle *Valens:* But that he might leave no Enemy, capable of making any Difturbance in his Abfence, behind him, he had a mind firft to punifh the *Lentienfes,* a People of *Germany* bordering upon *Rhætia,* who broke the League, and gave a Beginning to the late War. He therefore march'd his Army over the *Rhine* with all the Secrefie imaginable, intending by Surprize if poffible to conquer, or extirpate fo inconftant and faithlefs a People. The *Lentienfes* being inform'd of his fudden Approach were

were in a great Confternation what to do; after a fhort Deliberation they remov'd with their Families, and whatever elfe they could bear off with them, into the Mountains, where they fortify'd themfelves with great Precipitation, refolving to make good the Place at the Hazard of their Lives. Hither *Gratian* follow'd 'em, and finding upon Trial that they were not eafily to be remov'd, he block'd 'em up, and fo refolv'd by degrees to ftarve 'em. Of this the *Germans* were quickly fenfible, and therefore they broke up without much Concern, and remov'd to other Mountains, higher and more inacceffible than the former. They were no fooner gone, but *Gratian* mov'd after 'em, and endeavouring to difcover the Paffes that led to the Top of the Hills, he gave 'em to underftand what they were to expect from him. They imagin'd by this his obftinate Refolution, that nothing would fatisfie him but their Deftruction; whereupon they furrender'd themfelves, and in a very fubmiffive manner begg'd his Pardon, which was granted them upon Condition they deliver'd up their Youth, who ferv'd to recruit the *Roman* Army. By this laft Advantage the Weftern Nations were reftrain'd for the prefent, and now *Gratian* was at leifure to purfue his intended Expedition into the Eaft, whither the Fame of his late Exploits was gone before him. He had indeed gain'd much upon his Subjects by his generous Carriage, being a Youth of great Hopes, well difpos'd, Eloquent, Courteous, and Liberal.

Having fettled all his Affairs in *Gaul*, he began his March, and mov'd with great Expedition by *Lauriacum*, call'd at prefent *Lork*, to the Affiftance of his Uncle. In the mean time, whilft *Frigeride* was behaving himfelf with great Prudence and Caution, and fortifying the Straights of *Succi*, a Place of the greateft Importance, he was unaccountably difmifs'd

Gratian begins his March into the Eaft.

dismiss'd from his Employment, at a season when such a Man ought to have been courted to the Service, and been entrusted in the highest Commands. This was a great Loss to the Army, and was aggravated by the Inabilities of *Maurus* who succeeded him, being a Man of a quite contrary Temper, rash, sullen, and inconstant.

Valens was by this time arriv'd at *Constantinople*, where he discharged *Trajan* from any farther Service, and made *Sebastian* General of the Foot. He was a brave experienc'd Commander, bed up in the Army, to which his Inclinations led him, from his Youth; and was now detach'd by the Emperor with a good Body of Forces under his Command against the Barbarians, lying then with a great Booty about *Berœa* and *Nicopolis*. At *Adrianople* he refresh'd his Men, and issuing out the next Day, he fell undiscover'd upon a Party of the *Goths*, who without any apprehensions of an Enemy were roving about the River *Hebrus*, whom in great Numbers he kill'd, and recover'd their Plunder. *Fritigern* was much perplex'd at this unexpected Defeat, and fearing lest the rest of his Countrymen, roving about the Country, should fall into *Sebastian*'s Hands, he gave 'em Orders to join him with all speed, and march'd towards the Coasts of *Cabyle*.

Sebastian defeats a Party of the Goths.

During these Occurrences in *Thrace*, *Gratian* had inform'd his Uncle of the Success of his Arms against the *Germans*, and was by this time come to *Sirmium*, where he stay'd four Days to refresh his Army, and then proceeded along the *Danube* to a Fort call'd *Castra Martis*, having in his March lost some of his Men through the sudden Incursions of the Barbarians, and being himself afflicted all the while by an Ague.

Valens by this time began to think his own Reputation eclips'd by that of his young Nephew, and
there-

therefore resolv'd to do something that might equal his Exploits against the *Germans*. This Emulation, had it been rightly conceiv'd, might have been of great use to the publick Affairs, but it made *Valens* hasty and ungovernable, and thereby hasten'd his Destruction. He had a mind to enjoy without a Rival the Glory of a Victory, which he could not obtain without an Assistant. Marching therefore from *Melanthias*, an Imperial Town, he encamp'd with his Army near *Adrianople*, where he was presented with Letters from his Nephew *Gratian*, in which he earnestly press'd him not to hazard a Battle 'till he had join'd him, nor make that Victory doubtful, which the Conjunction of their Forces would render indisputable. In a Council of War, which was immediately call'd, some advis'd him to fight without delay, amongst whom was *Sebastian*, General of the Foot; but *Victor*, who commanded the Horse, and was a wary prudent Officer, advis'd him by all means to stay for his Collegue, and the Accession of the *Gallick* Troops, which would make him an equal Match for the Enemy.

Some say *Fritigern* at the same time sollicited him to a Peace, offering to accept of it upon very reasonable Conditions, which his Officers advis'd him by all means to embrace; remonstrating to him, that an honourable and certain Peace was always to be preferr'd to an uncertain Victory. Notwithstanding all which Considerations he was obstinate to fight, persuaded to it by his Flatterers, who told him he would thereby prevent that Honour his Nephew would share with him in the Engagement, and wear the Laurel alone. So that having sent all the Baggage into *Adrianople*, he order'd the Army to march, and about Noon the Enemy was discover'd preparing to fight; hereupon the *Roman* Officers drew up their Army in Order of Battel. Some of the Enemy that lay farther off with *Alatheus* and *Safraces* sent to the Emperor, and pretended to desire Peace: He receiv'd 'em with much Indignation, requiring the chiefest among 'em to be deliver'd up as Hostages; but they drew out the Time as long as they could 'till their Horse was arriv'd, which they hourly expected; besides, they design'd by their Delay to tire out the *Romans* with the Heat of the Season, which was very much increas'd by the multitude of Fires they had for that purpose kindled throughout the Country.

In the mean time *Fritigern*, farther to amuse the Emperor, promis'd by a Messenger to bring all his Forces over to him, together with Necessaries for the Army, of which they then stood in great need, but requir'd that some Noblemen might be sent as Hostages to him. The Message was very acceptable to *Valens*, who propos'd *Equitius*, a Tribune and his own Relation, to be one of the Hostages; but he refus'd the Employment, having experienc'd the Severity of the Barbarians when detain'd Prisoner among 'em, from whom he lately made his Escape. Upon this *Richomeres*, like a Man of Courage and Resolution, voluntarily offer'd himself to go; but as they were conducting him to the Enemies Camp, a Party of Archers and others, under the Command of *Bacurius* an *Iberian* and one *Cassio*, impatient to be doing, fell upon the *Goths*, and gave an unlucky Beginning to the War: For by this means *Richomeres* his Design was frustrated, and the *Gothick* Horse having join'd the rest of the Army, they came rolling like a Torrent down the Mountains, and with an impetuous Force overwhelm'd all that stood in their way. The *Romans* were over-power'd at the first Onset, and fell in great Numbers, however they made a very vigorous Resistance, and were resolv'd to sell their Lives at as dear a rate as

they

they could; never was Battel fought with more obstinate Resolution, where Death, like a raging irresistible Flame, first caught hold on those who turn'd it loose, and then enlarg'd and extended it self on every side with an implacable Fury. The Left Wing of the *Roman* Army pierc'd through to the Enemy's Carriages, and had undoubtedly done great Execution had they been supported by fresh Troops; but being deserted by the rest of the Horse, who were broken at the first Shock, the Barbarians fell like a mighty Tower upon 'em, and crush'd 'em in a Moment; by this means the Foot were left naked, and expos'd to the Enemy's Weapons, who surrounding 'em on every side did very great Execution. The *Romans* fought like Men in Despair, and seem'd to contemn that Death they found unavoidable; the Barbarians behav'd themselves with equal Bravery, encourag'd with the Prospect of a Victory which they began to think indisputable. They ow'd the Fortune of the Day not so much to their own Valour, as the Advantage of their Numbers, which made 'em insensible of the loss of Multitudes of their Countrymen, who lay scatter'd o're the Field, gnawing the Earth, and rolling their Eyes in Death, which for that reason only was unwelcome, because it took from 'em the means of Revenge. Through this Obstinacy on both sides the Plain became cover'd with heaps of dead Bodies, and the heavy Groans and Lamentations of them that were dying silenc'd the Shouts and Acclamations of those who still continu'd fighting. After the *Roman* Foot had done all that Men, whose Native Courage was embolden'd by Despair, could pretend to do, and had resisted an Enemy, 'till at last they found him to be irresistible, they betook themselves to their Heels and fled, but were closely follow'd by the Barbarians, who appear'd as obsti-

The Roman Army defeated.

obstinate in the Pursuit as they had been before in the Fight, sparing none that yielded, but quitting all those that made resistance. On the one side the *Romans* were hinder'd in the Flight by Multitudes of dead Bodies filling up the Ways, on the other they were favour'd by the Darkness of the Night which now was coming on upon 'em. When the Emperor perceiv'd to which side the Fortune of the Day inclin'd, and that the Relicts of his Army were quitting the Field to the Victorious Enemy, he fled in great Consternation to the *Lancearii*, who had hitherto stood the Shock without giving the least Ground; which *Trajan*, who was lately restor'd to a Command in the Army, observing, he cry'd out, *That the Emperor, deserted by his Guards, would unavoidably be lost unless he was instantly rescu'd*; whereupon *Victor* went in haste for a Body of *Batavians*, who had been plac'd as a Reserve for the Relief of the Prince, but by this time were either slain or fled. Thus *Valens* was left expos'd to the Fury of the Enemy, forsaken rather by Fortune, than deserted by his Soldiers, whom the Barbarians over-power'd rather than conquer'd. Those Officers that were left about him press'd him earnestly to fly for his Safety, and reserve himself for better Times, and the good of the Common-wealth, having provided him with Horses accordingly, that would convey him speedily out of Danger: But he thought it beneath his Dignity to out-live so great a Loss, and

Valens slain. therefore was slain by the Barbarians, together with several of his Followers, who in Heaps fell o'er him, covering his Body instead of a Monument. This Account of his Death we have from *Ammianus*, and *Libanius* in his Oration to *Theodosius*; tho' other Historians affirm he did not die upon the spot, but being wounded in the Field fled with some of his

Fol-

Followers to a Contryman's House hard by, which they made good for some time against the Barbarians, who ignorant of the Quality of the Person, and more intent upon the Prospect of a greater Booty, set Fire to the House, in the Flames of which the unhappy Emperor was consum'd. All Authors agree he ow'd his Ruin to his own Obstinacy, engaging with the Enemy in Envy to the Virtues of his Nephew *Gratian*, contrary to the Rules of Prudence, and the Advice of his most experienc'd Captains. Some say he receiv'd the *Goths* into the *Roman* Pale out of a Disgust to *Gratian*, who, when *Valentinian* had been chosen Emperor, without acquainting either of them with it, had confirm'd the Election without his Advice, and shar'd the Empire with him; to this may be added, the Disagreement that was between 'em in Matters relating to Religion; for *Valens* had from the beginning openly espous'd the *Arian* Party, whereas *Gratian* was a great Favourer of the Orthodox Professors.

With the Emperor fell near two Thirds of the Army, and among 'em several Eminent Persons, such as *Trajan* and *Sebastian*, two Principal Commanders, *Valerian* and *Equitius*, one Master of the Horse, the other great Steward of the Houshold, tho' none was more lamented than *Potentius*, a young Gentleman of extraordinary Hopes, highly esteem'd for his own Merits, and reverenc'd in Honour to the Memory of his Father *Ursicinus*. This great Overthrow, said to be equall'd by none but that of *Cannæ*, happen'd on the 9th of *August*, A. D. 378. in the sixth Consulship of *Valens* and of *Valentinian*, after *Valens* had reign'd fourteen Years and four Months, and had liv'd near Fifty.

The Character Heathen Authors have left us of him is agreeable to what we have already related *His Character* concerning him; but Ecclefiaftical Writers are more fevere againft him, and term his Death a juft Judgment from Heaven for the many Perfecutions he had rais'd againft the Faithful, and the great Encouragement he gave to that abominable Herefie of *Arius*, which flourifh'd and encreas'd more in his Reign than under any of his Predeceffors. In fome refpects he was like his Brother, for he was very cautious of preferring his Relations, and a rigorous Exacter both of Civil and Military Difcipline. He was likewife a watchful Guardian of the Provinces, to whom he was as affectionate in his Care, as he could be to his own Family. He had one very commendable Quality, for he never conferr'd an Eftate upon his begging Courtiers before he who had a Title to it had time allow'd him to plead his Right, and defend himfelf; and when ever upon Trial it appear'd he might lawfully difpofe of it, he never gave it all to him that begg'd it, but made him fhare it with fome others that were abfent, and by fuch Difappointments check'd the Importunity of thofe who were gaping after others Men Wealth; tho' he himfelf was fo intemperately covetous of Riches, that his rigorous and almoft daily Confifcations made his Government intolerable. He was of a clownifh furly Temper, which in a great meafure may be charg'd upon his want of Education, being brought up in his Youth neither to the Study of Arms, nor the liberal Sciences. He was fo jealous of his Authority, that the leaft fufpicion of Treafon made him cruel and inexorable, and his Ears were open continually to all manner of Accufations, which gain'd him but a few Friends, tho' where ever he profefs'd a Friendfhip himfelf he was firm and faithful. His want of Breeding made him Rude and Abufive, his Jealoufie made him Cholerick and Partial, and his want

of

of Merit Envious and Detracting; the laft of which, the moft unbecoming a Prince, threw him upon imprudent Courfes, and as we obferv'd before, brought him to an untimely End.

II. The Day after the Fight the *Goths*, inform'd by fome Fugitives that *Valens* had left many Perfons of Quality behind in *Adrianople*, where likewife the Imperial Treafure was lodg'd, march'd with great Expedition thither, and laid Siege to the City, by which means they prevented feveral, who had efcap'd the Battel, from getting into the Town; whereupon three Hunder'd of 'em went in a Body over to the Barbarians, who cut 'em all in pieces, and by that imprudent Severity prevented the like Treachery for the future. After they had for feveral times affaulted the Town with much Vigour, and were as vigoroufly repuls'd by the Inhabitants, they at firft endeavour'd by Letters full of Threats to perfuade the Defendants to Surrender, who anfwer'd 'em with much Indignation; then they attempted to feize on that by Fraud, which they could not obtain by Force, and encourag'd certain Fugitives to pretend they had made an Efcape from the Befiegers, and thereby gain Admittance into the Town, which they were to fet on Fire in fome convenient Place; which whilft the Defendants were bufied in extinguifhing, the Barbarians might Scale the Walls with greater Eafe, and fo mafter the Place. Thefe Fugitives came accordingly to the Trenches, where, with their Hands ftretch'd out, they defir'd of the *Romans* to be admitted, who without Sufpicion of any Treachery open'd the Gate and took 'em in; but when they came to be examin'd about the Enemy's Defigns, they difagreed in their Anfwers, which made 'em fufpected; and being put on the Rack they con-

The Goths *Befiege Adrianople.*

confess'd the whole Matter, and lost their Heads for their Treason. The *Goths* being by this Discovery deceiv'd of their Expectation, renew'd the Attack with Minds harden'd against Death and Danger, thinking by the Superiority of Numbers to do the Business; but in this the *Romans* had the Advantage, that whatever they discharg'd at 'em did *They raise* some Execution. This Attack was shortly after, *the Siege,* at the Instigation of their Officers, seconded by another, which they carry'd on with equal Obstinacy, but were again repuls'd by the *Romans*, and forc'd to retire towards the Evening with great Loss, fretting at their Success, and upbraiding each other for acting contrary to *Fritigern*'s Advice, who by all means desir'd 'em to avoid Sieges; so that they *and march* broke up the next Day, and march'd towards *Perin-* *to* Perin-*thus*, which they resolv'd to seize; but still feeling *thus;* the rough Entertainment they met with before *Adrianople*, they had not the Courage to approach the Walls, but wasted that Fertile Country on every side; and so dividing the Army into four Bodies, for fear of a Surprize, they mov'd towards *from thence Constantinople*, promising themselves nothing less than *to* Constan-the Possession of the great Wealth they knew to be *tinople.* in that City.

Some time before the Death of *Valens*, the *Saracens* in the East, encourag'd perhaps by the Success the *Goths* met with in *Thrace*, in Defiance of a Truce concluded between the Emperor and their Prince, who was lately dead, by which means the Truce was expir'd, rose up in Arms, and under the Conduct of *Mavia*, Widdow to the deceas'd, a Woman of Masculine Courage, surpriz'd the Towns situate on the Frontiers of *Palestine* and *Arabia*, and in several Encounters worsted the *Roman* Army, and thereby oblig'd the Emperor to grant 'em an Honourable Peace; one of the Principal Articles

cles in which was, that, the Queen, who had lately receiv'd the Light of the Gospel, might have a certain Hermit call'd *Moses*, renown'd for his Virtues, and the Miracles God wrought by his Hands, sent to her to convert and instruct her Subjects in the same Religion. *Moses* was sent accordingly, and was so successful in his Mission, that great Multitudes of People, who never before heard of Christianity or the Gospel, were enlighten'd by the Holy Ghost, and embrac'd the Faith. A great Party from this Nation were now sent by the Queen to defend *Constantinople*, and being more dextrous in sudden Onsets than regular Engagements, they issu'd out, and fell suddenly upon the *Goths* as they were facing the City. After a hot Dispute for some time they parted upon equal Terms, tho' the *Goths* were much terrify'd at an Action they observ'd in one of the *Saracens*. A Man whose Hair hung in a great length behind him, and who was naked all over his Body except his Privy Parts, ran with an hideous Noise into the midst of the *Goths*, and killing one of 'em, set his Mouth to the Wound and suck'd his Blood; tho' this was a customary thing with them of that Nation, as appears from the Testimony of several Authors, yet the Barbarians were so surpriz'd at such a prodigious Action, that they began to reflect on the Posture of their Affairs, and march'd with more Circumspection. Observing the large compass of the Walls, the Strength of the Place, and great Numbers of its Inhabitants, they decamp'd in the Night, and march'd Northward as far as the *Julian Alps*; having lost more Men than they destroy'd in this bold Attempt, which prov'd more Fatal to some of their Countrymen than themselves; for the Noise of their Devastations throughout *Thrace* were no sooner reported in the East, but all the Provinces were

A strange Action of a Saracen.

in a great Consternation, expecting the Storm would presently be at their own Doors, by reason of the great Multitude of *Goths* which were then Quarter'd in the several Forts and Cities of those Parts, tho' under the Command of *Roman* Officers, who they made no doubt would readily rise and join with their Countrymen, should they in the Course of their Rovings move that way; but *Julius*, who commanded in the East as General of the *Roman* Armies, enter'd upon a safe and wholesome, but a severe and bloody Course to prevent any Danger that might arise from 'em. By Letters sent secretly to their Officers, he order'd 'em all to be drawn out in the Fields adjoining to their respective Quarters at one and the same time, under a Pretence of receiving their Pay, and to be all put to the Sword. This prudent Council was put in Execution without any Noise or Delay, and the Eastern Provinces were thereby deliver'd from those great Dangers they had just reason to apprehend. *Gratian* being inform'd of his Uncle's Death, and the great loss the *Romans* had sustain'd in the late Battle, went presently to *Sirmium*, there to take such Measures, and follow such Councils as the Necessity of his Affairs suggested to him; and being join'd by all the Forces he could raise, he march'd through *Pannonia*, *Mysia*, and *Thrace*, and arriv'd at *Constantinople*, where considering with himself how many brave Officers the present War had destroy'd, and how much he stood in need of an able and faithful General, he pitch'd upon *Theodosius*, the Son of him who commanded with so much Success first here in *Britain*, and afterwards in *Africk*. He was a Person of great Abilities in Matters relating to the War, and no less capable of managing State Affairs, and governing in Times of Peace, of all which he had given extraordinary Proofs, tho'
upon

All the Goths put to the Sword in the East.

upon the Account of some Faction in *Spain*, his own Country, he was at present laid aside, and led a private retir'd Life. Him *Gratian* immediately sent for, and in the mean time named *Ausonius* and *Olybrius* Consuls for the Year ensuing. *Ausonius* was a Native of *Burdeaux*, had been the Emperor's Tutor, and was one of the most famous Poets of his Time; tho' he fell short of that Beauty and Purity in his Writings, which so evidently distinguish those of the *Augustean* Age.

Theodosius, in Obedience to the Emperor, arrived at Court, and had Orders to command in the East; and some say, that he immediately thereupon enter'd into Action with the Barbarians, and obtain'd a memorable Victory over 'em: This is not very likely, if we consider the Silence of the ancient Writers in this Particular, and that within a Month after, being with *Gratian* at *Sirmium*, he was declared by him his Collegue in the Empire.

THEODO-
SIUS.

For *Gratian* observing the Necessities to which the State was reduc'd, and the imminent Dangers that threaten'd the Empire, how the *Goths* on one side continu'd to infest it, and were raging in the very Bowels of it; how on the other the *Germans*, taking the advantage of his Absence, were again up in Arms, and were making Work enough for him in *Gaul*, he willingly inclin'd to the Advice of those, who persuaded him to assume *Theodosius* for his Partner in the Supream Power. Whereupon summoning the Nobility together, he addrels'd himself in a Speech to *Theodosius*, and told him he had resolv'd to commit the Care of the East to his Charge. *Theodosius* thank'd him, in a modest Answer, for the great Honour he intended him, but endeavour'd to excuse himself, declaring the Burden to be greater than he was able to undergo. However *Gratian* still persisted in his Design, and so *Theodosius* was
declared

A.D. 379.

declared Emperor on the 16th of *January*, when he was Thirty three Years old, *A.D.* 379. *Aufonius* and *Olybrius* being Confuls.

After *Gratian* had taken this Order for the Settlement and Security of the Eaft, he left *Sirmium* in order to return to *Gaul*, into which he heard the *Germans*, having broken through the Borders, were lately fallen. He march'd therefore towards it with all Expedition, and at *Milan* publifhes an Edict, forbidding any under the fevereft Penalties to harbour or conceal thofe who deferted their Colours, a thing at that time very much in practice. From *Milan* he proceeded on his Progrefs through *Rhetia*, and vifited the *Sequani* and *Germania Prima*, and by little more than his Appearance in thofe Parts reftrain'd the Motions of the *Germans*, and fettling the Affairs of that Country he return'd to *Triers*, having much about this time iffued out another Edict, forbidding Hereticks to form any publick Affemblies throughout the Empire.

Gratian being departed from *Sirmium*, *Theodofius* remov'd to *Theffalonica*, where he gain'd very much upon the Minds of the People, through the eafie Accefs to his Perfon, and his obliging Carriage to thofe who had any Bufinefs with him, relating either to the Publick, or their own private Concerns. Here he began his firft Preparations againft the *Goths*, who having in frefh Numbers pafs'd the *Ifter* grew very burdenfome to the Provinces. They were grown fo numerous in *Thrace*, all which they had by this time over-run, that the *Roman* Forces difpofed in Garrifons throughout the Country, dar'd not fo much as look abroad, much lefs come to any Engagement in the open Field. Here our beft Guide, *Ammianus*, has left us, who concluded his Hiftory prefently after the Death of *Valens*; and other Authors, who wrote of the Actions perform'd

againft

against the Barbarians, are so inconsistent with each other, so obscure in their Accounts, and frequently so contradictory to themselves, that a Writer ought to be very cautious of what he relates upon their Authority. Some say *Theodosius* march'd in Person against 'em, fought 'em, and gave 'em a total Defeat. Others, that whilst he continu'd at *Thessalonica*, one *Modares*, a Man of Royal Birth among the *Scythians*, having embrac'd the *Roman* Interest, and perform'd some signal Services under 'em, was preferr'd to a considerable Command in the Army. That he leading his Men up to a Hill, from whence he had a fair Prospect of the adjacent Country, discover'd the Barbarians, who had abus'd the Advantages the fruitful Plains afforded, and were for the most part overcome with Excess of Wine. Whereupon he order'd his Troops to leave their heavy Armour behind, and with their Swords in hand fall upon them who were by this time unable to defend themselves. This was speedily executed, and the Barbarians were put all to the Sword, many of 'em dying without being sensible who they were that hurt 'em. In their Camp, which they plunder'd, they found four thousand Waggons full of their Wives and Children, with an answerable number of Slaves, besides several who follow'd on foot, and were to ride when their Turns came, for there was not room sufficient in their Carriages to receive 'em all at once. And in this manner *Zozimus* tells us *Thrace* was preserv'd from an approaching Ruin, which he attributes to the Conduct of *Modares*, and not to the Prudence and Circumspection of *Theodosius*, who, if we may believe him, behav'd himself unworthy the high Dignity to which he was advanc'd; for he inveighs against him in Terms better becoming the Virulence of a Declaimer, than the Integrity of an Historian. But as he appears grosly parti-

al

al in many other Passages of his History, so is he no less to be suspected in this; for besides that he is not able to conceal the Rancor of his Heart, and his Zeal for the Pagan Worship, several Laws made by *Theodosius* at that time, especially some relating to the Army, wipe off those Aspersions he has flung at random upon him, and argue him as void of good Manners as of Judgment. To all which we may add, that in those things for which he reprehends and taxes *Theodosius*, few or no other Writers agree with him; but where he condescends to make him some Allowances due to his Prudence and Success, he therein concurs with the rest of the Authors, who have written of those Times, whether Christian or Heathen. He confesses that his generous Behaviour and Magnificence towards *Athanarich*, a *Scythian* Prince we had occasion to mention before, wrought so much upon the *Scythians* who attended him to *Constantinople*, that they return'd home, in high Admiration of *Theodosius* his Goodness, and resolv'd no more to molest the *Romans*; and some who staid behind undertook to defend the Bank of the River, and freed the *Roman* Territories from any Incursions for a long time after. He tells us he overthrew the *Scyri* and *Carpadoca*, who had join'd themselves with the *Hunns*, and compell'd 'em to return home; that by this, and some other successful Exploits, the Soldiers began to re-assume their former Courage, and breath with new Hopes, notwithstanding the many Difficulties which for a long time had lain heavy upon the Empire, which seem'd now by *Theodosius* his Vigilance to be recover'd from its former Distempers. This Account of *Theodosius* his Success is no more than what is attested by several other Writers, who agree with him in his Commendations of *Theodosius* his Clemency and singular good Nature; by the Force and Efficacy of which

which Weapon, more prevalent than his Garrisons, Legions and Cohorts, saith *Themistius*, he extinguish'd the *Scythian* Flame, though it had for a long time raged with a resistless Fury throughout *Thrace*, which groan'd with the Weight of the Barbarians that rush'd in upon it, whilst the Banks of the *Danube* vomited forth Battels that laid whole Provinces waste in a moment. *Orosius* writes further, that all the Nations of the *Goths*, charm'd with the Virtue and Mildness of *Theodosius*, renounc'd all farther thoughts of War and submitted themselves to the Laws of the *Roman* Empire: Adding, that at the same time the *Persians* voluntarily sent their Embassadors to *Constantinople* to sollicit a Peace, whereupon a League was concluded, of which all the East reaped the Benefit for a long time after.

Tho' *Zozimus* charges this Emperor with many enormous Corruptions, which he suffer'd to be intromitted into his Court and his Camp, yet we are assured that he effected a thorough Reformation in both. He put a stop to the ill Practices that had been us'd for a long time in raising the *Tirones*, or Recruits for the Army; publish'd a Law, which he caus'd exactly to be observ'd, against corrupt Judges; enlarg'd the Authority of the *Præfecti Prætorio*, who had thereby a full Power to punish the Misdemeanors of Governors in the Provinces; he restrain'd the unlimited Licence of Informers, and sufficiently discourag'd a great Vice, natural to Courtiers in almost all Reigns, that of begging Men's Estates; and whereas some Governors of Provinces, by a shameful Abuse of their Power, often terrify'd Men into Donations, wherein they gave a great part of their Estates to them, to the apparent Prejudice, and sometimes utter Ruin of their Families, he declared all such Donations to be void, whether made to the Governors themselves,

O   er

or any of their Relations; he reform'd several Abuses too much practised by the Receivers of the Revenue, which were thereby improved to a very great degree; and by a very wholesome Law ordain'd, that those who had been Governors of Provinces, should, after the time of their Government was expir'd, remain in the respective Province for two or three Months, there to answer whatever the Provincials could alledge against 'em in reference to their Male-Administration, and made 'em responsible not only for whatever Injuries they had done themselves, but for the Insolences committed by their inferior Officers. One *Natalis*, who had formerly commanded in *Sardinia*, gave occasion to this Law: He, in the former Reign, had cruelly oppress'd the Inhabitants of that Province, and was got out of their reach, before they had time to complain to those who had the proper Cognizance of it; but *Theodosius* sent him back into the Island, and subjected him to the Inquisition of the Law, and to prevent the like Oppressions for the future, publish'd the forementioned Edict.

These Laws and Ordinances sufficiently clear him from the Imputation of that heavy Charge *Zozimus* has brought against him, whose greatest Quarrel to him was that he was a Christian, in the Purity of which Faith he persisted, at a time when the Church was almost rent in pieces by innumerable Heresies and Schisms. One *Maximus*, a *Cynic* Philosopher, had lately embrac'd Christianity, in the Defence of which he writ with much Spirit and Judgment, both against the *Arians* and Heathens, for which in *Valens* his Reign he had suffer'd much Persecution, and was banish'd into the Desart of *O-*

Commotions at Constantinople *asis*. He was now return'd to *Constantinople*, and was recommended by *Peter* of *Alexandria* to *Gregory Nazianzen*, whom the People of the City had
elected

elected for their Bishop, into which Office the *Arians* had in *Valens* his Reign thrust one of their own Faction. *Gregory* received *Maximus* with much Tenderness, and recommended him to the People, as one whom Jesus Christ had thought worthy to suffer for his Name sake, and little thought a Man of his exemplary Sanctity should be animated with the Spirit of Pride and Ambition. *Maximus* had, either by the Appearance of his good Qualities, or his Promises and Presents, so far gain'd the Good-will of *Peter* Bishop of *Alexandria*, that he resolv'd blindly to espouse and favour his Interest: Accordingly he dispatch'd seven Orthodox Bishops to *Constantinople*, whom St. *Gregory* entertain'd with much Civility, and commended 'em in his Sermons as Prelates truly zealous for the Faith. Some time after an Indisposition of Health obliged him to retire into the Country for a few Days, for the Benefit of the Air; and in his Absence these Bishops got by Night into the Church *of the Resurrection*, where they ordain'd *Maximus* Bishop of *Constantinople* in the room of *Gregory*: In the Morning the People and the Priests, who were of *Gregory*'s Party, and even the *Arians* themselves, offended at so bold an Attempt, came in a great Body and forc'd *Maximus* and his Ordainers out of the Church; notwithstanding which they persisted still in their Design, and getting into a private House they cut off *Maximus* his Hair, which he wore very long after the Mode of the *Cynic* Philosophers, and confirm'd him Bishop. The People were so provok'd at this their Obstinacy, that they chaced the new Prelate out of the City, and sent for St. *Gregory*; who returning, convinc'd some who had been induced to adhere to *Maximus*, of his sinister Practices, and composed the Minds of the People. From hence we may learn, that the Life and Nature of Chri-

Christianity does not consist in an outward Profession of it, however formal and zealous, but in an inward Purity of the Mind, which none can counterfeit, and is the immediate Gift of God. These Practices at *Constantinople*, and some fresh Attempts of the *Arians*, caus'd *Theodosius* to summon the second General or Oecumenical Council, which was celebrated in that City by 150 Orthodox Bishops.

<small>Arcadius declared Augustus. A. D. 383.</small>

Sometime after this *Theodosius* advanc'd his Son *Arcadius*, whom he had by the Empress *Placilla*, to the Imperial Dignity. This Ceremony was perform'd on the 16th of *January*, *Arcadius* being then six, or as some will have it eight Years of Age. After he had made him Emperor, his first Care was to give him an Education proper for a Person that was to move in so high a Sphere, and to that purpose desired *Gratian* by Letters to send him some pious and learned Man, whom he thought fit for so great an Undertaking. Hereupon *Gratian*, at the Recommendation of *Damasus* Bishop of *Rome*, made choice of *Arsenius* a Deacon of the *Roman* Church, a Person eminent for Piety and Learning.

Upon his Arrival at *Constantinople* the Emperor resign'd up his Sons, together with *Nebridius* their Cousin-German, to his Care, telling him *That for the future he should look on him as their Father more than himself*: Implying by it, that he desired him to use the same Authority over, and Affection towards 'em, as a Father doth to his Children; and that he expected his Sons should pay him a Respect equal to that which is due to a Parent. Accordingly coming one Day into the School he found *Arsenius* standing, and *Arcadius*, whom he was instructing, sitting down, at which Sight he was angry, and reprehended *Arsenius* for not preserving the Dignity of his Office. To this *Arsenius* reply'd, *That it by no means became him to sit in the Pre-*

Presence of an Emperor; upon which *Theodosius* took the Diadem from off *Arcadius* his Head, and made *Arsenius* sit down whilst the young Emperor receiv'd his Instructions standing, and bare-headed, as a Scholar ought; adding, *That his Son would be unworthy the Empire, if to Knowledge he did not add Goodness and the Fear of God.* *Arsenius* omitted nothing requisite to the informing a Prince, in whose Education a great part of Mankind was so nearly concern'd; but he found his Scholar was not so Docile and Tractable as he desir'd, for being constrain'd to chastise him one Day for a very considerable Fault, he receiv'd his Correction with so much Indignation, that he immediately plotted against his Master's Life. *Arsenius* being inform'd of it retir'd secretly from Court, and join'd himself to some *Anchorets* in *Egypt*, where he liv'd all the rest of his Days, and dy'd Famous for his Sanctity.

Gratian had upon all Occasions show'd himself very averse to the Heathen Superstitions, depriving the Priests of the Revenue that had been assign'd for their Subsistance. He refus'd the Title of *Chief-Priest*, which had been offer'd him, being of Opinion it favour'd too much of the ancient Idolatry; these, and other Provocations, upon the account of Religion, render'd him odious to the Heathens, whose manner of Worship they were afraid he intended to extirpate; and this made 'em cast their Eyes upon *Maximus*, who was then aiming at great things here in *Britain*, where he had perform'd many brave Exploits against the *Scots*, whose King *Eugenius*, he defeated and kill'd in Battel. The Writers of those Times are not agreed upon the Place of his Birth; some say he was a *Spaniard*, others that he was Born in this Island; but of what Country soever he was, he gave out that he was

Maximus Usurps.

descended from *Constantine* the Great, and accordingly call'd himself *Fl. Clemens Maximus*; and the better to ingratiate himself with the Soldiers, pretended that he was join'd in Affinity with *Theodosius*, with whose Participation and Consent he had thus set up for himself. *Gratian* at first despis'd him as a mean Man, unable to accomplish his Treasonable Designs, and therefore sent only a few mercenary *Alans* against him, whom indeed some accus'd him for favouring too much. The old *Roman* Soldiers were highly affronted at this Preference, which they thought the Emperor gave the Barbarians, on whose Fidelity and Courage he seem'd chiefly to rely. This Dissatisfaction was improv'd by some who were disaffected to *Gratian*, and wrought so much upon the Army that in great Anger they revolted to *Maximus*, from whom they were promis'd all manner of Favours. A Revolt so unexpected made *Gratian* fly from *Triers* in great Consternation to *Paris*, whither the Usurper, after he had easily defeated the *Alans*, follow'd, and encamp'd near him. For five Days together both Armies continu'd in their Posts without any Action, except a few Skirmishes, in which the Advantage was great on neither side, 'till first the *Moors*, and then the rest of the Army shamefully deserted the Prince, and went over to *Maximus*. *Gratian* seeing himself thus abandon'd by his Subjects fled in great haste towards the South, attended by no more than three hunder'd Horse, and at last got into *Lyons*, after he had been refus'd Admittance into other Cities. *Maximus* follow'd him close upon the Heels with his whole Army, and attempted at first by plain Force to destroy him; but being disappointed in that, he had recourse to a Stratagem, in which he succeeded. He procur'd some about *Gratian* to inform him, that his Wife was

was coming to him, and intended to meet him on this fide the *Rhône*, which runs by the City. This News highly pleas'd the unfortunate Prince, who was over-joy'd to hear the Emprefs was fo near at Hand, and without any Hefitation went forth to meet her. In the mean time a Ruffian had by *Maximus* his Procurement difpos'd of himfelf in a Litter, in which *Gratian* was made to believe the Emprefs was. The Emperor with open Arms ftood ready to receive her, and the Villain fuddenly ftarted forth, and without any remorfe depriv'd him of Life, whom he ought to have defended at the certain hazard of his own. Thus fell *Gratian* by the Hands of a barbarous Traitor, call'd *Andragathius*, in the Flower of his Age, having hardly liv'd Twenty eight Years, and reign'd Sixteen. He was a Prince on whom the moft inveterate of Pagan Writers have faften'd no ill Character; for not to mention his School-mafter *Aufonius*, they all agree that he was Modeft, Gentle, Eloquent and Sincere; that he was Abftemious, Sober, Frugal, but not Parcimonious; Devout, but no way Superftitious. They charge him with following the Sports of the Field, and other Recreations too much, neglecting in the mean time the weighty Affairs of the Empire; this may juftly be imputed to his Youth, and want of Confideration, and for which there is great reafon to think he would have made large Amends in his riper Years; as may be gather'd from his Exploits againft the *Germans*, his Zeal in affifting his Uncle *Valens*, and Prudence in promoting *Theodofius*, and thereby providing for the Security of the Eaft. Indeed *Aufonius* launches out largely in his Commendation, tho' there is nothing contain'd in his whole Panegyrick, that feems to contradict the Senfe other Writers had of him, whether Chriftian or Heathen. In a Word, he was worthy

Gratian Slain.

His Character.

a longer Life, but is not the only good Prince whom Treason and Ambition have brought to an untimely Death.

III. We ought not to wonder if *Maximus*, who had stain'd his Hands in the Blood of his lawful Soveraign, should deny him decent Burial after he had procur'd him to be barbarously murder'd; it was an Inhumanity worthy of a Tyrant and Usurper, whose Cruelty was not satisfy'd with his Death, but rag'd with an implacable Thirst against those whose Loyal Services had rais'd 'em into any degree of Favour with their deceas'd Master. Some Writers have affirm'd that *Merobaudes*, the Consul for this Year, was privy to *Maximus* his Proceedings, and consenting to the Death of *Gratian*, for which, if it be true, the Tyrant made him but an ill return; for before the Year was expir'd he put him to Death, as he did *Ballio* and several others, whom he suspected to be favourable to the Memory of *Gratian*, who he thought still surviv'd in their Affections towards him, and render'd his Usurpation weak and insecure. As soon as he found all things succeeded according to his Desire and Expectation, either because he thought himself safe by this time in his new Dignity, or rather to strengthen and confirm himself in it, he sent his Embassadors to *Theodosius*, not to ask his Pardon for what he had acted against *Gratian*, but *to offer Peace, and upon his Acceptance of it to Unite himself in a League with him against the Enemies of the* Roman *Empire; or in case he rejected that Friendly Offer, to denounce War against him, which must be bloody in the Course of it, and doubtful in the Issue.*

Theodosius, concealing his Thoughts, receiv'd the Embassadors very honourably, and in appearance com-

comply'd with the Tyrant's Demands; for he was afraid left, upon his Refusal, he should Invade *Italy* and Surprize *Valentinian*, who had neither Experience, nor Forces sufficient to make Head against so powerful an Enemy, who was now become Master of *Gaul* and *Spain*; and *Valentinian* himself was so sensible of the Danger he was in, and jealous of the Integrity of some that were near him, that he sent St. *Ambrose*, Bishop of *Milan*, to see if upon the Reputation of his Wisdom and Sanctity, he could restrain the Usurper's extravagant Thirst of Empire, and perfuade him to continue on that side the *Alps*. *Maximus* seem'd well pleas'd with St. *Ambrose* his Errand, either because he had not as yet settled his Affairs in *Gaul* and *Britain*, or at present was in want of Mony, the Sinews of War, without which his future Attempts would be vain and ineffectual. He caress'd St. *Ambrose* in an extraordinary manner, and ask'd him why *Valentinian* himself did not come with him, affirming he would have been equally welcome to his Arms, as if he had been his own Son. St. *Ambrose* made a very handsome Excuse for *Valentinian*, telling him he was too Young to attempt a Journey over the *Alps* at so unseasonable a time of the Year; and concluded that he was not come to give him an Account of his Master's Actions, but settle a mutual Confidence and Agreement between 'em, if he thought fit to accept of it; and in short he so dexterously amus'd *Maximus*, that a Peace was concluded according to his Desire.

This Year *Theodosius*, who earnestly endeavour'd to establish a perfect Union in the Church, summon'd another Council to sit at *Constantinople*, sending not only for the Orthodox Bishops, but the *Arians, Eunomians, Novatians*, and others; and having propos'd a means of an Accommodation between

tween 'em, he outwardly caress'd the Heretick Prelates during the Conference, hoping, by such a Condescension, to make 'em more inclinable to a Compliance. This was observ'd by *Amphilochius*, Bishop of *Iconium*, a Person Eminent for his Doctrine and Piety, who now began to be afraid the Emperor would suffer himself to be seduc'd by the crafty Insinuations of the *Arians*; and when the other Bishops, upon his Entrance into the Place where the Council was celebrated, rose and paid *Theodosius* the accustom'd Honours, observing the same to his Son *Arcadius*, whom he had lately declar'd Emperor, *Amphilochius* saluted the Father, but took no manner of notice of *Arcadius*, which *Theodosius* imputing to a Mistake, commanded him to come and render the same Honours to *Arcadius*; the Bishop reply'd, He had done his Duty in that he had honour'd the Father: This Answer offended *Theodosius*, who thought both himself and his Son highly injur'd in it, upon which *Amphilochius* said aloud, *Your Majesty is in the right in requiring the same Honours to be paid to your Son, which are due to your self; be pleas'd to judge therefore what an heinous Offence they commit against God the Father, who are so far from giving the Son the Honour due to his Name, that they dare most impiously to revile and blaspheme it.* *Theodosius* was so touch'd with this seasonable Answer, that he ever after espous'd the Orthodox Interest with more Zeal, and prohibited the *Arians* from holding any Publick Assemblies.

He had lately by his Armies in the East obtain'd several Advantages over the *Persians*, who therefore by their Embassadors at *Constantinople* desir'd a Peace, which *Theodosius*, whose main Care was the Safety and Prosperity of the Empire, readily granted; and tho' he had then great Armies on Foot in several

several Quarters of the Empire, he at a great Expence beautify'd and improv'd the City, by building several Aqueducts, and a Capacious Port, from whence, as some have conceiv'd, the *Turks* at this Day call *Constantinople* it self, by way of Eminence, the *Port*; by several wholesom Laws and Royal Immunities he eas'd the Inhabitants of such Hardships, as either the Corruption or Remissness of former Reigns had thrown upon 'em. This Year was *Honorius* his second Son Born, in the Consulate of *Fl. Ricimeres*, and *Fl. Clearchus*, and the Year following had *Fl. Arcadius*, and *Fl. Bauto* for Consuls. About this time *Theodosius* lost his Wife *Placilla*, or *Flaccilla*, a Lady as remarkable for her Piety and Munificence, as she was illustrious for her Dignity, with which she never appear'd in the least Elevated, but rather the more Humble and Devout; she took care often to remind the Emperor of his former Condition, that he might behave himself in his exalted Fortune with a Heart full of Gratitude and Submission to the Will of God, by whom he Reign'd. She not only made a Provision for the Maintenance of the Sick and Infirm, but would her self often Visit 'em in Person, and Administer to 'em: These extraordinary Qualities endear'd her to the Fathers of the Church, who liv'd in that Age, and who have given Posterity large Commendations of her Virtues. The Emperor was sensibly touch'd at the loss of so excellent a Wife, which was follow'd by some new Commotions rais'd by the *Gruthingi*, a People unknown 'till then to other Nations, but who began now to appear on the other side of the *Ister*. They were many in Number, and provided with Arms, and whatever else was necessary for a bold Undertaking; so that breaking with ease through the Territories of other Barbarians, under the Conduct of *Odetheus*

A. D. 385.

The Death of the Empress Flaccilla.

their

their King, they came to the Banks of the River, and demanded a Paſſage over. *Promotus* was then Lieutenant for the Emperor in thoſe Parts, who, without making much Oppoſition, openly circumvented 'em by a Stratagem. He procur'd ſome in whom he could confide, and were ſkilful in the Language of the Barbarians, to go in the nature of Deſerters over to 'em; they being brought to the King undertook, upon the Promiſe of a good Reward, to conduct 'em ſafely over the River, and betray the *Roman* Commander and his Army into their Hands. The King readily accepted of the Conditions, and Matters were duly concerted between 'em for the Accompliſhment of the intended Deſign; but *Promotus* being inform'd of all by his induſtrious Emiſſaries, was ſo prepar'd to receive thoſe, who expected to meet with no Oppoſition, that they were all drown'd before they could reach the oppoſite Shore, and they who continu'd ſtill on the other ſide, were either taken or put to Flight; the *Romans* plunder'd their Camp, in which they found a very great Booty, beſides Multitudes of Women and Children, who with the Priſoners taken in the Fight were ſent to *Theodoſius*, who receiv'd 'em more favourably than they expected, releas'd 'em from their Bonds, regal'd 'em with Preſents, hoping by this his Humanity to purchaſe their good Will, and make uſe of 'em in the War he was now preparing againſt *Maximus*. But whilſt he was intent upon it a Sedition at *Antioch* diverted him from his Preparations, which as it was extraordinary in its kind, and brought the City into extream Danger, ſo in the Sequel it ſhow'd the Golden Temper of *Theodoſius* his Mind. His Son *Arcadius* was now in the Fifth Year of his Sovereignty, and he himſelf ready to enter into the Tenth of his own, ſo that this Year he celebrated his

Promotus Defeats the Gruthingi.

A. D. 387.

Son's

Son's *Quinquennalia*, and was making a Provision for the solemnizing his own *Decennalia*.

As it was usual with the Emperors to present the Soldiers with a Donative upon their first Promotion to the Imperial Dignity, so did they always do the like upon these Solemnities, at which time they were supposed to renew their Power, and in a manner begin their Reign afresh. The necessary Preparations for the War design'd against *Maximus*, and this Largess which the Emperor was to make, as well upon his own as his Son's Account, required a great Sum of Mony; for which reason he exacted an answerable Supply from the People. This seem'd so unreasonable an Oppression to the Inhabitants of *Antioch*, that they rais'd a great Sedition in the City, demolishing his Statues, together with those of the late Empress *Flaccilla*, those of his two Sons and of his Father *Theodosius*. *A Sedition at Antioch*

The Emperor, upon the first News of this Insurrection, was highly displeas'd, and sent away two Judges with full Powers to try and punish the Offenders; who arriving at *Antioch* first deprived the City of all her Privileges, degraded her from her Metropolitan Honour, and made *Laodicea* Metropolis of *Syria*; they commanded all the Baths, Theatres, *Forums*, and other Publick Places to be shut up; the most eminent of the City, who were known or suspected to be guilty, were apprehended, and committed to Prison, where they were presented with Tortures, and terrify'd with the sense of the Emperor's Indignation; a sufficient Number of Guards were placed in all the Quarters of the City to curb the Citizens, and restrain 'em from any new Insurrection; the Judges were busied in preparing the severest Inquisitions, and in seizing the Estates of those, who were suspected to have been the most Active, whilst the disconsolate Inhabitants had no Comfort,

Comfort, but in their Devotions, and the Sermons of St. *Chryſostome*, who then reſided in that City. A great part of the Inhabitants, and they who had been the Ring-leaders in the Uproar, when they heard how highly the Emperor was offended, eſpecially at the Indignity offer'd his deceas'd Empreſs, withdrew themſelves from the Storm which they ſaw gathering over 'em. Several Hermits, who led a retir'd Life in the adjacent Mountains, had no ſooner heard of the miſerable Condition the City was in, but they repair'd thither, and by their importunate Arguments prevail'd with the Judges to ſuſpend their farther Proceedings, 'till by ſome proper Meſſenger they had attempted to appeaſe the Emperor, and ſoften him into Pity towards 'em. The very principal Men in that flouriſhing City had been arraign'd and condemn'd, and there wanted nothing but the Execution of the Sentence pronounc'd againſt 'em; with very earneſt and repeated Importunities St. *Chryſostome* and theſe Hermits obtain'd a Reprieve from the Judges, 'till a Report of their whole Proceedings had been made to the Emperor, and his further Pleaſure were known. None ſeem'd more ready, or indeed more proper to appear before *Theodoſius* in behalf of the almoſt deſolate City, than *Flavian*, Biſhop of the Place; who foreſeeing the Danger undertook the Employment ſhortly after the Fact was committed, and before the Commiſſioners ſent by *Theodoſius* were arriv'd; and when he came to *Conſtantinople* found the Emperor highly incens'd againſt them, however by his perſuaſive Carriage and pathetical Entreaties he obtain'd his Deſire. The Emperor repreſented to him, in a long and lively Expoſtulation, the Kindneſs he had ever expreſs'd to that City, ask'd him *what ill Offices he ever had done 'em that could provoke 'em to ſo undutiful a Reſentment, which not content to offer In-*
dignities

Chap. II. XLVI. Vale. II. Theod. Arcadius.

dignities to the Living, broke out in most inhuman Fury against the Dead. He told him, *he had ever preferr'd* Antioch *to all other Cities, and in the height of his Prosperity earnestly desir'd to see it, promising more Satisfaction to himself from that than all his Imperial Pomp and outward Enjoyments.* Flavian began his Answer with a hearty Acknowledgment of their Insolence and Ingratitude, which he aggravated to the Emperor, confessing to him, *That Fire and the Sword were Punishments too mild and gentle for their Offences, of which they were now so truly sensible, and of their undutiful Returns to so indulgent a Prince, that they dreaded his Anger more than Exile or Captivity:* He reminded him of the Duty of a Christian, *who ought to imitate the Mercy and Forbearance of God Almighty*; and shew'd him how near he would approach that Divine Original, if he would restore the disconsolate City to his Grace and Favour. He told him, *he had now an Opportunity of making himself a lasting Example to all Posterity of Clemency and good Nature; that it was in his power to raise as from the dead his miserable Subjects, who in a just Sense and Apprehension of his Displeasure were dying already, even before the Sentence was denounc'd against 'em.* In a word, this admirable Speech, as it is represented at large in St. *Chrysostome*, proved so efficacious with the Emperor, that he could not restrain from Tears, but immediately sent *Flavian* back to put a stop to the Proceedings of the Commissioners, to restore the City to her ancient Liberties and Privileges, and the Citizens to his Love and Protection. The News of his Success flew quick before him to *Antioch*, and was receiv'd with so universal a Joy, that almost the whole City went out to meet their Holy Bishop on the Way, and usher'd him in with Songs and Acclamations, spending the Day in Feasts and Triumphs, as if *Antioch*

tioch had now begun, and the Day which restor'd her to her forfeited Honours, had been the first that gave a Being to 'em.

This Matter being so happily ended, *Theodosius* found himself more at leisure to prosecute his Designs against *Maximus*, who toward the latter end of this Year had broken into *Italy*, and driven away *Valentinian*, who with *Justina* his Mother, and his Sister *Galla*, fled to *Thessalonica* in *Illyricum*, whither *Theodosius* went to meet him.

For we are to understand that *Maximus*, after he had fully secured to his Obedience most of those Nations who obey'd *Gratian*, thought his Work but half done, 'till he had strengthen'd himself by the Addition of *Valentinian*'s share too, and sent him to follow his Brother's Fortune. *Valentinian* had lately sent *Domninus* a *Syrian*, in an Embassy to him. This *Domninus* was a Person of great Esteem, and particularly regarded by the Emperor, who had a great Confidence in him, and made him a Partner of all his Secrets. *Maximus* receiv'd this Embassador with great Civility, entertain'd him with much Magnificence, and express'd himself with so much Tenderness towards *Valentinian*, that he thought his Master infinitely happy in so sincere a Friend. The Tyrant had long been contriving in secret what Course he was to take to march his Army into *Italy*; the long and usual Way over the *Alps* would be dangerous for so great a Body of Men, and afford *Valentinian* time to prepare for his Reception; and to those nearer and more commodious Passages he was an utter Stranger: But now the better to compass his Designs, he deliver'd part of his Army into *Domninus* his Hands as for the Emperor's Use, to serve him against the Barbarians that began to infest *Pannonia*; with which unexpected Supply *Domninus* return'd, wonderfully exalted at the Success of his

Maximus his Policy.

his Negotiations, and march'd at the Head of his Forces the nearest and safest Way into *Italy*. *Maximus*, who found his Stratagem met with the desir'd Effect, follow'd with the rest of the Army at a convenient Distance behind, sending some light Parties before him, who were to observe the Way *Domninus* took, and intercept all they met, and by that Means keep his Expedition secret. His Orders were so exactly observ'd, that he got safe into *Italy* without meeting any Enemy to oppose him, and directed his Course immediately to *Aquileia*. *Valentinian* was so much terrify'd at his unexpected Approach, that he immediately embark'd with his Mother and Sister, and set sail for *Thessalonica*; where when he was arrived he sent and intreated *Theodosius* to chastise the Usurper, for the Injuries offer'd to the Family of *Valentinian*. Hereupon *Theodosius* remov'd with some of the Senate to *Thessalonica*, where it was resolv'd in Council to punish *Maximus*, who had not only by his treasonable Practices murder'd *Gratian* and usurp'd his Authority, but attempted the same upon *Valentinian*, and had now driven him out of his Dominions. Pursuant to this Resolution *Theodosius* prepared to march against him, and having promoted such Persons to the chief Offices in the Provinces, as he knew would in his Absence have a regard to the Good of his Subjects, he made *Promotus* General of the Foot, and *Timasius* of the Horse. He sent the Empress *Justina*, with her Son and Daughter under a good Guard to *Rome*, prudently conceiving that by their Presence they would encourage the Inhabitants to defend the City against any Attempts of *Maximus*, to whom he knew the Citizens were generally disaffected; resolving himself to march through the upper *Pannonia*, and fall on a sudden upon the Enemy from the *Appennine* Mountains. *Maximus*, who continu'd all this

Theodosius resolves to chastise Maximus.

A.D. 388.

P while

while at *Aquileia*, had notice of the Preparations that were making against him, and used all his Endeavours to disappoint and prevent him. He had by mighty Promises persuaded the Barbarians, in conjunction with the *Roman* Legions, by way of Diversion to revolt, and find *Theodosius* work in *Thrace*, and give him the more time to confirm his Power in *Italy*. Of these his Practices the Emperor had timely Intelligence, and broke all his Measures by sending a sufficient Number of Troops, that dispersed the Barbarians before they could unite themselves into any considerable Body, and having settled all things in those Quarters he prepared for his Expedition.

Maximus being inform'd that *Justina* design'd to cross the *Ionian* Gulf in her way to *Rome*, mann'd out a few Pinnaces, and sent *Andragathius* if possible to intercept her; who, tho' he used the utmost Expedition, fail'd of his Design, for she had pass'd the Gulf before his Arrival; whereupon he strengthen'd his Squadron by the Accession of several other Ships, designing to dispute the Passage with *Theodosius*, who he thought would transport his Forces over the Sea. But the Emperor, pursuant to his former Resolutions, directed his March towards *Pannonia*, and the *Appennines*; whilst *Maximus*, having as he thought secured himself of *Italy* and *Africk*, was intent upon raising Mony, making use of the vilest and most shameful Means that would serve to his Purpose, 'till the News of *Theodosius* his Preparations diverted him from his Extortions. As soon as he was inform'd of the Emperor's Motions he march'd at the Head of his Army over the *Julian Alps* into *Pannonia*, to make sure of the Passes in those Quarters, and having fortify'd *Petovio*, which was surrender'd to him, he moved with all Expedition to *Siscia*, call'd at present *Sescec*, where
he

he staid to refresh his Army. Thither *Theodosius* advanced against him, and having pass'd the *Save* he drew his Men out and offer'd him Battel, which he accepted and was defeated, tho' his Men fought with a great deal of Courage and Resolution. This Victory, which was very extraordinary, cost *Theodosius* but a few Men, the Loss of whom was more than supply'd by a part of *Maximus* his Army, which surrender'd themselves up to him. From hence he march'd against *Marcellinus*, Brother to the Usurper, who had strengthen'd himself at *Petovio*, not *Padua*, as some have mistaken it, whom he totally routed; and pursuing the course of his Fortune, he follow'd *Maximus* close upon the Heels, and sate down before *Aquileia*, where the Usurper had secured himself, and provided for a Siege, which *Theodosius* push'd on with much Vigour. They within defended themselves at first with much Bravery, but finding the Emperor resolv'd to carry the Town, and observing *Maximus* to despond, and as it were shake off that Sovereignty he had so tyrannically usurp'd, they seiz'd upon him, bound him, and presented him to *Theodosius*, having first stripp'd him of his Imperial Ornaments. The Emperor beheld him with Eyes of Compassion, and out of a just sense of Fortune's Inconstancy had pardon'd him, had not those about him perceiv'd it in his Looks, which melted with Pity towards him, and taking him out of his sight cut off his Head, without any Order from *Theodosius*. *Andragathius*, whom *Maximus* had made his Admiral, as we observ'd before, hearing of the Tyrant's Defeat as he was cruising to and fro upon the *Ionian* Bay, threw himself headlong into the Sea, there to receive the Reward due to his Cruelty and Treason: And *Victor*, the Son of *Maximus*, who had been declared *Augustus* by his Father, and left to command in *Gaul*, was defeated,

Maximus overthrown

retires to Aquileia,

where he is taken,

and beheaded.

P 2 taken,

taken, and slain, by *Arbogastes*, whom *Valentinian* had sent thither for that purpose. Thus did *Theodosius* by his Vigour and Conduct put a speedy End to a War, which at first promis'd it self a longer Continuance, and threaten'd the Empire with a great many Calamities. And the Honour and Reputation he acquir'd in his Success, was highly improv'd by his Moderation and Clemency in the Use of it; for he not only settled *Valentinian* in the peaceable Possession of *Italy*, his own Share of the Empire, but relinquish'd to him *Gaul*, and *Spain*, and *Britain*, with whatever else the Tyrant had seiz'd on after the Murder of *Gratian*, being satisfy'd with the Good he had done, without drawing any particular Advantage from it to himself. And so far was he from oppressing *Maximus* his Friends and Relations, that except two or three of the most seditious, who were put to Death as an Example of Terror to others, he pardon'd all those who had embrac'd the Usurper's Interest; so that under so merciful a Conqueror they felt not that they were conquer'd. He sent for *Maximus* his Wife and Daughters out of their Confinement, settled an honourable Pension upon 'em for their Lives, and charged a near Kinsman of their own to take care of their Interests, and see that no body oppress'd 'em.

Theodosius continu'd the rest of this Year partly at *Aquileia*, and partly at *Milan*, where he publish'd an Edict on the 9th of *October*, by which he revoked all the publick Acts made by *Maximus*, whom he terms *Infandissimus Tyrannorum*; but the Year following he went with *Valentinian* and his Son *Honorius* to *Rome*, and resided there the greatest part of the Summer. Here he was receiv'd with all the Respect due to his Person and Dignity; and whilst he was follow'd with Applauses and Acclamations from the Senate and People, for his late Success against

Marginalia: Theodosius his great Moderation and Clemency.

Marginalia: A.D. 389.

against *Maximus*, he behav'd himself in every respect with the profoundest Humility, appropriating nothing to himself, but referring all to God Almighty, who had chosen *Valentinian* and himself as his Instruments of Revenge upon a Tyrant and Usurper. During his Residence in this City he labour'd seriously in the Suppression of Idolatry, shutting up the Temples of the Heathen Deities, commanding their Statues to be remov'd from thence, and to be erected in the Publick Parts of the City to serve as Ornaments to it. The Christian Inhabitants, animated by the Zeal *Theodosius* express'd for Religion, broke down the Images, those detested Objects of Idolatry; and if we may believe *Zomsius*, seiz'd upon the precious Ornaments with which the Ignorance and Superstition of former Ages had wonderfully enrich'd 'em; and what seem'd to concern him more nearly than all the rest, burnt the Books of the *Sybills*, the Sacred Oracles of the Bigotted Heathens, and thereby gave a fatal Stroke to Paganism; from whence we may gather how much they are in the right, who affirm, that the Books that appear under that Quality at present are Suppositious, sent into the World by some Pestilent Pen in the early Days of Christianity, to pervert and corrupt a great many well-meaning Men in the Times succeeding, and give Birth to some dangerous and mortal Errors that by degrees crept into the Church. As the Emperor's Presence and Authority encourag'd the Christians at *Rome* to extirpate Idolatry, so did his Example inspire the *Alexandrians* in *Egypt* with the like Zeal, which however made a greater Noise, and occasion'd the Effusion of some Blood. *Theophilus*, Bishop of *Alexandria*, had begg'd of the Emperor an old Heathen Temple, at that time ruin'd and forsaken, to convert it to a Christian Church, to which the

He commanded the Heathen Temples at Rome to be shut up.

A bloody Tumult at Alexandria.

Emperor readily condescended. As they were clearing it of the Rubbish, the Workmen found among the Ruins several filthy obscene Figures of *Priapus*, which the Bishop order'd to be expos'd in Publick, to ridicule the Superstition of the ancient *Egyptians*; and about the same time they discover'd their Subterraneous Grottoes, where they usually perform'd their abominable Sacrifices. The Heathens, exceedingly scandaliz'd at these Affronts, fell in great Fury upon the Christians, some of whom they wounded, others they kill'd; and seizing upon the Temple of *Serapis*, built upon a Hill by one of the first Kings of *Egypt*, call'd *Sesostris*, they fortify'd it, and in their frequent Excursions seiz'd upon the Christians, whom they constrain'd to Sacrifice to their Idol, or upon their Refusal they fix'd 'em on a Cross, where they were put to unspeakable Torments. The Emperor being inform'd of this Tumult, gave Order to the Magistrates of the City, *Not to revenge upon the* Pagans *the Death of those who had obtain'd the Crown of Martyrdom at their Hands, but rather pardon 'em, and try by gentle Methods to win 'em over to Christianity*; but however he commanded 'em *to destroy all the Temples that had given Birth to the Sedition*; these Orders were exactly observ'd to the great Joy of the Christians, and Confusion of their Adversaries, who had been taught by their Traditions, that the Inundations of the River *Nile*, from whence proceeded the Fertility of their Country, was owing to the benign Influence of their God *Serapis*; and they concluded therefore, that now he was destroy'd, the River would no longer overflow, the Consequence of which would be an universal Famine; but when afterwards they observ'd on the contrary, that the *Nile* swell'd to a much higher degree than had been known in the Memory of Man, and thereby

thereby produc'd a great Plenty of all manner of Provisions, a great many of the Heathens renounc'd their ancient Errors, and worshipp'd the God of the Christians, who makes the Sun to rise, and the Rain descend upon the Earth.

Theodosius, before he left *Rome*, is said effectually to have reform'd two abominable Abuses, which were at that time a great Scandal and Disgrace to that Queen of Cities, as *Socrates* terms her; there were large and ancient Buildings in *Rome*, reserv'd as Store-houses of Bread wherewith the City was supply'd; under these Buildings were the Bakehouses, and on each side of 'em, through the Connivance of the Overseers, were built Victualling and Tipling Houses, where Women were entertain'd for lewd Purposes, and many who resorted thither, either to satisfie their Hunger, or gratifie their Lust, were stripp'd of all they had, and commonly so dispos'd of, by means of a private Conveyance out of those Tipling Houses into the blind Bake-house beneath, where they were compell'd to Grind, and so kept in perpetual Slavery, that their Friends could never hear of 'em after. It happen'd that one of the Emperor's Soldiers was thrown into this Hole, and so receiv'd into the blind Bake-house, where, finding himself like to be made a Slave, he drew his Dagger, of which they had forgot to Disarm him, and killing all those that oppos'd his Passage he escap'd, and got means to inform the Emperor of it, who immediately commanded the Overseers to be punish'd as they deserv'd, and order'd their Houses, the Receptacles of Theives, to be demolish'd. The other Abuse, which he took care to have remov'd, was this. It was customary in *Rome* to inflict such a Punishment on a Woman taken in Adultery, as remov'd not the Sin, but increas'd the Vice, for they confin'd her to narrow Stews, where

Theodosius reforms some things at Rome.

she was compell'd to Prostitute her self, without any Shame, to such Adventurers as were provided for her; and whilst the Deed was doing her Neighbours were inform'd by the means of some sounding Vessel prepar'd for that purpose, that she was that Moment under Correction; this horrible Custom *Theodosius* abolish'd, and enacted other Laws for the Punishment of Women taken in Adultery. For the last of these Stories the Reader has no more than *Socrates* his Word, and therefore he is at Liberty to believe it or not, but the other is supported with better Authority.

A. D. 390.

From *Rome* both the Emperors remov'd by the way of *Valentia* to *Milan*, when *Valentinian* was declared the fourth time Consul, together with *Neotherius*, and as if he had some Jealousie of what shortly after follow'd, he publish'd an Order that no one should be admitted to attend upon his Person, but such as had first receiv'd his own Approbation; the Year following *Theodosius* remov'd towards the East, being accompany'd by *Valentinian* as far as *Aquileia*, where he left him, and proceeding on his Way to *Constantinople*. He arriv'd at *Thessalonica*, where he found the Affairs of *Macedonia* to be in a great Confusion; for the Barbarians, who at the Instigation of *Maximus*, had revolted just as he was ent'ring upon his Expedition against the Usurper, and upon his sending a part of his Forces to reduce 'em, had secured themselves among the Lakes and Fastnesses in the Woods, taking the Advantage of his Absence, broke out of their Holds, and ravaged *Thessaly* and *Macedonia* without any Opposition, disposing of the Lives and Fortunes of the Inhabitants at their own Pleasures; but as soon as they heard of the Emperor's Success, and his Return, they again withdrew into their Dens, from whence they stole out secretly in the Night-time, and seizing on whatever came in their way, they

return'd

return'd with their Booty before the Morning Light. These secret Excursions, and nocturnal Depredations, made *Theodosius* imagine the Aggressors were Spirits and Apparitions, rather than Men; but being resolv'd, if possible, to find out the Truth, without discovering his Designs to any one, he made choice of Five Persons in whom he could trust to attend him, ordering 'em to take three or four spare Horses a-peice, that they might shift as often as there was occasion. Thus attended, and in a Disguise, he rang'd about the Country, receiving from the Peasants such Refreshments as their Cottages could afford him. At length he came to a small Inn, kept by an old Woman, who receiv'd him very civilly, entertaining him with Wine and what other Conveniences she had in the House, and Night coming on he was persuaded to Lodge there 'till the Morning; when he was retir'd into his Chamber he observ'd a certain Man, who declin'd Conversing with him, and seem'd desirous to conceal himself. The Emperor surpriz'd at his Carriage calls for his Hostess, and demands of her who that Person was; she answer'd, that who he was she knew not, but ever since the News of the Emperor's Return with the Army out of the West this Man had lodg'd at her House, going out in the Morning, and continuing abroad all Day, but at Night repaired home, as from Work, to his Supper and his Lodging, for which he honestly paid her. Upon this Information the Emperor order'd the Man to be seiz'd, and commanded him to declare who and what he was; which he refus'd with much Obstinacy, 'till the Emperor had declared himself to him, and his Followers had with several Tortures forced the Truth out of him; then he confess'd that he was employ'd, as a Spy, by the Barbarians that lay among the Bogs, to give 'em Intelligence from

time

time to time where he lay with his Army, and what Persons and Places lay the most commodious for their Incursions.

Defeats the Barbarians. Hereupon the Emperor caus'd his Head to be struck off, and returning early the next Morning to the Army, led his Soldiers to that Place where he had learnt from the Spy the Barbarians were lodg'd, and falling at an Advantage upon 'em destroy'd a great Number of 'em, killing the most resolute as they defended themselves in the Bogs, and dragging the rest out of their Retirements. One *Timasius* had at this time a Principal Command in the Army, who, according to *Zosimus*, could not but admire the extraordinary Courage of the Emperor, who appear'd the foremost in all Dangers; he conceiving the greatest number of the Barbarians to be Slain, and that the rest could not escape them, whom therefore they might pursue at their leisure, desir'd the Emperor would allow the weary and hungry Soldiers time to refresh themselves after so warm and desperate a Service, to which *Theodosius* readily consented, so that sounding a Retreat they gave over the Pursuit, and falling too with more Appetite than Discretion, they first overcame themselves with Wine, and then fell fast asleep, and thereby gave the Barbarians an Advantage they were too wary to omit. They fell with great Fury upon the *Romans*, who were unprepar'd to defend themselves against an Enemy they thought already vanquish'd, and had destroy'd the Emperor himself, had he not been seasonably reliev'd by *Promotus*, who rescu'd his Master at the great Hazard of his own Life. This piece of Service, undoubtedly deserv'd a great Reward, but such, according to *Zosimus*, was the unhappy Influence *Rufinus*, a Person we shall hear more of hereafter, had upon this Emperor, that he procur'd him to be

He is in great Danger.

murder'd; tho' whether this was done by *Theodosius* his Privity, or *Rufinus* his treacherous Practices with the Barbarians, by whose Hands he fell, remains still a Doubt among the other Historians of those Times. Certain it is *Rufinus* was a Person of great Interest with the Emperor, and being a Man of a bold aspiring Temper, he look'd on *Promotus* as a great Obstacle to his ambitious Designs.

The Emperor had hitherto try'd by Force of Arms to restrain those Rovers, but the more effectually to suppress 'em he publish'd a Law, by which the Provincials of *Macedonia* had Power to resist, and cut off those who enter'd upon their Possessions, or lay lurking in the High-way; thereby abrogating an old Edict, forbidding any private Man to levy War without the Knowledge and Approbation of the Emperor.

At his Arrival at *Constantinople*, Fl. *Arcadius* the second time, and *Rufinus* were declared Consuls; here finding himself for the present free from any Foreign Disturbances, he began diligently to enquire into the Corruptions that had lately crept into the State, reforming by several wholesom but severe Laws a great many Abuses, that during the Publick Calamities had been practised by his Officers. From this his Fatherly Care he was diverted by News out of the West, where *Valentinian* was found strangled in his Palace. *Theodosius*, during his Stay in *Italy*, had, as we observ'd before, us'd all means to extirpate Heathenism, restraining by his Authority those who appear'd the most zealous Patrons for it; but at his Return they began to conceive new Hopes, and apply'd to *Valentinian* for his Favour and Protection, which when they were deny'd they enter'd upon new Measures, and consulted how to purchase a Toleration at the price of Treason. *Arbogastes*, a *Frank* by Nation, had at this time

A. D. 392.

time the Chief Command in the Army; he ow'd his firſt Preferment to *Gratian,* and after his Death wonderfully gain'd upon the Soldiers, who eſteem'd him for his Experience in Military Affairs, and his great Contempt of Mony, and made him General without the Participation of *Valentinian,* ſo that he arrogated a Power to himſelf of controlling the Emperor, and reprehending him for whatever he thought done amiſs. To him the diſaffected Party apply'd themſelves; and encourag'd him to deſtroy that Power he had already ſupplanted. About this time *Valentinian* was inform'd the Barbarians began to threaten the Borders of *Italy,* and being then in *Gaul* reſolv'd to march againſt 'em, and chaſtiſe their Inſolence; but whilſt he was conſulting in Council the propereſt Means to forward his Expedition, he was thwarted in all his Deſigns by *Arbogaſtes,* with whoſe Inſolence he was ſo much provok'd, that he drew out his Sword, and attempted to kill him, declaring he had rather kill himſelf than bear the Title of Emperor without enjoying the Authority; but being with-held by ſome who ſtood near him, he threw *Arbogaſtes* a Paper, which contain'd an Abrogation of his Command: *Arbogaſtes,* when he had peruſ'd the Contents of it, tore it in pieces, declaring that he receiv'd not his Authority from him, nor ſhould it be in his Power to diveſt him of it; and from this time uſ'd the unfortunate Prince more like a Priſoner than his Soveraign; diſpoſing of the Chief Commands in the Army according to his own Pleaſure, and placing ſuch about him, who obſerv'd him rather as Spies, than obey'd him as Servants. In this melancholy Condition *Valentinian* ſent and deſir'd Aid from *Theodoſius,* but *Arbogaſtes* was gone ſo far now, that he found it neceſſary to proceed farther, and made good that old Saying, That there is but a ſmall diſtance between

the

the Prisons and Graves of Princes; and therefore got
him privately to be murder'd at *Vienna* in *France*; Valentini-
having corrupted some of the Officers belonging to an *mur-*
his Chamber, who strangled him whilst he was a- *der'd.*
sleep, and tying a Cord about his Neck hung him
up, that the World might be induced to think he
kill'd himself, and not tax them with his Murder.
Arbogastes had no mind to appear guilty of so barbarous a Treason himself, and therefore would not
openly usurp the Imperial Authority, but chose rather to confer it on *Eugenius*, who was to be Prince Eugenius
only by his Permission and Allowance. *Eugenius* *usurps.*
was a Man of great Learning, an accomplish'd Orator, elegant and facetious, but very uncapable of
the Sovereign Dignity to which he was design'd.
Tho' *Arbogastes* endeavour'd to divert from himself
the Odium of so unnatural a Treason, yet he is charged with it by all the Writers of that Age, who
however seem not to condemn him so much as his
Guilt deserv'd; whether this proceeded from the
Hopes they at first conceiv'd of *Eugenius*, or out
of Complaisance to *Theodosius*, who in the end was
a Gainer by his Death, having the Sovereign Authority united in his own Family, is hard to determine.

The Ecclesiastical Writers say his Death was a *The Cha-*
publick Loss to the World, and even *Zosimus* him- *racter of*
self raises no Charge against him. Had he been suf- *Valentini-*
fer'd to live longer he had undoubtedly proved an *an.*
excellent Prince, being of a lively Spirit, valiant,
sober, liberal, sincere in his Friendship, and devout
in his Religion. He had in his Youth been comit-
ted to the Care of St. *Ambrose*, Bishop of *Milan*,
whose Instructions made him an Enemy to Vice before he was capable of learning what it was. Tho'
he was young he was an absolute Master of his Passions, and was generally more severe to himself than

he

he was to others. He was murder'd at *Vienna* in *France*, after he had reign'd sixteen Years and a half, and lived upwards of twenty.

IV. Tho' all good Men were sensibly afflicted a the Death of this innocent Prince, none appear'd s nearly touch'd as *Theodosius*, who had now lost Collegue and Ally in the flower of his Age, destroy' by the treasonable Practices of those, of whom h had great Reason to be jealous; for *Arbogastes* wa bold and valiant, and *Eugenius* renown'd for his Learn ing and other Virtues; so that he made all Prepara tions possible for a War: In the midst of which Em bassadors arrived from *Eugenius* the Usurper, who without taking the least notice of *Arbogastes*, de manded of him if he would admit of *Eugenius* a his Collegue, or consider him as his Enemy. *The odosius*, according to his Custom, amused the Em bassadors with fair Words and Royal Presents, dis missing 'em with ambiguous Answers, whilst he ap ply'd himself with great Diligence to his Military Preparations, in which he spent almost two Years concealing as much as possible his Designs 'till he was able to put 'em in execution. Like a Christian he made use of the Means Christianity suggested to him, in order to obtain the Divine Favour, publish ing a new Edict at *Constantinople* against the Heathen Worship, and reviving the ancient Laws against He reticks, their Ordinations and Assemblies; and like a Father of his People abrogated an old Law, which punish'd those with Death, who spoke seditious Words against the Prince; *Because*, said he, *if they proceed from Levity they are to be despised, if from Madness to be pitied, if from Malice to be forgiven.*

A. D. 393. Honorius declared Emperor.

The Beginning of this Year *Theodosius* had de clared his Younger Son *Honorius* Emperor, and in tending to leave *Arcadius* behind at *Constantinople*, he he committed him to the Care of *Rufinus*, who was thereby vested with almost an unlimited Power. The Emperor strengthen'd his own regular Troops with the Addition of several Barbarians inhabiting the other side the *Danube* and *Euxine* Sea, who made him a voluntary Offer of their Service, and were of great use to him in this War, under the Coduct of *Alaric* the *Goth*, who afterwards took *Rome*, and was the first that led the Barbarians into *Italy*. For during this War they had an Opportunity of viewing the Country, of observing the most advantageous Passes, the Fruitfulness of the Soil, Strength of the State, and number of the Inhabitants; and so were the better encouraged to return afterwards with greater Numbers, and subdue those they were now come to serve. Having appointed *Timaius*, *Bacurius*, and *Stilicho*, who had marry'd his Brother's Daughter, Commanders in chief, he began his Expedition the thirteenth of *March* the Year following, directing his March through *Thrace* into *Pannonia*, and designing from thence to break through the *Julian Alps* into *Italy*, which the Usurper had lately got into his own Power, and being arrived at *Milan*, tho' he had hitherto made a Profession of Christianity, he turn'd aside to the heathenish Superstitions at the Instigation chiefly of *Flavianus* Præfect of *Rome*, who promis'd him mighty Advantages from the Inspection of the Sacrifices, and Observation of the Stars; assuring him he was design'd by Fate to restore the ancient Greatness and Religion of the *Romans*, and that he would in time be sole Emperor of the World. Hereupon he was persuaded to allow 'em the free Exercise of their Religion, to re-edifie the Altar of Victory, and whatever else had been formerly deny'd 'em by the Emperors *Theodosius* and *Valentinian*: And hearing of *Theodosius* his Forwardness he mustered his Forces,

ces, and so set out from *Milan,* accompany'd by *Arbogastes* and *Flavianus,* whom he had made his Lieutenant-Generals, swearing publickly at his Departure, that if ever he lived to return victorious he would put all the Priests to death, and make a Stable of the great Church; because looking upon him as an Apostate and Usurper they would not accept of his Offerings, nor suffer him to communicate in Prayer with the rest of the Faithful.

Eugenius used so much Diligence in his March, that a detach'd Party had seiz'd on the *Julian Alps* before *Theodosius* could come up, who however attack'd the Guards with so much Bravery and Resolution, that he easily beat 'em out of that advantageous Post. *Flavian* the Præfect, fighting with much Obstinacy, was slain in this Action, in whose Fall *Eugenius* his Party suffer'd a considerable Loss. *Theodosius* trusting to his Cause, and his propitious Fortune, push'd on with great Alacrity, and having without much Difficulty pass'd the Mountain, he descended with all his Forces into the Plain, where he offer'd his Enemy Battel, which *Eugenius* with great Readiness accepted. The Emperor disposed his Army into two Batallions, one consisting of the Barbarians, under the Command of *Gaines* and *Bacurius,* the other of the *Romans* led on by *Stilicho;* encouraging his Soldiers by his Presence and Discourse, admonishing 'em to behave themselves like Men, confiding in the Protection of their *Saviour,* under whose Banner they fought. On the other side *Eugenius* had erected the Standard of *Hercules,* and behaved himself like a Man sure of Victory, deluded by the vain Promises of the Heathen Priests, who in the Name of their Deities had promised him an entire Conquest. At a Signal given both Armies engaged, and *Zosimus* saith that during the Fight there happen'd so great an Eclipse that for a long time

Theodosius engages with Eugenius,

time the Sun was almoſt totally darkened; however the Fight continu'd with great Slaughter, 'till in the End *Eugenius* prevail'd, for the Barbarians being unable to ſtand the Shock of the *Roman* Legions gave ground, and were moſt of 'em cut off together with *Bacurius* their Commander. Night coming on both Parties retreated to their Camps, where *Eugenius*, concluding himſelf the Victor, and that nothing was to be fear'd from *Theodoſius* after ſo great a Defeat, rewarded ſuch of his Men as had behaved themſelves beſt, diſmiſſing 'em all to their Eaſe and Refreſhment. In the mean time *Theodoſius* was adviſed by ſuch as were about him not to hazard a ſecond Engagement, but rely upon the Fortune of another Campaign, againſt which time he would have leiſure to recruit his Army, and be able to match his Enemy with an equal Number of Men; but the Emperor collecting the Remainder of his Forces by Break of Day, fell with an unexpected Bravery upon the Enemy, ſecurely ſleeping in their Camp, killing all ſuch who had not time to make any Defence or beg for Quarter, and by this means reſcu- *and de-* ed the Victory out of the Hands of a preſumptu- *feats him* ous Uſurper, who ſeem'd to want nothing but the Head of *Theodoſius* to crown his Succeſs. This is chiefly the Account *Zoſimus* gives of the Fight, in the Subſtance of which he agrees with others that have writ concerning it, only they make no mention of an Eclipſe, inſtead of which they aſſure us, that in the ſecond Engagement ſo violent a Tempeſt aroſe, as the Memory of Man could not equal, that it drove ſo furiouſly upon the Army of the Uſurper that it turn'd their Arrows and Javelins back upon themſelves, and rais'd ſo great a Duſt as depriv'd them of their Sight, ſo that having two Enemies to encounter at once they were quickly overthrown. In the beginning of the Fight *Eugeni-*

us

us had promised a great Reward to those who should bring him *Theodosius* alive or dead, thinking it impossible for him to escape; but now astonish'd at the impetuous Violence of the Tempest, and concluding from thence that they fought against Providence, several of his Troops despairing of Success went and surrender'd themselves to the Emperor, begging Pardon for their Offence, and swearing an inviolable Loyalty for the future. *Theodosius* receiv'd 'em into Grace, and order'd 'em to bring *Eugenius* into his Presence. The Usurper observing some coming in great haste towards him concluded they brought him News of the Victory, and instantly asked if they had not secured *Theodosius*; they return'd him no Answer, but to his Astonishment bound him and hurried him away to the Emperor, who reproach'd him for his Cruelty towards his Master *Valentinian*, accus'd him for the Calamities he had by the War brought upon the Empire, and upbraided him for putting his Confidence in *Hercules*, in Distrust and Defiance of the only true God; and without waiting for his Answer order'd his Head to be struck off. *Arbogastes*, whose Conscience told him he had great reason to expect the same Punishment, turn'd his own Executioner, and laid violent Hands upon himself; tho' the good Emperor made the same Use of this Victory as he had done of those that preceded, bewailing the innocent Blood that had been spilt in the War, and as if he himself had been the Author of it, for which reason he abstain'd for some time from participating in the holy Mysteries of the Eucharist. The Children of *Eugenius* and *Flavian* had great reason to think they were to suffer for the Rebellion of their Fathers, and therefore betook themselves to Sanctuary, but by the Intercession of St. *Ambrose*, who came to *Aquileia* there to congratulate *Theodosius* for his late Victory, the Emperor not

Eugenius taken,

and beheaded.

Theodosius his Moderation.

only

only pardon'd them, but gave Order to have 'em instructed and confirm'd in the Principles of the true Religion, and to be advanc'd to honourable Employments in the State; acquiring not so much Glory from his Success in the Field, as from such Actions as these, truly worthy a Christian Prince, never enough to be commended, imitated, and admired. From *Aquileia* he removed to *Milan*, whither his Son *Honorius* came according to his Order from *Constantinople* to attend him; for he now found himself indisposed, and inclinable to a Dropsie, which carry'd him off in a short time after.

About this time several Countries were shaken with violent Earthquakes, others were drown'd with excessive Rains, attended by so great a Darkness as had not been observ'd for a long time before; all which the Historians of those times seem to apply as Omens design'd to usher in the Fall of that great Man, and the Loss the *Roman* Empire was to sustain in his Death. He was now arrived at the height of human Happiness, for he had not only vindicated the Imperial Authority from Usurpation and Tyranny, but exercised it without a Competitor, and united it in his own Family. He was faithfully served by his Subjects, and admired by his very Enemies; and tho' he found it impossible to extirpate the Barbarians that had taken too deep a Root within the *Roman* Pale, yet he repress'd and in some measure civiliz'd 'em: And now as he was preparing to remove to *Constantinople*, there to enjoy the Fruit of his Labours, he was seiz'd with a fatal Distemper at *Milan*, which put an end to his Life and all his future Designs. As soon as he perceived himself to be in danger he made his Will, in which he made a Division of the Empire, bequeathing the East to his eldest Son *Arcadius*, aged about 18 Years, and the West to *Honorius*, who was then

He falls sick.

almost

almost eleven; recommending the one to *Rufinus* his Care and Direction, and the other to that of *Stilicho*, who was made General of the Army. He at the same time eased the People of several Impositions, and pardon'd many Criminals; and resigning himself with a chearful Mind to the Will of God, he expi-

and Dies. red at *Milan* on the 17th of *January*, after a glorious Reign of sixteen Years, and in the fiftieth of his Age according to some, tho' others say he lived sixty, *An. Ur.* 1147. the 3d of the 293d Olympiad, in the Consulship of *Olybrius* and *Probinus, An. Dom.* 395.

His Character. The Reader will easily conclude *Theodosius* dy'd universally lamented, when he considers that he seem'd sent as a publick Blessing into the World; and that he was call'd to the Empire when the Necessities of the State requir'd a Person of Experience, Courage, Conduct, and Perseverance. He ow'd much to Fortune, but more to himself, and was made Emperor more for the sake of those he was to govern than his own. His Virtues were as great whilst he liv'd a private Life, but became afterward more conspicuous, and as at first he discountenanc'd Vice by his Example, so he afterwards suppress'd it by his Authority; his Modesty at first refus'd that Power which the most deserving of his Predecessor had courted with Ambition, but he made it appear in the Issue that no Man knew how to be Great better than himself. He was a Prince of exemplary Temperance; curious in the choice of his great Officers and Counsellors; just to his Friends, and generous even to his Enemies. In him we may say were collected all the rare Qualities that were so eminent in the first *Romans*, he had the Chastness of the *Pontifices*, the Moderation of the *Consuls*, the Grandure of the *Patricians*, and the Meekness and Humility of the *Clients*. The Wars he was engag'd in during his Reign were of other Mens kindling, not his own, and he only by his Courage and Conduct put a ſtop to what others by their Tyranny and Ambition had begun. How kind a Father he was to the Publick appears in his leſſening the Burden of Taxes, and that at a time, according to *Themiſtius,* when he had ſuch an Army on Foot as the *Roman* Empire hardly ever ſaw before. He was Juſt in his Dealings to all Men, but fond of thoſe that were good, making the Greatneſs of his Mind appear in his Liberality and Munificence towards 'em. He is ſaid both in Body and Mind to have reſembled *Trajan,* only *Theodoſius* was more Graceful and Majeſtick; beſides he was a Stranger to *Trajan*'s Vices, ſuch as Drunkenneſs, Incontinence and Ambition. In this Character of *Theodoſius* all the Heathen Authors of thoſe Times unanimouſly agree, except *Zoſimus,* who injuriouſly taxes him with Incontinency, Sloth and Voluptuouſneſs; tho' at the ſame time the force of Truth is prevalent in him, when he confeſſes, that as by Nature this Prince was idle and unactive, giving himſelf up to all manner of Debauchery, when the Affairs of the State left him at leiſure for it; ſo when ever he was call'd upon by any imminent Danger, which threaten'd the Publick Safety, he rouz'd himſelf as from a Dream, ſhook off thoſe Vices of his Nature, and went as readily to Work as if Labour and Difficulties had been familiar to him. Chriſtian Authors have deſervedly commended him upon another Account, his Zeal for the Chriſtian Religion, in which he equall'd, if not excell'd any of his Glorious Predeceſſors; many Inſtances they have given us of his great Care for, and Submiſſion to the Ordinances of the Church, and of his Spiritual Obedience. *Sozomen* tells us, that

whilſt

whilst the Emperor continu'd in *Italy* after the Defeat of *Maximus*, an Insurrection happen'd at *Thessalonica*, in which the Seditious kill'd *Botericus*, the Emperor's Lieutenant in *Illyricum*, and several of the Magistrates; that *Theodosius* being inform'd of it commanded a great number of the Mutineers to be put to Death, but at the Intercession of St. *Ambrose* he revok'd his Orders, and pardon'd them. Some time after several of the Great Men in his Court represented to him, that the *Thessalonians* had been encourag'd to this Sedition by his too great Indulgence shown to those at *Antioch*, and upon many other occasions, and that if he permitted 'em to go unpunish'd, his Officers for the future would be in continual Danger of their Lives, and that he would be constantly alarm'd with some new Commotions. The Emperor was sensibly affected with this Remonstrance, and instantly dismiss'd some of his Troops to *Thessalonica*, where in three Days time they cruelly massacred above seven Thousand People, without regard either to Age, Sex or Condition, murdering the Innocent as well as Guilty. At this time an Assembly of Bishops was held at *Milan*, who all express'd how much they abhorr'd so excessive a Severity in the Prince. Whereupon St. *Ambrose* writ a Letter to *Theodosius*, in which, with a Confidence no way injurious to the Respect he ow'd his Soveraign, he represented to him the Enormity of his Crime, and exhorted him to make an Atonement by a sincere Submission and Repentance. The Emperor being arriv'd at *Milan*, was going to perform his Devotions in the great Church, into which St. *Ambrose* deny'd him Entrance, 'till he had expiated so Publick a Crime by as Publick a Penance. To this the Emperor readily submitted, and return'd to his Palace with Tears in his Eyes,

Eyes, and a Heart full of Divine Contrition, and perform'd with a moſt Chriſtian Submiſſion all the Duties of an open Penance, as they were enjoin'd by the Cannons of the Church, and the Cuſtoms of thoſe Times; and to make the Empire an Honourable Amends for his Fault, he then publiſh'd, or at leaſt enforc'd the Obſervance of an Edict, by which all Criminals were to have a Reſpite of Thirty Days allow'd 'em, between the pronouncing of the Sentence and the Execution, and thereby prevented both himſelf and his Succeſſors from falling into the like Error for the future. I have given the Reader this Signal Example of a Divine Reſignation, and leave him to make what uſeful Obſervations he thinks fit upon it.

CHAP. III.

From the Death of Theodosius *the Great, to the Taking of* Rome *the first time by the* Goths.

Containing the Space of almost Sixteen Years.

I. THE World can never discern the Worth of a Prince sufficiently 'till they have lost him, of which the *Roman* Empire was too sensible after the Death of *Theodosius*. The Subject of the remaining part of this History will be the Decay and Ruin of the greatest State that ever gave Laws to the rest of the World, and the Reader must now behold the *Roman* Common-wealth struggling in Death, oppress'd by her own Slaves, and overpower'd by those she at first arrogantly contemn'd.

Theodosius, as we observ'd before, unhappily divided the Empire at his Death between his two Sons, who being too Young to govern of themselves were committed to the Care and Direction of such, who apply'd their Power more to the gratifying their own private Interest and Ambition, than to the Honour and Safety of the Empire. *Arcadius* immediately after his Father's Death repair'd to *Constantinople,* for fear the People should affect any dangerous Change upon the News of so general a Calamity, where he issu'd out several Edicts for the Confirmation of such Laws as had been pub-

The Ambition of Rufinus and Stilicho prejudicial to the Empire.

lish'd by *Theodosius* against the Hereticks and Heathens. In the mean time *Rufinus* and *Stilicho,* out of Envy to each others Greatness, grew such implacable Enemies, that in Prosecution of their several pernicious Projects they confounded all things
Divine

Divine and Human, and seem'd to rend that Empire asunder, which *Theodosius* design'd only to have divided. By this means the Barbarians, who had been receiv'd into the Empire, were inticed to make use of so favourable an Advantage, and began to think of setting up for themselves, of becoming Conquerors instead of Subjects, of sharing the Provinces amongst them, and erecting Principalities of their own. *Arcadius* and *Honorius* were indeed honour'd with the Imperial Titles, but the Sovereign Power rested solely in *Stilicho* and *Rufinus*, the one Commanding at his Pleasure in the East, and the other in the West. They undertook to determine all Suits and Controversies, which they did with a most Arbitrary Partiality, drawing the Wealth of whole Provinces into their own Coffers, and impoverishing Nations to enrich themselves. The Princes all this while were ignorant of their Practices, approving whatsoever they did or propos'd, which carry'd with it the Strength and Validity of a Law. *Rufinus* in a short time render'd himself odious to the People through his Pride and Arrogance. From an obscure Beginning he had been rais'd to the greatest Employments in the State, so that he began to think himself remov'd but one Step from the Imperial Dignity, to which he had a great Desire to attain, and the readiest way he thought was to Marry his Daughter to *Arcadius*; for being the Emperor's Father-in-law he concluded he could do no less than assume him for his Collegue. The Overtures were made by some of his Instruments with great Secrecy to *Arcadius*, which however by degrees became the Discourse of the People, and increas'd their Aversion to him; but none oppos'd his Designs so effectually as *Eutropius*, one of the Emperor's Eunuchs, and a Person in great Esteem with him. *Promotus* left two

Eutropius opposes Rufinus.

two Sons behind him, who in *Theodosius* his Lifetime were brought up with his own Children, one of which had at present a Virgin in his Family of extraordinary Beauty; some say she was *Gratian's* Daughter, others that she was the Daughter of *Bauto*, who had been Consul with *Arcadius*; this Lady *Eutropius* upon all occasions commended to the Emperor, extolling her in a high degree as the most perfect Workmanship of Nature, and so far prevail'd that he consented to Marry her. *Rufinus* was just return'd to *Constantinople* from *Antioch*, where he had given the World a new Instance of his Cruelty and Ingratitude. *Florentius*, who had been *Præfectus Prætorio* in *Julian's* Reign, had a Son call'd *Lucian*; this Gentleman made his Court to *Rufinus*, presenting him with Possessions of a very considerable value, upon which account *Rufinus* recommended him to the Emperor, who made him *Comes* of the East, in which Office he behav'd himself with the greatest Justice and Moderation, and was so far from being a Respecter of Persons, that he rejected a Proposal made to him by the Emperor's own Uncle *Eucherius*, in which he requir'd something that was not fit for him to grant; whereupon *Eucherius* complain'd of him to the Emperor, who reproach'd *Rufinus* for imposing so unworthy a Man upon him. *Rufinus*, instead of Protecting one who had purchas'd his Friendship at so great a Price, communicating his Thoughts to a very few made haste to *Antioch*, where he enter'd in the Night time, apprehended *Lucian*, and without any Accuser commanded him to make his Defence; he order'd him to be beaten on the Neck with Leaden Balls 'till he expir'd under the Torment, and then put him into a close Litter, endeavouring to persuade the People that he was still alive, and might expect some Favour at his Hands; but

Rufinus his Cruelty.

but they being too fenfible of the Truth highly refented fo barbarous a Proceeding: *Rufinus*, to appeafe 'em, built 'em a moft Magnificent *Portico*, and fo gave the City at once an Inftance of his Cruelty and Prodigality; and from thence he return'd to *Conftantinople*, pleafing himfelf with the Thoughts of his future Affinity with the Emperor, and the Eftablifhment of his own unlimited Power; but he had not been long there before he found the Emperor by *Eutropius* his means marry'd to *Eudoxia*, and himfelf difappointed of his airy Imaginations. This he was refolv'd to revenge upon *Eutropius*, and from henceforward he labour'd to poffefs himfelf of that Power by Treafon, which he could not purchafe by his Intrigues, to which he was the more incited by *Stilicho*'s fuccefsful Attempts in the Weft; for he had not only marry'd his Daughter to *Honorius*, but had the Command of the Flower of the *Roman* Army difpofs'd in Garrifon up and down the beft Cities, which by that means were all at his Devotion; for being Captain-General of the Army at *Theodofius* his Death, he referv'd the beft of the Troops to himfelf, and difmifs'd thofe of lefs Eftimation into the Eaft. *Rufinus* was inform'd that *Stilicho* had the Preference in *Theodofius* his Will, that he was left Governor to both his Sons alike, and was coming into the Eaft to make ufe of his Authority accordingly. This Journey *Rufinus* endeavour'd by all means poffible to prevent, endeavouring at the fame time to weaken, as much as he could, the Forces of *Arcadius*; in thefe Defigns he was affifted by Inftruments more wicked than he could have expected or defir'd. *Rufinus* thought it would be much to his Advantage if he could let the Barbarians into *Greece*, and therefore made *Antiochus* Governor of it, a Man bafely degenerating from the Virtue and Integrity both of his

Arcadius married to Eudoxia.

Rufinus his treacherous Practices.

his Father and his Brethren; at the same time he deliver'd the *Straits* of *Thermopylæ* into the Custody of *Gerontius*, who he was sure would second him in any Villanous Attempts upon the Commonwealth. *Alarich* had all this while the Command of the Barbarians, employ'd by *Theodosius* against the Usurper *Eugenius*. *Rufinus* observ'd him to be of an Unquiet, Seditious Temper, Haughty and Impetuous, and at present dissatisfy'd, for that he had been rewarded with no better Preferment. He *His Dealings with Alarich the Goth,* therefore sends privately to him, and advises him to be his own Carver; he encourages him to draw together those of his own Country, and all such of any other Nation as would follow his Fortunes, and march boldly at the Head of 'em, assuring him he should meet with no Opposition.

In Confidence of this Promise *Alarich* quits *who marches into Greece.* *Thrace,* and marches into *Macedonia* and *Thessaly,* destroying all the Country as he march'd, and coming near to *Thermopylæ,* by Messengers he inform'd *Gerontius* and *Antiochus* of his Approach. *Gerontius,* according to his Instructions, immediately withdrew his Guards from the *Straits,* and so open'd a free Passage for the Barbarians into *Greece,* where they rag'd with unexampl'd Fury, killing all the Males that were able to oppose 'em, and driving away the Boys and Women in great Numbers, together with the Wealth of the Country, which fell all into their Hands. All *Bœotia,* and those other Parts of *Greece* that felt their Fury, wore the Marks of it for a long time after. They peirc'd into *Argos, Corinth* and *Lacedemon,* rifling the Temples and pillaging all the wealthy Cities, which were unfortify'd through the Avarice of the *Roman* Magistrates, who were ready to serve the Lust and Ambition of those who were in Power, tho' at the Expence of their own Country. These Proceedings
of

of the Barbarians serv'd to feed the Ambition of
Rufinus, who hop'd to succeed better in his Designs
upon the Empire, whilst it labour'd under such
Publick Calamities; but *Stilicho*, who as yet had
more generous Thoughts, and was intent upon the
Preservation of the Common-wealth, having first
repress'd the *Franks*, the *Suevi*, and the *Germans*,
who were aiming at some Commotions in the West,
and thereby quieted all behind him, resolv'd to
march to the Succour of *Achaia*. Accordingly he
sets forward with the Western Troops, and those
of the East that had been left in *Italy* ever since
the Defeat of *Eugenius*, and landing safe in *Peloponnesus*, was in a fair way of ruining the Barbarians.
The whole Army express'd a great Forwardness for
the Expedition, and earnestly desir'd to come to an
Engagement with them, and revenge the Miseries
they had brought upon the Empire; which without
doubt they had effected, had not *Rufinus*, who concluded that when once the Barbarians were repress'd
the Storm would fall upon his own Head, prevail'd
with *Arcadius* to send for the Oriental Troops for
the Defence of *Constantinople*, and restrain the *Hunns*,
who by the like Artifices had broken into the Empire. *Stilicho* was extreamly surpriz'd at this Order, which he thought depriv'd him of a certain
Victory, and put the Empire into imminent Danger. The Chief Commanders in the Army were
as much concern'd as their General, however they
thought fit to march in Obedience to the Emperor's Orders, which they were sensible *Rufinus* had
by his Artifices procur'd, on whom therefore they
were resolv'd to be reveng'd, as on an Enemy to
the State; and so they set forward under the
Conduct of *Gaines*, a great Friend of *Stilicho*'s, who
had promis'd him to remove his Antagonist, and
promote his Interest in the East. About this time

Stilicho marches towards the East.

Theodosius his Corps was brought from *Milan* to *Constantinople*, where he was bury'd with more Solemnity of Grief than Pomp of State, the Ceremony serving to re-mind the People of what they had lost, and the defenceless Condition of the Empire. *Rufinus* had a great many brave Troops at his Devotion, commanded by Persons of the first Quality; who had conspir'd to proclaim him Emperor immediately upon the Arrival of that out of the West: The Purple was prepar'd, and the Donative ready for the Soldiers, who suffer themselves too often to be corrupted by Presents. *Gaines* being come at the Head of his Army within a few Hours March to *Constantinople* gave *Arcadius* notice of his Approach, and that pursuant to his Orders he was come to his Relief; of this the Emperor was highly satisfy'd, and was pleas'd to go out of the City and meet the Soldiers in Person, being inform'd 'twas an Honour his Predecessors usually paid to the Army. The Soldiers receiv'd him with the Respect due to his Dignity, but upon a Signal given by *Gaines* they surrounded *Rufinus*, whose Thoughts were puffed up with an imaginary Empire, and cut him in pieces; his Head was fixed upon the Top of a Lance, and expos'd to the View of the People, who abominated him for his excessive Cruelty and Extortion, and therefore beheld it with much Satisfaction: They were well pleas'd at the Invention of a certain Soldier, who took his right Hand, and by a witty Contrivance opening and closing his Fingers at pleasure, went up and down the City begging an Alms for that insatiable Creature. Thus fell *Rufinus*, who well deserv'd the Usage he receiv'd, having by his Ambition involv'd the Publick in great Difficulties, and procur'd the Ruin of many private Families. The *Hunns* and the *Goths*, who had been let into the Empire by his Means, could never afterwards

Rufinus slain.

terwards be expell'd, but took so deep a Root, and grew up by Degrees to such a Strength and Resolution, that at first they shook off the Yoke of the *Romans*, and at last brought 'em into Subjection, as we shall see hereafter. Upon *Rufinus* his Death *Eutropius*, who had concurr'd with *Stilicho* in all his Devices against him, was made chief Minister in his Room; securing the greatest Part of his Estate to his own use, but giving others liberty to re-assume what had been unjustly taken from 'em. His Wife and Children, fearing they should fall a Sacrifice to the Fury of the People, took Sanctuary in a Church, from whence by the Emperor's Permission they retir'd to *Jerusalem*, where they spent the rest of their Days.

Eutropius being thus confirm'd in his Master's Favour, succeeded *Rufinus* not only in his Power and his Employments, but what is worse in his Cruelty, his Avarice, and his other villainous Qualities, so that *Rufinus* seem'd still to survive in this wicked Eunuch. He was a declar'd Enemy to Virtue and virtuous Men; nor had he any farther Regard to Religion than as he could make it subservient to his Interest. He abus'd with much Insolence his Master's Power, who being young, and addicted to his Pleasures, resign'd the Government of his Affairs into his Hands. And the better to confirm himself in his Authority, he endeavour'd to remove all those out of the way, who seemed to bear any Sway in the Court. For this end he began his Practices upon *Timasius*, a Man who had been a long time a principal Commander in the Army, and had in many Wars served the Government with much Honour, Courage and Integrity. Being some time before this at *Sardis* he accidentally met with one *Bargus*, a Native of *Laodicea* in *Syria*, a mean inconsiderable Fellow, and who for some notorious

Eutropius as bad as Rufinus.

Crime

Crime had been forced to fly his Country; *Timasius* perceiving him of a facetious infinuating Conversation, without ever enquiring farther into his Character, admitted him to his Familiarity, preferr'd him to the Command of a Cohort, and took him with him to *Constantinople*; at which some of the Magistrates were highly displeas'd, because he had been formerly banish'd that City for some Offences committed by him. This Man *Eutropius* thinks a fit Instrument for his Villainy, and with many Gifts and more Promises persuades him to accuse *Timasius* of High-Treason. Hereupon the Villain counterfeits a Writing, in the Contents of which *Timasius* is charged with affecting the Imperial Dignity, and is therefore brought without delay to his Trial, where the Emperor himself presided first as Judge; but finding the People disliked the Proceeding, and were offended to see a Person of *Timasius* his Dignity forced to answer the mercenary Accusations of so insignificant and scandalous a Fellow, he quitted the Employment, and substitutes *Saturninus* and *Procopius* in his room. *Saturninus* was an ancient Man, and had gone through many great Offices, but was given to Flattery, and in the Court of Judicature to pass such Sentences, as were likely to please those who were in greatest Favour with the Prince. *Procopius* had been *Valens* his Father-in-Law, and was rigid and inflexible, pretending to have a great Regard to Right and Equity; as indeed he appear'd in this Case, for he endeavour'd to convince *Saturninus* how unreasonable a thing it was, that a Fellow so notorious as *Bargus* should be suffer'd to accuse so great a Person as *Timasius*, and after he had been obliged in so extraordinary a manner, endeavour to betray and destroy his Benefactor. However *Saturninus* his Sentence prevail'd in the End, notwithstanding this reasonable Remonstrance; and *Timasius*
was

Chap. III. XLVIII. Arcadius, Honorius. 241

was confin'd to *Oasis*, a barren uncomfortable Place, out of which there could be no Escape for those who were once brought thither; for it was surrounded with a large desolate Desart, full of Sand, which moving to and fro with the Wind suffer'd no Tract or Footsteep of any former Travellers to be seen: *Timasius* being thus removed, a Report was spread abroad that his Son *Syagrius*, assisted by a Company of Robbers, had intercepted him and forc'd him from the Guards, who were sent by the Emperor to conduct him to his Place of Exile. Whether this Report was true, or rais'd by some of *Eutropius* his Creatures, is uncertain, tho' neither the Father nor Son were heard of ever after.

Bargus receiv'd the Command of a Cohort, as a Reward for his extraordinary Service to *Eutropius*, and was deceiv'd with the Hopes and Promises of greater things, not thinking that his Treachery to his great Benefactor *Timasius*, would teach *Eutropius* to be upon his Guard, and deal with him accordingly; this his senseless Security drew upon him the Judgment he deserv'd, for *Eutropius* taking an opportunity of his Absence, persuaded his Wife, who was then at variance with her Husband, to present the Emperor with some Papers of dangerous Consequence, and among the rest many heavy Accusations against *Bargus*; whereupon *Eutropius* brought him instantly to his Trial, where he was convicted, sentenced, and executed accordingly. So certain is the hand of Justice to punish, first or last, those who are guided by no Rule, nor observe any Law that interferes with their private Interest, how unreasonably soever grounded or pursued.

A.D. 396.

Bargus *put to death by* Eutropius *his Procurement.*

And now *Eutropius*, grown drunk with Power, and arrogant through his Success, employs his Spies in all Quarters and in every Corner, by whose Informations he made his own Advantage, oppressing those

those who were considerable for their Authority, or conspicuous for their Estates, and excluding such from the Presence of the Emperor, who had the Courage to tell him how much he was abus'd. Among these was *Abundantius*, a Man considerable in the Common-wealth in *Gratian*'s time, and who had been Prætor and Consul under *Theodosius*. His Virtue, Experience, and Authority, were Qualifications no way agreeable to *Eutropius*, so that he prevail'd through his crafty Insinuations with the Emperor to have him stripp'd of his Honours and Estate, and confin'd to *Sidon* in *Phænicia*, where he dy'd. After this he found none in *Constantinople* able to dispute or rival his Power, and so was more at leisure to turn his Eyes towards the West, where he observ'd *Stilicho* governing with an unlimited Authority, belov'd by the Emperor, caress'd by the Soldiers, and inclinable to come to *Constantinople*, which it consisted with his Interest to prevent, and therefore he persuaded *Arcadius* to summon the Senate, in which *Stilicho* is declared a publick Enemy to the Empire. After which he so far practis'd upon *Gildo*, who was Governor in *Africk*, that he renounc'd his Obedience to *Honorius*, owning *Arcadius* for his Soveraign, or rather setting up for himself; restraining that Supply of Corn with which *Rome* us'd to be furnish'd, and thereby creating a great Scarcity in that populous City. This *Gildo*, as we observ'd before, was one of the Sons of *Nubel*, who whilst he lived was a potent Prince in *Mauritania*. In the time of his Brother *Firmus* his Rebellion *Gildo* stuck fast to the *Romans*, for whom he appear'd so zealous that *Theodosius*, as a Recompence for his Services, conferr'd many Honours upon him, and made him his Lieutenant in *Africk*. For some time he behav'd himself with much Respect and Obedience to the Empire, but finding it embroil'd upon *Eugenius*

Who gets Abundantius to be banish'd,

and practises against Stilicho.

Gildo revolts in Africk.

his Usurpation, he declin'd joining the Forces under his Command with *Theodosius*, and began then to entertain thoughts of a Revolt; but after his Death, presuming upon the Incapacity of his Sons, he struck in with *Eutropius*, and made himself absolute Master of *Africk*. *Gildo* had then a Brother, call'd *Mazescel* or *Mazezil*, who oppos'd him with so much Activity, that he was violently enrag'd against him, and had a Design upon his Life; upon which *Mazezil* fled into *Italy*, where he gave the Emperor and *Stilicho* a just Account of the Province, inform'd 'em of the readiest way to suppress the Usurper, and offer'd to undertake the Service himself, provided they would place him at the Head of a sufficient Army. The Emperor had great reason to distrust this Barbarian's Sincerity, but the City was reduced to such a Scarcity of Provisions through the Rebellion in *Africk*, that he was glad to embrace any Offer that was propos'd to extinguish it. Whereupon the War was declar'd against *Gildo* in the Senate, and committed to the Management of *Mazezil*. Of this when *Gildo* was inform'd, he in great Rage murder'd two of his Brother's Sons, whom he had left behind in *Africk*; which serv'd only to inflame his Brother with more Animosity against him, and to prosecute the War with greater Application, since to his Rebellion he had added the unnatural Sin of Paricide.

A. D. 397.

Against whom his Brother is sent.

In the mean time the People of *Rome*, tho' they were afflicted with a Famine at home, and threaten'd with great and almost unavoidable Dangers from abroad, in a senseless Security gave themselves up to all manner of Luxury and Prodigality. The *Goths*, and other Barbarous Nations, were by degrees grown so familiar to 'em, many of whom they had entertain'd within their own Walls, that they became fond of their Fashions, and began to imitate 'em in

their

their Dresses, thinking their own dull and unpolished: This was look'd upon as a fatal Prelude to what follow'd not long after; for 'tis almost a certain sign that that Nation will in time be subjected to those, of whose Fancies they are fond; and that they to whose Imaginations they submit their Reason, will in time become Masters both of their Persons and Estates. This Extravagance was attended by another altogether as unreasonable; they were infatuated with a Madness of Building, and that at a time when the City was already grown too great for the Inhabitants, and the Inhabitants too many for the Provisions that were brought to it. Both these Extravagancies *Honorius* endeavour'd to restrain by two several Edicts, but to little purpose, for they still persisted in their Imitation of the Barbarians and the humour of Building continu'd so long, 'til the City her self slid down from her Seven Hills and repos'd her self, as for Ease, in the *Campus Martius*.

The Death of St. Ambrose.

This Year was remarkable for a Council held at *Carthage*, wherein were framed several remarkable Cannons, by which we may judge of the pious and self-denying Temper of the Prelates that celebrated it. In the same Year dy'd St. *Ambrose*, Bishop of *Milan*, who is accus'd of some Doctrinal Errors whereby we are to know that the best of Men are not infallible; for he maintain'd, as well as St. *Hilary* that *all Men indifferently are to undergo a fiery Trial at the last Day*; that *even the Just are to pass through it, and be thereby cleansed from their Sins; but the Unjust are to continue in it for ever.* He likewise taught, that *the Faithful should be rais'd gradually at the last Day, according to the Degree of their particular Merits:* That *the Bow God promis'd Noah he would place in the Firmament after the Deluge, as a Token that he never intended to drown the World again*.

was not to be understood of the Rain-bow, which can never appear in the Night, but some visible Virtue of the Almighty; and several other Tenets, wherein he differ'd from the rest of the Orthodox Fathers, and which afterwards gave occasion to many Speculations.

The Year following *Honorius* was Consul the fourth time with *Eutychianus*: And *Stilicho* and *Eutropius*, who had hitherto appear'd publickly to be in good Terms with each other, now broke out into open Enmity, agreeing still however in pillaging and oppressing the Publick. All Employments were at their Disposal, the Power of Pardon and Punishment rested solely in them, so that all Men became their Courtiers and Dependants. At this no Man was more offended than *Gaines*, who thought his Services little regarded, his Person neglected, and none prefer'd but those who were able to pay the highest price for it. These Considerations made him turn Male-content, so that he began to think of raising new Commotions, and communicated his Thought to one *Tribigild*, a bold Couragious Soldier, fit for any desperate Undertaking. *Tribigild* had the Command of some Troops of Horse of the Barbarians that lay Quarter'd in *Phrygia*, and having concerted his Matters with *Gaines*, he left *Constantinople* under a Pretence of Mustering his Troops, and viewing the Condition they were in; but as soon as he had plac'd himself at the Head of 'em he laid all the Country waste before him, killing Men, Women and Children, and upon a Promise of free Booty got such a Company of pilfering Rascals together, that all *Asia* seem'd to be threaten'd with Destruction. *Lydia* was in an Uproar, from whence the Inhabitants drew down towards the Sea, and pass'd over into other Parts to avoid the Tempest they saw ready to break upon 'em. *Ar-*

A. D. 398.

Gaines *turns Male-content.*

Tribigild *Rebels.*

cadius

cadius being inform'd of all this had no Sense of the Publick Calamities, nor Discretion enough to remove 'em, but like a helpless unactive Prince resign'd all to the Management of *Eutropius*, who made Choice of *Gaines* and *Leo* for the Generals of the War, by whose Conduct and Fidelity he made no doubt but *Tribigild* would quickly be reduc'd. *Leo* had Orders to march into *Asia*, and disperse the Barbarians that were met in a confus'd manner together; and *Gaines* was to have an Eye upon *Thrace* and the *Straits* of the *Hellespont*, to prevent any Irruptions on that side. Thus was the Emperor shamefully abus'd, and the Empire cruelly afflicted by open and avow'd Enemies that were sworn to her Destruction, and by treacherous, unskilful Generals, who undertook the Care of her Defence: for *Leo* had no other Qualification that could warrant his Pretence to so high an Employment, but his Intimacy with *Eutropius*; and *Gaines*, by Birth and Inclination was an avow'd Enemy to the *Roman* State. However they both march'd from *Constantinople* according to their Instructions, and *Gaines*, pursuant to the Agreement between 'em, sent and advis'd *Tribigild* to draw with his Forces down towards the *Hellespont*. Had this Design been as warily executed, as it was cunningly suggested all *Asia* and the East must unavoidably have been lost, but Fortune had not yet totally abandon'd the *Roman* Common-wealth. He left *Constantinople* with a Heat and Impetuosity natural to Barbarians, and sent not his Advice to *Tribigild* 'till he was arriv'd at *Heraclea*, and then *Tribigild* was afraid to observe his Orders, lest he should fall in with the Forces that were by that time sent to Guard the Coast; so that having wasted all *Phrygia*, he fell with the same Barbarity upon *Pisidia*. The Inhabitants sent to *Gaines* for Relief, which he, with much

much Artifice, prolong'd sending, whilst *Leo* hover'd about the *Hellespont* without daring to encounter the Enemy, who ravag'd the Country at Discretion, roving up and down without meeting the least Opposition, being daily reinforc'd by some or other of his Countrymen, who instead of defending their friendly Neighbours, the *Romans*, join'd with their Enemies, and drew their Swords against 'em.

Gaines pretended all this while to be highly exasperated against him, but at the same time magnify'd his Stratagems and Sagacious Conduct, affirming he effected more by that than the Force of his Arms. He pass'd over into *Asia* with a Pretence to oppose and chastise him, but was so far from doing any thing that tended that way, that he sate down as a Spectator whilst *Tribigild* laid all the Country waste, and burnt the Cities about him. *Gaines* expected he would have march'd out of *Phrygia*, and have mov'd towards the East, to which he privately advis'd him, and assisted him underhand with some Forces for the Expedition. Indeed had *Tribigild* directed his Course into *Lydia* he had easily master'd *Ionia*, and from thence he might have pass'd over into the Islands with as considerable a Fleet as he pleas'd, and so have over-run all the East, and have march'd up as far as *Egypt* without any Opposition. But directing his Course towards *Pamphylia*, he fell into a craggy mountainous Country, where there was no possibility for his Horse to march. There indeed he found no Army to oppose him, but met with one *Valentine*, a Citizen of *Selga*, a small Town in *Pamphylia*, situate upon a Hill, who had rais'd a Body of Slaves and Countrymen, that by their frequent Disputes with the Robbers of those Parts had learn'd how to make sudden Onsets, and frame advantagious Ambushes. These Men *Valentine* plac'd upon such Hills as were near the Passage, and so dispos'd 'em with the best Skill he had, that they with ease, and unobserv'd, could behold all that came that way. As soon as they saw *Tribigild* was enter'd the *Straits*, with huge Stones tumbled down from the Mountains they kill'd great Numbers of his Men; and now he began to find his Error too late, and that he had *His Army* no room left him to escape; for on one Hand was *cut off.* a deep Lake and rotten Bogs, on the other a narrow Ascent in which two Men could scarce move a-breast, call'd *Cochlea* by the Inhabitants, from the Orbicular Shape of it; this Pass was guarded by one *Florentius*, who had Men enough to make it good against the Barbarians; however *Tribigild*, by the force of his Presents, got leave to pass with three hundred of his Men, the rest of his Army being lost either in the *Straits*, or the adjoining Lake. From hence he descended into the Plain, where he was reduc'd to greater Extremities than ever; for all the Inhabitants of the Country got together, and with such Weapons as they found shut him and his Followers up between the two Rivers, *Melane* and *Eurymedon*; from hence, in great perplexity, he sent to acquaint *Gaines* with the Condition of his Affairs, who was as much troubl'd at it as himself; but having not yet openly declar'd himself, he sent *Leo*, who lay near him, with Orders to assist the *Pamphylians* in Conjunction with *Valentine*, and hinder *Tribigild* from passing the Rivers. *Leo*, who was more a Fool than a Knave, punctually follow'd his Instructions, and by that means made *Gaines his Tribigild*'s Escape utterly impossible; whereupon *Treachery. Gaines* sent time after time such Cohorts of Barbarians as he had in his Camp to *Leo*'s Assistance, as he pretended, and to reinforce his Army; but his Orders to them were, to kill such of the *Romans* as they found straggling from the Camp, to lay waste

the

the Country, and by degrees destroy *Leo* and his Army, which the Barbarians executed accordingly. By this means the Country was entirely ruin'd, and *Tribigild* had leisure to withdraw out of *Pamphylia*, and return into *Phrygia*, where he made good *Gaines* his Design and Expectation, for he raged with greater Fury than ever.

The Emperor, being thus abus'd on every side, was in great Perplexity. *Gaines*, instead of reducing *Tribigild*, magnify'd his Exploits to the Emperor, threaten'd him and the Senate with his intended March towards the *Hellespont*, which would endanger the present Posture of Affairs, unless the Prince thought fit to incline to his Proposals; those Proposals had before-hand been concerted between him and *Tribigild*, and were such as, when granted, would enable him the better to prosecute his own Ambitious Designs. He was an inveterate Enemy to *Eutropius*, who being design'd Consul this Year in the East, and honour'd with the Title of Patrician, he was more exasperated at his Preferment, than offended for that he was not advanc'd himself, and therefore was resolv'd to be satisfy'd with nothing less than Death. Accordingly whilst he lay in *Phrygia* he acquainted the Emperor, that he had neither Strength nor Authority enough to oppose *Tribigild* any longer, whose Conduct and Experience was such that all *Asia* would of necessity be lost, unless he had his Demands granted him; the cheif of which was, that *Eutropius*, the grand Author of all the late Calamities, might be deliver'd up into his Hands. Hereupon *Arcadius* immediately stripp'd *Eutropius* of his Power and Dignity, who in great Consternation fled for Refuge to a Christian Church. This was not enough to satisfie *Gaines*, who still insisted, that *Tribigild* would be contented with nothing less than *Eutropius* his utter Ruin; so that he

A. D. 399.

was

was first banish'd to the Isle of *Cyprus*, and some time after brought to *Pantychium*, where, after a formal Trial, he was put to Death.

Eutropius put to Death.

Tho' *Eutropius* in a great measure ow'd his Fall to *Gaines* his inveterate Malice, yet his insolent Carriage to the Empress had made *Arcadius* himself from an indulgent Master become an offended Prince. Looking on himself as the great Instrument of her Promotion, he thought he might make more bold with her than consisted with his Duty and her Imperial Dignity. Among other Extravagancies he presumptuously threaten'd her one Day, upon some small Dislike, to turn her out of the Palace, and send her home; the Empress highly offended at such unusual Arrogance went with Tears in her Eyes, and her two little Daughters, *Pulcheria* and *Arcadia*, in her Arms, and complain'd of the Eunuch to the Emperor; who either immediately depriv'd him of his Wealth and Dignities, and banish'd him into *Cyprus*, or more easily listen'd to *Gaines*, and consented to his Ruin. Whatever the main Reasons of his Fall were, he met with a Fate common to those insolent Favourites, who being advanc'd by the Indulgence of the Prince, shamefully abuse his Power, and misapply his Favours.

We took notice before of *Gildo*'s Revolt in *Africk*, and how his Brother was sent by the Emperor and Senate of *Rome* against him, who put an end to the War much sooner than was expected; for *Orosius* tells us, that depending more upon the Divine Assistance, than the Strength of his own Arms, he invok'd the Name of Christ, who supported him in the Day of Battel, and gave him a miraculous Victory; for he had not above Five thousand Men, tho' *Gildo* was above Seventy thousand strong. *Zosimus* saith *Mazezil* fell upon his Brother unawares, and after a sharp Dispute defeated him; that presently

Gildo Overthrown.

sently after *Gildo* chose rather to Strangle himself, than fall into his Enemy's Hands. *Mazezil* having by this Victory reduc'd *Africk* to *Honorius* his Obedience, return'd into *Italy*, where he was rec.iv'd very favourably by the Emperor, and outwardly caress'd by *Stilicho*, in Consideration of his late Services, who however inwardly envy'd him for his great Deserts, and procured him to be drown'd not long after. The Death of *Gildo* deliver'd *Africk* from great Oppressions, which the War would of necessity have brought upon it, had he liv'd to have receiv'd the Assistance he had been promis'd by *Eutropius*, who was not yet in Disgrace; but the Disagreement between the two Brothers seem'd an Act of Providence, and prov'd very advantagious to *Honorius* his Affairs, revenging upon the Usurper the Dissentions he endeavour'd to create between the two Emperors. With *Africa*, all *Gildo*'s Paternal Dominions fell to *Honorius* his share, and was so large, that as a distinct Province it was govern'd by its proper Officer, call'd *Comes Gildoniaci Patrimonii*.

After this the Western Empire seem'd to enjoy some Repose, and the Year following, whither the Course of the Wars in the East have already conducted us, is distinguish'd with the Name of no more than one Consul, which was *Flavius Mallius Theodorus*, a Person Eminent in those Days for his Learning, Eloquence and good Manners, as well as his Quality and Fortune; 'tis true we observ'd before that *Eutropius* was design'd for his Collegue, but fell a Sacrifice either to the Emperor's Indignation, or the Malice of *Gaines*, before he was Vested with the Honour. *Gaines* was so far from being satisfy'd with his Death, that he still aim'd at greater and more dangerous Innovations. Having patch'd up a pretended Peace with *Tribigild* in the Emperor's Name,

Name, he return'd through *Phrygia* and *Lydia*, leaving *Tribigild* to follow close after him, who join'd him again at *Thyatira*. Here they both agreed to return and sack *Sardis*, the Metropolis of *Lydia*, but were prevented by the great Rains which had lately fallen, and swoln the Rivers over which they were to pass. Hereupon they separated once more, *Gaines* marching through *Bythinia*, and *Tribigild* toward the *Hellespont*, allowing their Men to seize and plunder whatever came in their way, which they did with great Licentiousness; and being advanced, the one as far as *Chalcedon*, the other into the Territories of *Lampsacus*, they not only put *Constantinople* into a great Consternation, but the whole *Roman* Empire seem'd to be in apparent Danger; for *Gaines* was now become so insolent, that he demanded a Meeting with the Emperor in Person, refusing to treat with any one else. *Arcadius* was forc'd to condescend, and so it was agreed between 'em, at a Place near *Chalcedon*, sacred to the Memory of *Euphemia* the Martyr, that *Gaines* and *Tribigild* should pass out of *Asia* into *Europe*, and that such eminent Men in the State as they demanded should be deliver'd up into their Hands: These were *Aurelius*, who was *Stilicho*'s Collegue in this Year's Consulate, *Saturninus*, a Man of Consular Dignity, whom we had occasion to make mention of before, and *John*, Secretary to the Emperor: *Arcadius* found himself obliged to comply with this Tyrannical Demand, and having deliver'd 'em up to *Gaines* he sent 'em all into Exile. Upon the Conclusion of this Treaty he passed over into *Europe*, follow'd by *Tribigild*, leaving *Asia* to breathe a little, and recover her self from her late Calamities.

After this he continu'd for some time at *Constantinople*, from whence he remov'd the Soldiers that had formerly lain in Garrison in the City, that he might the

the better effect the Designs he had upon it. He first demanded a Church for himself and Followers, being all obstinate *Arians* in opinion, in which they might have a free Exercise of their Religion. The poor Emperor, being afraid to give him an absolute Denial, referr'd him to St. *Chrysostome*, who being Bishop of the City had the Disposal of all Consecrated Places. St. *Chrysostome* oppos'd him with much Courage, told him 'twas not in the Emperor's Power to alienate any thing that was Sacred; that the Churches were daily open in the City, where he might go and pay his Devotions, and hear the Word of God: To this *Gaines* answer'd, that being of another Persuasion he could not join with them in their Religious Worship; and that the Services he had render'd the Empire very well deserv'd a Church to be appropriated to him and those of his Faith. St. *Chrysostome* reply'd boldly, that his Rewards already exceeded his Merits, for he had the Honour of being a General, and enjoy'd the Consular Dignity; that from a low and abject Condition he had been advanc'd to the highest Employments in the Government; that he ought to be contented with what he already enjoy'd, without demanding what was not in the Emperor's Power to grant: Whereupon he shew'd him an Edict publish'd by *Theodosius*, prohibiting all Schismaticks whatever to hold any Meetings in the City, and reminded him of the Oath he had made to that Emperor, by whom he was so signally obliged, of being true to the *Roman* Interest, obedient to the Laws, and loyal to him and his Children; advising him to have a Regard to that Oath, in the Breach of which he would so highly provoke the Divine Vengeance against him. This Discourse, so seasonably inforc'd by the Bishop, made him quit his Demand for the present, tho' he went away very much dissatisfy'd, and full

of

of turbulent ambitious Designs. About this time there appear'd a Comet of unusual Magnitude, that seem'd to sweep the Earth with its Tail, and to hang directly over the City; portending some great Disaster ready to fall not only upon the City, but the Empire. His first Attempt was to seize the Wealth of the Bankers, of which being disappointed, he order'd some of his Barbarians to fire the Palace, which, say the Ecclesiastical Historians, was preserv'd by a Miracle. After this he pretended himself possess'd by a Spirit, and seiz'd on the Church of St. *John Baptist*, seven Miles from the City, there to perform his Devotions; having order'd some of his Party to follow him, and the rest to stay behind, who at a convenient Time, and upon a Signal given, were to seize the City and deliver it up to him, who would be ready at the Gates to assist them. This Design had in all probability taken effect, had he not been too hasty, and unadvisedly anticipated his Time: For without any Signal given he appear'd before the Walls at the Head of his Men, with which the Watch being alarm'd gave notice to the Inhabitants, who at first made such Outcries as are usual in Towns that are storm'd, but uniting themselves by degrees they set upon the Barbarians that were left behind, whom they dispatch'd with such Weapons as came first to hand; and so gall'd *Gaines*, whom the Emperor in the very *Crisis* had proclaim'd Traitor, that he was forc'd to retire from the Walls, after he had in vain attempted to break into the City. In the beginning of the Tumult seven thousand of the Barbarians fled for Refuge into one of the Churches, as to a Sanctuary; but the Emperor not thinking it reasonable a Christian Church should serve as an *Asylum* to those, who were declared Enemies both to Church and State, gave Order to have 'em all destroy'd either by Fire

His Designs upon Constantinople

frustrated.

or

or Sword; whereupon they uncover'd the Roof which lay over the Altar, and from thence ply'd 'em so furiously with Brands of Fire that not a Man of 'em escaped.

This is the Substance of this History, as we have it both from *Zosimus* and other Writers, wherein they vary in some Particulars that are not worth our Observation. *Gaines*, after this Defeat, declared open War against the State, and falling into *Thrace* found the Towns not only fenced with Walls, but well defended by the Courage and Resolution of the Inhabitants, who having learn'd Experience by former Incursions, had now secured their Fruits, Cattle, and all other Provisions within the Walls, and putting themselves into a Posture of Defence knew how to sally out and distress the Besiegers; so that *Gaines* finding nothing there but Grass, resolv'd to leave *Thrace* and march into the *Chersonesus*, and return through the *Straits* of the *Hellespont* into *Asia*. In the mean time the Emperor and Senate made choice of one *Fraiutus* to manage the War against him; he was by Birth a Barbarian, but in other Respects a *Greek*, not only in his Disposition and Manners, but his Affections and Religion, being, as *Zosimus* tells us, a Pagan. He had behav'd himself with much Honour in several former Services, having cleared the East, from *Cilicia* as far as *Palestine*, from Robbers that had cruelly infested it.

Fraiutus readily undertook the Charge, restor'd the ancient Discipline of the Camp, inur'd his Soldiers to Labour and Industry, being himself vigilant and indefatigable; and as he took great Care to form and exercise his own Troops, so was he as diligent to observe and discover the Condition of the Enemy, preparing to engage with him as well by Sea as by Land; for he had a good number of Pinnaces,

naces, with which he intended to dispute *Gaines* his Passage over, if he should attempt. He being now in Distress for want of Forrage resolv'd to stay there no longer, framing therefore a sufficient number of Planks, he so artificially compacted 'em together, that they were capable of transporting both Men and Horse, which he order'd to embark, and at a convenient Season put out to Sea. The *Roman* General, who had his Eye upon him all this while, put off with his Pinnaces a little from the Shore, and suffering the Vessels of the Barbarians to make down with the Tide, he with his own Pinnace faced the foremost, and falling foul of her with his Brazen Beak after a short Grapple sunk her; the rest of those Vessels follow'd the same Fate, so that very few of the Barbarians escaped alive. This Loss exceedingly perplex'd *Gaines*, who doubtful what measures to take left the *Chersonesus* and passed farther into *Thrace*, where some say he fell into the Hands of the *Roman* Forces quarter'd in those Parts, as he waited in expectation of fresh Supplies, who put him and the Remainder of his Army to the Sword. Others say, that after he had robb'd *Thrace* of what former Depredations had left behind, and massacred such *Romans* as still continu'd to follow him, he intended to pass the *Ister*, and end his Days in his own Country, but was prevented by *Uldes*, or *Hudin*, at that time Prince of the *Hunns*, who thought it imprudent to permit him to pass with an Army of his own Nation, and settle on the other side the River; and conceiv'd he should do an acceptable piece of Service to the *Roman* Emperor if he forc'd him from thence; whereupon drawing all his Forces together he prepar'd to give him Battel, which *Gaines*, who knew it impossible for him now to return to the *Romans*, was forced to accept of, and after a sharp Dispute on both sides, in which he fought with a desperate Resolution,

Gaines kill'd.

tion, he was slain, and his Head sent by *Uldes* to *Arcadius*, who thereupon rewarded him with many Royal Presents, and admitted him into a League and Society with the *Romans*.

II. The East seem'd to be deliver'd, by *Gaines* his Death, from the Calamities under which it had labour'd for a long time: But a new Storm was now gathering in the West; which so violently assaulted it, that at length it tore up the Empire by the Roots, and robb'd *Rome*, which for so many Ages had been the Queen of Cities, of her Hereditary and Imperial Honours. We were told before, how that *Alarich*, at *Rufinus* his Instigation, had invaded *Greece*; from whence, after he had committed unheard of Cruelties up and down wherever he pass'd, he descended into *Epirus* and *Pannonia*, both which Countries, together with the adjacent Parts, he harass'd and depopulated. His Success made him bold and his Army couragious, so that he began to bend his Thoughts towards *Italy* it self, and had already devour'd in his Mind all the Wealth of that beautiful Garden of the West; in whose fertile Plains, and capacious Towns, he thought at last to settle. These his Thoughts he communicated to his Men, who with a barbarous Applause approv'd of his Proposal; he told 'em *Italy* was at present weak and defenceless, unable to oppose any sudden violent Attempt; he concluded it no difficult matter to take *Rome* her self, and thereby seize upon the innumerable Wealth which the Care, Industry, Avarice or Ambition of so many Ages had with a profuse Husbandry drain'd from the whole World, and hoarded up in her. The Army were so well pleas'd with his Design, that from their General they made him their King, and prepared all things for their intended March; which he thought not fit to begin 'till the

A.D. 402.

Alarich *prepares to invade Italy.*

Summer was pass'd, but chose rather to enter *Italy* in the Winter, the Rigour of which he and his *Goths* had from their Infancy been inured to, and must therein have an Advantage of the *Italians*, who had not been us'd to the Hardships of War in that Season. Having got a sufficient Army together, consisting of *Alans*, *Goths*, *Hunns*, and other barbarous Nations, he quitted the lower *Pannonia* and march'd into the upper, consisting at present of *Austria*, *Stiria*, and *Carinthia*; from thence he pass'd on to *Noricum*, or *Bavaria*, the Passes of which he with great Ease master'd; from hence he drove out *Ætius*, who had the Command of the Imperial Army, and took and pillaged all the Towns that came in his way. Hearing *Honorius* was in *Liguria* he pass'd through the Forest of *Trent* with an intent to attack him, seizing on all the little Towns that lay on the Coast of the *Adriatick*, and directing his Course towards the *Adda*, he enter'd all the Cities of that Quarter without any Opposition. Having made a Bridge for his Men to pass over the River he left a sufficient Number to secure it, and so directed his Course to *Liguria*, making what haste he could to *Hasta*, or *Ast*, where he was inform'd the Emperor then lay.

Upon the News of it the Romans are in great Consternation.   It is not to be express'd with how much Consternation the *Romans* receiv'd the Intelligence of the intended Invasion. All the Omens, or pretended Omens, that had been observ'd for a considerable Time pass'd, were, by the superstitious Fears of the People apply'd to the present Extremities: Not only the Voice of Thunder, but Chattering of Birds frighted 'em: Hail-stones of an unusual Bigness, and Bees attempting to swarm at an unseasonable time, like so many Oracles denounc'd the Calamities they already had in view. The frequent Eclipses of the Moon, and the appearance of a Comet of an extraordinary

dinary size impos'd upon their Ignorance, and awaken'd their guilty Consciences with the sense of Divine Vengeance. But nothing affected 'em so much as the Sight of two Wolves which as the Emperor was riding abroad presented themselves to his View, and had the Courage to set upon the Company. Being receiv'd upon the Points of their Spears and Swords they were easily dispatch'd; but when their Bellies were open'd, in one was found the Right Hand of a Man, to the great Amazement of the Beholders, and in the other the Left. This Prodigy they concluded apparently threaten'd *Rome* her self, the Founder whereof, according to their Tradition, had been nourish'd by a She Wolf; so that they now began to cast up the Age of the City, and to reckon her End approaching. Their Fears made 'em superstitious, and the Event prov'd they were Prophets.

And as if these unusual and sinister Practices were not sufficient for the publick Distractions, the People inhabiting *Rhætia*, the present Country of the *Grisons*, either at the Instigation of *Alarich*, or out of a Prospect of mending their Condition, revolted from the *Romans*, and so facilitated the Design of the *Goths*. To obviate all these apparent Mischiefs *Stilicho* took care to have all the Towns well fortify'd and provided, especially *Rome* it self; notwithstanding which *Alarich* was no sooner enter'd *Italy*, but the Inhabitants look'd upon it as already taken, and were for removing with their Wealth, some into the Islands on the *Adriatick*, others into *Sicily*, and the very Officers in the Emperor's Court were for flying into *Gaul* upon the Approach of the Barbarians. Indeed this general Horror, which had seiz'd on the Minds of the People, was no more than a seasonable Introduction to the Calamities that follow'd. *Italy*, that for many Ages had liv'd in a continu'd Serenity, in the full Enjoyments of Peace,

A Revolt in Rhætia.

Plenty, and Prosperity, from this time forward became the Stage of such Calamities, and for several Years together afforded Examples of such strange and frequent Revolutions, as the World can hardly parallel.

Stilicho was the only Man who stood unshaken at the Approach of this furious Tempest, silencing their Fears, and reviving their Hopes and Resolutions by his seasonable Speeches and vigorous Preparations. He told 'em *the Goths had taken the Advantage of their own Discord and Distractions, and had broken into* Italy *when their Forces were employ'd in* Rhætia, *and that they would dare to stay no longer than 'till the Troubles were compos'd on that side.* He reminded 'em how unsuccessful the Attempts upon Italy *had ever prov'd to Foreign Armies,* and promis'd *'em quickly to reduce their revolted Neighbours, and then chastise the Arrogance and Presumption of* Alarich. Accordingly he march'd with all Expedition into *Rhætia*, where the *Grisons* being confounded at his unexpected Approach began to repent of their Folly, and listen to an Accommodation. He taking the Advantage of their Fear reduc'd 'em by gentle Means to their Duty, and incited 'em to employ their Arms in the Defence of the Empire and *Honorius*. This Affair being happily concluded, he apply'd himself with great Diligence to the raising an Army for the Defence of *Italy*. To those Troops that had serv'd in *Rhætia* he added such as he could draw out of *Gaul, Britain,* and other Parts, and with his new Army, amounting to about Thirty five thousand Men, he return'd back into *Liguria*, inspiring new Life into the States and Cities of *Italy*.

A. D. 403.
Honorius besieg'd in Hasta,

Honorius was at this time in the City of *Hasta*, whither *Alarich* was advanc'd in the Depth of Winter to besiege him, there to force from him such unequal and dishonourable Terms, as the visible Extremity

Chap. III. XLVIII. Arcadius, Honorius.

tremity of his Affairs encourag'd him to propose to him. *Stilicho* being inform'd of the Danger the Emperor was in, hasten'd with the utmost Diligence to his Relief, which, with a true *Roman* Courage, he effected; for passing over the *Adda* he broke thorough the Enemy's Camp, and threw himself with a sufficient Force into the Town. *Alarich* was much disharten'd at this unexpected Bravery in the *Romans*, and began to be weary of his *Italian* Expediton, whereupon he summon'd a Council of War, in which it was resolv'd to raise the Siege, as they did accordingly. *Stilicho* placing himself at the Head of the Army, which by this time was come up, march'd after the *Goths*, and overtook 'em at *Pollentia*, or *Polenza*, seven Miles distant from *Hasta*, where he engag'd and defeated him. One *Saul*, a *Pagan* and Barbarian, had the Chief Command of the *Alan* Horse that serv'd in the Emperor's Army: He concluding the *Goths* out of respect to their Religion, being Christians, tho' of the *Arian* Sect, would not Fight on *Easter*-day, attack'd 'em upon that solemn Festival, promising himself an absolute Victory; but the *Goths* seeing themselves so hardly press'd upon took to their Arms, and fought with greater Animosity, so that *Paul* was Slain, and his Troops put to Flight, and thereby endanger'd the Miscarriage of the whole Wing, had not *Stilicho* come seasonably in with the Legions to their Assistance; he rally'd the Horse, drew up the whole Army, and so began the Fight afresh, which was maintain'd on both sides with much Resolution. At length the Victory inclin'd to the *Romans*; for after an obstinate Contest the Barbarians gave Ground, and lost as many in the Pursuit as they had done in the Fight. *Stilicho* remain'd Master of the Field of Battel, and the *Romans* pillag'd the Camp of the Enemy, where they

Roman is reliev'd by Stilicho.

Alarich defeated at Pollentia;

re-

recover'd many Captives, and found an inestimable Treasure which the *Goths* had plunder'd in the wealthy Cities of *Greece*, among which, if *Claudian* may be credited, were the Purple Robes of the Emperor *Valens*. *Stilicho* might have intercepted the *Goths* in their Flight, and have destroy'd *Alarich*, but he thought fit to let him escape over the *Po* with the remainder of his Troops, either because he conceiv'd it imprudent to press too hard upon Barbarians in Despair, or for that he intended to make some use of them afterwards, or desir'd to render himself by the War more considerable to the Empire; whatever the Reasons were, by an Agreement between them, they were immediately to quit *Italy*; in pursuance to which *Alarich* retir'd with his shatter'd Troops as far as *Verona*, but there, in Breach of his Promise to *Stilicho*, he put himself into a Condition of engaging a second time with the *Romans*, should they think fit to hazard another Battel; which *Stilicho*, provok'd at the Perfidiousness of the Barbarian, was the more inclinable to do, both because the Enemy was drawn farther off from *Rome*, and the River *Po* was betwixt 'em.

and again at Verona. Here the *Romans* had once more the Advantage, and *Alarich* narrowly escaping fled with the Remnant of his Army to the Mountains, over which he attempted to pass into *Rhætia* or *Gaul*, but was oppos'd by *Stilicho*, who kept him in so long 'till most of his Men forsook him and join'd with the *Romans*; and then, after he had undergone a multitude of Inconveniences, he retir'd with a few of his Companions into *Dalmatia*. *Stilicho*, by all appearance, might have prevented his Escape, but he is thought to have enter'd into a secret Confederacy with him, thinking his Grandeur and Authority with the Emperor could by no means be maintain'd so well as by the continuance of the War.

This

This Year, so remarkable for the Success of the *Romans* against *Alarich*, had *Theodosius*, the Son of *Arcadius*, and *Rumorodius* for Consuls. *Theodosius* was then but two Years of Age, and had the Year before been declared *Augustus* by his Father; the East all this while enjoy'd a perfect Peace, and *Arcadius* found himself at leisure to ease several of his Subjects by some wholesome and seasonable Laws, and reward such as had been zealous in his Service. About the latter end of the Year *Honorius* remov'd from *Ravenna* towards *Rome*, as well to triumph for his Victories over the *Goths*, as to satisfie the Senate and People, who by their several Petitions had desir'd the Honour of his Presence. At *Rome* he enter'd into his sixth Consulship, chusing *Aristænetus* for his Collegue. The People were overjoy'd to see him, especially upon such an occasion, and express'd their Satisfaction in costly Feasts, magnificent Shows, and other publick Demonstrations of their Joy. In the mean time *Stilicho* is said to have made a Peace with *Alarich*, and that with the Emperor's Participation; the Conditions of it were, *That* Alarich *should retire with all his Troops out of the Territories of* Honorius, *and break into the Eastern Part of* Illyricum, *which belonged to* Arcadius; *that* Honorius *or* Stilicho *should, in time convenient, send* Jovius, *Lieutenant for the Emperor in the Western* Illyricum, *who in Conjunction with the* Goths *should seize upon both Parts in Behalf of* Honorius; upon which *Alarich* went and possess'd himself of *Epirus*, a Branch of the Eastern Empire, where he waited in Expectation of *Stilicho*'s Promises.

A. D. 404.

St. Chrysostome *Persecuted.*

About this time began the Troubles of St. *Chrysostome*, that worthy Father of the Church, and Bishop of *Constantinople*, which ended not but with his Life. Being a declar'd Enemy to all Vice and vici-

vicious Practices, he often exclaim'd in his Sermons against the Pride, Wantonness and Vanity of the Female Sex, which drew upon him the ill Will of several Ladies in the Court, amongst whom were *Marsa*, or *Martia*, the Widdow of *Promotus*; *Castruccia*, *Saturnius* his Widdow; and *Eugraphia*; these three joining together persuaded the Empress *Eudoxia*, that St. *Chrysostome* in one of his Sermons had call'd her *Jezebel*, at which she was extreamly incens'd against him. Some Bishops, whom he had depos'd by reason of their corrupt Lives, and several Priests whom he had reprov'd and corrected for their Licentiousness, embrac'd so favourable an Opportunity of Revenge; among these was *John*, one of his own Deacons, who produc'd several Articles against him, to which a Synod of Bishops, summon'd for that purpose by *Theophilus*, Bishop of *Alexandria*, his declared Enemy, requir'd him to give in his Answer. The Principal of these Articles were, *That he sold several consecrated Vessels, had laid a Snare to entrap* Severian, *Bishop of* Gabala; *had ordain'd four Bishops at one single Ordination; had suffer'd Women to come into his Chamber when no one was by; had conferr'd Holy Orders on several Persons without Testimonials, or the Consent of his Clergy; that he eat by himself, and led a very beastly, gluttonous Life*; and the like. Among those who appear'd the most vigorous against him were *Severian* of *Gabala*, *Acacius* of *Berœa*, and *Antiochus* of *Ptolemais*; who tho' they were all Men remarkable in their Generation for their Eloquence and Knowledge of the Scriptures, yet did they suffer themselves to be miss-led by *Theophilus*, either out of Envy to his great Reputation, or some other private Regard. After several Citations this Mock-Synod presum'd to pronounce a formal Sentence upon him, tho' they all knew that the Particulars with which

he

he was charg'd were either false or insignificant. Having by an Unanimity of Voices declar'd him depos'd from his Function, they order'd their Sentence to be communicated as well to the Clergy as the Court, and undertook to inform the Emperor, that *Chrysostome* having had the Arrogance to call the Empress *Jezebel* was guilty of High-Treason. *Arcadius* confirm'd the Judgment of the Synod, banish'd him the City, and constrain'd him to Embark in an obscure, tempestuous Night, and retire to *Prenotus* in *Bithynia*.

But the Day following both the Emperor and the Empress were so alarm'd at a terrible Earth-Quake, in which the Emperor's Apartment suffer'd very much, that they resolv'd to recal him; he return'd accordingly, and was restor'd to his Bishoprick, from which however he was again thrust out not long after. For a Statue being erected in Honour of the Empress, near the great Church of St. *Sophia*, in *Constantinople*; those who had the Care of the Dedication represented several Idolatrous Shows to the People, who, pleas'd with the Performance, gave such a loud and tumultuous Applause, as disturb'd and interrupted the Divine Service; hereupon the Bishop exclaim'd, with his usual Zeal, against the Authors of such an unseasonable Disorder, and let fall some Words relating to the Occasion of it, which being reported to the Empress, were made to speak a Sense different from what he intended, which reviv'd her Dislike to him, and made her resolve to ruin him; whereupon she stirr'd his old Enemies up against him, supported 'em with her Authority and Interest in the Emperor, and never left off 'till he was once more Depos'd and Banish'd. For three Years together he liv'd an Exile, labouring under great Hardships in his own Person, and under no less in those his Friends were

made

made to endure for his sake. His Enemies still persisted to persecute him even in his Exile, procuring him to be remov'd, by the Emperor's Order, from place to place, and to be roughly us'd by the Soldiers who had the Charge of him; at last having suffer'd all the Fatigues of a three Months Voyage, during which they hurry'd him up and down with much Inhumanity, tho' he had a Feaver upon him, occasion'd by their barbarous Treatment, which they plainly told him they did by Order from the Court, that he might die upon the Road; they brought him to *Cumana*, in a Temple near which Place they lodg'd him for that Night; the next Morning the Holy Bishop finding his End approaching, and that he had not long to live, desir'd them to defer their Journey but for a few Hours, which they were so far from granting, that they press'd him with more haste than ordinary, but were scarce advanc'd a League and half on their Way before they found his Feaver so strong upon him that they were forc'd to return back to the Temple, where, upon the Fourth of *November*, he expir'd. In his Life he stood the main Champion for the Purity of the Christian Religion, and in his Death was a Reproach to several who openly profess'd, and ought to have been as shining Lights to the rest of the World, but had not arriv'd to that Purity of Spirit and Integrity of Heart, requir'd and enforc'd so often in the Gospel. We may learn from the Sufferings this Great Man endur'd, how requisite a Brotherly Love is to the Peace and Unity of the Church, and that the want of it does not proceed more from a Disagreement in Points of Doctrine, than from some private Ends and selfish Considerations, from which the Fathers of the Church themselves are not always free.

That

That St. *Chrysostome* ow'd all his Misfortunes to the Malice of the Empress *Eudoxia* we have no reason to doubt. She was, according to the Historian, a Woman insupportably Insolent, imposing upon her Husband, and being imposed upon by her Eunuchs, who committed great Disorders, and brought innumerable Corruptions into the Court, which was pester'd with Parasites and Informers; so that if St. *Chrysostome* tax'd her obliquely in his Sermons, it as well became the great Character he bore in the Church, as it became her Pride to resent it. The Night after his second Banishment the Episcopal Palace took Fire, the Flames of which laid hold on the Roof of the great Church adjoining to it, which was presently reduc'd to Ashes, together with the Hall where the Senate us'd to assemble. This Misfortune was imputed to St. *Chrysostome*'s Friends, as if they had set Fire to the Church with an Intent to have no other Bishop there but himself; upon which Consideration they were cruelly Persecuted, and thrown into Prison, where several of 'em dy'd of the Torments inflicted on 'em: But the Intelligence the Court had of some fresh Commotions put a stop to their violent Proceedings; for the *Isauri*, who inhabited the most inaccessible Places of the Mountain *Taurus*, fell in several Bodies down upon the adjacent Country, where they over-ran the Villages and unfortify'd Towns which they sack'd and plunder'd. The Court made Choice of one *Arbazacius* to oppose 'em and relieve *Pamphylia*. Upon his Approach they retir'd back into the Mountains, whither he pursu'd 'em, and apply'd himself with so much Vigour to the Service at first, that had he persisted he might have totally subdu'd 'em, and prevented the like Depredations for the future; but being a Man given up naturally to Ease and Pleasure he grew

A Fire in Constantinople.

remiss,

remiss, and suffer'd himself to be brib'd, preferring his private Gain to the publick Good. Of this great Complaint was made to the Court, whither he was sent for in order to be call'd to an Account for his Prevarication; but presenting the Empress with part of what he had gotten from the *Isauri* he evaded the Prosecution, and spent the rest in the fashionable Diversions of the City.

A. D. 406.
Radagaisus Invades Italy.

The Year following *Rome* was again threaten'd with no less than an utter Destruction, from an Inundation of Barbarians led on by *Radagaisus*, term'd by St. *Austin* King of the *Goths*. He observing *Alarich*, after his disgraceful Overthrow, was receiv'd into Confederacy with the *Romans*, and being honour'd and respected by 'em was averse from War, and willing to be at Peace with them, persuaded the Nations inhabiting the other side of the *Rhine* and the *Ister* to fall into *Italy*, and revenge upon it the late Slaughter of their Countrymen, alluring 'em with the Hopes of taking *Rome*, the Wealth of which he promis'd to give up to 'em. Hereupon a Body of four hundred thousand Men united themselves under him, and march'd directly for *Italy*. Upon the first Intelligence of their Motions, *Stilicho* advis'd *Honorius* to add to his *Roman* Legions such Numbers of the *Hunns* and *Alans* as were willing to serve him under the Conduct of *Uldes* and *Sarus*; and as if all these were not sufficient to Encounter such Swarms of Barbarians, he invited the Slaves to take Arms upon Promise of Liberty, a thing never known to be done, but when the Common-wealth was reduc'd to the greatest Extremity; and that those that were Free-men might be encourag'd to Arm themselves in Defence of their Country, he engag'd himself to pay them, that came in by such a time, a certain Sum by way of Advance or Gratuity.

Radagaifus having in the mean time ravaged all *Pannonia*, was pass'd the *Julian Alps* and got into *Italy*, directing his Course towards *Rome*, which he was already Master of in his Imagination. Being a Heathen he was very superstitious, performing his Sacrifices every Morning to his Gods. As he drew near the City the *Romans* were in the greatest Consternation; and the Heathens, who still made up a considerable Part of the Inhabitants, declared aloud that *Radagaifus* would assuredly prevail, not so much upon the Account of his numerous Forces as his Devotion to the Gods, who were banish'd by the ungrateful Citizens from *Rome*, which had deserted their Worship, and forsaken them that had so often defended her; therefore unless the ancient Religion was restor'd, and Christianity abolish'd, the City would certainly fall into the Hands of the Barbarians. With such Complaints as these was every Corner of the City fill'd, and Christ's Name blasphem'd as the Occasion of the present Calamities. *Stilicho* had prudently declin'd opposing himself against *Radagaifus* and his numerous Army, whilst he was in the open Champaign Country, where he might in a manner be surrounded by the Barbarians; but when he found him advanc'd as far as *Hetruria*, call'd at present *Tuscany*, a Region full of craggy Mountains and narrow Vallies, and that he was set down before *Florence*, which he had so well supply'd with Necessaries that it was able to make a very vigorous Defence, then like a wary Captain he thought fit to set upon him: Accordingly he advanced towards him, and after he had sufficiently weary'd out his Army in that Siege, he watch'd an Opportunity, and fell upon his Rear with so much Resolution, that no less than an hundred thousand of his Men were cut off, without the Loss of one Man on the *Roman* side. He drew up with the rest

Radagaifus defeated,

of

of his Army to the Mountains of *Fæsulæ*, where he secured his Men from the *Roman* Attacks, but expos'd 'em to the Inconvenience of a barren desolate Place, in which they were closely besieg'd by *Stilicho*. In this Condition he attempted to escape, and leave his Men to the Mercy of the *Romans*, into whose Hands he fell together with his Sons, and *and Slain*, was shortly after put to Death. The rest of the Barbarians, overcome with Hunger, submitted in such great Numbers that they were sold by the *Romans* like Beasts, a whole Drove at a time: But having contracted an ill Habit of Body by their long Fasting, and unwholesome Diet afterwards, they all dy'd in a few Days; and *Stilicho* had a Statue of Brass erected to his Memory, as a Reward for his great Industry, and extraordinary Service.

Whilst *Europe* was thus harass'd and oppress'd by the Barbarians, the State of *Africk* was serene and quiet; but the Repose of the Church was interrupted by the Donatists, who us'd the Catholicks with great Outrage and Violence. *Aurelius*, Bishop of *Carthage*, had summon'd a Synod against 'em, from whence *Theatius* and *Enodius*, two venerable Prelates, were deputed with Letters to the Emperors *Arcadius* and *Honorius*, in which they inform'd 'em that they had left nothing unattempted to reduce those Hereticks to the Church; but that they still continu'd obstinate, and instead of inclining to their Christian Proposals, they fell in a most outragious manner upon those Catholicks that came in their way, and had forcibly seiz'd upon several of their Churches. These Proceedings made 'em fly to their Majesties for Protection, beseeching 'em to have a regard to the Catholick Interest, and put a stop to the violence of those Hereticks, lest they compell'd the People by force to subscribe to their mischievous Doctrines. *Honorius* readily granted their Request,
and

and proceeded with great Rigour against the Donatists, by which means several of 'em relinquish'd their Errors, and return'd into the Bosom of the Church. But the most zealous among 'em would listen to no Accommodation, but exercis'd great Cruelties upon all those who were not of their Persuasion, whenever they could lay their Hands upon 'em.

This same Year the Barbarians pour'd themselves with fresh Forces into the Empire under the Conduct of *Godegisil*, King of the *Vandals*, who seeing *Italy* distracted with Wars on every side, thought he had now a fit Opportunity to invade *Gaul*; which being removed far from the Emperor's Presence, could not be so speedily reliev'd. Departing therefore out of *Scythia* at the Head of his *Vandals* and *Alans*, he first march'd through *Sarmatia*, where he was join'd by some of the *Quadi* and other Barbarians, who had formerly settled themselves there by the Permission of *Constantine* the Great. With these he enter'd into *Germany*, where great Numbers of the Inhabitants associated themselves with him, either forced to it through Fear, or allured by the hopes of Plunder. Having now a very numerous Army at his Command, he advanc'd with all Expedition to the *Rhine*, where the *Franks* at first oppos'd him, either out of regard to a League they had lately enter'd into with *Stilicho*, or for that they were willing to preserve a Province they hoped one day to be Masters of themselves, from the Incursions of so numerous an Enemy; but being overpower'd with Odds they were forced to retire, and suffer *Godegisil* to advance with his Army, who pass'd the *Rhine* the thirtieth of *December*, An. Dom. 406. *Arcadius* being the sixth time and *Probinus* Consuls.

A new Invasion of the Barbarians.

They

They were no sooner got on the other side the *Rhine*, but they miserably harass'd the Country on every side, whilst the Governors of the Provinces, who had been placed there by the Emperor, were in no Condition to oppose 'em. The first City that felt their Fury was *Mayence*, which they took by Assault; here many thousands of the Inhabitants fled for Refuge into their Churches, whom however they most cruelly massacred, and then rased the City. *Wormes* held out a considerable time, but despairing of any Relief they at last surrender'd at Discretion. The Cities of *Spires* and *Strasbourgh* followed the same Fate, being taken and pillaged. From hence they marched on to *Rheims*, which they took by Storm; after which they cut off the Head of *Nicasius*, Bishop of the Place, and put his Sister *Eutropia*, and great Multitudes of the other Inhabitants to Death. From *Rheims* they went to *Arras*, *Tournay*, *Amiens*, and up as far as the Sea-Coasts about *Calice* and *Bologne*, sacking and pillaging all the Towns they met in their March.

The Britains rebel, and set up a new Emperor.

This Misfortune was attended by another; for the Inhabitants, and Troops that were quarter'd in *Britain*, fearing lest the *Vandals* should pass over the Sea and subdue them with the rest, revolted from their Obedience to *Honorius*, and set up one *Mark*, whom they declared Emperor. Presently after, being on a sudden grown weary of their new Prince, they deprived him of his Life and Dignity together, and placed one *Gratian* in his Room, who was a Countryman of their own. Him they vested with an Imperial Robe, and dutifully attended him for four Months together, but then upon some Dislike they murder'd him, and conferr'd the Sovereignty upon one *Constantine*; not so much in respect to his Courage, for he was a very inconsiderable Man in the Army, but in regard of his Name, which they

look'd

look'd upon as fortunate, and importing good Success: For they were in hopes he would deliver 'em from the Barbarians who had over-run *Gaul*, and govern the Empire with Honour and Reputation, as *Constantine* the Great had done in the foregoing Age, who was of the same Name, and had been advanced to the Imperial Dignity in the same Island. This new Prince, immediately after his Promotion, pass'd over into *Gaul*, and taking with him the very Flower of all the *British* Youth, so utterly exhausted the Military Force of the Island, that it was wholly broken, and the Island left naked to new Invaders, by which means she lost her old Inhabitants, and submitted to the Power of other Lords.

Constantine, as soon as he was got on the other side, laid Siege to *Bologn*, which he carry'd with little Opposition, after which all the *Roman* Forces in the Country came readily in and join'd him; by whose Assistance he made himself Master in a short time of all *Gallia Celtica* and a great part of *Aquitain*, whilst *Limenius, Præfectus Prætorio*, and *Cariobaudes*, General of the Foot, concluding it impossible to resist *Constantine* and the *Vandals* both at once, fled into *Italy* with the Relicks of their Army; leaving the *Vandals* to waste the Country on one side, and *Constantine* to pursue his Success on the other.

Honorius receiv'd the first Intelligence of this Revolt at *Ravenna*, where he was intent upon raising an Army, which was to march into *Illyricum* and join *Alarich*, as it had been formerly agreed between 'em, and together with him fall upon his Brother's Territories; to which he had been induced either at the Instigation of *Stilicho*, who found he had great Enemies in *Arcadius* his Court, or because *Honorius* thought himself affronted in his Embassadors, by the rough Usage they receiv'd from *Arcadius*,

cadius, to whom they were sent with Letters from his Brother in behalf of St. *Chrysostome*. But as soon as he was inform'd of these strange Revolutions in *Gaul*, he chang'd his Design, and so the *Illyrian* Expedition was interrupted.

A.D. 408.

Arcadius dies.

The Year following, on the first of *May*, in the Consulship of *Bassus* and *Philippus*, *Arcadius* the Emperor dy'd at *Constantinople*; he left behind him one Son, and four Daughters; *Pulcheria*, *Placilla*, *Arcadia*, and *Marina*; who became all of 'em illustrious for their Piety, and Zeal for the true Religion. *Arcadius* dy'd in the Flower of his Age, being not full one and thirty Years old; of which he had reign'd twelve with his Father, and thirteen Years three Months and fifteen Days after his Death.

His Character.

He was himself a Prince well inclined, a great Lover of his Subjects, and a Friend to Justice and Sobriety, but he suffer'd himself to be too much ruled and imposed upon by his Favourites, who abusing his Authority most grievously oppress'd his Subjects. He was something too uxorious, especially at the latter end of his Reign, which involv'd the Government in a great many Difficulties, and introduced strange Corruptions into the Court. He left for his Successor *Theodosius* sirnamed the Younger, being at his Father's Death no more than seven Years old, but he reign'd above two and forty Years after his Decease. *Arcadius* found by the Measures his Brother *Honorius* took, and his Practices in *Illyricum*, that he had little reason to depend upon him; fearing therefore left after his Death he should strip

He makes the King of Persia his Son's Guardian.

his Son of the Empire, he left him to the Care and Protection of *Isdegerdes*, King of *Persia*, with whom he had lately enter'd into a strict League and Alliance for an hundred Years, and in whose approved Honour and Virtue he knew his Son would find a sure Refuge. *Isdegerdes* undertook the Charge with

Sincerity, and acquitted himself as faithfully; for being unable to quit his own Dominion, and take care of *Theodosius*, or attend to the Administration in person, he sent *Antiochus* in his room to *Constantinople*, a prudent, honest, and experienc'd Statesman; to whom was join'd in Authority *Anthemius*, the *Præfectus Prætorio*, who had been Consul three Years before: He was one of the greatest Men of the Age, being a zealous Christian, a vigilant Statesman, an honest Courtier, and a valiant Soldier. *Socrates* saith he encompass'd *Constantinople* with new Walls and Fortifications, that he never undertook any thing without the Advice and Approbation of the ablest Men in the State, but above all others he rely'd much upon *Troilus* the Sophist, a wise Man, and of much Experience. Some say *Anthemius*, the better to secure the Empire to *Theodosius*, procur'd the Peace between the *Romans* and *Persians* for an hundred Years; which however was confirm'd in his Father's Life-time, as we observ'd before, tho' it's very likely he might be instrumental in the causing it to be renew'd.

This Peace contributed very much to the Advancement of the Christian Faith in *Persia*, whither *Maruthas*, Bishop of *Mesopotamia*, being sent in an Embassy, he is said to have cured the King by his Prayers of a Distemper under which he had been long afflicted, and deliver'd his Son who was possess'd with a Devil. These Cures were look'd upon as miraculous, in consideration of which the Prince gave *Maruthas* leave to build several Churches throughout his Dominions; and was almost persuaded to embrace the Faith himself, having discover'd the Impostures of his own false Doctors, among which this was not the least remarkable. The *Magi*, who were afraid Christianity was going to be built upon the Ruins of Paganism, convey'd a

Socrat. L. 7. C. 8.

Man privately under the Temple of the Sun, who when the King came thither to perform his Sacrifices, cryed out from beneath with a hollow and dismal Voice, that *Ifdegerdes* *ought to be dethron'd, having provok'd the God of the* Perfians *by his impious Favours shown to the Christians*. This Voice, which he thought came from Heav'n, at firft much furpriz'd the fuperftitious Prince, but he was foon undeceiv'd by *Maruthas*, who advis'd him to open the Ground near that Place where the Voice feem'd to be deliver'd; which was no fooner done but they difcover'd a Hole wherein a Man lay conceal'd, who was immediately put to Death by the King's Order, together with feveral of the *Magi*. This Relation will not feem ftrange to thofe, who are not ignorant of the many Impoftures put upon the World now-a-days, by the villainous Artifices of the *Roman* Priefts.

Honorius had not as yet heard of his Brother's Death, but had his Thoughts intent upon *Conftantine*, and his Progrefs in *Gaul*, againft whom *Stilicho* had fent one *Sarus* at the Head of a fufficient Army; who meeting with *Juftinian*, one of the Ufurper's Officers, a Man ignorant and uncapable; he kill'd him upon the Place, with the greateft part of his Forces; and having got a very rich Booty, he march'd towards *Valentia*, whither he heard *Conftantine* was remov'd, and where he refolv'd to befiege him. *Nevigaftes* was another of the Ufurper's Generals, whom *Sarus* by fair Promifes drew off to his Party, but afterwards order'd him to be flain, contrary to the Faith he had given him. Into their Places *Conftantine* advanc'd *Gerontius* and *Edobechus*, the one a *Frank*, and the other born in *Britain*. *Sarus* was too fenfible of the Courage and Experience of thofe two Perfons to wait their coming, and therefore he rofe up in hafte from *Valentia*, after he had

laid

laid Siege to it seven Days. They pursu'd him with so much Vigour and Execution, that with long Marches and many Dangers he got to the *Alps*, where he was forc'd to buy his Passage into *Italy* by quitting all his Booty to the *Bacaudæ*, an hardy desperate People inhabiting those Parts.

After this *Constantine* united all his Forces together, and with much Diligence fortify'd the *Alps* that lay between *Gallia Celtica* and *Italy*, and that he might secure himself from the Insults of the Barbarians, as well as of the *Romans*, he fortify'd the *Rhine*, and then made *Constans* his eldest Son *Cæsar*; having recall'd him from *Winchester*, as our Writers say, where he had devoted himself to a Monastical Life. After this *Constantine*, having made sure of the greatest part of *Gaul*, which submitted to him, settl'd his Imperial Seat at *Arles*, from whence he sent *Constans* with a powerful Army into *Spain*, where he proceeded with much Success, and took *Didymius* and *Veronianus* Prisoners; these were two of *Theodosius* his Relations, and if we may believe *Zosimus* had much disturb'd the Affairs of their Country, which therefore with more readiness submitted to *Constans*; who having committed the Command of the Army, and the Care of the *Pyrenees* to *Gerontius* his Lieutenant, he return'd into *Gaul*, and presented the Prisoners to his Father, by whose Order they and their Wives were immediately put to Death. All this while *Godegisil* was pursuing his Conquests, proceeding out of *Gaul* into *Spain*; for by a private Agreement betwixt him and *Constantine*, whilst *Constans* was Conquering the Eastern Parts, he was to seize on the West; whereupon the *Vandals* took *Gallicia*, where they settl'd: The *Suevi* push'd their Conquests farther, and the *Alans* fix'd themselves in *Portugal* and *Andalousia*. From these Barbarians descended

Constantine's Progress.

the Ancient Kings of *Spain*, the firſt of which in the Catalogue is *Hermenric*, King of *Gallicia*.

<small>Honorius Marries his firſt Wive's Siſter.</small> During theſe Tranſactions in *Gaul* and *Spain*, the Emperor *Honorius*, who had lately loſt his firſt Wife, the Eldeſt Daughter of *Stilicho*, was marry'd to *Thermantia* her younger Siſter. This inceſtuous Match, to which *Stilicho* is ſaid to have been very averſe, was effected by the Procurement of his Wife *Serena*, who hop'd by this means to preſerve her Authority over *Honorius*, who indeed was very much guided by her. Tho' he had Cohabited many Years with *Mary* the Elder, he never had any Chidren, which made *Serena* more deſirous to Marry him to the Younger, being ambitious of Royal Iſſue, but ſhe likewiſe continu'd Childleſs; the reaſon of this we have from *Zoſimus*, who tells us that when *Honorius* was firſt contracted to Marry, her Mother knew ſhe was too young for his Bed, and yet was not able to prevent or defer the Nuptials; fearing therefore her Daughter's Life to be in Danger, ſhe had recourſe in this Extremity to an old Woman, who by her Charms work'd ſo far with the Emperor, that her Daughter liv'd and dy'd a Virgin; for it ſeems the Spell had a ſtronger Power than was deſign'd, and never forſook the Emperor 'till his Death. If this Account be true they muſt be in an Error, who impute the want of Conſummation to the ſudden Death of *Thermantia*, as well as her Elder Siſter. *Thermantia* was depos'd after her Father's Death, and ſent back to her Mother, as we ſhall ſee hereafter.

Before the Nuptial Solemnity was well over, News was brought to Court that *Alarich* having quitted *Epirus*, and paſs'd the *Straits* between *Pannonia* and *Venetia*, was encamp'd at a Town call'd *Æmon*, from whence he advanc'd into *Bavaria*, and

and sent to demand of *Stilicho* Mony to pay his Army, which, upon his Account, had been Quarter'd so long in *Epirus*, and likewise to defray the Charges of the present Expedition, otherwise he threaten'd to peirce into *Italy*, and lay all waste before him. Hereupon the Senate was assembl'd, and the Question put what was to be done in this Affair; after a short Consultation most of the Senators were for a War, in which *Stilicho* and his Party oppos'd 'em with great Earnestness. They that were on the other side desir'd to know why he was so fond of a Peace, which was to be bought to the great Dishonour of the *Roman* Majesty, urging that it became the Dignity of the Empire to chastise the Insolence of a Barbarian, that presum'd to make a Market both of Peace and War; to this he answer'd, That *Alarich* had by *Honorius* his Orders continu'd thus long in *Epirus*, in Expectation of being employ'd against *Arcadius*, and in Conjunction with the *Roman* Forces to have wrested *Illyricum* from him, and have join'd it to *Honorius* his Dominions; that the thing had long since been put in Execution, had he not been recall'd by the Emperor's Letters, procur'd by *Serena*'s means, who was careful to preserve a good Intelligence between the two Brothers. Whether the thing was just and reasonable or no, *Stilicho* was thought by the Senate to have given a very good Answer, and so it was agreed that *Alarich* should be paid four thousand Pounds of Gold to keep him quiet, tho' many consented against their Judgments meerly for fear of *Stilicho*; and *Lampadius*, a Man of great Birth and Reputation, openly oppos'd it, affirming boldly, *That they were not now buying a Peace, but signing a Contract of Servitude*; but fearing this Liberty of Speech might draw the Fury of the Court upon him, as soon as the Senate

A War propos'd in the Senate against Alarich, which is oppos'd by Stilicho.

was up he fled into the next Church for Sanctuary. *Stilicho* having, by Virtue of this Act of Senate, purchas'd a Peace from *Alarich*, prepared all things for his intended Expedition against *Constantine* in *Gaul*. *Honorius* himself had a mind to take a Progress to *Ravenna*, there to view and encourage the Army that was to defend him and the Empire against so considerable an Enemy; to this *Stilicho* was very averse, for he had no mind the Emperor should keep any Correspondence with the Army, and therefore endeavour'd, by all Persuasions possible, to divert him from it; but finding him firm to his Resolution, he procur'd *Sarus*, Captain of the Barbarians that lay at *Vienna*, to raise some Disturbance, not aiming by it at any Innovation, but only to frighten the Emperor, and deter him from his intended Progress.

About this time the Emperor heard of the Death of *Arcadius*, and sent for *Stilicho* to *Bononia* to confer with him about the Publick Affairs of the Empire. *Honorius* had a mind to take a Journey into the East, to look after his young Nephew's Interests, and settle the Affairs in those Parts; this *Stilicho* oppos'd with many weighty Arguments, by showing him how expensive such an Expedition must needs be, how necessary his Residence was in *Italy* at this Conjuncture; that *Constantine*, who had already over-ran all *Gaul*, would take the Advantage of his Absence, and bring more Mischiefs upon the Empire; he added, that *Alarich* himself, tho' now in Peace with him, was deceitful and a Barbarian, having a powerful Army at his Command, and therefore not too far to be trusted. He rather propos'd that *Alarich*'s Forces should be join'd to the *Roman* Legions, that the Army so united should be under the joint Command of *Alarich*, and the Officers belonging to those Legions; that they
should

should march with all Expedition against the Usurper, and that he himself should be dispatch'd with Letters from the Emperor to *Constantinople*, containing the Substance of what he would have transacted in the East.

Tho' *Honorius* already began to entertain a Jealousie of *Stilicho*, yet he approv'd of all he propos'd, and having sign'd his Letters for *Theodosius* and *Alarich*, he departed from *Bononia*, attended by one *Olympius*, born nigh the *Euxine* Sea, a Man, says *Zosimus*, who upon the Reputation of Christian Piety, which he outwardly affected, and a great Pretence to Modesty and Sobriety, was in very great Esteem with the Emperor, who advanc'd him to a Principal Post in the Court, and employ'd him about his Person. He discoursing with *Honorius* upon the Road, encreas'd the Suspicions he had lately conceiv'd of *Stilicho*'s Designs, and particularly endeavour'd to perswade him, that he so earnestly desir'd to be sent into the East for no other reason, but that he might have the better Opportunity to remove *Theodosius*, and transfer the Sovereignty of those Parts upon his Son *Eucherius*; to which purpose he held private Correspondence with *Alarich*, with *Godegisil*, and even the Usurper *Constantine*, with whom he had hitherto prolong'd the War on purpose to make himself considerable to the State, and powerful in the Army. He so throughly convinc'd the Emperor of this, and whatever else he had to alledge against *Stilicho*, that he resolv'd to get rid of him as soon as he could, and gave *Olympius* and *Sarus* Orders to destroy him. At *Ticinum*, or *Pavia*, *Olympius* wrought so cunningly with the Soldiers, who had no Kindness for *Stilicho*, that they all mutiny'd, and in a tumultuous manner flew all those who were known to be well affected to *Stilicho*; among these were *Limenius, Præfectus Prætorio*

Honorius grows jealous of Stilicho.

A Mutiny at Ticinum.

in *Gaul*, and *Chariabaudes*, who had lately fled from *Conſtantine*, as we obſerv'd before, and were now come to the Emperor to *Ticinum*; together with theſe they ſlew *Vincentius, Salvius, Nemorius, Patronius* and *Longinianus*, who was *Præfectus Prætorio* of *Italy*. Theſe were all Men Eminent in the State, but of the Inferior ſort there fell Multitudes without number. *Stilicho* was ſtill at *Bononia* when the Report of this Sedition was brought to him, and in great Conſternation call'd the Officers of the Confederate Barbarians together, with whom he conſulted what Courſe was proper to be taken. *Stilicho* at firſt was inform'd that the Emperor himſelf had miſcarry'd in the Tumult, and therefore it was unanimouſly agreed among 'em, that if *Honorius* was Slain, all the Confederates ſhould fall upon the *Roman* Soldiers, and by chaſtiſing them reſtrain the reſt; but if the Tempeſt fell only upon the Magiſtrates, then the Ringleaders of the Mutiny ſhould be puniſh'd as an Example to the reſt. By a ſecond Expreſs *Stilicho* was inform'd that no Violence had been offer'd to the Emperor's Perſon, that the Mutiny was begun by *Olympius* his Procurement, and that none but his own Friends had ſuffer'd in it; by this he ſaw they aim'd ſolely at him, and that it was time for him to conſult his own Safety; whereupon he reſolv'd to remove to *Ravenna*, a ſtrong Town well inhabited, and at his Devotion; but *Sarus*, who commanded the Barbarians that were in Garriſon there, ſeiz'd upon *Stilicho*'s Guards by Command from the Emperor, and order'd him to be taken into Cuſtody; he having notice of it fled by Night into a Church of the Chriſtians, from whence he was taken out the next Day by his own Conſent, after the Soldiers had affirm'd upon Oath, in Preſence of the Biſhop, that they had no Orders from the Emperor to kill,

but

but secure him; however he was no sooner remov'd out of the Church, before they produc'd fresh Letters from *Honorius* with a Warrant for his Death, which was executed accordingly on the Twenty third of *August*, A. D. 408. the Senate at the same time ordering his Name to be ras'd out of all Publick Places, and his Statues to be demolish'd. The Historians of those Times are not agreed in the Circumstances of this Execution, but concur so far in the Substance as we have related it. *Zosimus* indeed disagrees with himself, for whereas at first we were told of his Rapine and Oppression, his Luxury and Debauchery, he at parting represents him as a Man the most Modest of all others, who at that time were entrusted with the Management; for tho' he was nearly ally'd to the Emperor *Theodosius*, and had marry'd both his Daughters to his Son *Honorius*, tho' he had exercis'd the Office of General for three and Twenty Years together, yet was his Son advanc'd to no higher Employment than *Tribune of the Notaries*, nor was he ever known to prefer any Person in the Army for the sake of his Mony, so that upon the whole he seems neither pleas'd with his Advancement nor Disgrace; but in this he follows his old Maxim of arraigning, as much as he can, the Actions of all Christian Princes, and might probably bear a greater Respect to the Cause and Person of *Stilicho* for the sake of his Son *Eucherius*, who to make himself acceptable to the Heathens threaten'd, that if ever he should be advanc'd to the Imperial Dignity, he would begin his Reign with the Restitution of the Temples, and Destruction of Churches. Those, who are less partial to *Stilicho*'s Memory, say he justly deserv'd the Death he suffer'd, that he introduc'd *Alarich* into *Honorius* his Dominions, and call'd the barbarous Nations into the West. After all we must

(margin: Stilicho put to Death.)

must allow him to have been a very great Statesman, and a Person of very Excellent Qualities, but that he was too much perverted by Ambition, which blinded and destroy'd him. He was a Valiant Soldier, and Experienc'd General, ready in forming any Design, and as successful in the Execution of it. *Honorius* was so implicitely guided in his Counsels by him, that for a long time he did nothing without his Approbation, so that he seem'd to be more Absolute in the Empire than the Emperor himself, having a vast Capacity in the Management of Affairs relating either to War or Peace.

Immediately after his Death his own Estate, and that of his Friends and Adherents, were by Publick Edict Confiscated to the Emperor's use. *Thermantia*, the Empress, was depos'd and sent home to her Mother: *Eucherius* was seiz'd at *Narny*, and convey'd from thence to *Rome*, where, by the Emperor's Order, he was put to Death. *Theodosius* was acquainted by Letters from *Honorius* of his Favourite's Death, and the occasion of it; a strict Alliance was concluded between 'em, and in pursuance of it they enter'd together into the Consulate, tho' this happen'd not 'till the Year following. The Emperor's Officers proceeded with great Severity against the Friends of *Stilicho*, and when the Soldiers that were Quarter'd up and down in the Cities of *Italy* heard of his Death, they flew instantly upon the Wives and Children of the Barbarians, who, upon *Stilicho*'s Account, had enter'd into the Emperor's Pay, and putting all to the Sword seiz'd on whatever they had. This prov'd of very ill Consequence, for when their Husbands, Fathers and Relations heard of this abominable Cruelty, and the impious Violation of the Faith given them in a Solemn manner by the *Romans*, they vow'd Revenge, and resolv'd to join with *Alarich*, and in

What follow'd upon Stilicho's Death.

Con-

Conjunction with him enter into a War againſt the *Romans*. Accordingly above thirty thouſand of 'em quitted the Emperor's Service at once and retired toward *Alarich*, who at firſt ſeem'd cautious of receiving 'em, or giving ear to their Propoſals; for a full Year was not expired ſince his laſt Peace with the Emperor, to whom he ſent Meſſengers with Offers to confirm it, and to propoſe to him, That if he would raiſe him a ſmall Sum of Mony to pay his Army their Arrears, and deliver up as Hoſtages for performance of Articles *Ætius* the Son of *Gaudentius*, and *Jaſon* the Son of *Jovius*, he in exchange would ſend him ſome among the chiefeſt of the Nobility in his own Nation, and withdraw his Troops out of *Noricum* into *Pannonia*. *Honorius* being miſs-led by ill Counſel rejected his Propoſals, and ſo loſt an Opportunity of making, if not a very honourable, at leaſt a very advantagious Peace; and yet at the ſame time made no Proviſions for a War. Had he muſtered his Forces together from all Quarters, and ſo diſpos'd of 'em as to have ſtopp'd the Enemy in his Paſſage, or prevented his farther Progreſs; had he made choice of *Sarus* for his General, whoſe very Name was a Terror to the Enemy both for his Courage and Experience, and who had with him a great Number of Barbarians that upon trial would have been found able to make a great Reſiſtance, he had in ſome meaſure provided againſt the Attempts of ſo powerful an Adverſary: But relying wholly upon the Advice and Humours of *Olympius*, he involv'd the State in great Calamities, chuſing ſuch Perſons for his Generals, as at once created Contempt and Confidence in the Minds of his Enemies; for he gave the Command of the Horſe to *Turpillio*, of the Foot to *Varanes*, and made *Vigilantius* General of the Troops of the Houſhold; Men of little Courage, and leſs Experience.

Alarich's Offers rejected by Honorius.

The

A.D. 409.

The Year following *Alarich* sent for *Ataulfus*, his Wife's Brother, out of *Pannonia*, to come and join him with the *Hunns* and *Goths* which he had in great Numbers under him, and be his Associate in the War; but without staying for his Arrival he began his March, in execution of his mighty Designs; and quitting *Noricum* he pass'd the *Alps*, and descended into *Friuli*, leaving *Aquileia* and *Padua* on the left Hand: Passing the *Po* without any Opposition, he drew near to *Ravenna*, and encamp'd with his Army in the Country adjoining to it. From thence he sent Embassadors to *Honorius*, who was then lying in the Town, with Offers not only of Peace but of his Service, provided he and his Men might have some Habitations assign'd 'em in *Italy*; promising, upon that consideration, to serve him and the Empire faithfully. Tho' *Honorius* was sensible *Alarich*'s Forces were much superior to his, and that he was unable to give him Battel, yet relying upon the Strength of *Ravenna*, and other Cities that were well fortify'd, together with the Supplies he expected out of the East, he was deaf to his Proposals, and answer'd him with much Assurance, that he was resolv'd never to condescend to any Offers he should make whilst he continu'd in *Italy*; out of which he advis'd him instantly to retire with his Army, unless he had a mind to be driven out by main Force, as he had been once before, which he had great reason to remember. *Alarich*, incens'd at this haughty Answer, moved with his Army towards *Rimini* and the *Picentin*, from thence into *Umbria*, call'd at present St. *Peter*'s Patrimony; raging with Fire and Sword on every side as he pass'd, to render himself the more terrible; and in this manner march'd directly to *Rome*, stopping up all the Passages that led to it: By which means the City which was crouded with Inhabitants, was presently

He enters Italy,

and marches to Rome.

fently reduc'd to Famine, which was attended by a Peſtilence, proceeding from the unwholſome Diet they were forced in that Exigence to make uſe of, and the Infection of the Air ariſing from great numbers of the Dead that lay up and down the Streets unbury'd, which made that great City look like a large Charnel-Houſe. In this Extremity the Senate diſpatch'd their Embaſſadors out to *Alarich*, to deſire him either to grant 'em a Peace upon reaſonable and moderate Terms, or give 'em leave to come out in Battle-Array, and fight it out with him in the open Field like true *Romans.* Upon this he burſt out into a loud Laughter, and anſwer'd, *Thick Graſs was eaſier cut than thin.* When they came to debate about a Peace he demanded with an inſolent Barbarity all their Gold and Silver, all their rich Moveables, together with their Slaves, without which he was reſolv'd never to raiſe the Siege; and when he was ask'd what he would leave the Inhabitants, he reply'd ſternly *Their Lives.* Hereupon they deſir'd he would grant 'em a ſhort Truce in order to a farther Treaty, which having obtain'd they return'd into the City. The Heathens that were then in *Rome,* ſeeing themſelves reduced to ſuch Hardſhips, began to cry aloud, that Recourſe ought to be had to the Gods who had heretofore ſuccour'd and preſerv'd the City in the greateſt Extremities; and when ſome *Hetruſcan* Augurs affirm'd that the only way to preſerve the City was publickly to reſtore the uſual Sacrifices, the Senate conſented to it: But ſo far was this from relieving the City, that it labour'd every Day under ſome new Difficulties. So that they were forc'd to treat a ſecond time with the Barbarian, who agreed to raiſe the Siege upon Payment of five thouſand Pounds of Gold, thirty thouſand of Silver, four thouſand ſilk Garments, three thouſand Skins of Purple Dye, and as many

many Pounds of Pepper; and for as much as a Sum so immense could not be rais'd by any Tax to be laid upon the Citizens, they had therefore recourse to the Temples of the Heathen Gods, taking from thence the Silver and Gold, and whatever rich Ornaments they found in 'em, and which had hitherto been apply'd to Idolatrous Purposes, wherewith they made good the Deficiency. *Alarich* having receiv'd the Sum they agreed upon, retir'd with his Army into *Tuscany,* without the Concurrence of *Honorius* to the Peace, tho' the Senate had sent and desir'd him to be included in it. For *Constantine,* who as we observ'd before had been declared Emperor, and had settled himself in *Gaul* and a great part of *Spain,* about this time sent his Embassadors to *Honorius,* who were to ask his Pardon for that he had assum'd the Imperial Title which had been forc'd upon him.

Honorius makes Constantine his Associate in the Empire. *Honorius* not only admitted of his Excuse, but sent him back the Imperial Habit, and associated him in the Empire, expecting he would come to his Assistance against *Alarich,* as he had promis'd; and besides the Advantage of having but one Enemy to deal with at a time, he thought it the readiest way to procure the Safety of his Kinsmen, *Veronian* and *Didymius,* of whose Murder he was at that time ignorant. This new Accommodation made *Honorius* averse to any Thoughts of a Treaty with *Alarich,* tho' the Senate had sent their Deputies expresly to him upon that account, and *Alarich* insisted upon nothing but being made Commander in chief of the *Roman* Armies, as well Horse as Foot; to which *Honorius* could by no means be brought to consent, urging that it would be a Disgrace to the Dignity of the *Roman* Majesty, and very prejudicial to the Empire, and so the Messengers were sent back without any satisfactory Answer.

About

About this time *Ataulfus*, whom *Alarich* had sent for, as we obferv'd before, had pafs'd the *Julian Alps*, and was advanc'd into the Coafts bordering upon the *Adriatick*, with an Intent to join and reinforce *Alarich*'s Army. *Honorius* drew out the beft of his Forces garrifon'd in the Towns thereabouts, and fent 'em under the Conduct of *Olympius* to hinder fo dangerous a Conjunction; and they behav'd themfelves fo well that they kill'd above fifteen hundred of the Enemy with the lofs of no more than feventeen Men. Notwithftanding which great piece of Service, *Olympius*, who had been accus'd as Author of all the prefent Calamities being difmifs'd from Court, was glad to fly into *Dalmatia* for fear of any further Mifchief; after whofe Difgrace, *Jovius*, the *Præfectus Prætorio* of *Italy*, fucceeded as chief Minifter of State to *Honorius*, and drew the Emperor into new Troubles. For being fent to propofe fome new Conditions of Peace to *Alarich*, in which he appear'd too forward, and therein offended the Emperor; upon his Return he thought to re-ingratiate himfelf by over-acting his part on the other Hand, and having firft obliged the Emperor by Oath never to make Peace with *Alarich*, but wage perpetual War with him, he made the fame himfelf, by touching the Head of the Emperor, and exacted it from all others that were in any Place or Authority. *Alarich*, enraged to fee all his Propofitions for an Accommodation rejected, march'd from *Rimini* towards *Rome*, and refolv'd to lay Siege to it a fecond time; but obferving that the Emperor was raifing great Bodies of Forces on every fide, that he had entertain'd ten thoufand *Hunns* in his Service, and confidering that the Fate of War is doubtful and precarious, he procured fome Bifhops to go to the Emperor, and conjure him not to fuffer through his Neglect that City, which for so many Ages had been Mistress of the World, to be exposed as a Prey to the Barbarians, nor give up her beautiful Buildings to be burnt and destroy'd, but to admit of such moderate Conditions as he now propos'd; which were only a small Sum of Mony, and Provisions for his Army, together with Upper and Lower *Bavaria* for their Habitations, which paid but an inconsiderable Tribute to the Empire, and were subject to the continual Invasions of their Neighbours: In consideration of which he was ready to contract a perpetual Friendship and Society in War with the *Romans*, and oblige himself to defend the Common-wealth against all her Enemies whatever. All the World were surpriz'd at this sudden and unexpected Modesty in *Alarich*, who declining all former Pretension, had of himself offer'd Conditions so just and advantagious to the Empire, as the Affairs of the Emperor then stood. Notwithstanding which, *Jovius* and those of his Faction oppos'd all Overtures of Peace, alledging they had bound themselves by a solemn Oath, sworn by the Head of the Emperor, never to make any Peace with *Alarich*; as if the Observance of a rash, and indeed an unjust Oath, was to be preferr'd to the Welfare of the State. *Alarich* therefore, finding himself abus'd, marched directly for *Rome*; and as he approach'd near to the City, he sent for the principal Inhabitants, and acquainted 'em with *Honorius* his invincible Obstinacy, and threaten'd to take the Town by Force, unless the Citizens would join with him in a War against *Honorius*: Which when the Inhabitants could by no means be persuaded to do, he laid close Siege to the Town, took the Haven, and in it all the Publick Provisions, which he threaten'd to distribute among his own Men, unless they instantly submitted. They, seeing the Necessity to which they were reduc'd, and that they must unavoidably

New Proposals from Alarich rejected by Honorius.

voidably perish for Hunger, consented to what *A-larich* had propounded; so that inviting him into the City they deliver'd him up *Placidia*, the Emperor's Sister, as an Hostage of their Fidelity, and according to his Command created *Attalus*, Præfect of the City, Emperor; who in return made *Alarich* General of the Army, and *Tertullus*, a Heathen, Consul for the Year ensuing; distributing the other great Offices among Heathens and *Arians*, being himself an *Arian*. *Alarich* advised him to send some Troops of Barbarians into *Africk*, under the Command of *Drumas*, to remove *Heraclian* who commanded there for the Emperor, and might be a great Hindrance to him in the Progress of his Affairs: But in this and other things he acted contrary to the Advice of *Alarich*, and behav'd himself in every respect like a Man whose Authority was like to be of a very short Continuance.

Alarich makes Attalus Emperor;

With the Succours he receiv'd from *Alarich* he undertook to besiege *Honorius* in *Ravenna*, who, much terrify'd at the Approach of so many Enmies sworn to his Destruction, sent and offer'd to receive him as his Partner in the Empire; but was answer'd, that *Attalus* was so far from suffering him to enjoy so much as the simple Name of Emperor, that after he had stripp'd him of his Imperial Robes, he would confine him to some remote and desolate Island, where he should spend the rest of his Days in Obscurity, glad he had so escaped with his Life. The poor Emperor was so confounded at this prodigious Arrogance, that he thought of escaping to his Nephew *Theodosius*; but at that instant six *Cohorts*, consisting of four thousand Men, that had been formerly sent for out of the East, arriv'd to his Assistance, which encourag'd him to continue at *Ravenna* in expectation of the Success of his Arms in *Africk*; concluding if *Heraclian* prevail'd he he should, with the Accession of his Forces, be able to make head against *Attalus* and *Alarich*.

Whilst the War raged with such Violence in the midst of *Italy*, the Provinces abroad labour'd under equal Difficulties, for whilst some were daring to throw off the Authority of the Empire, others presum'd to usurp it; but *Honorius* was too much employ'd at home to have any leisure to look abroad. So that all things were managed in *Gaul* and *Spain*, according to the Will and Pleasure of those that were strongest.

Alarich had a mind more closely to besiege *Honorius* in *Ravenna*, which *Attalus* had block'd up by the Forces under his Command, expecting the Success of his Arms in *Africk*; and when *Alarich* understood they had been defeated by *Heraclian*, he began to be weary of his new Emperor, whom he found unequal to so great a Charge. His Aversion to him was improved by some near *Attalus*, who had been regain'd to the Emperor's Interest, and made the *Goth* believe that *Attalus* had a Design upon his Life, the better to assure himself of the Empire, which he scorn'd to hold upon precarious Terms. This the King was more inclinable to believe, when he observ'd that by the ill Conduct of *Attalus* their Affairs were quite ruin'd in *Africk*; that *Heraclian* had seiz'd upon all the Ports, and thereby put a stop to the Importation of any Corn, or other Merchandise, into *Italy*. This created a great Famine throughout the Country, which was increased for that the Lands, by reason of the Wars, had not been till'd for several Years; but no Place felt it so grievously as *Rome*, where Men were ready to devour one another, and several Mothers were reported to have fed upon their own Infants; so that *Alarich* seeing the publick Calamities encrease through the Folly of those who had the Government of Affairs,

fairs, sent his Embassadors once more to Treat with *Honorius*, promising to strip *Attalus* of that Dignity with which he had invested him. The Conditions were readily accepted by the Emperor, who on his part offer'd to agree to all his Demands. Hereupon *Alarich* return'd with his Army towards *Rome*, where he publickly depriv'd *Attalus* of the Imperial Purple, which he sent to *Honorius*, detaining the Usurper and his Son *Ampelius* Prisoners. After which he return'd towards *Ravenna*, there to confirm the Peace, on Condition he was made Co-Partner in the Empire, and some Commodious Part of *Gaul* was assign'd him for himself and his Men; in Consideration of which he would be ready to assist *Honorius* and the Empire upon all Occasions whatsoever. Both the Heathens and the *Arians* were much offended at this Accommodation, for the one had promis'd themselves mighty Advantages, *Attalus* himself being an *Arian*, and the other no less than a Re-establishment of their Idolatry, which he had promis'd them. But this peaceable Face of Affairs was shortly after chang'd by the means of *Sarus*, because it no ways countenanc'd his particular Interest. He had great Numbers of Barbarians under his own Independent Command, with which he had for some time observ'd a Neutrality; but when he found *Ataulfus*, who was his Mortal Foe, join'd with *Alarich*, he began to apprehend his Power, and declare openly for *Honorius*: Tho' he knew a Treaty of Peace had been concluded between him and the *Goths*, yet with three hundred of his Men he fell upon the *Goths*, who expected no such Usage, and kill'd a great number of 'em. *Alarich*, who concluded that what *Sarus* had done was by *Honorius* his Participation and Consent, departed in a great Rage, and went to his Army that continu'd

and Degrades him again.

Sarus prevents an Accommodation.

Rome Taken.

Encamp'd

Encamp'd near *Rome*, which he press'd closer than ever, and at last took it, whether by Force or Stratagem is hard to be determin'd, for the Historians that have written of it are not agreed among themselves in that Point, any more than to the particular time of the Year in which it was taken; for some say it was on the First of *April*, others on the Twenty fourth of *August*, which seems the most likely. Thus that City, which for many Ages together had pillag'd the rest of the World, and enrich'd her self with the Spoils of other Nations, suffer'd now in her turn, and beheld that with which she us'd to feed her Pride and Luxury fall into the Hands of Barbarians, her declar'd Enemies; there was hardly a House throughout that vast and opulent City, but what suffer'd in the common Calamity, several of 'em being set on Fire by the insolent Soldiers after they had been rifl'd. *Alarich*, before he broke into it, forbad his Soldiers, at the Peril of their Lives, from molesting those that fled for Sanctuary into the Churches, especially those of the Holy Apostles. He gave 'em free Liberty to plunder where they pleas'd, only they were commanded to abstain from things consecrated to Holy Uses, and to spill the Blood of none but such as they found in Arms, and endeavouring to make Resistance. Several *Pagans* observing the particular Favour shown the Christians turn'd Christians too, and fled with them for Safety into their Churches, the Preservation of which, and the extraordinary Respect shown 'em by the *Goths* in the midst of so horrible a Confusion, whilst their own Idolatrous Temples were industriously burnt and destroy'd, they look'd upon as miraculous. Three Days did the City suffer under the Tyranny of the Barbarians, who on the third quitted it of their own accord, and left it in a much better Condition than the *Gauls* or *Nero ro* had done, whose brutish Wantonness exceeded the more generous Anger of the Victorious Barbarian; so that this seem'd a shaking of the Rod over the Proud City, rather than a thorough Correction; a Denunciation of God's Anger, and not an Execution of his Judgments: Happy had it been for her if she could have taken Warning, and not after so many Trials have forc'd the Divine Vengeance down upon her Head. This Captivity of *Rome* fell out in the 18th Year of *Honorius*, the second of the 297th *Olympiad*, in the Consulship of *Varanes* and *Tertullus*, in the 1163d after her Foundation, *A. D.* 410.

CHAP. IV.

From the Taking of Rome *by the* Goths, *to the total Failure of the Western Empire in* Augustulus.

Containing the Space of Sixty Six Years.

I. A *Larich* having now in his Power the Imperial City, might easily have fix'd himself there, and with his Triumphant and Victorious Army have made War upon *Honorius,* and by degrees have united the Body of the Empire to the Head; but whether it proceeded from the want of good Counsel, or the secret Pleasure of Divine Providence, he knew not how to make an advantagious use of his Victory, nor secure the Conquest he had with much Labour and Difficulty obtain'd. Driven out by an Almighty Hand, rather than of his own Accord, his straggling Troops rov'd through *Campania, Lucania,* and *Calabria,* wasting the Country, and loading themselves with the Wealth of it; of which when he thought it sufficiently drain'd, and had gratify'd his Humour to the full upon the Continent, he thought of passing, with his Army, over into *Sicily,* there to act the same Cruelties over again. Accordingly he drew his Forces down to *Rhegium,* where they were Embark'd; but by that time he was got out to Sea a violent Tempest seiz'd him, which beat him back upon the Coasts of *Calabria,* where he fell upon *Consentia,* a strong Town, that refus'd to admit him, and having taken it by Force he gave it up to be plun-

A. D. 411.

plunder'd by his Soldiers. Here, as he was considering what farther Course he was to take for the Advancement of his Affairs, he was suddenly seiz'd with a Fit of Sickness, which carry'd him off in a few Days. The *Goths* exceedingly lamented the Death of their King, under whose Conduct they had perform'd such great Exploits, and met with such extraordinary Success. Lest the *Romans*, who had been so often defeated by him, should come and offer an Indignity to his Bones after he was bury'd, they turn'd the Course of the River *Busento*, by digging a great Canal for the Reception of the Water, and in the midst of the Channel they bury'd their King, and with him abundance of their Wealth, after which they restor'd their Waters to their right Course, and kill'd all the Slaves they had employ'd in the Work, that no Discovery might be made of the Place. This Solemnity being over they consulted about the Choice of a new King, and, after a short Deliberation, it fell upon *Athaulph,* or *Adolph,* Brother-in-Law to the Deceas'd; who, being thus promoted, marry'd *Placidia,* Sister of *Honorius,* who had been detain'd as an Hostage by *Alarich,* but us'd with much Honour by him. This happen'd well to the *Roman* Empire, for being a Woman of good Address, and great Discretion, she so far insinuated her self into him, that she inclin'd him which way she pleas'd. He had a Design of returning back to *Rome,* of taking it a second time, of settling himself there, and intended to call it *Gothia* instead of *Rome,* the very Name of which he had a great Ambition to obliterate; but she so temper'd him by her Prayers, Entreaties and Persuasions, that a Treaty was concluded betwixt him and the Emperor upon the same Foot with his Brother's, which was that he should quit *Italy,* and retire into *Gaul,* where a commodious Tract should

The Death of Alarich.

Athaulph, made King, marries Placidia.

be

be assign'd for him and his new Subjects; accordingly he went and settl'd in *Gallia Narbonnensis*, where he was acknowledg'd as King and Ally of the *Romans*, whom he honestly assisted afterwards in their *Galtic* Wars; presently after this the Inhabitants of *Rome*, who had left it in the time of Danger, seeing the Storm at last blown off, and that there was some appearance of Peace, return'd in such great Numbers, that shortly after the Town was grown as populous as ever.

Constantine breaks out again; And now there was hardly any left able to disturb the Publick Peace but *Constantine*, who, as we observ'd before, was receiv'd by *Honorius* into a Partnership of the Empire, upon a Promise of his Fidelity for the future, which he had not Honour enough to observe, but broke out shortly after in hopes of seizing *Italy* in the midst of so many Publick Confusions; whereupon *Honorius*, in Consideration of his restless turbulent Spirit, was resolv'd, if possible, to destroy him; and making *Constantius*, a *Roman* of great Nobility, Valour and Prudence, his Lieutenant-General, he sent him into *Gaul* with a powerful Army. *Constantine* was at that time besieg'd in *Arles* by *Gerontius*, who had been formerly his Commander in *Spain*, but having receiv'd some Unkindness from him, fought at present neither for him nor *Honorius*, but labour'd to raise one *Maximus* an Emperor of his own chusing; whilst he was pressing the Siege *Constantius* arriv'd with the Army under his Command, whereupon *Gerontius* knowing his Forces to be inferior to his rais'd the Siege, and fled into *Spain* with as many of his Troops as would follow him, for a great many of his Men, neither approving of his Conduct nor his Cause, went over to *Constantius*. *Gerontius* his ill Fortune pursu'd him into *Spain*, where the Soldiers, offended at him for his shameful Flight, attack'd attack'd him in his own House, which he defended with much Courage; and being assisted by no more than one Friend, and a few Slaves, he kill'd above three hundred of them, fighting obstinately 'till all their Weapons were spent, and then the Slaves consulted their own Safety and fled. *Gerontius* might with ease have sav'd himself too, but was detain'd by his Love to his Wife, whom he could not be persuaded to forsake, who begg'd him to kill her rather than suffer her to fall into the Hands of his Enemies; wherefore when he found there was no room left for Hope, he first cut off the Head of his Friend, after that his Wife's, and then dispatch'd himself.

In the mean time *Constantius* had taken up his Post, and was laying close Siege to *Constantine*, who after a Defeat of a Party that was marching to his Relief, and a Defence for four Months, divested himself of the Purple, and retir'd into the Church, where he got himself to be Ordain'd a Priest, thinking that Character sufficient to preserve his Life. As soon as it was known to the Inhabitants, and *Constantius* had taken an Oath for their Indemnity, he was receiv'd into the Town, and immediately sent away *Constantine* and his Son *Julian* to *Honorius*, by whose Order they were put to Death upon the Road. *and is put to Death.*

The Fate and Punishment of *Constantine* could not deter others from aiming at the like Usurpations; for at this time *Jovinus*, a Man of great Power and Quality in *Auvergne*, usurp'd the Imperial Title, and by the assistance of the *Franks*, *Burgundians* and *Germans*, was preparing to make good his Pretensions, but was overthrown by *Constantius*, who follow'd him so close that he was forc'd to fly out of the Country, after *Constantius* had taken most of his Adherents and put 'em to Death. *Jovinus usurps in Gaul,*

After

and Hera-   After *Jovinus* follow'd *Heraclian*, who the same
clian *in* A- Year usurp'd in *Africk*; he being a Man of Power,
frick.   Interest and Authority, put *Italy* at first into a
great Consternation, especially when by detaining
the Annual Supply of Corn they began to be in
great want of Provisions. *Heraclian* had commanded
the Emperor's Armies in *Africk*, had been very
successful in his Services in that Province, and was
design'd Consul for the ensuing Year, all which
Considerations made his Rebellion more extraordi-

A. D. nary, and the Issue more doubtful; he Mann'd out
413. a very strong Fleet of Ships, and no less, according
to *Orosius*, than three thousand seven hundred Sail,
therein out-doing the Naval Strength of *Xerxes* and
Alexander the Great. With this Fleet he set Sail,
and after he had rov'd along upon the *Italian* Coast
he landed his Men, and put *Rome* into a great Consternation; but *Marinus*, one of the Emperor's
Commanders, march'd out against him at the Head
of the *Roman* Youth, and *Veterane* Troops of the
Empire, which made a brave Appearance, and quite
disheartn'd the Usurper; who, without trusting to
the issue of an Engagement, fled in great Precipitation, and getting on Board a small Chaloup, set
Heraclian Sail for *Carthage*, where he was kill'd the Year
kill'd. following by one of his own Soldiers.

   In the mean while *Constantius* was busily employ'd in *Gaul*, which by this time was so far
settl'd through his Industry and Success, that of
all those barbarous Nations that first follow'd *Godegisil* thither, none remain'd but the *Burgundians*,
Natives originally of that Tract of Land that lyes
between the *Oder* and the *Vistula*, but quitting
their own Country came with the rest of the Barbarians into *Gaul*. *Constantius* thought fit to march
against 'em, but they finding he was likely to prove
too strong for 'em, petition'd him for Peace, and
desir'd

desir'd they might be admitted as Friends and Allies to the *Romans*. *Constantius* thought it not prudent to provoke 'em too far, lest some unexpected Miscarriage should sully the Reputation of his Arms; and therefore granting their Demands, gave 'em leave to settle themselves upon the Banks of the Rivers *Rodanus* or the *Rhône*, and the *Soane*, call'd by the Ancients *Araris*. After this *Constantius* was sent for by the Emperor to *Rome*, where for his signal Services he was rewarded with the Honour of Consul and Patrician, but had not long continued at *Rome* before new Commotions recall'd him abroad; for *Adolph*, King of the *Goths*, a warlike and restless People, taking his Advantage of the Wars he saw the *Romans* engaged in, began to disturb the Empire. He had brought *Attalus* with him out of *Italy*, and now persuaded him once more to re-assume the Imperial Purple, and act the Emperor: *Attalus* being a Man of a fickle ambitious Temper readily embraced the Occasion, and by his Patron's Assistance rais'd a very powerful Army, consisting of turbulent unruly People, fond of Novelty and Confusion. Hereupon *Honorius* declared both him and *Adolph* Enemies to the Empire, and made *Constantius* his General, who was at that time esteemed the Emperor's Right Hand, and Buckler of the State. *Constantius* the more readily accepted the Service because he had no great Kindness for the *Gothick* King, so that departing from *Arles* at the Head of his Army in the Beginning of the Spring he march'd up to *Narbonne*, where *Adolph* kept his Court, whom he threaten'd with a Siege unless *Attalus* was deliver'd up to him. *Placidia* advised her Husband to quit the Interest of the Usurper, and comply with *Constantius*; but when the King could by no Persuasions be prevail'd upon to do it, *Constantius* laid Siege to the Place, and press'd him so hard that *Adolph*

A.D. 414.

Adolph makes Attalus Emperor again

Attalus and Adolph declar'd Enemies to the Empire.

dolph seeing there was no possibility of a Relief thought of leaving the Town and transporting his *Goths* into *Africk*; of which *Constantius* being aware he seiz'd upon all the Gallies and other Vessels riding near the Coast, so that he was forced to alter his Measures, and fly, together with *Attalus*, into *Spain*, where he seiz'd upon *Barcellona*. Here some of the *Gothick* Soldiers, who had no great Kindness for *Attalus*, laid hold suddenly upon him, and carry'd him Prisoner to *Constantius*, who put him in Chains and sent him to the Emperor, by whom he was reserv'd to be led in Triumph at the End of the War.

<small>Attalus taken.</small>

As soon as the *Vandals* understood the *Goths* were settling themselves in *Spain*, and like to be their Neighbours, they thought it their Business to prevent 'em before it was too late, and accordingly by their Embassadors to *Honorius* advis'd him to be at Peace with both Parties, and leave 'em to fight it out between themselves, for whatever Side prevail'd he was sure to be a Gainer; which was a Maxim *Honorius* afterwards observ'd, to the great Ease and Benefit of the Empire. In the mean time *Placidia* had again importun'd her Husband to renew the Peace with *Honorius*, which he could no longer refuse to a Wife he lov'd so tenderly, and who had so great a Power over him. But the *Goths*, who were of a quite contrary Inclination, and thought Peace prejudicial to their Honour and their Interest, murder'd him and six of his Children, promoting *Sigerich* to be King in his stead; who being of the same Principles in a short time after suffer'd the same Fate, and was succeeded by *Wallia*, a Man of a more warlike Genius, whose first Attempt was to transport his *Goths* into *Africk*; but being driven back by a Tempest he enter'd into a Treaty with *Constantius*, to whom he delivered up *Placidia*, the Emperor's Sister, and was to be esteemed a Friend and

<small>Adolph slain by his own Subjects.</small>

and Ally of the *Romans*, upon Condition he made perpetual War with the *Vandals* in *Spain*. The Peace being thus concluded *Conſtantius* return'd with *Placidia* to *Rome*, where by the Conſent and Encouragement of *Honorius* he was marry'd to her, to the great Satisfaction of the People, whoſe publick Rejoycings were prolong'd by the Solemnity of *Honorius* his Triumph, in the Concluſion of which *Attalus* had his Right Hand cut off, and was confin'd to the Iſle of *Lipare*.

Conſtantius marry'd to Placidia. A.D. 417.

During all theſe Commotions and publick Calamities, with which the Weſtern Empire had been almoſt overthrown, the Eaſt by a particular Favour of Providence enjoy'd a profound Peace, under the Government of *Theodoſius*, an Infant; God ſeeming in an eſpecial manner to favour him, for the Encouragement Chriſtian Piety found, not only in his own Court but almoſt throughout his Empire. Eccleſiaſtical Writers are very particular in their Commendations of this Prince, and of his Siſter *Pulcheria*, who was two Years older than the Emperor, and in conſideration of her great Wiſdom, Virtue, and Piety, was created *Auguſta*, and ſhared with him the Imperial Power, or rather had all reſign'd up to her ſelf; for ſhe govern'd both him and the Empire with an abſolute Authority, and adminiſter'd Affairs with ſo much Prudence, that he was belov'd by his Subject, and formidable to his Enemies. Yet could not all her Care and Circumſpection prevent frequent Feuds ariſing upon the Account of Religion, which as they begun in an ungovernable Zeal, ſo they very often ended in Blood, as it happen'd at this time in *Alexandria*, a City notoriouſly remarkable for Tumults and Seditions. Some ſlight Diſputes between the Chriſtians and the Jews, who inhabited there in great Numbers, ſo far exaſperated the latter, that they reſolv'd upon a cruel Revenge, eſpecially

A Sedition at Alexandria.

cially when they found themselves favour'd and protected by the Præfect of the City, who was at Enmity with *Cyrill*, Bishop of the Place. They agreed among themselves to set upon the Christians in the Night-time, and massacre all they could get into their Hands: And the better to execute their Bloody Design, they hired some Apostate Christians to cry out in the dead of Night, that one of the chief Churches in the City was in Flames; whereupon the Christians ran in great Confusion out of their Houses to extinguish the Fire: But the Jews, who were all arm'd, and knew each other by a certain Mark of Distinction which they wore for that purpose, kill'd all as they came out into the Streets, without any Mercy. The Bishop, being highly provok'd at so great a Barbarity, went attended with multitudes of Christians to the Synagogues, whilst the Jews were assembled there, where infinite Numbers of 'em were murder'd, the rest forc'd out of the City, and their Houses plunder'd. The Præfect was so much offended at this, that tho' St. *Cyrill* did all he cou'd to appease and mollifie him, he never would listen to any Accommodation. The Noise of this Uproar came to the Ears of the Monks living upon the neighbouring Mountains, who to the number of five hundred came down and insulted the Præfect as he was riding in his Chariot, calling him Idolater, Heathen, and Unbeliever; tho' he at the same time declared himself a Christian, and that he had been baptized by *Atticus*, Bishop of *Constantinople*. This serv'd only to enrage 'em the more, insomuch that one among 'em, call'd *Ammonius*, broke his Head with a Stone, and had almost kill'd him, whilst his Attendants forsook him for fear of being murder'd, and hid themselves in the Croud. But the People, provok'd at the outragious Insolence of these Monks, fell upon 'em, and drove 'em out

A bloody Massacre.

The Monks raise Disturbances.

of

of the City, seizing on *Ammonius* their Ringleader, and deliver'd him up to the Governor, who immediately put him to Death. This serv'd to widen the Breach between the Bishop and the Præfect, which occasion'd great Disorders in the City, and was fatal to *Hypatia*, the Daughter of *Theon* the Philosopher; a young Lady, so well acquainted with all the Sects in Philosophy, that for Learning and Quickness of Apprehension she exceeded all the Philosophers of that Age; and which was a greater Ornament than all the rest, she was no less remarkable for her Modesty, Meekness, and Chastity. These extraordinary Qualifications made her Conversation courted by the Princes and Great Men of the Province, but she was intimate with none more than the Præfect, which Intimacy cost her her Life, for she was accus'd as one that hinder'd an Accommodation between the Governor and the Bishop; whereupon several of the People, among whom one *Peter* a Lecturer in a Church was Ringleader, forced her out of her Coach, drag'd her into a Church, where they stripp'd her, mangled her Body, kill'd her, and then burnt her to Ashes. *This Action*, saith *Socrates*, *brought a great Scandal upon* Cyrill *and his Flock, being so much unbecoming those who make a Profession of Christianity*: And we may likewise observe the Temper of the Monks of those Times. About this time *Innocent*, the Pope of *Rome*, began to assert his Authority over other Bishops, and to claim a Supremacy, which was as earnestly challeng'd by his next Successor *Zosimus*, nor has the Claim been dropp'd ever since.

The Year following was remarkable for the Birth of *Valentinian* the Third, of whom *Placidia* was deliver'd at *Ravenna*; but more for a great Eclipse of the Sun, and other Accidents, that much alarm'd the Minds of the People, for it was follow'd with

Valentinian III. Born.

so great a Drought, that Men and Cattle dy'd in great Numbers; after which enfued moſt dreadful Earthquakes, accompany'd with Fire that fell from Heaven, which put Men into a mortal Fear but did little Hurt, for whilſt like ſo many Waves it was overwhelming whole Countries, a ſudden and great Wind aroſe, by which it was driven into the Sea and quench'd in the Waters.

Not long after this *Honorius*, who had no Children, began to think of an Aſſociate and Succeſſor, who might ſhare with him in the Difficulties of the State whilſt he liv'd, and be a Support to the Empire after his Death. His own Experience and the Peoples Vows made him caſt his Eyes upon *Conſtan-* <small>Conſtanti-</small> *tius*, who was accordingly proclaim'd *Auguſtus* with <small>us *declar'd*</small> much Solemnity, and his Son *Valentinian* declar'd <small>Auguſtus, *and* Valen-</small> *Cæſar*. But as this was done without the Conſent <small>tinian Cæ-</small> or Knowledge of *Theodoſius* he never approv'd of it, <small>ſar.</small> nor would he give Audience to the Embaſſadors ſent by *Honorius* upon that account, nor receive the Picture of *Conſtantius*, ſent, as the Cuſtom was, to be placed with his own. This Indignity highly concern'd *Conſtantius*, who thought his ten Years ſuccefsful Service in the Wars againſt Uſurpers and Barbarians well deſerv'd the Honour *Honorius* had conferr'd upon him, and therefore he prepar'd to force *Theodoſius* to a Recognition, and be reveng'd <small>Conſtanti-</small> upon him for the Affront, but dy'd at *Ravenna* of <small>us *dies at*</small> a Pleuriſie, occaſion'd by an immoderate Grief con-<small>Ravenna.</small> tracted upon that Account. 'Tis not improbable but *Theodoſius* might be the more averſe to *Conſtantius* his Promotion becauſe he then began to think of marrying himſelf, as he did not long after to *Eudocia*, Daughter of *Leontius* the *Athenian* Philoſopher: Her firſt Name was *Athenais*, which at her Baptiſm was changed, by *Atticus* Biſhop of *Conſtantinople*, for *Eudocia*. Her Father had ſo well inſtructed

structed her in Philosophy, in the Mathematicks, the Languages and the Sciences, that she equall'd if not exceeded the greatest Professors in those Times. These Riches of the Mind *Leontius* thought a competent Fortune for his Daughter, for which reason he disinherited her by his last Will, and left all his Estate to her two Brothers; whereof, as soon as he was dead, she went and complain'd to *Pulcheria*: *Pulcheria* admiring her extraordinary Beauty, and the great Endowments of her Mind, persuaded *Theodosius* to marry her; which she did, as some have imagin'd, out of Policy, and Regard to her own Interest, concluding that *Athenais*, who ow'd her Advancement entirely to her, would suffer her to continue absolute in the Management of publick Affairs. *Theodosius marries.*

These Occurrences happen'd not 'till after the War was broken out between *Theodosius* and the King of *Persia*, who had broken the League with the Empire, and horribly persecuted the Christians in his Dominions. Whilst *Isdegerdes* liv'd, who, as we observ'd before, had been appointed Tutor to the Emperor, he preserv'd a good Understanding betwixt the two Crowns; but his Son *Vararanes* who succeeded him was of a different Temper, and at the Instigation of the *Magi* rais'd a bloody Persecution against the Christians throughout all his Dominions, which was imputed in a great measure to the indiscreet Zeal of a Bishop call'd *Audas*, who burnt one of the *Persian* Temples, and when he refus'd to re-build it, according to the Sentence pronounc'd against him, the King put him to Death, and order'd all the Christian Churches to be demolish'd, and proceeded with such Violence against the Faithful, that they came in great Numbers to *Constantinople*, where *Atticus* receiv'd 'em with much Compassion, and stirr'd up the Emperor in their Behalf. *A Persecution in Persia.*

A. D. 419.

Behalf. But left this Provocation should not be thought Grounds sufficient for a War, the *Persians* detain'd some Workmen they had hired out of the *Roman* Territories, who were to dig in some Mines of Gold they had lately discover'd, and were to be return'd back after they had perform'd the Work they were hired for; and as an Aggravation of all the rest, they robb'd and abus'd several *Roman* Merchants that traded into their Country. The King of *Persia* first began, by demanding back his Subjects, whom he had driven out of his Country by the Heat of his Persecution: But the *Romans* were so far from delivering those miserable People into his Hands, that they declar'd War against him; and *Theodosius* immediately rais'd an Army, constituting *Ardabarius* his General, who overthrew *Narses*, Commander of the *Persian* Army, in the Province of *Azazena*, slew a great multitude of his Men, and forc'd him to fly. *Narses* thought to redeem his lost Credit by invading the *Roman* Borders, which he hoped to effect on the Side of *Mesopotamia*, destitute at that time, and unprepar'd for a Defence: The *Roman* General was quickly sensible of his Motions, and therefore marched with all speed into *Mesopotamia*, frustrated his Design, and besieg'd him in *Nisibis*, at that time in the Hands of the *Persians*. *Vararanes* having by this time receiv'd Intelligence of his General's Overthrow, and the Danger his Army and the City was in, made all the haste he could to his Relief, calling into his Assistance *Alamundurus*, Prince of the *Saracens*, a haughty vainglorious Man, who promis'd the King not only to raise the Siege of *Nisibis*, but deliver the beautiful City of *Antioch* into his Hands. But his Attempts were no way answerable to his arrogant Promises, nor his Success to either; for a Dissention first rose among his Men, and after that a Panick Fear seiz'd

A War with Persia,

so violently upon 'em, that flying away in great Confusion at the very appearance of the *Romans*, they took the River *Euphrates*, where an hundred thousand of 'em are said to have perish'd. After which the *Romans* being inform'd the King was approaching with a great number of Elephants to relieve the Town, they rais'd the Siege, but in several Engagements which followed soon after got the Advantage, and very much weaken'd the Enemy; notwithstanding which, *Theodosius*, who had the Character rather of a good Prince than a great Emperor, was inclinable to Peace, and sent his Embassadors to Treat with *Vararanes* accordingly; but he being reinforced with a fresh Supply of Ten thousand Men, who call'd themselves *Immortals*, thought fit to try his Fortune once more before he listen'd to an Accommodation; but when he heard that all his bold *Immortals* were cut off by the *Romans*, he attended seriously to the Proposals of Peace, which was granted to him by *Theodosius*, upon Condition he put a stop to the Persecution he had rais'd against the Christians, and restored 'em to their Estates and Privileges. The Valour and Conduct of the *Roman* Generals in this War was very remarkable, but the Charity of *Acacius*, Bishop of *Amida*, was more extraordinary. The *Romans* had in this Town above seven thousand Prisoners, who must all have perish'd with Hunger had not this Bishop reliev'd 'em. He summon'd his Clergy together, and told 'em God was not so much serv'd by the Vessels of Gold or Silver, which the Piety of Devout Christians had dedicated to the use of their Church, but in Actions of Charity, Brotherly Love and Munificence, and that it would be a Deed worthy their Holy Profession to sell those Vessels, and apply the Mony to the Relief of such miserable Wretches that were now ready to perish

in which the Romans have the better.

The Charity of Acacius, Bishop of Amida.

among 'em. Hereupon, by the Approbation and Confent of all his Clergy, he melted the Plate, converted it into Mony, with part of which he ranfom'd the Captives, and diftributed the reft among 'em for their Subfiftance. The King of *Perfia* was fo nearly affected with fuch a tranfcendent Act of Charity, that he confefs'd the *Romans* knew how to Conquer as well by their Liberality as the Power of their Arms, and earneftly defir'd to fee the Bifhop that had fo highly oblig'd 'em. *Acacius* receiv'd Orders from *Theodofius* to fatisfie his Curiofity, and by his Prefence encreas'd the great Opinion *Vararanes* had conceiv'd of him, who after that grew more mild and indulgent to the Chriftians.

A. D. 422.
A War in Spain.

In the mean time *Honorius* obferving how much the *Goths* and *Vandals* had by their continual Wars weaken'd each other in *Spain*, thought their Divifions gave him a fair Opportunity of recovering it to the *Roman* Empire, to which purpofe he fent two powerful Armies thither, one by Land under the Command of *Caftinus*, and the other by Sea from *Africk* under the Command of *Boniface*, who was Governor in that Country. They were, without Contradiction, two of the moft experienc'd Soldiers *Honorius* had in all his Dominions, and therefore he join'd 'em in Commiffion, that they might with equal Power and Command promote his Service in *Spain*. At firft there appear'd an happy Underftanding and Unanimity between 'em, which produc'd Effects very advantagious to the Emperor's Intereft and their own Reputation; for they got *Jovinus* and *Maximus* into their Hands, two of the late Ufurpers, who were ftill aiming at Innovations; they worfted the Barbarians in feveral Encounters, and forc'd 'em almoft to a Neceffity of Submiffion; but this friendly Correfpondence,

Fel-

Fellowship and Success, was interrupted by the haughty, arrogant Temper of *Castinus*, who valuing himself upon the Success of his Arms, began to despise *Boniface*, and claim a Precedency over him; but the other, who would by no means be persuaded to acknowledge him for his Superior, embark'd his Forces, and set Sail for *Africk*. This unseasonable Arrogance in *Castinus* prov'd very prejudicial to the Emperor's Affairs; for the *Vandals*, who by their united Forces were reduc'd to the last Extremity, upon this Division took Courage, engag'd *Castinus*, defeated him, and kill'd near twenty thousand of the *Romans*.

The Romans defeated.

Honorius receiv'd the News of this Defeat with much Concern, but did not live to punish his Generals, who by their untimely Disputes occasion'd it. From the time of *Constantius* his Death, *Honorius* had entertain'd his Sister *Placidia* with much Friendship and Affection, and the Communication was so close between 'em, that it gave ground to several scandalous Reflections, as if their mutual Love was more than what ought to pass between a Brother and Sister. But this Year some unfortunate Differences fell out betwixt 'em, and were improv'd to that degree, that *Placidia* with her two Children, *Valentinian* and *Honoria*, retir'd into the East, where she was kindly receiv'd by her Nephew *Theodosius*, tho' he had formerly refus'd to own *Constantius*, her Husband, for Emperor. *Honorius* was made to believe, by some about him, that his Sister held secret Correspondence with the *Goths*, who still look'd upon her as their Queen; that she betray'd all his Councils to 'em, and invited his Enemies into the Empire; whether this was the reason of his Dislike, or any other Provocation he had receiv'd, he contracted so great an Aversion to her, that he readily gave her leave to depart, but fell

A. D. 423.

Honorius dies.

His Character.

Honorius fell sick presently after, and dy'd of a Dropsie on the Fifteenth of *August*, after he had lived thirty nine Years, of which he Reign'd two with his Father, and twenty eight Years and seven Months after his Decease. The Historians of those Times vary very much in the Character they have left us of him; for they who writ of the *Byzantine* Empire are very severe to his Memory, whereas those who were his Cotemporaries highly commend him for his Zeal and Perseverance in the Orthodox Faith, to which they attribute his Success against the Barbarians and Usurpers. He seldom or never appear'd himself at the Head of his Armies, but executed all by his Officers, by whom he may be said to have extinguish'd more Rebellions than any Christian Emperor whatsoever. They must all allow his Reign to have been very unfortunate, for in his Time *Rome* was first taken by the *Goths*; the *Hunns* invaded *Pannonia*, the *Alans*, *Suevi*, and *Vandals* broke into *Spain*, the *Burgundians* settl'd in *Gaul*, where the *Goths* also fixed themselves at last. So many Enemies, with which the Empire was on all sides assaulted, requir'd a Prince of more Activity upon the Throne than *Honorius*, who is accused by some of so supine a Negligence and invincible Stupidity, that when he first was told *Rome* was taken, he answer'd the Messengers, *'Twas very strange, for he but that Moment had been playing with it,* supposing they meant a Game-Cock call'd *Rome*, in which he took great Delight.

John Usurps.

II. *Honorius* left no Children behind him, nor design'd any for his Successor at his Death. *Placidia* was absent with her Son *Valentinian* in the Court of *Theodosius*, so that the Imperial Purple seem'd to belong of Right to him who first laid hold upon it. This encourag'd one *John*, who from an ob-

obscure Beginning was first made Secretary to *Honorius*, and afterwards *Præfectus Pratorio*, to take upon him the Imperial Title, being encourag'd in it by *Castinus*, who was now return'd out of *Spain*, and design'd Consul for the Year following, whom he made General of his Armies, and *Ætius*, the Son of *Gaudentius*, a *Scythian*, who had been an Hostage with *Alarich* and the *Hunns*, and was now made great Master of the Palace by the Usurper. His first Care was to remove all those Magistrates he had reason to suspect, and supply their Places with others that were more affectionate to his Cause; he depriv'd the Church of several Privileges it had obtain'd from the Grace and Favour of former Emperors, and sent an Army into *Africk* to secure his Interest, and set up his Authority in those Parts, and then dispatch'd away his Embassadors, as he would have 'em call'd, to *Theodosius*, to desire he would own and declare him Emperor. *Theodosius* had before this receiv'd the News of his Uncle's Death, but thought not fit to discover it 'till he had secured the Borders of the Eastern Empire, by a sufficient number of Troops placed at *Solonæ* in *Dalmatia*; and tho' he had been inform'd of *John*'s Usurpation, he thought him a Man of no Interest, and did not much regard it; but when he found he had the Arrogance to send and make his Demands of him, he receiv'd the Messengers with much Indignation, and sent 'em back with a very unwelcome Answer, or, as some say, banish'd 'em into *Propontis*. *John*, no way discourag'd at *Theodosius* his Displeasure, sent *Ætius* into *Pannonia* with a great Sum of Gold to draw the *Hunns* over to his Assistance, with whose Commanders *Ætius* was intimate, who was farther order'd to fall upon the Rear of *Theodosius* his Troops if they march'd into *Italy*, whilst he himself charg'd 'em in the Front. In the mean time *Valentinian* being declared *Cæsar* by *Theodosius,* who had conferr'd the Dignity of *Augusta* on his Mother *Placidia,* was arriv'd at *Salonæ,* attended by *Ardaburius,* who was made General of the War, and his Son *Aspar,* where it was resolved between 'em, that *Ardaburius* with part of the Forces should go by Sea and Besiege *John* in *Ravenna,* and that *Asper,* with the rest of the Army, should convoy *Placidia* and *Valentinian* by Land thither. Hereupon the General set to Sea with a good Fleet, and was got just upon the Coasts of *Ravenna,* where he was going to land his Men, when a violent Storm arose that scatter'd his Fleet, and drove his own Vessel a-shoar, where he was taken by the Usurper's Soldiers, and carry'd into his Presence. *John,* who was highly elevated with a Victory that cost him nothing, and a Purchase he never dream'd of, knew *Ardaburius* to be a Man of such Consequence, that he hop'd *Theodosius* would for his sake condescend to his own Terms, and admit him for his Companion in the Empire; for which reason he treated him very honourable, and allow'd him the Liberty of the City, which he made his Prison. *Ardaburius* made good use of this Favour from the Usurper; some he found at *Ravenna,* who having been disoblig'd by him, were grown disaffected to his Government, with whom he took Care to ingratiate himself; and observing the Negligence and Security in which the Tyrant liv'd, he sent Intelligence of it to his Son *Aspar,* who was by this time got to *Aquileia,* which he surpriz'd and fortify'd; his Father advis'd him to advance speedily with his best Troops and seize on the City Gates, which stood open and unguarded; this Advice *Aspar* executed with that Success, that after a little Opposition he took *John,* and sent him away to *Placidia,* who us'd him with an Insolence incident to the Weakness of her Sex; for having cut off

John taken Prisoner.

off his Right Hand, she set him upon an Ass, and had him led in Derision through the Streets of *Aquileia*, after which he was Beheaded. He was a Man, according to *Procopius*, of a mild Disposition, and much Temper and Moderation in all his Affairs. Three Days after he had been taken Prisoner by *Aspar*, *Ætius* arriv'd with an Army of Sixty thousand *Hunns*, between whom and *Aspar* began a very obstinate Fight, 'till being inform'd of *John*'s Captivity he thought it advisable to make the best Terms he could for himself. *Placidia* promis'd to receive him into Favour, upon Condition he sent his *Hunns* home into the Country, and continu'd Obedient for the future; this he perform'd very honourably, and was afterwards serviceable to the Empire in a great many respects. After this *Valentinian* was declared Emperor, and *Placidia* Regent of the Empire during her Son's Minority. She began her Administration with venting her Fury upon the City of *Ravenna*, which she suffer'd the Soldiers to pillage, and after she had stripp'd *Castinus* of all his Employments, she sent him into Exile, and by this Severity forc'd him upon violent means for his own Safety and Support; so that inviting such of the Army to him as had been lately Disbanded, or were willing to follow his Fortunes, and espouse his Cause, he in a little time found himself in a Condition to begin new Disturbances, and with a good Body of experienc'd resolute Soldiers invaded *Africk*, out of which he hop'd he should be able to drive his old Competitor *Boniface*, who notwithstanding maintain'd his Post so well that *Castinus* was defeated and taken Prisoner. This piece of Service turn'd much to the Reputation of *Boniface*, and reviv'd an old Grudge *Ætius* had to him, who therefore by his cunning Insinuations persuaded *Placidia* that *Boniface* had preserv'd *Africk* for himself, rather than the Empire; that he watch'd an Opportunity

Valentinian.

A. D. 426. *Castinus Invades Africk, and is taken Prisoner.*

to

to Revolt, and Establish an Independent Sovereignty in those Parts; that he held secret Correspondence with the King of the *Vandals*, having marry'd one of that Prince's Relations; that the only way to prevent him was to Abdicate his Authority there, and recal him home. On the other side he writ to *Boniface*, and in his Letters pretended a great Friendship for him, told him he had been secretly accus'd of High-Treason; that therefore the Empress intended to recal him home, but he advis'd him by all means to consult his own Safety, for if once he came within the Power of the present Government, the Danger would be unavoidable. Tho' *Boniface* was well assur'd of his own Innocence and Integrity, yet taking *Ætius* for a Man of Honour, and his faithful Friend, he refus'd to quit his Command, and began to put himself into a Posture of Defence. *Placidia* was convinc'd by his Disobedience to her Orders, that *Ætius* his Information was true, and therefore sent *Mavortius*, *Galbio* and *Sinox* with a good Army into *Africk* to reduce him, and Treat him as an Enemy to the *Roman* Empire.

Boniface being inform'd of the Forces that were marching against him, shut himself up in *Carthage*, where he was resolv'd to stand the Shock, and held out against the *Romans* so long, 'till the three Generals disagreed among themselves, and *Mavortius* and *Galbio* were kill'd by the Practices of *Sinox*, whether at the Procurement of *Boniface*, or to satisfie his own Ambition and Revenge, is not easily to be determin'd; however he did not long survive 'em, but was dispatch'd shortly after, and left *Boniface* a Victory without the loss of one Man on his side. *Placidia*, hearing of the ill Success of her three Generals, grew the more enrag'd, and resolving to renew the War and push it on with more Vigour, she rais'd fresh Forces, and made choice
of

of *Sigesvultes* to command 'em; whilst *Boniface* in the mean time concluded himself unable alone to oppose the Strength of the Empire, and therefore resolv'd to draw others into his Quarrel, and so applying himself to *Guntharius* and *Genserich*, Kings of the *Vandals* in *Spain*, he agreed to divide *Africk* between 'em, and accordingly the two Brothers embark'd with their Forces at the *Straits* of *Gibralter* and landed in *Africk*, where they made themselves Masters of the Country without any Resistance, executing that Vengeance upon the miserable Provincials, which their enormous Crimes had pull'd down upon their Heads. *The Vandals call'd into Africk.*

Whilst *Italy* stood amaz'd at so unexpected a Revolution, and already gave *Africk* for lost, several of *Boniface* his Friends in *Rome* were deeply afflicted, when they beheld his Valour, with which he had often defended the Empire, was now turn'd against it; and wonder'd how a Man, who had given so many Instances of his Integrity, Honour and Loyalty, should, without any Provocation, be thus alter'd on a sudden, and contract a Friendship with the Enemies of his Country: They therefore made Application to *Placidia*, and obtain'd her Permission to go into *Africk*, and at *Carthage* met with *Boniface*, who, when they charged him with Treason and Rebellion, produced *Ætius* his Letters, by which he convinc'd 'em that he took up Arms in his own Defence. With these Letters they return'd to *Placidia*, who was sensible of *Ætius* his Treachery, but concealed her Indignation for the present, because *Ætius* was at the Head of a victorious Army in *Gaul*; where he had lately obtain'd many Advantages over the *Franks*. But to *Boniface* and his Friends she express'd her Resentments; she assured him by her Letters that she detested the Injury had been practised against him, and that for the future he A. D. 428.

he might be assured of her Favour and Protection. She advis'd him to apply himself diligently to the Good and Safety of the Empire, and be as zealous in his Endeavours to remove the *Vandals* out of *Africk*, as he had been to call 'em in. *Boniface* readily undertook it; but found upon trial that it's easie to receive a powerful Enemy into a Country, but very difficult and often impossible to drive 'em out on't. He first attempted to remove 'em by the Promise of an immense Sum of Mony; when he found 'em deaf to that, he represented to 'em the Strength and Power of the *Roman* Empire; told 'em it was to be fear'd *Theodosius* and *Valentinian* would unite their Arms, and send such puissant Forces against 'em, as they would find it impossible for 'em to resist: But *Gunderich*, for his Brother was lately dead, was not to be moved either by his Threats or Promises. He is described, by the Writers of those Times, as a warlike Prince, of a low Stature, but Ambitious, capable of great Designs, wary in Contrivance, and vigorous in Execution; a Man of few Words, but weighty Sense; very expert at sowing Divisions among those he had a mind to weaken, and watchful upon all Opportunities, which he always husbanded to the best Advantage. *Boniface* perceiving he was not to be mov'd by fair means, join'd with *Aspar*, who was lately arriv'd with a gallant Army out of *Italy*, and gave him Battel; in which the *Romans* were beaten, and great Numbers of 'em taken Prisoners, among whom was *Martian*, who was afterwards Emperor.

A.D. 430.
The Vandals *conquer* Africk.

Genserich meeting nothing to oppose him after this Victory in *Mauritania*, proceeded up into *Numidia* and the rest of *Africk*, destroying all the Country as he pass'd, and like an irresistible Flame devouring all before him; whilst *Boniface*, who had not Forces sufficient to make head against him, retired

tired into the fortified Towns with those Troops that were able to join him. There were but three of these Towns that were not exposed to the Fury of the Enemy, those were *Carthage*, *Hippo*, and *Cirtha*, all of 'em built upon the Sea, and well provided. Towards the latter end of the Year *Genserich* came with his Army and sate down before *Hippo*; *Boniface* had just before thrown himself into it with a good Body of Men, and made a very couragious Defence: But the King being resolv'd to take it push'd on the Siege with great Vigour, and block'd it up both by Sea and Land. The Siege continu'd for fourteen Months together, and was manag'd with great Obstinacy on both Sides; but at length, after the Garrison had been quite spent with the Heat of the Service, and despair'd of any Relief, the Place was deliver'd up to the Mercy of the Barbarians, who put all they found to the Sword, pillag'd the Town, and destroy'd every thing of Value in it, except St. *Austin*'s Library, who dy'd a Month before the Town was taken. *Hippo taken.*

After the Loss of this Town the *Vandals* grew more outragious than ever, committing such barbarous Cruelties wherever they mov'd as surpass'd Imagination.

Theodosius had some time before sent *Aspar* at the Head of a very powerful Army, to assist *Valentinian* in *Africk*; he was now join'd by *Boniface*, and with the united Forces both of the Eastern and Western Empire endeavour'd to put an end to the Depredations of the victorious Barbarian; who fought and entirely defeated him, kill'd the very Flower of his Army, and forced the rest to fly for their Safety up and down the Country. *Aspar* with much ado return'd to *Constantinople*, and *Boniface* upon *Placidia*'s Invitation embark'd for *Italy*; where he challeng'd *Ætius*, fought him, and overcame him, A. D. 433. but

but dy'd three Months after, and enjoin'd his Wife *Pelagia* upon his Death-Bed never to marry any other Man but *Ætius:* Who after his Overthrow was for some time asham'd to appear at Court, and therefore retired into *Pannonia*, where he became more familiar with the *Hunns*, and by degrees rais'd himself up to his former Reputation, being shortly after employ'd by *Valentinian* against the *Burgundians*, who had pass'd their Bounds and invaded *Gallia Belgica*, wasting the Country with Fire and Sword; 'till *Ætius* appear'd against 'em, and with his usual Courage and Success overthrew, and made 'em glad to return home.

A War with Persia *concluded by a single Combat.* About this time a new War had like to have broken out between *Persia* and the Empire; for *Theodosius* observing the *Persians* crouded the Frontiers of the Empire with great numbers of Troops, sent *Bocopius* against 'em with a very strong Army. *Vararanes* finding himself too weak to give 'em Battle, propos'd to decide the Difference by a single Combat between two Champions chosen respectively out of each Party, and that that Side whose Champion was vanquish'd should pay Tribute to the other. *Theodosius* is said to have accepted of the Proposal, and made choice of *Arcobinda* or *Areovindus* for his Champion, who overcame the *Persian*, and was rewarded with the Consulship the Year following; and a Peace was concluded betwixt the *Romans* and the *Persians*, which was to last for fifty Years.

Some time after this a private Misfortune much afflicted the Court at *Ravenna*; where *Honoria*, Sister to the Emperor *Valentinian*, had stolen a great Belly. She first sent to *Attila*, King of the *Hunns*, and offer'd to marry him if he approved of the Match; but receiving no Answer agreeable to her Wishes, she prostituted her self to the Lust of one *Eugenius*, Steward of her Houshold; with whom she

she plotted against her Brother's Life and Dignity. The thing being discovered she was only sent away to *Constantinople*, there to be censur'd as *Theodosius* should think fit.

Whilst the Empire was thus afflicted by the cruel Insults of the Barbarians, the Church was no less assaulted by the Rise and Propagation of most damnable Heresies; it being observable, that Errors both in Doctrine and Discipline are never so fruitful, as in times of publick Calamities. *Nestorius* was at this time Bishop of *Constantinople*, to which he had been advanced by *Theodosius*, having been before a Priest at *Antioch*, where he had gain'd much Reputation for his Eloquence, Doctrine and Piety; but was naturally of a haughty seditious Temper, as he made it appear to the World after his Promotion. Tho' at first he prosecuted the *Arian* and *Novatian* Hereticks with so much Zeal, that *Constantinople* had like to have been in an Uproar, yet he shortly after published his own pernicious Tenets, which created much Trouble in the Church, infected great Multitudes of People, and continues at this Day in a great measure throughout the East. He held *that it was not lawful to call the Virgin* Mary *the Mother of God, who could not be born; but the Mother of Jesus Christ, who after his Birth obtain'd, by vertue of his good Works, to be united to the Word, not by an Hypostatick or Personal Union, but by a Residential Union of the Word in the Humanity, as in a Temple*; so that it was no more than a communicative or moral Society. By this Doctrine he did not only assert two Natures in Jesus Christ, but two Persons, the Divine and Human, and so destroy'd the Mystery of the Incarnation. He did not at first venture to publish the Errors himself, but made *Anastatius*, a Priest he had brought with him from *Antioch*, broach 'em

Nestorius, Bishop of Constantinople.

His Heresie.

'em to the People, who were aftonifh'd at his blafphemous Impieties. *Neftorius,* inftead of condemning fuch pernicious Doctrines, as the Duty of his Office required him, boldly afferted and maintain'd 'em; openly denying to the Virgin *Mary* the Title of *The Mother of God;* and procured one *Dorotheius,* who had been lately depofed from the See of *Marcianople,* to Anathematize from the Pulpit all thofe who prefum'd to give her that Honour. Thefe Errors, which *Neftorius* defended with much Obftinacy, caus'd *Celeftin* Bifhop of *Rome,* and *Cyrill* of *Alexandria,* to fummon a Synod each in his Diocefs, where they were univerfally condemn'd, and *Neftorius* depos'd, if within ten Days after the Signification of that Act of their refpective Synods he did not recant and difavow his Herefie; but he was fo far from a Recantation, that by his Artifices he rais'd Divifions among the Orthodox Bifhops themfelves, and fo far impos'd upon the Emperor *Theodofius* that he efpous'd his Intereft, and reprov'd *Cyrill* as one that by his Calumnies difturb'd the Unity of the Church. Thefe Practices made the Breach wider, and the Schifm irreparable without the Intervention of a General Council, which therefore *Theodofius* fummoned to meet at *Ephefus,* where, inftead of the Bifhop of *Rome, the Holy Scriptures* were placed in an eminent Throne, as a Guide to their future Controverfies; as appears from the firft Act of the Council, and *Cyrill*'s Apology to *Theodofius. Neftorius* was cited to appear at the firft Seffion, and upon his Non-Appearance depos'd; the Sentence of his Depofition, fign'd by above two hundred Bifhops, was fent to him, and publifh'd in the City to the great Joy and Satisfaction of the People. And the Day following St. *Cyrill* in a Sermon gave the Virgin *Mary* fuch Elogies, which tho' they were drawn from the concurring fenfe of the Scriptures,

The Third General Council at Ephefus.

ptures, and favoured nothing of the Extravagances they now-a-days throw upon her, yet did they make the Church from that time forward honour her with a greater Zeal than it had ever done before.

Five Days after the Condemnation of *Nestorius*, *John* Bishop of *Antioch* arriv'd at *Ephesus* with those of his Party, and being offended at what the Council had done without his Presence and Consent, he united himself with about thirty others, some of whom had been depos'd for their Crimes, and others were known openly to espouse the Errors of *Pelagius*. These Prelates assembled at his Lodgings, and calling themselves a Synod or Council, depos'd *Cyrill* and *Memnon* of *Ephesus*, and pronounc'd a Sentence of Excommunication against all the Bishops of the lawful Council, unless they restor'd the *Pelagians* who had been depos'd; and declared with them, that Adam's *Soul did not die for his Offence, and that Original Sin was not transmitted from Father to Son*. The Emperor at the beginning of the Council had appointed *Candidian*, Master of his Houshold, to appear there on his behalf, and by his Authority to prevent any Disorders, whereby the Fathers might be molested. *Candidian* had implicitly espous'd the Passion and Interest of *Nestorius*, and therefore intercepted the Couriers that had been deputed to *Theodosius* with the Proceedings of the Council, and Letters from the Fathers, and at the same time inform'd the Emperor that Matters were handled with much Heat in the Assembly, and that they had proceeded against *Nestorius* with too much Precipitation: But he permitted the Anti-Council from time to time to transmit their Decrees to the Emperor; to accuse *Cyrill* and others of Heresie, and the Spirit of Revenge; and condemn every thing the Fathers had done: Whose Silence in the Matter the Emperor interpreted as a Confession of the Fact; and so gave Orders for the Imprisonment of St. *Cyrill* and *Memnon*; who were not releas'd 'till the Emperor some time after had been inform'd of the Truth in each particular; and then he dissolv'd the Council, set the two Bishops at liberty, and confirmed the Condemnation of *Nestorius*. But whereas the Fathers had proceeded to depose *John* and his Adherents, the Emperor thought fit to suspend the Ratification, for fear of exasperating those turbulent Spirits, and making 'em more averse to an Union; which they were so far from embracing, that they protested they had rather die a thousand times than partake of *Cyrill*'s Communion, or his Doctrine. As for *Nestorius*, the Emperor permitted him to retire to his Monastery, that he might have the better Opportunity to acknowledge his Errors, and abjure 'em: But he was so far from acknowledging this Grace of *Theodosius* towards him, that he persisted to poison the World with his Heresie, both in his Discourses and his Writings; for which reason he was banish'd four Years after into *Oasis*, where, after his Tongue had been eaten out with Worms, he dy'd a miserable Death; but in his Life-time rais'd a spiritual War against the Church, which has been continued to this very Day.

The Wars all this while were continued in *Gaul* and *Africk* with various Success, the *Burgundians* had for some Years been opposing the *Roman* Arms, and put the Empire to a vast Expence; nothing but the Conduct and Resolution of such a General as *Ætius* was able to hinder 'em from breaking farther into the Empire, and involving the State in new Difficulties. This Year he obtain'd so many Advantages over 'em, that *Gundicarius* their King was glad to listen to Reason, and agree to a Peace very honourable and advantagious to the *Romans*. At the

A. D. 435.
A Peace in Gaul and Africk.

the same time *Trigetius*, who had been sent to succeed *Boniface* in *Africk*, forc'd *Genserich*, King of the *Vandals*, to condescend to a Peace, upon Condition the *Romans* resign'd up to him that part of *Africk* that lyes round *Hippo*, which was accordingly deliver'd up to 'em, and prov'd in the Consequence highly prejudicial to the Empire. The Joy the People conceiv'd at these two Agreements was improv'd at *Rome*, where *Valentinian* celebrated his *Decennalia*, and publick Vows were made for the continuance of his Reign, which were reasonably thought to have more of Form than Substance in 'em, he behaving himself already like a loose, dissolute Prince, regardless of the State, and abandon'd to his Pleasures.

Peace being thus concluded between the *Vandals* and *Burgundians*, the Empire seem'd to breath a little after the long Fatigues of War, and to put on a Face of Gaiety; for tho' *Theodorick*, King of the *Goths*, had, contrary to his Agreement with the *Romans*, broken out lately in *Gaul*, yet *Littorius*, with a Body of *Hunns*, watch'd him so narrowly that the Mischief he did at present was inconsiderable, and his Attempts carry'd more of the Name of War with 'em than the Inconveniences of it, so that *Valentinian* had time to listen to the Advice of those who persuadeed him to Marry *Eudoxia*, and for that purpose demanded her by his Embassadors of her Father *Theodosius*, who inclin'd willingly to the Proposal, and *Valentinian* himself went to fetch her from *Constantinople*, but was hardly return'd back to *Ravenna* before new Commotions interrupted the Solemnity of his Nuptials. For *Littorius*, who had hitherto commanded with much Success against the *Goths*, presum'd too much upon his good Fortune, and out of Emulation to *Ætius* was so far transported as to Besiege *Tholouse*, the Capital of the *Goths*, *New Troubles in Gaul.*

promising to himself, if he could once be Master of that Place, he should be able with ease to drive the *Goths* out of the Country. *Theodorick* was at first so much frighten'd, that he sent some Bishops out to him with Offers of a Peace; but he trusting to the Promises and Encouragement he receiv'd from his *Pagan* Idols, would listen to no Terms of Accommodation, but gave the *Goths* Battle, who fighting like Men in Despair, not only defeated his Army, and kill'd a great many of his Men, but took him Prisoner, and led him bound into that City as a Slave, where he not long before threaten'd to enter as a Conqueror, and where, by *Theodorick's* Command, he was put to an Ignominious Death. The *Goths* after this Defeat ravag'd up and down the Country without Control, and *Theodorick* advanc'd with his Army as far as the *Rhône*, thinking he now had an Opportunity to enlarge his Dominions. But *Valentinian*, as soon as he was inform'd of the loss both of his General and his Army, dispatch'd *Ætius* with all Expedition into *Gaul*, whose very Name was grown so terrible to the *Goths*, that without daring to appear in the Field against him they earnestly desir'd a Peace, which was granted 'em upon the Mediation of *Avitus*, *Præfectus Prætorio* of those Parts, and kept the *Goths* in tolerable good Order for some Years after.

A. D. 439. *A new War in Africk.* But whilst *Ætius* was employ'd in the quenching the Flame in *Gaul*, a greater broke out in *Africk*, which prov'd of more weighty Consequence to the Empire. *Genserich*, who had concluded a Peace with the *Romans* about four Years before, thought himself oblig'd to observe it no longer than it appear'd advantagious to his Interest, and serv'd to strengthen and confirm his Pretensions in *Africk*; so that not content with the Conquest he had already made, nor the vast Provinces that were

in

in his Possession, he broke the Peace he had lately sworn to, and after having rag'd with all imaginable Liberty throughout the Country, he set upon *Carthage*, which he well knew was weakly Garrison'd, and took it on the 20th of *October*, before the Emperor could be inform'd of the Danger the City was in. He threw the Senators into Chains, and commanded the Inhabitants, upon Pain of Death, to discover to him all their Gold, their Silver, Jewels, and most valuable Moveables, and so made himself Master of the Riches of that wealthy City; from thence he pass'd with a powerful Fleet into *Sicily*, where, meeting with little or no resistance, he behav'd himself with his usual Barbarity. Among his many other Severities, which he exercis'd without any remorse upon the Orthodox Clergy, this was one which carry'd not the least Terror with it. He forc'd *Quod-Vult-Deus*, Bishop of *Carthage*, and a great part of his Clergy to be put naked on Board several Leaky Vessels prepar'd for that purpose, and in that helpless Condition to be thrust out to Sea, where, after they had for a long time been toss'd up down by the violence of the Waves to their great Consternation, and certain hazard of their Lives, they were all driven safe a-shoar near *Naples* in *Campania*. He left *Sicily* sooner than he intended, upon an Information that *Sebastian*, Son of the late General *Boniface*, was arriv'd in *Africk* with a very strong Army; this brought him back with all speed to *Carthage*, for fear the *Romans* should in his Absence recover that City out of his Hands. But *Sebastian*, instead of behaving himself like a *Roman* General, and pursuing *Genserich* as an Enemy to the Empire, sate down idly in the Province, and enter'd into Terms of Accommodation with him. Hereupon *Genserich*, who had a Mind to bind him firmer to his Interest,

rest, endeavour'd by his Persuasions to make him turn *Arian*, which when he could by no means be prevail'd upon to do, he got him to be murder'd, either out of an Aversion he had to the Orthodox Faith, or because he knew *Sebastian* was an experienc'd Commander, and was afraid he intended to circumvent him. This insolent Demeanour in the King of the *Vandals* highly provok'd *Theodosius*, who thought it time to provide against so prevailing an Enemy, and therefore Mann'd out a Fleet of Sixty Sail, on Board of which he order'd a good Army to Embark, and committed it to the Conduct of *Areobindas*, and two others, who were Commission'd to land in *Africk*, and by all possible means endeavour to drive *Genserich* out of it. These Generals instead of following their Orders wasted a great deal of their time in *Sicily*, and then crossing over into *Africk*, carry'd more Terror than Execution along with 'em; for without performing any great Matters they return'd back into *Scicily*. However their Expedition had this good Effect, that *Genserich* perceiving what Power *Theodosius* had, which at another time might be better manag'd, he sent his Embassadors to *Constantinople* to Treat about a Peace, which *Theodosius* was forc'd to conclude the Year following, for Reasons that made that Year famous to Posterity.

A. D. 442.
The Hunns *Invade the Roman Empire.*

The *Hunns*, who had formerly driven the *Alans*, *Goths* and *Vandals* out of their ancient Seats, and forc'd 'em to pass over the *Rhine* and *Ister* into the *Roman* Territories, began now to follow 'em; and taking the Advantage of the Wars the *Romans* were engag'd in with their Neighbours, especially the *Vandals* in *Africk*, muster'd all the Forces they could raise among the Inhabitants on the other side the *Euxine*, and with an Army, terribly prodigious for its Numbers, fell upon the Frontiers of the Em-

Empire, where they seiz'd on the Forts and Garrisons built formerly upon the Banks of the *Ister* for the Defence of it. Here the Army was divided into two Bodies, with one of which *Attila* their King invaded *Mysia*, and with the other his Brother *Bleda* fell upon *Thrace*, where, bearing down all Opposition before 'em, they rag'd in all Places with Fire and Sword, they took and surpriz'd many Cities, and among the rest *Naissus* and *Singidunum*, two Cities of *Mysia Prima*.

Theodosius was too sensible of the ill Consequence of such Irruptions, especially at a time when the Empire was so much weaken'd already, not to think of some timely Resistance, and stop 'em, if possible, in their first Motions; whereupon he sent two of his Generals, *Arnegistus* and *Joannes*, with a strong Army against 'em. *Arnegistus* engaged *Attila* near *Marcianople*, at the same time that *Joannes* fought *Bleda* in *Thrace*; and they both met with such Success that the Barbarians were worsted, and seem'd at first more desirous of returning than capable of proceeding forward; but the Fate of the Empire began now to press hard upon it, and its Ruin seem'd inevitable; for the two Generals, instead of pursuing the publick Interest, fell into private Quarrels between themselves, in which *Joannes* was kill'd by the Fraud of his jealous Antagonist.

The *Hunns* taking the Advantage of these untimely Dissentions pursu'd their Conquests, and seiz'd upon all the Cities in *Thrace*, except *Adrianople*; they enter'd into *Macedonia*, *Greece* and *Illyricum*, in all which Places they made such horrible Havock as they never felt before. Being not only sworn Enemies to Christianity, but even to Civility, and the Knowledge of the true God; they exceeded the *Goths* and *Vandals* in their barbarous Cruelties, and when ever the *Romans* had

the

the Courage to Face 'em, they seem'd rather to harden and provoke, than repel or distress 'em. This reduc'd *Theodosius* to the last extremity, and tho' he had formerly resolv'd never to let *Genserich* possess a Foot in *Africk*, but by main Force to drive him out, yet being now press'd by a nearer Calamity, and unable to contend with two Enemies at once, he was persuaded to listen to the Overtures made by the *Vandals*, and granted 'em better Terms than they could otherwise have desir'd or expected. For *Genserich*'s Affairs at home were in a great Confusion; his insufferable Insolence, which he had contracted from the long Course of his Success, had so incens'd his Subjects, that they conspir'd against him, and when his Vigilance had discover'd and prevented the Plot, he us'd both the Innocent and Guilty with so much bloody severity, that he could not have been more weaken'd by a Defeat in Battel. These Domestick Disasters made him sollicite a Peace both at *Constantinople* and *Ravenna*, which *Valentinian* and *Theodosius*, for the Reasons above mention'd, readily granted. The Emperors, more for State than any other Consideration, reserv'd some ruin'd Provinces to themselves, and left the *Vandals* the quiet Possession of the rest of *Africk*, upon Condition he paid a Tribute to the Emperor for three Years together, and deliver'd his Son *Honoric* up to *Valentinian* as a Pledge and Assurance of his Faith, which he had so often violated.

Peace with the Vandals.

III. The Peace being concluded, *Theodosius* recall'd his Army out of *Sicily*, to be employ'd under the Conduct of *Areobindas* and *Aspar* against the *Hunns*, who were now got so far into the Country that all Opposition seem'd to come too late; so that *Theodosius* was forc'd, to the great prejudice of his

Chap. IV. XLIX. The. II. Valentinian III.

Reputation, to try the Power of his Gold, when he found the Force of his Steel ineffectual. He sent his Embassadors to *Attila* to Treat about a Peace, which he offer'd to purchase at the price of Six thousand Pounds of Gold to be paid in Hand, and an Annual Pension of Five hundred, or as some say, a Thousand more, provided he would instantly retreat, and confine himself and his Subjects within his own Bounds. The Proposals seem'd so fair that *Attila* found no reason to reject 'em, so that upon Payment of the Mony he prepar'd to be gone, enrich'd not only with so vast a Sum, but infinite other Treasure, and an hundred and twenty thousand Captives, leaving *Illyricum* in a much worse Condition than ever it had felt before, tho' frequently subject to such Calamities; as an Aggravation to which, so dreadful a Snow fell this Year, and lay so long on the barren Ground, which the Barbarians had burnt up and wasted, that not only great quantities of Cattle, but multitudes of Men, Women and Children perish'd for want of the Conveniences of Habitations and Fuel, of which the Savage *Hunns* had depriv'd 'em; at the same time happen'd an Earth-quake at *Rome*, which overthrew several Buildings both publick and private. These Accidents were look'd on as prodigious, and seem'd to forerun that mighty Storm, which, tho' quell'd for the present, broke in shortly after, and like an Hurricane tore up both the Eastern and Western Provinces.

In this Interval *Theodosius*, as if he foresaw the ensuing Calamities, reinforc'd and fortify'd the Borders, and by several Acts of State and publick Edicts put himself into the best Condition of Defence his Affairs would admit of; for at present the Empire enjoy'd a Tranquility both in the Eastern and Western Provinces, greater than any it had

D. D. 443. Theodosius buys a Peace of the Hunns.

had known for a long time before; it look'd like a Calm presaging the Tempest that was to follow, for except some Motions of the *Burgundians* in *Gaul,* who were easily reduc'd by *Ætius,* we hear of nothing that disturb'd the Publick Peace, 'till it was broken again by *Attila.* However *Theodosius* met with some Disturbances in his private Family, that gave him as much trouble almost as a War would have done; his Sister *Pulcheria* had hitherto assisted him at the Helm of State, and by her Care, Vigilance and Sagacity eas'd the Burden of the Empire, that would otherwise have lain heavy upon his Shoulder. *Chrysaphius* the Eunuch, and great Favourite of the Emperor, was highly displeas'd with *Flavianus,* Patriarch of *Constantinople,* and very desirous to have him remov'd, but knew all his Attempts would be ineffectual whilst *Pulcheria* continu'd in Power, whom therefore he labour'd to involve in some Difficulties; accordingly he endeavour'd to raise a Jealousie and Emulation between her and the Empress *Eudocia,* whom he persuaded to remove from *Pulcheria* the Steward of her Houshold, who manag'd all her Concerns; this *Eudocia* try'd all means with her Husband to effect, but *Theodosius* was resolv'd against it, nor would he so far disoblige his Sister, to whose prudent Management he was so much indebted. But at length she prevail'd so far that the Emperor requir'd *Flavianus* to make her a Deaconess; for as they often in those Parts drew great Men by force to Bishopricks, so the Bishops themselves very often made choice of Ladies of more exalted Virtue and Honour than the rest of their Sex, and by force ordain'd 'em Deaconesses of the Church. *Flavianus* knew not how to disobey the Emperor's Order, but admonish'd *Pulcheria* of it, and advis'd her to avoid him, lest he should be forc'd against his

Pulcheria remov'd from Court.

his Will upon a very ungrateful Office. *Pulcheria* was no sooner inform'd of it, but she voluntarily retired from the Administration, and led a private Life in the Country. From this we may form a lively Image of Court Intrigues, where its very often the Business of one Courtier to supplant another, because he thinks he is in a better Post than himself. They who have a mind to absolve *Eudocia* from the Sin of Ingratitude to *Pulcheria*, to whom she ow'd her Greatness, give another Reason for the Emperor's Displeasure, and affirm *Pulcheria* ow'd her Disgrace to none but her self. They tell us, that upon Observation of the Emperor's Easiness in signing whatever Papers were offer'd him, without ever examining the Contents of 'em, she thought to convince him of his Folly, by representing to him how dangerous it might one Day prove in the Consequence; she one day presented him with a Paper in which he sold his Wife as a Slave to *Pulcheria*, which he sign'd, as usual, without ever reading the Substance of it: Some time after she detain'd *Eudocia* as she came to visit her, and when the Emperor himself came to demand her, she told him that she having bought her of him he had no Right in her, and thereupon produced the Contract. *Theodosius* was so distasted at this home Reproof, that, like other Princes who are fond of Flattery but averse to Reprehension, he ever after that entertain'd a Prejudice to her, which its more than probable his Wife took care to aggravate, the better to re-ingratiate her self with him; for she had lately been in Disgrace, and that upon an Occasion which may serve to show us how cautious Persons in an high Sphere ought to move. Some Person had presented *Theodosius* with a Fruit, admirable for its Largeness and Beauty; this he sent as a Rarity to *Eudocia*, who made a Present of it to *Paulinus*, with whom
she

she was so intimately acquainted upon the Account of his great Learning, that her Familiarity with him gave occasion to some scandalous Reflections. He, ignorant from whence the Empress had receiv'd it, carry'd it to *Theodosius* as a thing new and singular, and *Theodosius* presently after ask'd his Wife what was become it; she, for fear of displeasing him, answer'd she had eaten it, whereupon *Theodosius* producing the Fruit convicted her of Falshood, order'd *Paulinus* to be put to death, and for some time was alienated in his Mind from the Empress.

Eudocia, the Empress, in Disgrace.

Pulcheria being remov'd from the Administration, *Chrysaphius* thought he might now with ease work *Flavian*'s Ruin, and was shortly after presented with a fair Opportunity of effecting it. *Eutyches*, an Abbot of a Monastery in *Constantinople*, had very vigorously oppos'd *Nestorius* his Heresie, but, as it often happens in the like Cases, fell out of one Extream into another: For whereas *Nestorius* deny'd the Hypostatick Union in Jesus Christ, *Eutyches* deny'd the Distinction of the two Natures, confounding the one in the other. This Doctrine was immediately condemn'd in a Synod at *Constantinople*, where *Eutyches* was summon'd to appear, but refus'd to stir out of his Monastery; tho' he presently after apply'd himself to *Chrysaphius*, whose Relation he was, and who was now the great Favourite of *Theodosius*. *Chrysaphius* persuaded the Emperor to summon the Second Council of *Ephesus*, where by the Activity of *Dioscorus*, Bishop of *Alexandria*, the *Eutychian* Heresie was approv'd, and *Flavian*, who had got it to be condemn'd in the Synod, was not only depos'd but most barbarously abus'd at *Ephesus*, and banish'd into *Lydia*, where he dy'd of his Wounds in a short time after, and is commemorated as one of the Martyrs of the *Greek* Church. This Violence and Injustice against *Flavian* demonstrates to us the Corruption

ruption of the Bishops that compos'd that Council, and that the Ancients upon good Grounds call'd it an *Assembly of Thieves.*

Attila, who had hitherto observ'd the Peace concluded with the Empire, did now again declare War against *Theodosius*, because the Tribute he was to have receiv'd by the Articles of Peace had not been punctually paid him; and taking the Advantage of a great Frost, which had frozen up the *Danube*, he pass'd his Army over, and wasted *Pannonia* and *Illyricum*. *Theodosius* sent *Anthemius* and *Arnegistus* to oppose him, who did great Service to the Empire; especially *Anthemius*, who was afterwards Emperor of the West, finding the Barbarians dispers'd up and down the Country, and intent upon the Pillage, he set upon 'em at several times, destroy'd a great number of them, and constrain'd the rest to unite themselves into one Body near *Sardica*, where he gave 'em Battel; and tho' *Arnegistus* at the beginning of the Engagement abandon'd his Collegue and deserted to the Enemy, yet he got an entire Victory, and oblig'd 'em to sue for a Peace, which he granted upon Condition they hung up the Traitor *Arnegistus*, who accordingly fell a Sacrifice to Justice, and the Peace was ratify'd both by *Theodosius* and *Valentinian*. Some time after this the Western Empire suffer'd a great Loss in the Death of *Galla Placidia*, *Valentinian*'s Mother, a Princess of great Prudence, who had been toss'd to and fro in the World, and run through several Changes of Fortune. She had the chief Management in the Affairs of State, not only during her Son's Minority, but afterwards when he arriv'd to a Ripeness of Years; for he was of himself an effeminate voluptuous Prince, resigning himself up entirely to the Government of those that were near his Person: His Mother, whilst she liv'd, restrain'd him in a great measure by her Autho-

A. D. 447.

Placidia Dies.

thority and good Counsel; but as soon as she was dead the Depravity of his Nature appear'd visible to the World, who thereby grew sensible how beneficial *Placidia* had been to the Empire. And as *Valentinian* was miss-led by Parasites and evil Counsellors in the West, so was *Theodosius* abus'd by the Artifices of his Favourite *Chrysaphius* in the East, where he ruled with an unlimited Authority, tyrannizing in a particular manner over the Clergy.

Pulcheria returns again to Court. His villainous Practices provoked *Pulcheria* to quit her Solitude and return again to Court, where she made it appear to *Theodosius*, that *Eutyches* was an infamous Heretick; that *Chrysaphius* had supported him out of Malice to *Flavian*; and had abus'd his Bounty in many respects. Hereupon *Theodosius* turn'd him out of all his Employments, confiscated his Estate, and banish'd him. This was thought too mild a Proceeding against one, who had not only most shamefully abus'd the Favour of his Prince, but troubled the Repose of the Church, and horribly persecuted her faithful Pastors. *Theodosius* at the same time severely reproved his Wife *Eudocia*, for concurring with *Chrysaphius* in his Intrigues, and procuring a Disagreement between him and his Sister *Pulcheria*, reproaching her besides for her private Correspondence with *Paulinus*, and appear'd so displeas'd at her, that to avoid his Indignation she got leave to visit the Holy Places at *Jerusalem*, where she led a very devout retired Life. After this publick Justice done to the great Satisfaction of his Subjects, and a Desire to repair the Injuries done to the Church by the late Council at *Ephesus*, *Theodosius* dy'd on the twenty ninth of *July* at *Constantinople*, in the fiftieth Year of his Age, and forty third of his Reign. Historians are not agreed upon the manner of his Death; some say he dy'd of Sickness, and particularly of the Plague; others, that

that he fell off from his Horse whilst he was a Hunting, and dy'd the Night following.

He was a Prince exemplary for his Piety, and a great Friend to the Church; but he was of a weak Spirit, and too much guided by those that were about him. Whilst he suffer'd himself to be directed by his Sister *Pulcheria* the Administration was blameless, which indeed redounded more to her Reputation than his own; but he lay too open to the Practices of intriguing Courtiers, who often persuaded him to Actions unjust and unwarrantable. He was so far from revenging any Injury offered him, that it's said of him he never was seen to be angry. As he resign'd the Civil Affairs up to the Government of his Sister and chief Ministers, so did he manage all his Wars by his Generals, addicting himself wholly to his Devotions and Recreations. *Theodosius* dy'd in the seventh Consulate of *Valentinian* and of *Avienus*, in the 1202d Year of *Rome*, An. Dom. 450.

His Character.

Immediately upon the Death of *Theodosius Pulcheria* got *Martian* to be declared Emperor by the Senate, to which the Officers in the Army afterwards consented. She thought the readiest way to continue both him and her self in the Authority was to marry him, which she did, but continu'd a Virgin 'till her Death notwithstanding, as we are told by *Evagrius*. *Martian* was by Birth a *Thracian*, and being the Son of a Soldier he always follow'd the Wars: It happen'd, as he was going in his Youth to list himself at *Philippopolis*, he found a Man that had been lately kill'd lying upon the Road; being surpriz'd at the Sight, he deferr'd his Journey 'till he could conveniently bury the Corps: But some who came by, and observ'd what he was doing, preferr'd an Information against him to the Magistrates of *Philippopolis*, by whose Order he was ap-

A.D. 450. Martian.

prehended, indicted, and condemn'd for the Murder; but as they were ready to lead him out to Execution the true Author of the Fact was discover'd and convicted, and *Martian* was left at liberty to follow his Inclinations, which led him to the Wars. *Evagrius* relates several Passages of him, which he faith portended the Imperial Dignity: *Martian* serving in *Africk* against the *Vandals* was taken Prisoner, as we observ'd before, with several others, in that Battle which *Aspar* lost to *Genserich*, and was order'd to be brought with the rest into a Field, where the King might have the Opportunity of viewing 'em, and where *Martian* was fallen fast asleep before the King's Arrival, who coming at last to visit the Prisoners, observ'd an Eagle hovering over *Martian* whilst he slept, to protect him with her Wings from the Heat of the Sun, which in that Country, and at that Season of the Year was very intense. Upon this Sight he conjectur'd what in the Course of Time was to befal him, and therefore upon a Promise given him, that when he came to be Emperor he would never wage War with the *Vandals*, he gave him his Liberty; which Promise he religiously observ'd after his Promotion.

Three Days after his Establishment he publish'd a severe Law against such Clerks and Monks as quitted the Orthodox Religion, and follow'd *Eutyches* his damnable Doctrine. He restor'd all those Bishops that had been depos'd by the Council at *Ephesus*, recall'd all that had been banish'd, and re-establish'd 'em in their several Dioceses; and the Year following this Emperor summon'd the fourth General Council, which was to be celebrated at *Nice*, but by an Order from the Emperor was transferr'd to *Calcedon*, where *Dioscorus* was depos'd, together with all those that had espous'd *Eutyches* and his Heresie.

Martian summons the Fourth General Council.

This

Chap. IV. L. Valentinian III. Martian.

This Year *Valentinian*, or his Ministers, were busily employ'd in warlike Preparations, and the Defence of the Empire, which was threaten'd by *Attila*; who observing *Valentinian* to be a vitious unactive Prince, regardless of the Publick, and devoted to his sensual Pleasures, thought it no difficult matter to possess himself of the Empire; especially having at present an Army on foot consisting of no less than seven hundred thousand Men, rais'd promiscuously out of *Tartary*, *Poland*, *Germany*, and *Muscovy*. The Writers of those Times have aim'd at several Reasons, or rather Conjectures, for this War, and why *Attila* chose to begin in *Gaul* sooner than other Parts of the Empire adjoining nearer to him. *Jornandes* saith, that *Honric*, Son of *Genserich*, having marry'd the Daughter of *Theodorich*, King of the *Goths* in *Gaul*, upon some Suspicion that she had a Design to poison him cut off her Nose, and sent her home to her Father; that *Genserich* apprehending upon good grounds *Theodorich* would resent so barbarous an Injury, endeavour'd to strengthen himself by an Alliance with *Attila*, and accordingly sent great presents to him, desiring him to invade *Theodorich*, and promising to join him with a very strong Army. *Attila*, who was intent upon nothing but his own Advantage, embraced the Opportunity; and that he might first divide those he intended to destroy, he sent his Embassadors to *Valentinian*, conjuring him by no means to assist *Theodorich*, and assuring him at the same time that all his Designs were upon him: On the other hand, he made *Theodorich* believe all his Preparations were against the *Romans*, and advis'd him not to intermeddle in the Quarrel. These crafty Practices in the fraudulent King were discover'd by the noble *Ætius*, who foreseeing what a mighty Storm was ready to discharge it self upon the Subjects of the

Empire, prevail'd with *Theodorich*, and his Son *Thorismond*, to suspend for the present their particular Quarrels to the Empire, and by an Union with it oppose the furious Torrent, which seem'd to threaten both alike. In the mean time *Attila* was marching at the Head of his numerous Forces out of *Scythia* into *Gemany* in the very midst of Winter, encouraging the People as he march'd along to throw off their Obedience to the *Roman* Empire, and joining with him have their share in the Spoils of *Gaul*; and by this means rais'd so powerful an Army, as seem'd design'd not only for the Destruction of *Gaul*, but the whole Earth. When he was advanc'd as far as the *Rhine*, he built so many Boats for the Transportation of his Forces that the vast *Hercinian* Forest seem'd unable to supply him with a sufficient quantity of Timber. Having pass'd the River, he took and pillaged *Cologn*, *Tongri*, and *Mets*; from thence he pass'd on to *Arras*, which met with the like Treatment, for wherever he came he put all to Fire and Sword, and so grew amazingly terrible to all Mankind: He order'd himself to be call'd *The Scourge of God*, and as such he behav'd himself, the Instrument of Divine Wrath, and a publick Plague to the rest of Mankind.

Attila invades Gaul.

Ætius being inform'd of the Barbarian's Progress, mustered his Forces at *Arles*, as well those of the Empire, as the Confederates under *Theodorich* King of the Western *Goths*, *Meroveus* of the *Franks*, *Sangiban* and *Gundicarius* Kings of the *Alani* and *Burgundians*, between whom at present *Gaul* was divided. *Anian*, Bishop of *Orleance*, hearing of *Attila*'s Approach towards that City, went speedily to *Ætius*, to acquaint him with the dangerous Condition the City would be in without a timely Relief, and was sent back with the Promise of a speedy Succour by *Ætius:* He was hardly return'd before *Attila*

tila laid Siege to the City with his whole Army, battering it on every side with his Warlike Engines; but here his Arms first met with a check, for *Ætius*, *Theodorick*, and *Thorismond* arriving forc'd him to raise the Siege, tho' some say he broke into the City, but upon the approach of the Confederates was forc'd to retire, before he had time to pillage it, to the *Campi Catalaunici*, or Plains of *Chalons*, angry and enrag'd at his Disappointment, and there he resolv'd to provoke *Ætius* to Fight, whom he had already conquer'd in Imagination, depending upon the Multitude of his Forces. *Ætius*, who was as willing to engage as *Attila*, soon presented himself, and stood prepar'd for a bloody Battel; he was at first in a great suspence, and suspected the King of the *Alans*, who he was inform'd had an Intent to Desert the *Romans* in the Fight, and run over to *Attila*; having therefore made a treble Division of his Forces, he plac'd him in the midst; the Right Wing he committed to *Theodorick* and his Son *Thorismond*, the Left he commanded himself, and both in the Front and Rear he dispos'd the most Valiant of the *Roman* Legions, the better to oblige the rest to fight. The Fight was very obstinate and bloody on both sides, continuing from Noon 'till Midnight; at which time neither Party yielded, but were rather parted by the Inconvenience of the Night; and *Attila* sounding a Retreat retir'd behind a Rampart he had formerly made, and left *Ætius* Master of the Field, who posted his Men in the best manner he could 'till the Morning, for fear the Enemy should take any Advantage, and snatch that Victory out of his Hands which he began already to think himself secure of, and was the next Morning assur'd of his Success. *Attila* is said to have lost in the Battel no less than one hundred and seventy thousand Men. On the

He lays Siege to Orleance,

and raises the Siege.

Ætius engages him,

and beats him.

Romans side *Gundicarius,* King of the *Burgundians,* and *Theodorick* was Slain, at which his Son *Thorismond* was so enrag'd, that he resolv'd instantly to Attack *Attila* in his Camp, and revenge his Father's Death; but *Ætius,* who was sensible of the Strength and aspiring Genius of the *Goths,* was afraid if the *Hunns* should be totally overthrown, that then they would turn their Forces against the Empire, and therefore in Policy chose to let him escape at present, that he might awe the *Goths* and *Franks,* and divert 'em from any dangerous Attempts upon the Empire; whereupon, after he had given *Thorismond* large Commendations for his extraordinary Valour, he advis'd him with speed to go and take Possession of his Father's Dominions both in *Gaul* and *Spain,* before his Neighbours had time to raise him any Disturbance there. *Thorismond* approv'd of his Advice, and so deferr'd his Revenge to another Opportunity. This Proceeding of *Ætius* towards *Attila* was very much blam'd by some, and gave others an opportunity of representing him as a dangerous Person to *Valentinian,* and one that had a Design of making himself Emperor; to which end he held private Correspondence with *Attila,* whom he forbore to destroy when he had him in his Power, and suffer'd him to escape, to bring more Mischief upon the Empire. These Suggestions, how ill soever they were grounded, prov'd in time the Ruin both of *Valentinian* and *Ætius,* as we shall see hereafter.

A. D. 452.
Attila having been beaten in *Gaul* retir'd with his Troops into *Pannonia,* which was now become the Seat of the *Hunns,* part of it being call'd from them *Hungaria;* here having refresh'd his Army, and reinforc'd it to that degree that it was far more numerous than the Year before, he resolv'd now to Invade *Italy* it self, which was more plentiful than any of the Provinces, and where he thought he
should

Chap. IV. L. Valentinian III. Martian.

should meet with no *Goths*, *Alans*, *Franks* or *Burgundians*, who in Confederacy with the *Romans* could oppose his Arms. The News of his Designs and Preparations were no sooner known in *Italy*, but the People were in a greater Consternation than at the Expeditions of *Alarich* and *Radagaisus*; for they consider'd *Attila* as a Barbarian, more fierce and savage than either of the former, who profess'd himself delighted in Destruction, and rejoic'd at the Calamities he brought upon his Fellow Creatures. At the same time there was a Report of several new Prodigies, particularly of three great Stones that fell from Heaven; besides *Italy* had been lately afflicted by a great Dearth, which was attended by a grievous Pestilence, Calamities terrible enough in themselves, without the Aggravation of any other Mischiefs.

Attila having pass'd the *Danube* towards the end of Winter, and repuls'd the Garrisons plac'd by *Valentinian* for the Defence of the *Julian Alps*, enter'd into *Friuli* and *Istria*; and the Inhabitants of *Venetia*, who expected the first Violence of the Storm, betook themselves to the Islands and inaccessible Marshes of the *Adriatick*, upon the first terrible noise of *Attila*'s Preparations; here they laid the Foundations of the City, call'd from the Name of the Country *Venice*, which exceedingly encreas'd by the Destruction of *Aquileia*, and the other Neighbouring Cities which felt the Fury of *Attila*'s Arms, and is at present one of the most glorious Common-wealths in Christendom, or perhaps in the World. *Valentinian* had fortify'd *Aquileia*, the Metropolis of *Venetia*, a strong Town, design'd to protect the Borders of *Italy* from the Incursions of the Barbarians. This Place *Attila* Besieg'd, and batter'd it furiously for the space of three Months together; but the Besieg'd defended them-

Attila Invades Italy.

The first Foundation of Venice.

Attila Besieges Aquileia.

themselves with so much Bravery, that the Barbarians were ready to Mutiny, and murmur'd at the King for spending his Time, and the Strength of his Army in a Siege, where they got nothing but Blows to encourage them; whereupon *Attila* had thoughts of raising it, but was prevented by an Omen, which gave him fresh Encouragement; for he observ'd a Stork, that had built her Nest upon the top of a great Tower in the City, to take her young ones and fly with 'em far off into the Country. This he show'd to his Army, and told 'em what the Stork did was by Instinct, and a natural Foresight, that she could expect no more Safety in a City that was going to be taken by a Victorious Enemy; he advis'd 'em therefore not to be wanting to themselves, but patiently expect the Possession of what was due to their unweary'd Labours. This Speech so inflam'd his Men that they once more apply'd their Engines to the Walls,

and takes it, and after a very vigorous Assault took the City; tho' some say it had been first deserted by the Inhabitants, who taking the Advantage of a dark Night escap'd by Sea with their Bishop *Nicetas.* The better to amuse the Enemy, and gain time for their Retreat, they plac'd certain Wooden Statues upon the Walls, which were to pass upon the Barbarians for Soldiers put there to guard 'em: The *Hunns* were not sensible of the Stratagem 'till they observ'd several Birds to perch unmolested upon 'em, and then they scal'd the Town, took it without any Resistance, pillag'd it for several Days together, kill'd all the Men that had been left behind, and ravish'd the Women, designing by this barbarous piece of Severity to strike an Awe into the rest, and terrifie 'em into Submission. This made the Inhabitants of the Neighbouring Cities quit their Dwellings, by which means all the Towns there-

thereabouts fell into the Hands of *Attila,* who inſtead of marching on towards *Rome,* declin'd towards the Right, and fell upon *Treviſa, Verona, Mantua, Cremona, Breſcio* and *Bergamo,* all which ſhared in the Fate of *Aquileia;* towards Winter he paſs'd the *Po,* and proceeded with the like Barbarity againſt *Placentia, Parma,* and other Places, ſo that all that Tract of Land, which lyes between the *Alps* and the *Appennine,* was reduc'd to Aſhes. *Ætius* had by this time rais'd a very formidable Army, and having quitted *Rome* was now upon the Borders of *Æmilia,* ready to oppoſe *Attila;* this Conſideration made the Barbarian liſten more readily to the Advice of his Commanders, who were loaden with the Riches of *Italy,* and were deſirous of enjoying it peaceably at home in their own Countries, rather than run the hazard of loſing all again by engaging with *Ætius,* who in ſeveral Skirmiſhes had already cut off ſome of their advanc'd Guards. For this reaſon they remonſtrated to *Attila,* " That he had done enough for the
" preſent, and ought to defer the Deſign he had up-
" on *Rome* 'till ſome other time; for that *Ætius,* a
" brave experienc'd Commander, was ready at the
" Head of a powerful Army to ſtop his March,
" ſhould he direct it towards that City; that he
" ought to remember the bloody Defeat he met with
" two Years before in *Gaul,* and not run the hazard
" of the like Diſaſter in *Italy,* but rather reflect on
" the Fate of *Alarich,* who liv'd but a little while
" after he had taken and plunder'd that City. Theſe Conſiderations made him turn back towards the *Po,* where *Leo,* Biſhop of *Rome,* came to him in an Embaſſy from *Valentinian,* and reaſon'd with ſo much Courage, Gravity and Eloquence, that he both ſurpriz'd and mollify'd him, and perſuaded him to return over the *Danube,* upon Promiſe of

He returns back over the Da-nube.

an

an Annual Tribute; tho' upon his Departure he threaten'd to afflict *Italy* more heavily than ever, unless they sent him *Honoria*, Sister to the Emperor *Valentinian*, who is said to have invited him to this War, hoping to draw some particular Advantage to her self out of it, chusing rather to sacrifice the Publick Peace and Safety to her private Lust, than live in that Restraint, which for the Reputation of the Court she was continu'd under.

A. D. 453.

He is again defeated in Gaul.

His Death.

The next Year *Attila*, as if he disdain'd either to be at ease himself, or indulge it to others, fell with his usual Fury upon the *Alans* in *Gaul*; but *Thorismond* concluding himself concern'd in his Neighbours Calamities, join'd his Troops with the *Alans*, fought, defeated and sent him ingloriously home; where Marrying himself to a beautiful Virgin, call'd *Hildico*, or *Indicto*, he drunk so much Wine upon his Wedding Night, that he was suffocated in his Bed by a great Effusion of Blood which usually issu'd out at his Nose; but being hinder'd of that Passage, whilst he lay bury'd in Wine and Sleep, pour'd it self down into his Throat and choak'd him. After his Death a Dissention arose among his numerous and ambitious Sons about the Succession, which in the end prov'd the Ruin of that Nation, who just before were thought to have aim'd at nothing less than the Destruction of Mankind; for *Ardarich*, King of the *Gepidæ*, who had follow'd *Attila* in all his Expeditions, rose up against his Sons, and shook off the Yoke, in which he was follow'd by the other Nations, who asserted and procured their former Liberty; for they fought the *Hunns*, kill'd *Ellec*, the eldest of *Attila*'s Sons, together with thirty thousand of his Adherents; and by the Consent of the Emperor made a Division of their Territories.

Chap. IV. L. Valentinian III. Martian.

Valentinian finding himself deliver'd from so terrible an Enemy, follow'd his vicious Pleasures with a more unbounded Appetite than ever, which this very Year drew upon him the Punishment he had long deserv'd. There was among the Senators one *Petronius Maximus*, Grandson to that *Maximus* who was overthrown by *Theodosius* the Great, that had marry'd a Wife not more extraordinary for her Beauty than Chastity. With this Lady the Emperor became deeply in Love, and when he found that all his Threats, Promises and Presents were to no purpose, he resolv'd to seize on that by Force, which he could not purchase by his Importunity. He one Day sent for *Maximus* to Court, and playing with him at Dice won a considerable Sum of Mony from him, and receiv'd a Ring off his Finger as a Pledge for the Payment of it. This Ring he sent privately to his Wife, and requir'd her, in her Husband's Name, to come and wait upon the Empress *Eudoxia*; the Lady knowing it to be her Husband's Ring without any Hesitation came to Court, and was conducted, by some the Emperor employ'd for that purpose, into a remote Chamber, where *Valentinian* by force enjoy'd her. She at first imagin'd her Husband privy to the Outrage by reason of the Ring, so that upon her Return home she severely reproach'd him, as the Author of his own Dishonour and Infamy. *Maximus*, surpriz'd at this Discourse, acquainted his Wife with the wicked Artifice of the Emperor, and from that Moment resolv'd to be reveng'd upon *Valentian*, but knew it impossible to effect his Destruction whilst *Ætius* liv'd, and therefore thought how to remove him first out of the way; and that he might make *Valentinian* the more odious to the Army, who ador'd *Ætius*, he effected it by the Emperor's own Hands; for he got some that were

Valentinian Ravishes the Wife of Maximus;

near

near his Person to persuade him that *Ætius* was a dangerous Man, that he was contriving how to set up for himself, and usurp the Imperial Dignity, in order to which he kept Correspondence with the Enemies of the Empire. *Valentinian*'s natural Depravity inclin'd him to be jealous of those he knew to be better than himself, so that he easily believ'd these Suggestions, and concluded his Safety consisted in the Death of *Ætius*, for which reason the ungrateful Prince kill'd him himself, and order'd all his intimate Friends to be Slain; the Death of *Ætius* was much lamented by the whole Army, who consider'd him as the Bulwark of the Empire, which made a *Roman* answer *Valentinian*, when he ask'd him if he had not done well in dispatching *Ætius, That he thought he had cut his Right Hand off with his Left*; he was at that time the greatest Soldier in the Empire, being a perfect Master in the Art of War, but withal he had an ambitious aspiring Spirit, which made him an Enemy to all those whose Merit seem'd in any degree to equal his. *Valentinian* was so far from imagining any one would presume to revenge upon him the Death of *Ætius*, that he preferr'd several of the Army who had a profound Veneration for that Great Man to be of his Body Guard; to some of these *Maximus* address'd himself, and prevail'd with two of 'em, known to Posterity by the Name of *Ostila* and *Transila*, to dispatch *Valentinian*; accordingly they fell upon him as he was making a Speech to the Soldiers from the Tribunal in the *Campus Martius*, on the 17th of *March*, and kill'd him, together with *Heraclius* his Favourite Eunuch, who couragiously interpos'd and endeavour'd to save his Master.

Valentinian was Slain in the Thirtieth Year of his Reign, and Thirty fifth of his Age. During his Government the Empire, which in the time of

Honorius

Chap. IV. LI. Martian, Maximus.

Honorius began to decline, may be said to have been seiz'd with a mortal Distemper, especially after the Death of his Mother *Placidia*; for all the great Offices of Honour and Profit were at the Disposal of Eunuchs, who sacrificed the Good of the publick to their own private Interest and Ambition. After he grew up to Years of Discretion he never undertook any Voyage or Journey farther than from *Rome* to *Ravenna*, and from *Ravenna* back again to *Rome*. He continued lock'd up in his Palace, where he plung'd himself into all sensual Pleasures; this encouraged the Barbarians to strip him, as they did, of so many of the Provinces, for in his Reign *Rome* was taken and pillaged, *Africk*, *Spain*, Great *Britain*, and almost all *Gaul*, *Germany* and *Illyricum* were dismember'd from the Western Empire: Tho' we must own he was not unhappy in his Wars with that Scourge of God, *Attila*, whom by his Generals he often defeated, and drove out of his Dominions. Certain it is he was the last that seem'd to be Emperor indeed, in whom a true Imperial Majesty resided; for they that succeeded him in the West were like Meteors and Exhalations, that vanish'd as soon as they appear'd.

As *Valentinian*'s Life was scandalous and unserviceable to the Empire, so did his Death prove fatal and destructive to it. Leaving no Sons behind him, it was easie for *Maximus*, the Author of his Ruin, to seize on the Purple in the general Confusion, being a Man very rich and powerful, and was accordingly proclaim'd Emperor by the Guards in the Imperial Palace. His own Wife being lately dead, his first care was to marry *Eudoxia*, Widdow to *Valentinian*, thinking by such a Match to add Reputation and Vigour to his Authority: *Eudoxia* was averse to the thing, but the Tyrant forc'd her to comply, and by that means stain'd *Valentinian*'s Bed,

Maximus Usurps.

Bed, as he had dishonour'd his. He made his Son *Palladius Cæsar*, and marry'd him to *Eudoxia*, *Valentinian*'s Daughter, who had been formerly promis'd to *Gaudentius*, the Son of *Ætius*. Some Writers say he had not held the Empire twenty four Hours before he began to be weary of the Toil, and repented of his Advancement, reputing *Damocles* happy, for that he was cumber'd with Royalty for no longer than the space of one Dinner: However, considering that to descend from so high an Eminence would endanger a Fall, he resolv'd to maintain himself in his new Authority, and, if possible, restore it to its ancient Splendor; for which purpose he made *Avitus*, who had been *Præfectus Prætorio* in *Gaul*, General of his Armies. *Avitus* was descended from one of the most noble and ancient Families in that Country, he was a Man of Learning and Eloquence, and had given many signal Proofs of his Valour and Conduct; him *Maximus* sent to conclude a Peace with all the neighbouring Crowns from whom he had reason to apprehend any Disturbance, concluding that when once he had establish'd himself, and settled his Affairs at home, he might then deal with 'em at his leisure, and subdue 'em: But God blasted the Designs of this Parricide, and made his own Folly the Instrument of his Ruin. Tho' he had marry'd *Eudoxia* only for Reasons of State, yet in a short time he grew fondly enamour'd, and thought the readiest way to ingratiate himself with her, and gain her Affections, was to tell her that his Love to her made him desirous of *Valentinian*'s Ruin, which was propos'd and effected purely by his Contrivance for her sake. She hated and mistrusted him before, but being now confirm'd in her Suspicions she was resolv'd to be reveng'd whatever it cost her, and took such a Course to effect it as in the Issue prov'd fatal to her self, to *Rome*, and
all

Chap. IV. LI. Martian, Maximus.

all *Italy*. Early in the Morning she rose, and sent a trusty Servant with Letters to *Genserich* in *Africk*, conjuring him to come and revenge the Death of his Friend and Ally *Valentinian*, and deliver her out of Captivity, and from the Arms of a Tyrant and Usurper. This Message was very acceptable to *Genserich*, who had long wish'd for such an Opportunity, which he was resolv'd to embrace; and immediately rigg'd out a very powerful Fleet of *Vandals* and *Moors*, and set sail for *Italy*, where he was little expected. *Maximus* was, before the News of his Arrival, in a disconsolate, desponding Condition; the Burden of Empire made him uneasie in the Day-time, and the Terrors of a guilty Conscience distracted him in the Night: But upon *Genserich*'s Approach he was seiz'd with the utmost Consternation. Instead of providing for the necessity of his Affairs, and comforting by his Presence and Application his unhappy Subjects, who thought their Safety in so imminent a Danger consisted in their Flight, he participated with 'em in their Fears, and was one of the first that prepared to fly. This being observ'd by some Senators that were his Enemies, and that he deserted those whom it was his Duty to protect, they pursu'd him on the twelfth of *June*, and having stoned him, they dragg'd his Corps about the Streets, and then threw it into the *Tiber*. Three Days after this Execution *Genserich* enter'd *Rome* without any Opposition, that now lay expos'd to his Lust and Avarice. Tho' he had promis'd *Eudoxia* to abstain from Plunder, and behave himself with the greatest Moderation; tho' *Leo* the Great, who was then Pope of *Rome*, went attended by the chief of the City to meet him, and conjur'd him by all things holy to have Compassion of that City, which even *Attila*, a sworn Enemy to Christ, had lately exempted from Violation; notwithstand-

Genserich invades Italy.

Maximus Slain.

ing all which, this barbarous King, who made a Profession of Christianity, in spite of his Faith given to *Eudoxia*, and unmov'd by the Eloquence and more prevailing Tears of the venerable Prelate, gave it up to the Mercy of his Soldiers, who for fourteen Days together raged with implacable Fury in the midst of it, sparing neither private Dwellings nor publick Buildings; pillaging the very Churches of all the rich Ornaments and consecrated Vessels; among which were those taken formerly by *Titus* out of the Temple at *Jerusalem* and brought to *Rome*, where they had been hitherto very carefully preserv'd. The Tyrant himself forced the Imperial Palace, where he seized upon all the Treasure and rich Moveables, affording the Empress too much reason to repent of the cruel Vengeance she had drawn upon her self and the City; for he carry'd her and her two Daughters, *Placidia* and *Eudoxia*, Captive with him into *Africk*, where he marry'd the Eldest to his Son *Honoric*, and sent the Empress to *Constantinople*, together with her younger Daughter *Placidia*, who was afterwards marry'd to *Olybrius*, one of the Western Emperors.

Martian was much concern'd at the Calamities of the Western Empire, but being grown old and infirm he could not provide any Remedies against 'em, nor think of naming a new Emperor, as the Senate had desired him. One indeed bore the Title of Emperor in the West, tho' he held it but a few Months. *Avitus*, as we observ'd before, had been sent by *Maximus* into *Gaul*, where, upon the News of the Tyrant's Death, he was persuaded by *Theodorich*, King of the *Goths*, to assume the Purple; who represented to him, that there was no other Person in the Empire fit to bear the Burden, and support the Dignity of it; that the publick Interest, and the Safety of the State required it of him; that he

might

Marginal note: Genserich sacks Rome

might do it without injuring any one, becaufe there appear'd no Pretenders to it; that the Soldiers and the People prefented it to him, and begg'd him to accept of the Imperial Scepter; that as for his part he might affure himfelf of all the Power and Affiftance he could expect from him, the better to fupport his Title. *Avitus*, who well forefaw how difficult a thing it would be to preferve himfelf in that Dignity they were now courting him to accept of, however fuffered himfelf to be prevail'd upon by the Officers that were about him, and the Perfuafions of *Theodorich*, fo that he was declar'd Emperor on the tenth of *July*, and immediately fent to acquaint the Senate of *Rome* with his Promotion, and to inform 'em, that as foon as he had compos'd the Affairs in *Gaul* he intended to appear in Perfon among 'em. Accordingly he gave Orders for the Defence of thofe Parts lying on the other fide the *Loire* from the Incurfions of the *Franks*, and thofe on the South fide from the Violence of the *Goths*, and engaged his Friend *Theodorich* to defend that Portion of *Spain* which as yet acknowledged an Obedience to the Empire from the Infults of the *Suevi*; after which he fet forward for *Rome*, attended by a very gallant Army, compos'd for the moft part of fuch *Goths* as *Theodorich* had appropriated to his Service. This made the Senate and People receive him at firft with an outward Show of Joy and Submiffion, becaufe indeed they were not ftrong enough to oppofe him; but as foon as he had difmifs'd his Troops, upon a Prefumption that he fhould have no farther Occafion for 'em, then they began to teftifie their Averfion to him, efpecially out of an Abhorrence to the Memory of *Maximus*, who firft advanc'd him, and whom they condemned as the Spring of all their prefent Calamities; they therefore expell'd him out of the City, and forced him to di-

Avitus declared Emperor.

veft

and is deposed. vest himself of the Imperial Purple, after he had worn it eight or ten Months. This he did at *Placentia*, of which Place he got himself to be ordain'd Bishop, but finding that Character could not secure him from the Fury and Indignation of the Senate, he resolved to take Sanctuary in the Church of St. *Julian* in *Auvergne*, where he was born, but dy'd upon the Road as he was travelling thither.

In the mean time *Theodorich*, according to his Promise given *Avitus*, march'd with a numerous Army out of *Aquitain* into *Spain*, where he fought with *Ricciarius*, King of the *Suevi*, six Leagues off from the City of *Astorga*, overthrew him, took him Prisoner in his Flight, and put him to death; after this Victory he wasted at his pleasure *Gallicia* and *Portugal*. But whilst he with his *Goths* was diverted thus in *Spain*, and the *Roman* Army followed *Avitus* into *Italy*, the *Franks* laid hold of the Opportunity they had been often wishing for, and settled themselves in the middle of *Gaul*, establishing their Kingdom at *Paris*, and by that means tore another Principality out of the Body of the Western Empire.

A.D. 457. This Loss was follow'd by another in *Africk*, where *Genserich*, not contented with the late Violation of the Peace, crown'd one Injustice with another, and seiz'd on that part of *Africk* which in the Partition of the Country had been resign'd to *Valentinian*; so that the *Romans* now had nothing left there, for it continued entire in the Possession of the *Vandals* 'till the Reign of *Justinian*. In this miserable defenceless Condition was the Empire of the West, an Empire in name, but in reality no other than the Shadow of her former Greatness, deserted by her Friends, insulted by her Enemies, and grown the very Sport of Fortune, that in every respect had abandon'd her. 'Tis true the Emperor
Martian

Chap. IV. LII. Leo, Majorianus.

Martian was nearly touch'd at her Confusions, but as he was preparing to relieve and restore her, and revenge upon the Barbarians the Affronts the *Roman* Majesty had sustain'd, he was prevented by Death, which put an end to all his future Designs, after a peaceable Reign of six Years: For in his time the Barbarians gave little or no Disturbance on that side of the Empire, which is imputed by most Writers to his extraordinary Wisdom and Cirrumspection. He is much commended for the Innocence and Simplicity of his Manners, and his Zeal for the Defence and Purity of Religion; and especially in that at his Death he left the Army subject to the Directions of the Senate, and the Senate so modest and unanimous that no Heats, Divisions, or sinister ambitious Practices appear'd in the Choice of a Successor, the Election falling upon *Leo*, a *Thracian* by Birth, who had signalized himself upon many extraordinary Occasions, and was acknowledged by all to be worthy the Imperial Dignity. *Leo*, as soon as he was Crown'd by *Anatolius*, Patriarch of *Constantinople*, thought it high time to supply the Western Empire with a worthy Head, and resolv'd to promote *Majorianus* to that high Dignity, a Man of great Wisdom and Virtue, and the most capable to restore the Peace of *Europe*: Having therefore made him General of the Armies, as the next Step to the Imperial Power, he sent him with a noble Train into *Italy*, where by the general Consent of all he was declared *Augustus*; and applying himself seriously to the Administration of publick Affairs, he made choice of the ablest Men in the Empire to be the Ministers of State; making *Ricimer*, a *Goth* by Nation, but a Man of great Experience, and on whom he entirely depended, Commander in chief of all his Forces; his first care was to secure *Italy* against the Insults of *Genserich*, who rigg'd out a Fleet this

Martian Dies.

His Character.

Leo elected Emperor.

Majorian Emperor in the West.

Year with an intent to fall upon *Campania*, and enrich himself with the Spoils of that Country whilst the Empire was without a Governor; but *Majorianus* march'd against him, with a strong Army and gave him Battel, in which the *Vandals* were overthrown, and forc'd to fly to their Ships for Safety.

A. D. 458. After this he supply'd all the Coasts of *Italy* that lye towards *Africk* with good Garrisons, and in the beginning of the Year following fitted out a strong Fleet, with an intent to follow the *Vandals* into *Africk*, and make that the Seat of the War. All this while *Theodorich* was pursuing his Conquests in *Spain*, piercing with his Troops into the Heart of *Portugal* without any Resistance, and was sate down before the City of *Merida*, but rais'd the Siege upon an Intelligence of some Commotions in his own Dominions in *Gaul*, which obliged him to return home; where, during the Absence of the Forces of the Empire in *Africk*, he fell upon some of the *Roman* Dominions in *Gaul*, and extending his Conquests up as far as the *Rhône*, he besieg'd, took and pillaged the wealthy City of *Lyons*, but was at last compell'd to submit to *Majorian*, who granted him Peace upon Condition he lent him some of his Forces, which he design'd to employ against the *Vandals* in *Africk*, which he was very ambitious of recovering out of the Hands of the Barbarians. The better to inform himself of the Strength of the Enemy, the State of the Country, and how the Inhabitants stood affected to the *Roman* Interest, he is said to have enter'd upon a Design full of Danger for a Person of his Dignity; for he disguis'd himself, and went in the Quality of an Embassador from the *Roman* Emperor, sent into *Africk* to make *Genserich* some Overtures of a Peace. *Genserich* receiv'd him very kindly, show'd him the Magnificence of his Court, his Treasury and *Arsenal*; all which when *Majorianus*

had

Chap. IV. LII. Leo, Severus.

had sufficiently contemplated, and discover'd all he had a Desire to be inform'd of, he return'd to his Army, and immediately besieg'd *Carthage*, which he was in a fair way of taking when he fell dangerously sick, and so was oblig'd to raise the Siege and Embark for *Italy*, after a great part of *Mauritania*, surpriz'd at his sudden Expedition, had submitted to him, and they were not without Hopes that the whole Country might be reduc'd. Indeed the Empire seem'd to receive new Life from his great Abilities and Industry, by Virtue of which he had forc'd the *Goths* to sue for a Peace, as we observ'd before, and not long after, by his vigorous Preparations, struck such a Terror into *Genserich*, who was aw'd by his Virtue, that he grew weary of the War, and sollicited a Peace, which was granted him by *Majorianus* upon Terms very advantagious to the Empire. But the Hopes the State conceiv'd of a Recovery under his Hands, were no other than a lightning, as it's call'd, before Death; for whilst he was busied in settling the Affairs of *Gaul*, *Ricimer* and *Severus* form'd a Conspiracy against him, in which it was agreed that *Ricimer* should dispatch him, and *Severus* seize on the Empire; for *Ricimer* being a Barbarian had not the Confidence to usurp the Purple himself. Before *Majorianus* left *Gaul* he press'd the *Alani* so close, that to divert him they Invaded *Italy*, which he made haste to relieve, and follow'd 'em as far as *Tortona* in *Liguria*, where he was met by *Ricimer*, who at first pretended he had brought some Forces to his Assistance, but murder'd him on the Seventh of *August*, and so gave a Mortal Wound to the Empire in the West. After he had done his Business *Ricimer* return'd to *Ravenna*, where the Soldiers, who had been prepar'd before Hand, declar'd *Severus* Emperor without waiting

A. D. 461.

Majorianus murder'd by Ricimer.

for any Orders or Approbation from *Constantinople*. This new Emperor, after some successful Enterprises against the *Vandals*, who had upon the Death of *Majorianus* attack'd the Islands adjoining to *Africk*, and had defeated the *Alani* who had Invaded *Liguria*, was in the Fourth Year of his Reign poison'd by his Friend *Ricimer*, after which was an *Inter-Regnum* for some time in the West.

The Death of Leo the Great, Pope of Rome. Not long before this dy'd *Leo* the Great, who had been Pope of *Rome* for one and twenty Years together, a Man of a great Mind and extraordinary Qualifications, remarkable as in several other respects, so particularly in this, that whereas his Predecessors founded their Pretensions to a Superiority upon the Dignity of the Imperial City, and the Constitutions of some precedent Councils, he observing the Distractions under which the Western Empire labour'd, and which threaten'd it with a Dissolution, and that the City of *Rome*, which had been often taken and pillag'd, was in great Danger of losing her Sovereignty, chose rather to establish the Precedency he claim'd, as Pope of *Rome*, over all other Bishops whatever, upon those Words of Christ, *Thou art* Peter, *and upon this Rock I build my Church*; from thence claiming a peculiar Prerogative, as the immediate Successor of St. *Peter*. The Christian World has too much reason to know how this Title has been since prosecuted.

After the Death of *Severus*, who, tho' an Usurper, fell lamented by the Senate and People of *Rome*, *Genserich* once more broke out into Hostilities, and behav'd himself more like a Pirate than a Prince, sometimes infesting the Coasts of *Italy*, at others falling upon *Gaul*, or the Neighbouring Islands, where, after having seiz'd on whatever things of value the Country afforded, he return'd loaden with his Spoils to *Africk*; and was usually

Chap. IV. LII. Leo, Anthemius.

so uncertain in his Expeditions, that they never knew where to expect or oppose him; being very often at a loss himself what Course to steer upon his first putting out to Sea, as appear'd by his Answer one Day to his Admiral, who demanding of him to what Parts he would have him Sail, he reply'd, *Thither where God shall call, and the Wind drive us.*

These his continu'd Depredations made *Leo* at length resolve to nominate an Emperor for the West, where *Ricimer*, ever since the Death of *Severus*, had govern'd as he pleas'd, tho' without the Marks of Empire, and done the State no small Service against the *Vandals*. *Leo* made choice of *Anthemius*, a Man of Noble Extraction, and very wealthy, who, after he had behav'd himself with much Courage in the Wars against the *Hunns*, over whom he had obtain'd many Advantages, was advanc'd to the Principal Command in the Army; these Qualifications, and the Personal Kindness *Leo* had for him, made him consider him as the fittest Man for a Collegue, and accordingly declar'd him Emperor in the West. Some say this Choice was not only confirm'd by the Consent of *Ricimer* himself and the Senate, but conferr'd upon him at their united Requests; accordingly *Anthemius* set out from the East, and arriv'd at *Rome* on the Twelfth of *April*, where he was receiv'd, and declar'd *Augustus* with the general Applause and Acclamation of the People: For as much as *Ricimer*'s Power was known to be absolute in the West, it was at first agreed that he should marry *Anthemius* his Daughter, and by that means the better confirm the Sovereign Power in the Hands of his Father-in-Law, and to make the Empire stronger, if possible, by Alliances, *Leo* marry'd his Daughter *Leontia* to *Martian*, the Son of *Anthemius*, so that

A. D. 467.

Anthemius

for some time both Courts were employ'd in Publick Triumphs and Diversions, as if the ancient Glories of the Empire were blooming afresh, and there were no Enemies able to disturb 'em; tho' *Leo* in the midst of these Solemnities had his Thoughts upon *Genserich*'s Depredations and Piracies, and what Course was to be taken to restrain him; for he had lately infested *Illyricum* and *Peloponnesus*, which being Members of the Eastern Empire more particularly concern'd him; for this reason he fitted out a very strong Fleet, said to consist of no less than Eleven hundred Sail well equipp'd, and provided with all sorts of Ammunition and Provision, and made *Basiliscus*, Brother to his Wife *Verina*, Admiral; and at the same time desir'd and advis'd *Anthemius* to make what Forwardness he could in his Preparations for the War. *Genserich* in the mean while had recourse to his usual Devices, and privately inform'd *Olybrius*, a Senator, very Rich and of great Interest, that if he would join with him at that Conjuncture against the two Emperors, he would employ all his Forces to make him Emperor of the West; *Olybrius* willingly listen'd to his Proposals, and from that time forward fell off from his Affections to *Anthemius*.

Basiliscus, Admiral of Leo's Fleet;

Before *Leo* suffer'd his Fleet to put to Sea, he thought it Prudence to secure *Mercellianus* to his Interest, who had been formerly a great Friend to *Ætius*, after whose Murder he revolted from the Emperor, and persuaded others to follow his Example, with whom he retir'd into *Dalmatia*, where he fortify'd himself in Defiance of the Empire, and grew very rich and powerful in the Country; but *Leo* so effectually prevail'd upon him by the Intervention of some who had a Friendship for both, that he enter'd into his Service, and commanded

manded an Army in *Sardinia*, which had been lately seiz'd by the *Vandals*, whom he drove out of the Island, and having restor'd it to the Obedience of the *Roman* Empire proceeded into *Sicily*, for which he hop'd to effect the same Deliverance. About the same time *Leo*'s Forces landed in *Africk*, where *Heraclius* with an advanc'd Party took the Town of *Tripoly*, and had *Basiliscus* march'd on directly to *Carthage* he might easily have master'd that City, and with it the rest of the Country, and so have put an end to the War at once. For the News of the loss of *Tripoly* and *Sardinia*, and the appearance of so powerful a Fleet, so distracted the Barbarians that they were seiz'd with a Panick Fear; but by his dilatory Proceedings and ill Conduct he gave *Genserich* time to look about him, and learn to despise him; whether this proceeded from his Fear and Cowardice, or his Avarice, being corrupted by a great Sum of Mony sent him from *Genserich*, or whether he was persuaded to it by *Aspar*, who advis'd him to prolong the War, and thereby make himself more considerable to the Empire; the readiest way to attain the Imperial Power, to which he promis'd in time to advance him, is uncertain. *Aspar* is thought to have given him this wicked Counsel for fear *Leo*, upon his Success, should grow too Bold and Potent, and have it in his Power to ruin him and his Factious Heretical Family. Whatever the reasons were, *Genserich* improv'd the Advantage, rais'd all the Forces he could, Mann'd out his Fleet, and that he might gain time sufficient to provide himself, he desir'd, by his Embassadors sent to *Basiliscus*, time to resolve either to submit to the Emperor, or continue the War. *Basiliscus* without any scruple consented to a Cessation, and in the mean time had no Care of the Fleet, but lay open to the Practices of the Enemy, who one Night,

who miscarries in the Expedition.

A. D. 368.

Night, whilst the *Romans* were a-sleep, took the Advantage of a favourable Wind, and bore down upon 'em with some Fire-Ships prepar'd for that purpose, which they let drive with full Sail upon the *Roman* Navy, and the next Morning before the *Romans* could have time to Tack, and recover themselves out of their Disorder, they drew up into a Line of Battel; but *Basiliscus* was so far from venturing an Engagement, that he tack'd about, and made away with the best Sail he had; the rest of the Fleet seeing the Admiral quit his Station follow'd his Example, and crowded after him, saving themselves where and in what manner they could. The Land Army left behind in *Africk*, being thus abandon'd, was easily defeated by the *Vandals*, who kill'd some and made the rest Prisoners; whilst *Basiliscus* made haste to *Constantinople*, where the People were so incens'd against him, that he was forc'd to fly for Refuge into the great Church, and at last, by the Emperor's Permission, retir'd into *Thrace*. Thus all these mighty Hopes and Warlike Preparations vanish'd into Air; *Genserich* grew more Bold and Presumptious upon his Deliverance, and the great Check and Diappointment of the Empire. *Marcellianus*, who had hitherto met with great Success in *Sicily*, was overpower'd by the *Vandals*, who, after the Miscarriage of the Imperial Fleet, were sent in great Numbers to the Relief of the Island, and the *Romans*, frustrated of their great Expectations, grew heartless and dispirited.

Aspar's Son made Cæsar.

Leo knew very well that *Aspar* was in a great measure the Author of these Misfortunes; he was the great Patron of the *Arian* Faction, and so potent in Friends and Dependants, that *Leo* found it necessary to dissemble with him in order to ruin him, for which reason he created his Son *Cæsar*, gave him his Daughter in Marriage, and by that means

means endeavour'd to allure him into a senseless Security, if he found it impossible to reduce him to his Duty and Loyalty. The Inhabitants of *Constantinople* were much displeas'd at this Promotion, for they knew *Aspar* and all his Family were obstinate *Arians*, and were enrag'd when they beheld a Son of that Family design'd Successor to an Old Man in the Imperial Seat. In the mean time *Aspar* grew more Insolent upon his Son's Advancement, and could not conceal from the People his ambitious Designs; this provok'd the Citizens to that degree that they insulted him in the *Hippodrome*, and so terrify'd him with their Threats, that he was forc'd to fly and take Sanctuary in the Church of *Chalcedon*. The Emperor sent *Gennadius*, Patriarch of *Constantinople*, after him, and promis'd him and his Sons all the Security they could desire, if they would return; but they refus'd to stir, unless the Emperor himself would come in Person, and Protect 'em from the Insolence of the Rabble; he went accordingly, took 'em home to his Palace, seated 'em at his own Table, and by his Condescention persuaded 'em to imagine he had either forgot or forgiven their Practices against him. But finding they were Persons in no measure to be trusted, and that he must either prevent them, or be prevented by 'em, he order'd *Zeno*, an *Isaurian*, to cut off their Heads the next time they came to Court. *Zeno*, being a hardy resolute Man, punctually executed his Commission, by which means the most potent Family in the Empire, which had brought great Difficulties upon the State, and had no less afflicted the Church, was destroy'd in the height of their Ambition, to the great Safety of the Emperor and Satisfaction of the People. From hence Princes may draw this useful Maxim, Never to suffer their Ministers to grow too great, lest in

Aspar takes Sanctuary at Chalcedon

A. D. 370. *Aspar and his Sons Slain.*

time

time they become more powerful and popular than themselves; and ambitious Courtiers ought to be cautious in their exalted Fortunes of making their Masters jealous of their Greatness, lest they provoke the same Power that lifted 'em up to turn to their Destruction.

The *Arian* Hereticks, who were then very powerful and numerous throughout both the Empires, were highly affronted at the Death of *Aspar* and his Sons, but no one was more displeas'd and irritated than their Friend and Countryman *Ricimer*; who knowing himself powerful in his Interest at home, having the Chief Command in the Army, and no less formidable in his Friends abroad, began at this time to practice against *Anthemius*, and study'd how to deprive him both of his Life and Dignity. *Evarich*, King of the *Goths* in *Spain* and *Gaul*, and *Genserich*, King of the *Vandals* in *Africk*, the Terror as well of the East as the West, were his great Friends upon account of his Original and Religion, both which were glad to create or countenance any Disturbances in the Empire, so that he made no doubt of destroying *Anthemius*, and in his Destruction revenge upon *Leo* the Death of *Aspar*. However he either wanted Art or Care enough to weave his Designs so fine, as to make 'em pass unobserv'd by the watchful Eye of *Anthemius*, who began first to distrust, and then express his Resentments against him, and the Coals of Dissention were by their Friends on both sides blown up to that degree, that *Ricimer* was glad to provide for his Safety in *Milan*, where in appearance he desir'd to live at Peace, but was inwardly resolv'd upon *Anthemius* his Ruin. The Nobility of those Parts were very much concern'd at this Breach, which they were afraid would at length plunge *Italy* into new Mischiefs; they therefore undertook

Ricimer angry at it.

dertook to mediate betwixt him and the Emperor, and perfuaded him to a Submiffion; they recommended *Epiphanius*, Bifhop of *Pavia*, to negotiate a Reconciliation with the Emperor. *Epiphanius* was a Man in great Efteem for his Probity, Prudence, Eloquence and Capacity; which Confiderations made *Ricimer* willing enough to comply with their Defires, and accordingly the Bifhop accepted of the Employment. *Anthemius* knew the fcope of *Ricimer*'s Defigns, in his choice of a Perfon fo celebrated for his Sanctity; for if now he refus'd to liften to *Ricimer*'s Propofitions of Peace, he fhould lofe himfelf in the Opinion of honeft well-meaning Men, and if he embrac'd 'em he put it once more in his Power to undo him. The Bifhop deliver'd his Meffage to him in a very elegant, pathetical Speech, and obtain'd his Defire: *Anthemius* confented to a Peace, which he knew in his own Thoughts would not be long obferv'd, and difmifs'd the Bifhop highly pleas'd with the Succefs of his Negotiation.

After this there feem'd for fome time to be a good Correfpondence between 'em, but the Year following *Ricimer* broke out into open Rebellion, and with a very ftrong Army befieg'd *Anthemius* in *Rome*, where the Inhabitants, fenfible of the Injuftice of *Ricimer*'s Caufe, were well affected to *Anthemius*, but were afraid to declare themfelves becaufe the Rebel appear'd the more powerful. *Ricimer* prefs'd on the Siege with much Vigour, and fo clofely block'd up the Town, that firft a Famine, and after that a grievous Plague raged within the Walls. In this condition the Emperor's whole Dependance lay in the Succours he expected from the *Goths* in *Gaul*, who were moving to his Affiftance under the Comduct of *Bilimer*, but *Ricimer* turn'd head againft 'em, fought, and deftroy'd a great Number of 'em, a-

A.D. 472. Befieges Anthemius in Rome;

mong

mong whom was their Commander; and exalted by this Success renew'd the Siege with redoubled Vigour: And the City being much weaken'd by Detachments, by Famine, and the Plague, he broke into it on the eleventh of *July*, where he raged with as much Fury as *Alarich* or *Genferich* had done before him: Thus was the Capital City of the World taken no less than three times, within the space of sixty three Years, by her most implacable Enemies. He permitted his Soldiers to plunder the Citizens, exempting only two Regions in which he had settled his own Quarters. He laid hold of *Anthemius*, and without any regard had to him as his Emperor or *puts him* Father-in-Law he put him to death, and establish'd *to Death,* *Olybrius* Emperor in his room. But God thought fit shortly after to punish him for his inhuman Cruelties, for he was seiz'd with a violent Pain in his *and dies* Bowels, of which he dy'd on the eighteenth of *Au-* *himself.* *gust*, and went to give a just Account of his Actions to the Impartial Judge of the Universe, after he had domineer'd like a second *Stilicho* ever since the Death of *Valentinian*. From a common Soldier he advanc'd himself by his Valour to the highest Posts in the Army, and dispos'd of the Western Empire according to his own Fancy. He had seiz'd upon the Church of St. *Agatha* in *Rome* for the Service of his *Arian* Hereticks, who could not be removed out of it 'till the Popedom of *Gregory* I, near 120 Years after.

Olybrius was scarce warm in his new Dignity before he followed his great Patron *Ricimer*, in Gratitude to whose Memory he made his Grandson *Gundibarius* a Patrician; an Honour first created by *Constantine* the Great, and in so great Esteem from the very beginning, that they who were dignify'd with that Title took place of the *Præfecti Prætorio* themselves.

Oly-

Chap. IV.   LII. Leo. Glycerius.

Olybrius in his Death left two Competitors to the Succeſſion, one ſupported by *Gundibarius,* who following the Example of his Grandfather *Ricimer* had proclaim'd *Glycerius* Emperor at *Ravenna;* the other promoted by *Leo,* who much reſenting the late Revolutions in *Rome,* eſpecially the Death of *Anthemius,* made choice of *Julius Nepos,* the Son of *Nepotianus,* to whom he marry'd his Niece, and deſign'd him *Cæſar.* Whilſt *Italy* was thus diſtracted and broken by Factions, *Genſerich,* her ancient and avow'd Enemy, did not only oppreſs her by his Arms in her *African* Provinces, but encouraged the *Oſtrogoths* at once to invade the Eaſtern and Weſtern Empire, to which they were animated by the Proſpect of a great Booty. Hereupon *Theodomir* their King, obſerving the diſtracted Condition of the *Roman* Empire, thought he had now an Opportunity of encroaching upon it, and enlarging his Borders, and accordingly order'd his Brother *Vindemir,* or *Windemir,* to break into *Italy,* whilſt he forc'd himſelf into *Illyricum,* a Country ſtronger and better guarded. *Vindemir* dy'd in his March, and left the execution of his Enterprize to his Son, who was met by Embaſſadors from *Glycerius* with Offers of a great Sum of Mony, if he would forbear his Deſigns upon *Italy* and divert his March into *Gaul,* where he had Relations of his own that reign'd in full Power. *Vindemir* accepted of the Conditions, and went and join'd with the *Viſigoths* in *Gaul,* and by that Junction added much to the Power of thoſe Nations both in *Gaul* and *Spain.* In the mean time *Theodomir,* having defeated the *Sarmatæ,* attack'd *Naiſſus,* the Capital City of all *Illyricum,* took it, and fortify'd it. After this he march'd into *Theſſaly,* where he took *Heraclea* and *Lariſſa,* and had the like Deſign upon *Theſſalonica;* but *Clarianus* a Patrician was got into the Town before him, and

Glycerius.

with

with a good Garrison defended it, 'till by the Emperor's Order he sent out some Embassadors with very rich Presents to *Theodomir*, who condescended to a Peace upon condition that the Eastern Part of *Illyricum* was resign'd up to his *Ostrogoths*, to which *Leo* readily consented. By this we may see how much the present Emperors were degenerated from the Virtues of their Predecessors, since instead of protecting and enlarging their Dominions by their Courage, they were content to preserve 'em by their Presents and Entreaties.

As these Barbarians distress'd and distracted the Empire by their Arms, so they afflicted and divided the Church by their Heresies. The whole Nation of the *Goths* were obstinate *Arians*, for the Emperor *Valens*, who was himself the great Patron of *Arianism*, when requested to send 'em some Bishops for their Conversion, made choice of none but such as were the great Assertors of that damnable Heresie, who by their Doctrine took care to convert 'em from Idolatry to Blasphemy, and taught 'em to deny the Divinity of the Eternal Son of God, to the great Detriment of the Church, and Scandal of Christianity.

These *Goths*, wheresoever they planted themselves by the force of their Arms, took care by the same means to establish their Heresie; and rais'd such cruel Persecutions against the true Believers, as the Church hardly ever suffer'd from Idolaters. By this means the Western Empire became polluted with *Arianism*, whilst the East was no less distracted by the Heresies of *Eutyches* and *Nestorius*; and herein the Father of Lies had a great Advantage, for whoever zealously oppos'd the *Nestorian* Errors was branded with the *Eutychian*, and so on the contrary, by which means the Church was rent asunder, and the truly Catholick were to move as between two

Rocks,

Rocks, to the great Hazard of their Faith, that on each side was threaten'd with a Shipwreck.

Leo, in recompence of the great Services *Zeno* had done him upon the Family of *Aspar*, marry'd him to his Daughter *Ariadne*, and made him Governor of the East, the Capital of which being *Antioch* he went to reside there, carrying with him one *Peter* sirnamed the *Fuller*, who had formerly been a Monk in the Monastery of the *Acæmites*, but had been expell'd from thence for his Debaucheries, and Adherence to the *Eutychian* Heresie, of which he made open Profession. Having met with some Persons of Quality who were infected with the same Errors, he insinuated himself by his Flatteries into their Friendship, and by that means got Access to *Zeno*, and was favourably receiv'd by him. At *Antioch* he grew acquainted with several *Apollinarists*, call'd so from an Arch-Heretick in the Fourth Century, who taught *that Jesus Christ was not animated with a Human Soul, the want of which was supply'd by the Divinity; that the Flesh he receiv'd from the Virgin descended originally down from Heaven, and only pass'd through* Mary *as through a Conveyance; and that in adoring it we are to believe it co-essential and co-eternal with the Divinity; that in Jesus Christ there were two distinct Sons, one of God, the other of the Virgin; that he was at first conceiv'd purely like other Men, but that after his Conception the Word descended, and operated in him as it had done before in the Prophets, without being united to him; that by his good Works he had obtain'd his Grandure and Perfection, and was now without a Body; that the Divinity suffer'd upon the Cross; that it dy'd, and was rais'd again;* with several other as absurd Dogma's, in which he resembled the *Manichees* and *Sabellians,* and some of which were afterwards copy'd by the *Eutychians.* With these Hereticks *Pe-*

Zeno marries Leo's Daughter.

ter join'd himself, to calumniate *Martyrius* Bishop of the Place, accusing him for a *Nestorian*, because he receiv'd the Council of *Chalcedon*, wherein *Eutyches* and his Doctrine were condemn'd; and that he might be the better able to usurp his See, he persuaded *Zeno*, either by himself or some other Apostates of the same Opinions, that the Church of *Antioch* would never be in order whilst *Martyrius* presided in it; of which *Leo* being advised, he sent for the Bishop of *Constantinople*, the better to inform himself of the Truth of the Allegations urg'd against him. *Martyrius* was so powerfully protected at *Constantinople* by *Gennadius*, Patriarch of the City, that the Emperor was made sensible of his Innocence, and the Malice of his Adversary *Peter*, who in his Absence had seiz'd upon the Episcopal Chair, and created one *John* Bishop of *Apamea*, who had formerly been depos'd. The Emperor being inform'd of his wicked Practices, order'd *Peter* to be banish'd, and sent *Martyrius* back to his Church; who upon his Return finding a great Division among the People, and that *Zeno* favour'd and protected his Adversaries, publickly abdicated himself from the Bishoprick, saying, *I renounce a disobedient Clergy, a rebellious People, and a defiled Church, reserving no more to my self than the Sacerdotal Dignity*; and so divested himself of the Episcopal Ornaments, to the great Detriment of the Truth, and Encouragement of its Enemies.

A.D. 474.
Leo Dies.

About this time *Leo*, who had held the Reins of the Empire almost eighteen Years together, was seiz'd with a *Diarrhea*, which was attended with a Feaver, and carry'd him off in a short time. He was a great Prince, wise and virtuous, and truly affectionate to the Catholick Religion, as appears by several Laws he made in favour of it; and the many Churches he built for Religious Worship. However

ver he is justly taxed for his too great Indulgence to the *Arians*, and blam'd for that he was not sufficiently cautious whom he preferr'd, such as *Basiliscus* and *Zeno*, who both prov'd bold Assertors of Heresie, and drew great Calamities upon the Empire. Some say he ordain'd his Grandson *Leo*, Son of *Zeno* and his Daughter *Ariadne*, his Successor in the Empire, and appointed *Zeno* for his Guardian, 'till he was at Years of Discretion to govern the State himself: However it were, he surviv'd not his Grandfather above ten Months, and dyed when he was no more than two Years of Age, and so uncapable of regretting the Dignity he lost.

In the mean time *Julius Nepos*, whom *Leo*, as we observ'd before, had appointed for Western Emperor, hearing *Glycerius* had possess'd himself of that Dignity, set sail for *Italy* with a very strong Fleet, and landing near *Rome*, oblig'd *Glycerius* to quit the Imperial Purple, and retire to *Salonæ* in *Dalmatia*; of which Place he made him to be ordain'd Bishop. After which *Nepos* was declar'd Emperor at *Rome*, the Affairs of which City after he had settled, he went and resided at *Ravenna*.

Nepos declar'd Emperor at Rome.

During these Troubles *Evarich*, or *Eurich*, King of the *Goths* in *Gaul*, encouraged by so many Varieties and Alterations, which had in so high a measure weaken'd the Empire, fell into the Territories the *Romans* had still left in that Country. *Nepos* sent *Epiphanes*, Bishop of *Pavia*, whom we had occasion to make mention of before, to treat of a Peace with the *Goth*: The Bishop manag'd the Negotiation very prudently, and concluded a Treaty in no Point disadvantagious to the *Romans*. But *Eurich* soon after, tho' he had sworn religiously to observe the Agreement, forcibly seiz'd upon *Armagnac, Rovergne, Perigueux* and *Limosin*, and at last attempted *Clermont*, the Capital of *Auvergne*; but was coura-

giously

giously repuls'd by Ecdicius, Son of Avitus, the late Emperor, assisted by Sidonius Apollinaris, his Brother-in-Law, who was Bishop of the Place, who is said to have wrought Miracles by his Prayers, his Exhortations, and Letters to several Persons of Quality, in which he implor'd their Succour in behalf of the distressed City. Ecdicius is reported to have made a Sally in the Day-time, attended with no more than eighteen Horse, with which he struck such a Terror into the Enemy that he put 'em into Disorder, travers'd through their whole Army, kill'd all that came in his way, forc'd 'em for some time to retire from the Walls, and return'd safe into the City without the Loss of one Man. An Action, if true, worthy to be compar'd with the Exploits of the first *Roman* Heroes, and sufficient to prove that their ancient Valour was not quite extinct, tho' like the departing Soul it surviv'd only in Particulars, whereas before it animated the whole Body.

However *Eurich* failing in his Attempts upon the State, raged with equal Fury against the Church, expelling or impoverishing all those who would not embrace *Arianism*; and when any of the Pastors of the Church dy'd he suffer'd none but *Arians* to succeed 'em, insomuch that in several Places the Churches lay in Ruins, the Entrances choak'd with Brambles, and Grass growing about the Altars; and this was observable not only in Country Villages but in great and populous Towns, where the People refus'd to frequent the Publick Assemblies. With such Calamities was the Church then oppress'd, in *Africk* under the Tyranny and Persecution of *Genserich*, in the West under the Cruelties of the *Arians*, and under the like Cruelties of the *Eutychians* in the East; where *Zeno* upon the Death of his Father *Leo* was acknowledg'd for Emperor, and was suspected to have contributed to his Death. He was no sooner

The distracted Condition of the Church.

Zeno Emperor at Constantinople;

sooner advanc'd to the Imperial Power, but he plung'd himself into all manner of Vices, refraining from no filthy or flagitious Act, but so wallow'd in his Debaucheries, that he thought it the Weakness of a base and low Spirit, to cover themselves in Darkness at the Commission of their Wickedness, but like the Grandeur of an Emperor, to Sin in broad Day-light; and as he was thus deform'd in his Mind, so was his Body said to resemble a Satyr more than any Human Appearance, for he was covered all over with Hair, his Shape was deform'd, and his Physiognomy ridiculous, tho' they who beheld him, and knew the Temper of his Mind, found more reason to tremble than laugh at the sight of him. As he was thus Deform'd in his Body, and Debauch'd in his Morals, so was he no less Corrupt in his Religious Principles; for he openly avow'd himself the Protector of Heresie and Schism, and therefore drew upon the Church Calamities unexpressible. As soon as the Citizens of *Antioch* heard of his Advancement to the Imperial Throne, those of *Peter*'s Faction sent their Agents to *Constantinople*, who, in the Name of the rest, desir'd his Re-establishment, and brib'd several of the Courtiers to favour 'em in their Petition to the Emperor, who immediately granted their Request, and *Peter* was once more seated in the Apostolick Chair of that Province; from whence he immediately denounc'd an *Anathema* against the Council of *Chalcedon*, and maintain'd the Errors of the *Apollinarians*, and restor'd such Bishops to their respective Sees, as had been formerly depos'd for adhering to *Eutyches*. But God suffer'd not the Impiety of *Zeno* to go long unpunish'd; for *Basiliscus* observing him to be a lewd, effeminate Prince, despis'd and abhor'd by the People for his abominable Vices, drew together a Company of Malecontents,

contents, to whom he join'd several of his own Friends and Adherents, who, united together, rais'd a great Sedition against *Zeno* in *Constantinople*. *Zeno*, terrify'd at the Uproar, fled in a great Fright with his Wife into *Isauria*, where he was well belov'd; and *Basiliscus* was by the Soldiers saluted Emperor, who, having assum'd the Title, conferr'd that of *Cæsar* upon his Son *Marcus*; and tho' *Basiliscus* did not long enjoy this Dignity, but was Dethron'd, put to Death, and *Zeno* restor'd; yet, because he grew no better for his Misfortunes, but persever'd in his brutish sensual way of Life, he at length came to a violent End, procur'd by his own Wife, who caus'd him one Day, Drunk, as he was after an excessive Debauch of Wine, to be shut up in a Sepulchre, and dispos'd some Guards about it, in whom she could confide, to prevent him from getting out. As soon as he was recover'd from his Lethargy he made an hideous noise, and desir'd to be releas'd, but was answer'd, The State had no farther Occasion for him, since another was now promoted to his Place; he reply'd, He was not at all concern'd at that, he only begg'd 'em to deliver him out of that noisom Place, and confine him to a Monastry if they thought fit, where he might end his Days in Peace; the Soldiers were deaf to all his Lamentations, so that he dy'd in that horrible Restraint, having been first constrain'd, through Hunger, to devour one of his Arms before his Death. Some, I know, give another Account of this Emperor's End, tho' they all agree in this, that it was violent; and *Ariadne's* Carriage after his Death, especially her great Care in promoting his Successor, and marrying him speedily upon it, leave no room to doubt what a large share she had in it.

flies into Isauria,

All

Chap. IV. LIII. Zeno, Augustulus.

A.D. 475.

All this while the Siege continu'd before *Clermont*, but this Year, after the Besiegers had made several Breaches in the Wall, and most of the Defendants were destroy'd, either by the Sword or some other Accidents, too obvious upon those Occasions, *Ecdicius*, in Despair of any Succour, yielded it up; and being sent for by *Nepos*, was honour'd with the Dignity of Patrician, and *Orestes* was sent into *Gaul* to succeed in the Command of the Troops in those Parts.

This *Orestes* was by Birth a *Goth*, and having acquir'd a great Reputation in the Wars, he was made General of the Auxiliary Forces of that Nation in *Italy*. He had upon all Occasions appear'd very vigorous in his Service to the Empire, and was therefore entrusted at this time with an Army to watch *Eurich* in *Gaul*, and be a Curb to his ambitious Practices. But this Barbarian, instead of executing his Commission like a Man of Honour, turn'd his Arms against his Master, and besieg'd him in *Ravenna*. He knew *Nepos* was in a weak Condition, and could easily be suppress'd, having stripp'd himself of those Troops that should have defended him, and committed 'em to his Conduct; so that *Nepos* finding himself unable to resist him, fled to *Salonæ* in *Dalmatia*, where he was entertain'd by the Bishop *Glycerius*, whom the Year before he had depriv'd of the Empire, whilst *Orestes*, meeting with none strong enough to oppose him, seiz'd on the Imperial Power, and made the Army Proclaim his Son *Augustulus* Emperor. Thus we see the Title, rather than Power, of the Western Empire bandy'd from one to another, and the Imperial Dignity toss'd from Hand to Hand, without any Reverence or Respect, by those Brokers of Majesty, who adorn'd their Creatures with the Purple, to strut upon the Stage for some time, and as soon

Orestes expels Nepos, and proclaims his Son Augustulus Emperor.

soon as they displeas'd 'em thrust 'em off again. We have seen no less than Ten appearing upon it within the space of Twenty Years, most of whom came to a violent End in their Persons, and all of 'em in their Dignities, as if Fortune had been angry with those who dar'd assume the Title, after she had been pleas'd to break or remove the Power.

A. D. 476. *Orestes*, having by this means comply'd with his Ambition in providing for his Family, endeavour'd to establish it by an Alliance with *Genserich*, King of the *Vandals*, the most powerful of all his Neighbours, and took Care to preserve the *Roman* Territories in *Gaul* against the *Goths*, the *Burgundians* and *Franks*, who very much encroach'd upon 'em. But all his Precautions were to no purpose, for those of the Nobility who had been oblig'd by *Nepos*, and espous'd his Interest, disdain'd the Tyranny and Usurpation of a Barbarian, who had dar'd to set up for himself without their Consents; and if of Necessity they must obey a Stranger, they resolv'd it should be one of their own Choice.

Odoacer invited into Italy. Whereupon they sent an Invitation to *Odoacer*, King of the *Heruli*, to come to their Assistance, and deliver *Italy*. *Odoacer* was well acquainted with *Orestes*, having serv'd as his Officer in the Wars; he knew the Eastern Empire was distracted with Civil Dissentions, that the West was divided and broken, that the Principal Inhabitants had fix'd their Eyes upon him, and that therefore it would be a madness in him to omit so fair an Opportunity of aggrandising his Family and gratifying his Ambition, for which reason he was resolv'd to go whither he was call'd; accordingly he rais'd a very powerful Army consisting of his own Subjects, and such of his Neighbours as he had allured by fair Promises, and hopes of Plunder. In the beginning

ginning of the Spring he pafs'd over the *Danube*, and enter'd into *Bavaria*, where *Severin*, Bifhop of the Country, who was in great Reputation for his Sanctity, came to meet him. *Odoacer* receiv'd him with a great deal of Refpect, and demanded his Bleffing, which the Bifhop gave him, and affur'd him of a fuccefsful Expedition. From thence *Odoacer* enter'd into *Trent*, and fo into the *Veroneze*, and meeting nothing to oppofe him in his March, he proceeded on to *Lodi* in *Liguria*, where he underftood *Oreftes* expected him with all the Forces, both Horfe and Foot, he was able to draw together. *Odoacer* came up to him, and gave him Battel, defeated and forc'd him to fly into *Pavia* with thofe Troops that ftuck by him; for the *Goths* forfook him in the Engagement, becaufe he had not divided the third part of the Land among 'em, as he had formerly promis'd. With thefe Troops he enter'd the Town, thinking to make it good againft *Odoacer*, becaufe it was well fortify'd, and fecur'd with a good Garrifon; but *Odoacer* follow'd clofe at his Heels, laid Siege to the Place, and, after fome vigorous Affaults, took it by Force, and expos'd it to the Pillage of his Soldiers, who deftroy'd all with Fire and Sword. *Epiphanius*, the renown'd Bifhop of the Place, with much a-do prevail'd to have his Sifter and fome of the beft Ladies in the Town exempted from the Outrage of the infolent Soldiers, a Favour he bought at the Expence of almoft all he was worth. Here *Odoacer* was faluted *King of* Italy, on the 29th of *Auguft*, a Title which at once fatisfy'd and made him proud. From *Pavia* he march'd to *Placentia*, which open'd her Gates to him, where he put *Oreftes* to Death in the Prefence, and amidft the Acclamations of the Victorious Army. After this he proceeded to *Ravenna*, which he took by Compofition,

Slays Oreftes.

on, and flew *Paul*, the Brother of *Orestes*, whom he had left Governor in the Town. Hearing *Augustulus* had fled for Security to *Rome*, he directed his March with an Intent to Besiege the City, taking in all the Towns in his way, some of which were forc'd to Surrender, and others voluntarily submitted to his Government; as he drew near to *Rome* all the Inhabitants of the City, who expected again to be pillag'd, as they had been several times before, went out to meet him, and receiv'd him with Acclamations as their Lord and Soveraign.

and Dethrones Augustulus. *Augustulus*, seeing it in vain to contend, threw off the Imperial Purple, and implor'd the Grace of the Conqueror, who gave him his Life, and confin'd him to *Lucullanum*, a Castle in *Campania*.

The end of the Western Empire. In *Augustulus* fell the very Name of an Empire in the West. *Britain* had long since been quitted by the *Romans*; *Spain* was divided among the *Goths*, *Suevi*, *Alans*, and the like; *Africk* was possess'd by the *Vandals*; the *Goths*, *Burgundians* and *Franks*, had erected their several Tetrarchies in *Gaul*, and now at last *Italy* it self, that for some Ages had triumph'd over the rest of the World, became enslav'd to a Barbarian King; and *Rome*, which was once the Capital of a large and flourishing Empire, is made the Member of a petty Kingdom.

And as there was this thorough Change in the State, so was there almost as great an Alteration in the Church, and the Purity of Religion suffer'd little less than a total Eclipse, when the Majesty of the Empire was expiring; for as on one side Irreligion and Prophaneness naturally spring out of War and Confusion, so on the other all the Christian World was at present under the Dominion either of Heathen or Heretical Princes. The Kings of *Persia*, and of the *Franks* were Heathens; in the East was

was reigning either *Basiliscus*, an *Arian*, or *Zeno*, a debauch'd, dissolute *Eutychian*. All *Africk* was in the Possession of *Genserich*, an obstinate *Arian*, and a cruel Persecutor of the Catholick Christians. *Eurich* was of the like Temper in *Gaul*, *Odoacer* in *Italy*, and the Kings in *Spain* were as zealous Asserters of the same damnable Heresie. So that from these Considerations we may reasonably conclude, it requir'd the same Almighty Power to preserve the Christian Faith pure and undefil'd, as it did at first to establish it; nor are we to wonder if, in that long Night of Ignorance and Error, the Enemy took the Advantage of Sowing his Tare among the good Seed, which in succeeding Ages brought forth so plentiful an Harvest.

Odoacer continu'd for some time at *Rome*, where he assum'd the Sovereign Power and Absolute Dominion, which however he us'd with much Moderation, for he refus'd the Purple, and other Imperial Ornaments, contenting himself with the Marks of Royalty. He diligently apply'd himself to the Settlement of Affairs in his new Kingdom, and the Security of his late Conquests; for this reason he courted the Friendship of the *Goths*, which *Orestes* had call'd in to his Assistance, assigning 'em a third part of the Lands in *Italy*, which he had promis'd 'em; for the present he set aside the Dignity of Consuls in *Rome*, because they seem'd to assume too great and unseasonable a Power; and that his Subjects might be induc'd both to fear and respect him, he gave 'em some publick Examples of his Justice and Severity. When he had dispos'd of all things according to his Will and Pleasure at *Rome*, he went and settled at *Ravenna*, where he usually kept his Court.

From this time forward we hardly meet with the very Shadow of the ancient *Roman* Greatness,
which

which as it exceeded all that ever went before it, so has it been equall'd by none since. The various Fortunes of this mighty State afford our Thoughts a Prospect full of Admiration and Curiosity, whether we consider it in its Birth, in its Establishment, or Dissolution; for certainly no People ever experienc'd so many Forms of Government, and yet flourish'd with equal Vigour in 'em all. Such Changes and Revolutions, as like Earthquakes would have torn up other Nations, made them the stronger; and Difficulties, that would have weigh'd down and dissolv'd other Governments, render'd them the more invincible. Their Greatness, at which the rest of the World stood amaz'd, was in few respects accidental, in most essential, and their Rise, as well as Fall, was owing not so much to Fortune as themselves. From a Pack of loose Vagabonds and wand'ring Shepherds, they form'd themselves, by degrees, into a Civil Society, and before they knew what Law and Government mean'd learn'd to obey, first a Succession of Kings, different in their Tempers, and contradictory in their Maxims; the gentle Dispensation of a Legal Monarchy grew, by degrees, corrupted to an unbounded Tyranny; and that on a sudden was soften'd into the Freedom of a Common-wealth; and yet in all these Revolutions they push'd on without Intermission, to that which from the beginning they seem'd to have in view, the Universal Empire. That Maxim, which compares different Forms of Government to different Climates, and supposes this agreeable to one Nation, and that to another, would not have held with them; for they who were one Day to be the Commanders of the whole World, ought to have a Genius as extensive as their Dominions. Their Power became more enlarg'd abroad under the Imperial Dignity, but

but then by degrees they grew more enslav'd at home, and their Greatness being arriv'd at its Meridian shone with too intense a Heat, and foretold a Declension; which however proceeded not so much from the Depravity of the People in general, as from the Luxury, Sloth, Pride and Ambition of their Emperors; some of whom holding the Reins too straight, others too remiss, are an Instance to us how much the Welfare of a Nation depends upon the Dispositions of its Prince, whose Heart is in the Hand of Providence, the great Ruler of the Universe.

This great Revolution in the West happen'd about 522 Years after the Battel of *Pharsalia*, which gave a Beginning to the Empire; 501 after the full Settlement of it under *Augustus*; 380 after the last of the Twelve *Cæsars*; 146 after the Removal of the Imperial Seat to *Byzantium*; about 101 after the Admission of the *Goths* into *Thrace*; 66 from the first Captivity of *Rome*; and 476 after the Nativity of our Saviour.

AN INDEX

Of the Principal

Men and Matters

IN THIS

HISTORY.

A

ACacius, *Bishop of* Amida, *his extraordinary Charity*, Page 309
Adaulfus, *Brother to* Alarich, *defeated in* Italy, 289. *Made King of the* Goths, 297. *Marries* Placidia, *Sister to* Honorius, ibid. *Makes* Attalus *Emperor a second time*, 301. *Slain by his own Subjects*, 302
Ætius *espouses the Interest of* John *the Usurper*,

INDEX.

surper, 313. *Reconcil'd to* Placidia, 315. *Imposes upon her,* 316. *Fights* Boniface, 319. *His great Services in* Gaul, 326, 332. *Frustrates the Designs of* Attila, 339. *Relieves* Orleance, 341. *Slain by* Valentinian's *Order,* 348

Africk *conquer'd by the* Vandals, 318

Alarich *brought the* Goths *to assist* Theodosius, 223. *Marches into* Greece, 236. *Prepares to invade* Italy, 257. *Besieges* Honorius, 260. *Is defeated by* Stilicho *at* Pollentia, 261. *And at* Verona, 262. *Makes a Peace with* Honorius, 263. *Raises new Troubles,* 279. *Offers an Accommodation, which is refus'd,* 285. *Enters* Italy, 286. *Lays Siege to* Rome *and raises it,* 287. *Enters* Rome, 291. *Makes* Attalus *Emperor,* ibid. *And degrades him,* 293. *Takes* Rome, 294. *Forc'd on Shoar by a Tempest,* 296. *Dies at* Consentia, 297

Alans *fix in* Spain, 277

Alavivus *leads the* Goths *into* Thrace, 167. *begins a War upon the Empire,* 173

Aliso *his bold Attempt,* 112

Ambrose, *Bishop of* Milan, *his Embassy to the Usurper* Maximus, 201. *His Death,* 244. *His Doctrinal Errors,* ibid.

Amida *besieg'd by* Sapor, 46. *Taken,* 48

Ammianus Marcellinus *the Historian, his narrow Escape out of* Amida, 49

Amphilochius, *Bishop of* Iconium, *his seasonable*

INDEX.

sonable Answer to Theodosius *the Great*, 202

Andragathius *murders* Gratian, 199. *Is made Admiral of the Usurper* Maximus *his Fleet*, 210. *Drowns himself*, 211

Annibalianus *made Governor of* Cappadocia *and* Armenia *the Less*, 5. *Slain by* Constantius, 8

Anthemius, *chief Minister of State during the Minority of* Theodosius *the Younger*, 275

Anthemius, *Emperor of the West*, 359. *His Death*, 366

Antiochians *offend* Julian, 74. *Raise a Sedition*, 205

Antoninus *injur'd at Court flies to* Sapor, 45

Apodemius *instrumental in the Death of* Gallus, 24. *Put to death by* Julian, 67

Apollo, *his Temple near* Antioch *burnt*, 76

Arbetio *sent against the* Germans, 27. *Defeated by 'em*, 28. *A corrupt Judge*, 49. *Provok'd by* Procopius, 113. *Adheres to* Valens, 114

Arbogastes *procures* Valentinian II. *to be murder'd*, 220. *Kills himself*, 226

Arcadius *declar'd Emperor*, 196. *Marries* Eudoxia, 235. *His Remissness*, 246. *Persecutes St.* Chrysostome, 264. *Dies*, 274

Arintheus *sent to assist the* Armenians, 132. *prevents the King of* Persia's *Designs*, 133

Arsaces, *King of* Armenia, *assists* Julian *in his Wars against the* Persians, 79. *Deserted by* Jovian, 93. *He is murder'd by* Sapor, 130

C c Arse-

INDEX.

Arsenius *made Tutor to* Arcadius, 196, *Retires into* Ægypt, 197
Artabanes, *deserting the King of* Persia's *Service,* 131. *Is kill'd by* Paras, 133
An Assembly of Thieves, 335
Aspar *seizes on the Usurper* John, 314. *Defeated in* Africk, 319. *Slain with his Sons,* 363
Athanarich, *over-power'd by the* Hunns, *kills himself,* 167
Athanasius, *Bishop of* Alexandria, *banish'd,* 3. *Highly esteem'd by* Jovian, 100
Attalus *made Emperor by* Alarich, 291. *Degraded,* 293. *Once more made Emperor by* Adolph, 301. *Taken,* 302. *And confin'd to the Island of* Lipare, 303
Attila *invades the Empire,* 328. *Sells a Peace to* Theodosius, 331. *Breaks out again,* 335. *Invades* Gaul, 339. *Besieges* Orleance, 340. *Engages* Ætius, *and is overthrown,* 341. *Enters* Italy, 343. *Takes* Aquileia, 344. *His death,* 346
Augustulus *proclaim'd Emperor,* 375. *Dethron'd,* 379
Avitus *made Emperor in* Gaul, 353. *Dethron'd by the People at* Rome, 354

B

Barbatio *sent to dispatch* Gallus, 24. *Opposes* Julian, 38. *Beheaded,* 44
Boniface *Governor of* Africk, 310. *Sent against the Barbarians in* Spain, ibid. *Defeats*

INDEX.

feats Caſtinus, 315. *Deceiv'd by* Ætius, *rebels*, 316. *Calls the* Vandals *into* Africk, 317. *And endeavours in vain to send 'em back*, 318. *Returns into* Italy, 319. *Challenges* Ætius, ibid. *Dies*, 320
Britains *rebel, and ſet up a new Emperor*, 272

C

Calocerus *ſets up for himſelf in* Cyprus, 4. *Taken, and burnt alive*, ibid.
Caſtinus *ſent with* Boniface *into* Spain, 310. *Defeated by the* Vandals, 311. *Made General by* John *the Uſurper*, 313. *Taken Priſoner in* Africk, 315
Chalcedon *beſieg'd by* Valens, 111
Chryſoſtome, St. *his Chriſtian Courage*, 253. *Perſecuted*, 263. *Dies*, 266
Chriſtians perſecuted by Julian, 70
Church, the State of it in Conſtantius *his Reign*, 56. *In that of* Valens, 119. *Oppreſs'd by the* Donatiſts *in* Africk, 270. *Depreſs'd by the* Goths, 368
Conſtans *created* Cæſar, 4. *His Share at the Diviſion of the Empire*, 8. *His Wars in* Gaul, 9. *Murder'd by* Gaiſo, 10
Conſtantine *the Great dedicates* Conſtantinople, 2. *Delivers the* Sarmatæ, 3. *Divides the Government of the Empire*, 4. *Is baptiz'd*, 5. *Dies*, 6
Conſtantine, junior, *made Governor in* Gaul, &c. 4. *Slain near* Aquileia, 8
Conſtantin *uſurps in* Britain, 272. *His*

Cc 2 *Pro-*

INDEX.

Progress in Gaul, 277. *Made Partner in the Empire by* Honorius, 288. *But acts against him,* 298. *And is put to death,* 299

Constantina *marry'd to* Gallus, 14. *Her extravagant Behaviour,* 19. *Her Death,* 23

Constantius *marry'd to* Eusebia, 4. *Murders his Relations,* 8. *Creates* Gallus, Cæsar, 14. *Overthrows* Magnentius, 15. *Resolves to destroy* Gallus, 23. *Grows Cruel and Jealous,* 25. *His Vanity,* 27. *Defeats the* Germans, 28. *His Ingratitude,* 31. *Makes* Julian, Cæsar, 33. *Takes a Progress to* Rome, 36. *Marches against the* Quadi, 41. *And Suppresses 'em,* 42. *Enters* Sirmium *in Triumph,* 44. *Grows Jealous of* Julian, 50. *Protects the* Arians, 57. *Marches against* Julian, 62. *Baptiz'd at* Antioch, 63. *His Death,* 64

Constantius, *a Noble* Roman, 298. *Made Lieutenant-General by* Honorius, ibid. *Grants a Peace to the* Burgundians, 301. *Marries* Placidia, 303. *Declar'd Augustus,* 306. *Dies at* Ravenna, ibid.

Courtiers, *their Ambitious Practices,* 28

Cylaces *Deserting the* Persians, 131. *Is murder'd by* Paras, 133

Cyrill, *Bishop of* Alexandria, 304. *Justly Condemn'd,* 305. *Procures the third general Council to be Summon'd at* Ephesus, 322. *Accus'd to the Emperor,* 323. *Imprison'd and releas'd,* 324

D

Dagalaiphus *his bold Anſwer to* Valentinian, 103. *Sent againſt the* Germans, 105

Dalmatius *Defeats* Calocerus, 4. *And is made* Cæſar, ibid. *He is murder'd*, 8.

Domitian *murder'd by the Procurement of* Gallus, 21

Dynamius *his Forgery*, 29

E

Eudocia *marry'd to* Theodoſius II. 307. *Her Ingratitude*, 332. *Goes to* Jeruſalem, 336

Eudoxia *calls* Genſerich *into* Italy, 351. *Is led into* Africk, 352

Eugenius *Uſurps*, 221. *Turns Heathen*, 223. *Engages* Theodoſius, 224. *Defeated*, 225. *Taken and Beheaded*, 226

Euſebia *marry'd to* Conſtantius, 4. *Perſuades him to make* Julian, Cæſar, 32. *Her Practices upon* Helena, 37. *Her Death*, 56

Euſebius *his Enmity to* Gallus, 25. *And* Urſicinus, 49. *Puniſh'd with Death by* Julian, 67

Eutropius *oppoſes* Rufinus, 233. *Succeeds him in his Power*, 239. *His treacherous Practices*, 241. *Put to Death*, 250

Eutyches *his Hereſie*, 334

F

Firmus *revolts in* Africk, 142. *Submits himſelf to the* Roman General, 143. *His Treachery,*

INDEX.

Treachery, 144. *He flies,* 146. *Hangs himself,* 147
Flavian, *Bishop of* Antioch, 206. *His Intercession with* Theodosius *the Great,* 207
Fritigern, *a Captain of the* Goths, 171. *His good Advice,* 173

G

Gabinius, *King of the* Quadi, *treacherously murder'd by the* Romans, 148
Gaines, *a great Friend to* Stilicho, 237. *Procures* Rufinus *to be Slain,* 238. *Turns Male-content,* 245. *Made General in the East,* 246. *His Treachery,* 248. *And Insolence,* 252. *Reprov'd by St.* Chrysostome, 253. *His Designs upon* Constantinople *frustrated,* 254. *His Death,* 256
Gaiso *murders* Constans. 10
Gallus *created* Cæsar, 14. *His extravagant Behaviour,* 18. *And Cruelty,* 21. *His Carriage at* Constantinople *provokes* Constantius, 23. *Who orders him to be put to Death.* 25
Gauls, *their desperate Attempt at* Amida, 47
Genserich *call'd by* Boniface *into* Africk, 317. *Conquers the Country,* 318. *Takes* Hippo, 319. *Breaks the Peace,* 326. *His Cruelties,* 327. *Concludes a Peace with the Emperor,* 330. *Sacks* Rome, 351. *His Piratical Excursions,* 359

George,

INDEX.

George, *the* Arian *Bishop, his Character,* 75

Gildo *serves the* Romans *against his Brother,* 142. *Revolts,* 242. *Murders his Brother's Sons,* 243. *Overthrown,* 250. *Strangles himself,* 251

Godegisil, *King of the* Vandals, *Invades the Empire,* 271. *Settles in* Spain. 277

Goths, *assisting* Procopius, *are punish'd by* Valens, 121. *Beg leave to be admitted into* Thrace, 167. *Defeat the* Romans, 172. *Besiege* Adrianople, 173. *Cut off a* Roman *Legion,* 175. *Overthrow* Valens, 181. *Destroy'd in the East,* 188

Gratian, *Son of* Valentinian, *declar'd* Augustus, 125. *Sends some Forces to the Assistance of* Valens, 174. *Defeats the* Germans, 176. *Marches into the East,* 177. *Makes* Theodosius *his Partner in the Empire,* 190. *Slain by* Andragathius, 199

H

Helena *marry'd to* Julian, 33. *Circumvented by the Empress* Eusebia, 37. *Dies,* 56

Heraclian *Commands for* Honorius *in* Africk, 291. *Defeats the Enemy,* 292. *Usurps, and is kill'd.* 300

Honorius *declar'd Emperor,* 222. *Marry'd to* Stilicho's *Daughter,* 235. *Besieg'd by* Alarich *in* Hasta, 260. *Reliev'd by* Stilicho, 261. *Makes Peace with* Alarich, 263. *Marries his first Wive's Sister,* 278. *Grows Jealous of* Stilicho, 281.

281. *Orders him to be put to* Death, 283. *Rejects* Alarich's *Proposals of a Peace,* 285. *Makes* Constantine *his Associate in the Empire,* 288. *Besieg'd in* Ravenna, 291. *Makes War upon the* Barbarians *in* Spain, 310. *His Death,* 312
Hunns *Invade the Empire,* 328
Hypatia, *Daughter of* Theon, *a Philosopher, massacred in an Uproar,* 305

I

John *Usurps in the West,* 312. *Taken Prisoner,* 314. *Beheaded,* 315
Jovian *Elected Emperor,* 90. *Concludes a Peace with the* Persians, 93. *Found dead in his Chamber,* 99
Isauri *their Inroads into the Empire,* 20. *Their Depredations,* 267
Isdegerdes *made Guardian to* Theodosius *the Second,* 274
Julian, *the Apostate, created* Cæsar, 33. *His Exploits in* Gaul, 34. *His Progress there,* 37. *His Victory at* Argentoratum, 39. *Declar'd Emperor by the mutinous Army,* 52. *Prepares to march against* Constantius, 58. *His Speech to the Army,* 59. *Enters* Sirmium, 61. *His Reformations after the Death of* Constantius, 68. *He opens the Heathen Temples,* 69. *Oppresses the Christians,* 70. *Begins his Expedition against the* Persians, 72. *An Instance of his Justice,* 73.
Quarrels

INDEX.

Quarrels with the Inhabitants of Antioch, 74. *Endeavours to Re-build the Temple at* Jerusalem, 77. *His Progress,* 78. *His Order of Marching,* 80. *His Success,* 82. *He is in great Danger,* 83. *His Obstinacy and Rashness,* 84. *He Defeats the* Persians, 85. *He is wounded,* 86. *And dies,* 87

Julius *puts all the* Goths *to Death in the East,* 188

L

Lampadius *his bold Saying in the Senate,* 279
Leo *Elected Emperor at* Constantinople, 355. *Puts* Aspar *and his Sons to Death,* 363. *Marries his Daughter to* Zeno Isauricus, 369. *His Death.* 370
Libanius, *the Sophist,* Julian's *Instructor in the Pagan Superstitions,* 70. *His Blasphemy,* 88
Limigantes, Sarmatæ, *their Obstinacy,* 42. *Punish'd by the Emperor* Constantius, 43
Lupicinus *his corrupt Practices in* Thrace *pernicious to the Empire,* 171

M

Magi, *their Religious Artifices,* 275
Magnentius *Rebels in* Gaul, 10. *His Cruelty,* 11. *Overthrown,* 15. *Kills himself,* 17
Majorianus *declar'd Emperor of the West,* 355. *Defeats the* Vandals, 356. *Murder'd by* Ricimer, 358

Martian *declar'd Emperor in the East.* 337. *Summons the fourth general Council,* 338. *His Death,* 355

Maximus *the Philosopher and Magician,* 72. *Put to Death,* 139

Maximus *Usurps in* Britain, 197. *His Cruelty,* 200. *And Policy,* 208. *Enters* Italy, 209. *Defeated and Beheaded,* 211

Maximus *see* Petronius,

Mazezil *opposes his Brother* Gildo *in* Africk, 243. *Drown'd by* Stilicho's *Procurement,* 251

Monks *raise Disturbances in* Alexandria, 304

Mutinies *in* Gaul *in the East,* 91. *At* Ticinum, 281

N

Nepos Julius *declar'd Emperor in the West,* 371. *Expell'd by* Orestes, 375

Nepotianus *sets up for himself, and is Slain,* 11

Nestorius, *Bishop of* Constantinople, *his Heresie,* 321. *Condemn'd in the Council at* Ephesus, 323. *His miserable End,* 324

Negrinus *his Loyalty to* Constantius, 62. *For which he is put to Death by* Julian, 67

O

Odoacer *invited into* Italy, 376. *Slays* Orestes, 377. *Makes himself be declar'd King of* Italy, 379

Olybrius, *Emperor in the West.* 366

Olympius

INDEX.

Olympius *practices against* Stilicho, 281. *After some Services dismiss'd from Court*, 289

Orestes *Rebels in the West*, 375. *Slain by* Odoacer, 377

P

Paras, *King of* Armenia, 132. *Destroys his two Friends at the Instigation of* Sapor, *King of* Persia, 133. *Detain'd Prisoner by the* Romans, 151. *Escapes into* Armenia, *and is treacherously murder'd*, 152, 153

Peter, *Sirnam'd the* Fuller, *his Heresie and Insolence*, 369, & Sequ.

Petronius Maximus *murders* Valentinian *the Third*, 348. *Usurps the Empire*, 349. *He is Slain*, 351

Placidia, Honorius *his Sister, marry'd to* Adolph, *King of the* Goths, 297. *And to* Constantine, 303. *Retires to* Constantinople, 311. *Made Regent of the Empire*, 315. *Her Death*, 335

Procopius *conceals himself after the Death of* Julian, 98. *Usurps*, 105. *Takes* Cyzicus, 112. *Grows Insolent*, 113. *Taken and Beheaded*, 115

Promotus *Defeats the* Gruthingi, 204. *Made General of the Foot by* Theodosius, 209. *Rescues the Emperor*, 218. *He is murder'd*, 219

Pulcheria *persuades* Theodosius *to Marry*, 307. *Forc'd to retire from Court*, 333. *Marry'd to* Martian, 337

Q

Quadi *invade the Empire,* 41. *Suppress'd by* Constantius, 42. *Insult the Empire,* 148. *Cut off two* Roman *Legions,* 150. *Waste* Illyricum, 155. *Sue for a Peace,* 157

R

Radagaisus *invades* Italy, 268. *Defeated,* 269. *And slain,* 270
Rando, *a noble* German, *seizes on* Ments, 134
Remigius *his corrupt Practices,* 127, 142
Ricimer, *a Goth, made General of the* Roman *Army,* 355. *Kills* Majorianus *the Emperor,* 357. *Besieges* Rome, 365. *Kills* Anthemius, 366. *And dies,* ibid.
Romanus *tyrannically governs in* Africk, 126. *His Policy,* 129
Rome *overflown by the* Tiber, 151. *Imitates the* Gothick *Fashions,* 243. *Besieg'd by* Alarich, 287. *Taken by him,* 293. *And by* Genserich, 351
Rufinus *his great Interest at Court,* 219. *Made Tutor to* Arcadius, 223. *His Ambition,* 232. *Renders himself odious to the People,* 233. *His Cruelty,* 234. *And Treachery,* 235. *Slain,* 238

S

Sabinianus, *a decrepit old Man, made General of the* Roman *Army,* 44

Sabinus,

INDEX.

Sabinus, *his bold Reflection*, 97

Saluſt *made Prefect of* Gaul, 60. *His good Advice to* Julian, 79. *Refuſes the Empire*, 89

Sapor, *King of* Perſia, *beſieges* Niſibis, 9. *His Wars with* Conſtantius, 44. *Beſieges* Amida, 46. *Takes it*, 48. *Concludes a Peace with* Jovian, 93. *Invades* Armenia, 130. *His Artifice*, 132

Saracens *converted to the Chriſtian Faith*, 186. *A ſtrange Action of a* Saracen, 187

Sarus *receiv'd into the* Roman *Service*, 268. *His Exploits in* Gaul, 276. *Acts againſt* Stilicho, 282. *Prevents an Accommodation between* Honorius *and* Alarich, 293

Sebaſtian *a Commander in* Julian's *Army*, 79. *Defeats the* Goths, 178

Sedition *at* Rome, 120. *At* Conſtantinople, 194. *At* Antioch, 205. *At* Alexandria, 213, 303

Severus *declar'd Emperor at* Ravenna, 357. *Slain by* Ricimer, 358

Stilicho *made a General in the* Roman *Army*, 223. *His Ambition*, 232. *Marries his Daughter to the Emperor* Honorius, 235. *Marches into the Eaſt*, 237. *His Exploits in* Rhætia, 260. *He relieves* Honorius, ibid. *Defeats* Alarich, 261. *His Policy*, 262. *Procures a Peace between* Alarich *and* Honorius, 263. *Defeats* Radagaiſus, 269. *Rewarded by the* Romans, 270. *His Power in the Senate*,

INDEX.

nate, 279. *Put to Death*, 283
Suevi *settle in* Spain, 277
Sylvanus *sent into* Gaul, 28. *Sets up for Emperor*, 29. *Murder'd*, 31
Sylvanus, *an Advocate, his confident Reflection*, 97

T

Thalassius *his imprudent Behaviour*, 19. *Renounces Christianity, and is reconcil'd to* Julian, 73
Themistius *in Favour with* Julian, 70
Theodosius, senior, *sent into* Britain, 123. *His prudent Management*, 124. *Sent against the* Moors *in* Africk, 142. *Hazards his Army*, 145. *His Victory*, 146. *Put to death*, 147
Theodosius *the Great declar'd Emperor by* Gratian, 190. *His Virtue*, 193. *His exemplary Justice*, 194. *Summons the second General Council*, 196. *His remarkable Saying*, 197. *Summons another Council*, 201. *Concludes a Peace with the* Persians, 202. *His Clemency*, 207. *His Proceedings against* Maximus, 209. *Conquers him*, 211. *His great Moderation*, 212. *Shuts up the* Roman *Temples in* Rome, 213. *Reforms some Abuses there*, 215. *His Exploits in* Macedonia, 216. *In great Danger*, 218. *His Proceedings against* Eugenius, 223. *Defeats him*, 225. *Falls sick*, 227. *His Death, and Character*, 228. *A great Instance*

INDEX.

Instance of his Christian Resignation, 230
Theodosius, junior, *declar'd* Augustus *by his Father,* 263. *Marries* Athenais, 307. *His Wars in* Persia, 308. *Buys a Peace of the* Hunns, 331. *Displeas'd with his Sister* Pulcheria, 332. *And his Wife,* 334. *His Death,* 336
Tribigild *rebels,* 245. *Loses his Army,* 248

V

Valens *declared Emperor by his Brother* Valentinian, 103. *Displeases his Subjects,* 107. *His Cowardice,* 110. *Success against* Procopius, 114, 115. *His great Severity,* 116. *A Friend to the* Arians, 120. *Wars against the* Goths, 121. *His Tyranny,* 136. *Admits the* Goths *into* Thrace, 168. *Engages with the* Goths, 181. *Defeated and slain,* 182. *His Character,* 183
Valentinian I. *elected Emperor,* 101. *His Speech to the Army,* 102. *Associates his Brother in the Empire,* 103. *His generous Resolution,* 105. *Makes his Son* Gratian *Augustus,* 125. *His Cruelty,* 126. *His Exploits in* Germany, 134, 135. *His Expedition against the* Quadi, 155. *His Death,* 158. *And Character,* 159
Valentinian II. *declar'd Emperor,* 162. *Flies to* Theodosius, 209. *Murder'd,* 221
Valentinian III. *made Emperor,* 315. *Marry'd*

ry'd to Eudoxia, 325. *Ravishes the Wife of* Maximus, 347. *Is slain,* 348
Valentine, *his great Service against* Tribigild, 247
Vandals *conquer* Africk, 318
Venice, *when founded,* 343
Veteranio *sets up for himself,* 12. *Depos'd,* 13
Ursicinus *sent into* Gaul, 29. *Procures* Sylvanus *to be murder'd,* 31. *Recall'd from his Command,* 44. *Oppos'd by* Sabinianus, 47. *Accus'd at Court,* 49. *His generous Defence,* 50

Z

Zeno *kills* Aspar *and his Sons,* 363. *Marry'd to* Leo's *Daughter,* 369. *Made Emperor in the East,* 372. *Flies into* Isauria, 374
Zosimus *his great Partiality,* 191

FINIS.

www.ingramcontent.com/pod-product-compliance
Lightning Source LLC
Chambersburg PA
CBHW030557300426
44111CB00009B/1019